EXCEL 97
FOR
WINDOWS®
FOR
DUMMIES®

by Greg Harvey

IDG
BOOKS
WORLDWIDE

IDG Books Worldwide, Inc.
An International Data Group Company

Foster City, CA ♦ Chicago, IL ♦ Indianapolis, IN ♦ New York, NY

Excel 97 For Windows® For Dummies®

Published by
IDG Books Worldwide, Inc.
An International Data Group Company
919 E. Hillsdale Blvd.
Suite 400
Foster City, CA 94404
www.idgbooks.com (IDG Books Worldwide Web site)
www.dummies.com (Dummies Press Web site)

Library of Congress Catalog Card No.: 96-79272

ISBN: 0-7645-0049-X

Printed in the United States of America

10 9 8

1B/QW/QR/ZZ/IN

Distributed in the United States by IDG Books Worldwide, Inc.

Distributed by Macmillan Canada for Canada; by Transworld Publishers Limited in the United Kingdom; by IDG Norge Books for Norway; by IDG Sweden Books for Sweden; by Woodslane Pty. Ltd. for Australia; by Woodslane (NZ) Ltd. for New Zealand; by Addison Wesley Longman Singapore Pte Ltd. for Singapore, Malaysia, Thailand, and Indonesia; by Norma Comunicaciones S.A. for Colombia; by Intersoft for South Africa; by International Thomson Publishing for Germany, Austria and Switzerland; by Distribuidora Cuspide for Argentina; by Livraria Cultura for Brazil; by Ediciencia S.A. for Ecuador; by Ediciones ZETA S.C.R. Ltda. for Peru; by WS Computer Publishing Corporation, Inc., for the Philippines; by Contemporanea de Ediciones for Venezuela; by Express Computer Distributors for the Caribbean and West Indies; by Micronesia Media Distributor, Inc. for Micronesia; by Grupo Editorial Norma S.A. for Guatemala; by Chips Computadoras S.A. de C.V. for Mexico; by Editorial Norma de Panama S.A. for Panama; by Wouters Import for Belgium; by American Bookshops for Finland. Authorized Sales Agent: Anthony Rudkin Associates for the Middle East and North Africa.

For general information on IDG Books Worldwide's books in the U.S., please call our Consumer Customer Service department at 800-762-2974. For reseller information, including discounts and premium sales, please call our Reseller Customer Service department at 800-434-3422.

For information on where to purchase IDG Books Worldwide's books outside the U.S., please contact our International Sales department at 317-596-5530 or fax 317-596-5692.

For information on foreign language translations, please contact our Foreign & Subsidiary Rights department at 650-655-3021 or fax 650-655-3281.

For sales inquiries and special prices for bulk quantities, please contact our Sales department at 650-655-3200 or write to the address above.

For information on using IDG Books Worldwide's books in the classroom or for ordering examination copies, please contact our Educational Sales department at 800-434-2086 or fax 317-596-5499.

For press review copies, author interviews, or other publicity information, please contact our Public Relations department at 650-655-3000 or fax 650-655-3299.

For authorization to photocopy items for corporate, personal, or educational use, please contact Copyright Clearance Center, 222 Rosewood Drive, Danvers, MA 01923, or fax 978-750-4470.

About the Author

Greg Harvey is a product of the great American Midwest, born in the Chicagoland area in 1949 (thus his saying "I'm only as old as China," — Red China, that is) in the dark ages of the Cold War before the age of McDonald's, MTV, and, certainly, personal computers. On the shores of Lake Michigan, he learned his letters and numbers and showed great promise in the world of academia (quickly achieving Red Bird reading status after being put back as a Yellow Bird due to an unforeseen bout of chicken pox at the start of the school year). After earning many gold stars along with a few red, he graduated from Roosevelt School (named for Teddy, not that socialist Delano) in 1963.

During his stint at Thornridge High School in the perfectly boring Chicago suburb of Dolton, Illinois (named for Tom Dolton, the gunslinger?), he found great solace in Motown music (thanks, Phil!) and the drama department. (To this day, he can recite every line from the play *Auntie Mame,* verbatim.) Bored with what passed for academic studies, he went through high school in three years. Looking back on these formative years, Greg was sure thankful for the great tunes and Auntie's philosophy, "Life's a banquet, kid, and some poor suckers are starving."

In 1966 (ah, the Sixties), he entered the University of Illinois at Urbana, Illinois where he was greatly influenced by such deep philosophers as Abbie Hoffman and Mahatma Gandhi. In the summer of 1968, he purchased his first pair of handmade sandals (from Glen, a hippie sandal maker who'd just returned from the Summer of Love in San Francisco).

During his college years, he became quite political. He holds the distinction of being one of a handful of men and women to attend the "camp-out" protest against women's dorm curfews (back then, not only were dorms not sexually integrated, but women were locked up at 11 p.m. on weeknights, 1 a.m. on weekends) and the last one to leave after all the others went back to their dorms. During his subsequent college years, he became a regular at the Red Herring coffee house, the veritable den of SDS activity on campus.

In addition to anti-war protests, Greg attended various and sundry classes in the Liberal Arts (such as they were in the last half of the 20th century). In the end, he took a major in Classical Studies (Ancient Greek and Latin) and a split minor in American History and French. (Greg showed a facility for foreign language, probably stemming from the fact that he's always had a big mouth.) In the course of his Classical studies, he was introduced to his first computer-based training, learning basic Latin with a CAI program called, what else but, PLATO!

At the beginning of 1971 (January 12, in fact), Greg migrated West from Chicago to San Francisco (with flowers in his hair). Deciding it was high time to get a skill so that he could find a real job, he enrolled in the Drafting and Design program at Laney College in Oakland. After that, he spent nine years working over a hot drafting table, drawing (by hand, mind you) orthographic and perspective plans for various and sundry engineering projects. During his last engineering gig, he worked with a proprietary CAD software package developed by Bechtel Engineering that not only generated the drawings, but kept track of the materials actually needed to create the stuff.

In 1981, following his engineering career, Greg went back to school at San Francisco State University, this time to earn his secondary teaching credential. Upon completion of his teacher training, he bought one of the very first IBM personal computers (with 16K and a single 160K floppy disk!) to help with lesson preparation and student bookkeeping. He still vividly remembers poring over the premier issue of *PC World* for every piece of information that could teach him how to make peace with his blankety, blankety personal computer.

Instead of landing a teaching job at the high school or community college (since there weren't any at the time), Greg got a job with a small software outfit, ITM, that was creating an online database of software information (well ahead of its time). As part of his duties, Greg reviewed new software programs (like Microsoft Word 1.0 and Lotus 1-2-3 Release 1) and wrote articles for business users.

After being laid off from this job right after the Christmas party in 1983 (the first of several layoffs from high-tech startups), Greg wrote his first computer book on word processing software for Hayden Books (as a result of a proposal he helped to write while still employed full-time at ITM). After that, Greg worked in various software evaluation and training jobs. After a few more high-tech software testing and evaluation jobs in Silicon Valley, Greg turned to software training to get, as he put it, "the perspective of the poor schmoe at the end of the terminal." During the next three years, Greg trained a whole plethora of software programs to business users of all skill levels for several major independent software training companies in the San Francisco bay area.

In the fall of 1986, he hooked up with Sybex, a local computer book publisher, for whom he wrote his second computer training book, *Mastering SuperCalc*. And the rest, as they say, is history. To date, Greg is the author of over 30 books on using computer software, with the titles created under the *Dummies* aegis for IDG Books Worldwide, Inc., being among his all-time favorites.

In mid-1993, Greg started a new multimedia publishing venture called mind over media. As a multimedia developer, he hopes to enliven his future computer books by making them into true interactive learning experiences that will vastly enrich and improve the training of users of all skill levels. You can send him e-mail at:

gharvey@mindovermedia.com

and visit his Web site at

http://www.mindovermedia.com

ABOUT IDG BOOKS WORLDWIDE

Welcome to the world of IDG Books Worldwide.

IDG Books Worldwide, Inc., is a subsidiary of International Data Group, the world's largest publisher of computer-related information and the leading global provider of information services on information technology. IDG was founded more than 25 years ago and now employs more than 8,500 people worldwide. IDG publishes more than 275 computer publications in over 75 countries (see listing below). More than 90 million people read one or more IDG publications each month.

Launched in 1990, IDG Books Worldwide is today the #1 publisher of best-selling computer books in the United States. We are proud to have received eight awards from the Computer Press Association in recognition of editorial excellence and three from *Computer Currents'* First Annual Readers' Choice Awards. Our best-selling *...For Dummies®* series has more than 50 million copies in print with translations in 38 languages. IDG Books Worldwide, through a joint venture with IDG's Hi-Tech Beijing, became the first U.S. publisher to publish a computer book in the People's Republic of China. In record time, IDG Books Worldwide has become the first choice for millions of readers around the world who want to learn how to better manage their businesses.

Our mission is simple: Every one of our books is designed to bring extra value and skill-building instructions to the reader. Our books are written by experts who understand and care about our readers. The knowledge base of our editorial staff comes from years of experience in publishing, education, and journalism — experience we use to produce books for the '90s. In short, we care about books, so we attract the best people. We devote special attention to details such as audience, interior design, use of icons, and illustrations. And because we use an efficient process of authoring, editing, and desktop publishing our books electronically, we can spend more time ensuring superior content and spend less time on the technicalities of making books.

You can count on our commitment to deliver high-quality books at competitive prices on topics you want to read about. At IDG Books Worldwide, we continue in the IDG tradition of delivering quality for more than 25 years. You'll find no better book on a subject than one from IDG Books Worldwide.

John Kilcullen
CEO
IDG Books Worldwide, Inc.

Steven Berkowitz
President and Publisher
IDG Books Worldwide, Inc.

Eighth Annual Computer Press Awards ≥ 1992

Ninth Annual Computer Press Awards ≥ 1993

Tenth Annual Computer Press Awards ≥ 1994

Eleventh Annual Computer Press Awards ≥ 1995

IDG Books Worldwide, Inc., is a subsidiary of International Data Group, the world's largest publisher of computer-related information and the leading global provider of information services on information technology. International Data Group publishes over 275 computer publications in over 75 countries. More than 90 million people read one or more International Data Group publications each month. International Data Group's publications include: ARGENTINA: Buyer's Guide, Computerworld Argentina, PC World Argentina; AUSTRALIA: Australian Macworld, Australian PC World, Australian Reseller News, Computerworld, IT Casebook, Network World, Publish, Webmaster; AUSTRIA: Computerwelt Osterreich, Networks Austria, PC Tip Austria; BANGLADESH: PC World Bangladesh; BELARUS: PC World Belarus; BELGIUM: Data News; BRAZIL: Annuário de Informática, Computerworld, Connections, Macworld, PC Player, PC World, Publish, Reseller News, Supergamepower; BULGARIA: Computerworld Bulgaria, Network World Bulgaria, PC & MacWorld Bulgaria; CANADA: CIO Canada, Client/Server World, ComputerWorld Canada, InfoWorld Canada, NetworkWorld Canada, WebWorld; CHILE: Computerworld Chile, PC World Chile; COLOMBIA: Computerworld Colombia, PC World Colombia; COSTA RICA: PC World Centro America; THE CZECH AND SLOVAK REPUBLICS: Computerworld Czechoslovakia, Macworld Czech Republic, PC World Czechoslovakia; DENMARK: Communications World Danmark, Computerworld Danmark, Macworld Danmark, PC World Danmark, Techworld Denmark; DOMINICAN REPUBLIC: PC World Republica Dominicana; ECUADOR: PC World Ecuador; EGYPT: Computerworld Middle East, PC World Middle East; EL SALVADOR: PC World Centro America; FINLAND: MikroPC, Tietoverkko, Tietoviikko; FRANCE: Distributique, Hebdo, Info PC, Le Monde Informatique, Macworld, Reseaux & Telecoms, WebMaster France; GERMANY: Computer Partner, Computerwoche, Computerwoche Extra, Computerwoche FOCUS, Global Online, Macwelt, PC Welt; GREECE: Amiga Computing, GamePro Greece, Multimedia World; GUATEMALA: PC World Centro America; HONDURAS: PC World Centro America; HONG KONG: Computerworld Hong Kong, PC World Hong Kong, Publish in Asia; HUNGARY: ABCD CD-ROM, Computerworld Szamitastechnika, Internetto online Magazine, PC World Hungary, PC-X Magazin Hungary; ICELAND: Tolvuheimur PC World Island; INDIA: Information Communications World, Information Systems Computerworld, PC World India, Publish in Asia; INDONESIA: InfoKomputer PC World, Komputek Computerworld, Publish in Asia; IRELAND: ComputerScope, PC Live!; ISRAEL: Macworld Israel, People & Computers/Computerworld; ITALY: Computerworld Italia, Macworld Italia, Networking Italia, PC World Italia; JAPAN: DTP World, Macworld Japan, Nikkei Personal Computing, OS/2 World Japan, SunWorld Japan, Windows NT World, Windows World Japan; KENYA: PC World East African; KOREA: Hi-Tech Information, Macworld Korea, PC World Korea; MACEDONIA: PC World Macedonia; MALAYSIA: Computerworld Malaysia, PC World Malaysia, Publish in Asia; MALTA: PC World Malta; MEXICO: Computerworld Mexico, PC World Mexico; MYANMAR: PC World Myanmar; NETHERLANDS: Computer! Totaal, LAN Internetworking Magazine, LAN World Buyers Guide, Macworld Netherlands, Net, WebWereld; NEW ZEALAND: Absolute Beginners Guide and Plain & Simple Series, Computer Buyer, Computer Industry Directory, Computerworld New Zealand, MTB, Network World, PC World New Zealand; NICARAGUA: PC World Centro America; NORWAY: Computerworld Norge, CW Rapport, Datamagasinet, Financial Rapport, Kursguide Norge, Macworld Norge, Multimediaworld Norge, PC World Ekspress Norge, PC World Nettverk, PC World Norge, PC World ProduktGuide Norge; PAKISTAN: Computerworld Pakistan; PANAMA: PC World Panama; PEOPLE'S REPUBLIC OF CHINA: China Computer Users, China Computerworld, China InfoWorld, China Telecom World Weekly, Computer & Communication, Electronic Design China, Electronics Today, Electronics Weekly, Game Software, PC World China, Popular Computer Week, Software Weekly, Software World, Telecom World; PERU: Computerworld Peru, PC World Profesional Peru, PC World SoHo Peru; PHILIPPINES: Click!, Computerworld Philippines, PC World Philippines, Publish in Asia; POLAND: Computerworld Poland, Computerworld Special Report Poland, Cyber, Macworld Poland, Networld Poland, PC World Komputer; PORTUGAL: Cerebro/PC World, Computerworld/Correio Informático, Dealer World Portugal, Mac*In/PC*In Portugal, Multimedia World; PUERTO RICO: PC World Puerto Rico; ROMANIA: Computerworld Romania, PC World Romania, Telecom Romania; RUSSIA: Computerworld Russia, Mir PK, Publish, Seti; SINGAPORE: Computerworld Singapore, PC World Singapore, Publish in Asia; SLOVENIA: Monitor; SOUTH AFRICA: Computing SA, Network World SA, Software World SA; SPAIN: Communicaciones World España, Computerworld España, Dealer World España, Macworld España, PC World España; SRI LANKA: Infolink PC World; SWEDEN: CAP&Design, Computer Sweden, Corporate Computing Sweden, Internetworld Sweden, it.branschen, Macworld Sweden, MaxiData Sweden, MikroDatorn, Nätverk & Kommunikation, PC World Sweden, PCaktiv, Windows World Sweden; SWITZERLAND: Computerworld Schweiz, Macworld Schweiz, PCtip; TAIWAN: Computerworld Taiwan, Macworld Taiwan, NEW ViSiON/Publish, PC World Taiwan, Windows World Taiwan; THAILAND: Publish in Asia, Thai Computerworld; TURKEY: Computerworld Turkiye, Macworld Turkiye, Network World Turkiye, PC World Turkiye; UKRAINE: Computerworld Kiev, Multimedia World Ukraine, PC World Ukraine; UNITED KINGDOM: Acorn User UK, Amiga Action UK, Amiga Computing UK, Apple Talk UK, Computing, Macworld, Parents and Computers UK, PC Advisor, PC Home, PSX Pro, The WEB; UNITED STATES: Cable in the Classroom, CIO Magazine, Computerworld, DOS World, Federal Computer Week, GamePro Magazine, InfoWorld, I-Way, Macworld, Network World, PC Games, PC World, Publish, Video Event, THE WEB Magazine, and WebMaster; online webzines: JavaWorld, NetscapeWorld, and SunWorld Online; URUGUAY: InfoWorld Uruguay; VENEZUELA: Computerworld Venezuela, PC World Venezuela; and VIETNAM: PC World Vietnam.
5/7/98

Dedication

To Shane, my partner in business and life, and truly the best friend a person could ask for.

Acknowledgments

Let me take this opportunity to thank all the people, both at IDG Books and at mind over media, Inc., whose dedication and talent combined to get this book out and into your hands in such great shape.

At IDG Books, I want to thank Tim Gallan for his help and good humor, and Regina Snyder, Anna Rohrer, Jane Martin, Angie Hunckler, and Brent Savage on the Production team.

At mind over media, Inc., thanks to Robert Prokupek and Jane Vait for taking care of the myriad details related to getting this revision done and out the door in record time (kudos all around). Also thanks to Shane Gearing for his great work on the example files (Mother Goose would be proud).

Publisher's Acknowledgments

We're proud of this book; please register your comments through our IDG Books Worldwide Online Registration Form located at http://my2cents.dummies.com.

Some of the people who helped bring this book to market include the following:

Acquisitions, Development, and Editorial

Project Editor: Tim Gallan

Acquisitions Editor: Gareth Hancock

Copy Editors: Suzanne Packer, Gwenette Gaddis

Technical Editor: Publication Services

Editorial Manager: Kristin A. Cocks

Editorial Assistant: Constance Carlisle

Production

Project Coordinator: Regina Snyder

Layout and Graphics: Cameron Booker, Elizabeth Cárdenas-Nelson, J. Tyler Connor, Dominique DeFelice, Angela F. Hunckler, Todd Klemme, Jane E. Martin, Drew R. Moore, Anna Rohrer, Brent Savage, Rashell Smith, Michael A. Sullivan

Proofreaders: Kelli Botta, Henry Lazarek, Nancy L. Reinhardt, Rachel Garvey, Robert Springer, Carrie Voorhis, Karen York

Indexer: Sherry Massey

General and Administrative

IDG Books Worldwide, Inc.: John Kilcullen, CEO; Steven Berkowitz, President and Publisher

IDG Books Technology Publishing: Brenda McLaughlin, Senior Vice President and Group Publisher

Dummies Technology Press and Dummies Editorial: Diane Graves Steele, Vice President and Associate Publisher; Mary Bednarek, Director of Acquisitions and Product Development; Kristin A. Cocks, Editorial Director

Dummies Trade Press: Kathleen A. Welton, Vice President and Publisher; Kevin Thornton, Acquisitions Manager

IDG Books Production for Dummies Press: Michael R. Britton, Vice President of Production and Creative Services; Cindy L. Phipps, Manager of Project Coordination, Production Proofreading, and Indexing; Kathie S. Schutte, Supervisor of Page Layout; Shelley Lea, Supervisor of Graphics and Design; Debbie J. Gates, Production Systems Specialist; Robert Springer, Supervisor of Proofreading; Debbie Stailey, Special Projects Coordinator; Tony Augsburger, Supervisor of Reprints and Bluelines

Dummies Packaging and Book Design: Patty Page, Manager, Promotions Marketing

♦

The publisher would like to give special thanks to Patrick J. McGovern, without whom this book would not have been possible.

♦

Contents at a Glance

Cartoons at a Glance

By Rich Tennant

page 7

page 103

page 209

page 257

page 365

page 329

Fax: 978-546-7747 • E-mail: the5wave@tiac.net

Table of Contents

Introduction

• •

*W*elcome to *Excel 97 For Windows For Dummies,* the definitive work on Excel 97 for those of you who have no intention of ever becoming a spreadsheet guru. In this book, you find all the information that you need to keep your head above water as you accomplish the everyday tasks that people do with Excel. The intention of this book is to keep things simple and not bore you with a lot of technical details that you neither need nor care anything about. As much as possible, this book attempts to cut to the chase by telling you in plain terms just what it is that you need to do to accomplish a task using Excel.

Excel 97 For Windows For Dummies covers all the fundamental techniques that you need to know in order to create, edit, format, and print your own worksheets. In addition to showing you around the worksheet, this book also exposes you to the basics of charting and creating databases. Keep in mind, though, that this book just touches on the easiest ways to get a few things done with these features — I make no attempt to cover charting and databases in a definitive way. In the main, this book concentrates on spreadsheets because spreadsheets are what most people need to create with Excel.

About This Book

This book is not meant to be read from cover to cover. Although its chapters are loosely organized in a logical order (progressing as you might when studying Excel in a classroom situation), each topic covered in a chapter is really meant to stand on its own.

Each discussion of a topic briefly addresses the question of what a particular feature is good for before launching into how to use it. In Excel, as with most other sophisticated programs, there is usually more than one way to do a task. For the sake of your sanity, I have purposely limited the choices by usually giving you only the most efficient ways to do a particular task. Later on, if you're so tempted, you can experiment with alternative ways of doing a task. For now, just concentrate on performing the task as described.

As much as possible, I've tried to make it unnecessary for you to remember anything covered in another section of the book. From time to time, however, you come across a cross-reference to another section or chapter in the book. For the most part, such cross-references are meant to help you get more complete information on a subject, should you have the time and interest. If you have neither, no problem; just ignore the cross-references as if they never existed.

How to Use This Book

This book is like a reference where you start out by looking up the topic you need information about (either in the table of contents or the index) and then refer directly to the section of interest. Most topics are explained conversationally (as though you were sitting in the back of a classroom where you can safely nap). Sometimes, however, my regiment-commander mentality takes over, and I list the steps you need to take to accomplish a particular task in a particular section.

What You Can Safely Ignore

When you come across a section that contains the steps you take to get something done, you can safely ignore all text accompanying the steps (the text that isn't in bold) if you have neither the time nor the inclination to wade through more material.

Whenever possible, I have also tried to separate background or footnote-type information from the essential facts by exiling this kind of junk to a sidebar. These sections are often flagged with icons that let you know what type of information you will encounter there. You can easily disregard text marked this way. (Icons used in this book are shown a little later.)

Foolish Assumptions

I'm going to make only one assumption about you (let's see how close I get): You have access to a PC (at least some of the time) that has Windows 95 and Excel 97 installed on it (and I'll bet there isn't much room on your hard disk for anything more!). However, having said that, I make no assumption that you've ever launched Excel 97, let alone done anything with it.

This book is written expressly for users of Excel 97. If you have a previous version of Excel for Windows (like Excel 5.0) running under the previous version of Windows (version 3.1), please put this book down and instead pick up a copy of *Excel For Dummies,* 2nd Edition, or *MORE Excel 5 For Windows For Dummies,* both published by IDG Books Worldwide, Inc. If you have a version of Excel for the Macintosh, you also need to put this book down, walk over to the Macintosh section of the store, and pick up a copy of *Excel 5 For Macs For Dummies.*

If you happen to be using Excel 7.0 for Windows 95 (either because you just haven't seen the need for upgrading yet, you're just too cheap to purchase the upgrade, or after installing Windows 95 you simply don't have enough disk space left for Excel 97), you can use this book to learn Excel 7.0 for Windows 95, provided that you promise to pay strict attention to the Excel 97 icon shown in the left margin. Anytime you see this baby, it means that I'm talking about a feature or set of features that are brand-new in Excel 97 (which means that they weren't yet invented in your version of Excel). I don't want any flame mail from you saying how the book's all wrong about some feature that doesn't appear in your copy of Excel. If that happens, I'll have to write you back and tell you that you weren't paying attention to the Excel 97 icon. Shame on you.

How This Book Is Organized

This book is organized in six parts (which gives you a chance to see at least six of those great Rich Tennant cartoons!). Each part contains two or more chapters (to keep the editors happy) that more or less go together (to keep you happy). Each chapter is further divided into loosely related sections that cover the basics of the topic at hand. You should not, however, get too hung up about following along with the structure of the book; ultimately, it doesn't matter at all if you learn how to edit the worksheet before you learn how to format it, or you learn printing before you learn editing. The important thing is that you find the information — and understand it when you find it — when you need to perform a particular task.

Just in case you're interested, a brief synopsis of what you find in each part follows.

Part I: Getting In on the Ground Floor

As the name implies, Part I covers such fundamentals as how to start the program, identify the parts of the screen, enter information in the worksheet, save a document, and so on. If you're starting with absolutely no background in using spreadsheets, you definitely want to glance at the information in Chapter 1 to discover what this program is good for before you move on to how to create new worksheets in Chapter 2.

Part II: Editing without Tears

Part II gives you the skinny on how to edit spreadsheets to make them look good as well as how to make major editing changes to them without courting disaster. Refer to Chapter 3 when you need information on formatting the data to improve the way it appears in the worksheet. Refer to Chapter 4 when you need information on rearranging, deleting, or inserting new information in the worksheet. And refer to Chapter 5 when you need information on how to print out your finished product.

Part III: Getting Organized and Staying That Way

Part III gives you all kinds of information on how to stay on top of the data that you've entered in your spreadsheets. Chapter 6 is full of good ideas on how to keep track of and organize the data in a single worksheet. Chapter 7 gives you the ins and outs of working with data in different worksheets in the same workbook and gives you information on transferring data between the sheets of different workbooks.

Part IV: Life beyond the Spreadsheet

Part IV explores some of the other aspects of Excel besides the spreadsheet. In Chapter 8, you find out just how ridiculously easy it is to create a chart using the data in a worksheet. In Chapter 9, you discover just how useful Excel's database capabilities can be when you have to track and organize a large amount of information. In Chapter 10, you find out about adding hyperlinks to jump to new places in a worksheet, to new documents, and even to Web pages, as well as how to convert worksheet data into HTML tables so that they can be published on your company's Web site.

Part V: Doing a Custom Job

Part V gives you ideas about how to customize the way you work with Excel. In Chapter 11, you discover how to change the display options in Excel. In Chapter 12, you find out how to record and play back macros to automate tasks. In Chapter 13, you see how to customize the built-in toolbars and create new toolbars of your own.

Part VI: From the Home Office in Indianapolis

As is the tradition in these ...*For Dummies* books, the last part contains lists of the top ten most useful and useless facts, tips, and suggestions. Don't worry, you won't have to read ten more chapters when you flip to this part.

Conventions Used in This Book

The following information gives you the lowdown on how things look in this book — publishers call these the book's *conventions* (no campaigning, flag-waving, name-calling, or finger-pointing is involved, however).

Keyboard and mouse

Excel 97 is a sophisticated program with lots of fancy boxes, plenty of bars, and more menus than you can count. In Chapter 1, I explain all about these features and how to use them. Be sure to review Chapter 1 if you have any questions about how to get around the program.

Although you use the mouse and keyboard shortcut keys to move your way in, out, and around the Excel worksheet, you do have to take some time to enter the data so that you can eventually mouse around with it. Therefore, this book occasionally encourages you to type something specific into a specific cell in the worksheet. Of course, you can always choose not to follow the instructions. When I tell you to enter a specific function, the part you should type generally appears in **bold** type. For example, **=SUM(A2:B2)** means that you should type exactly what you see: an equal sign, the word **SUM**, a left parenthesis, the text **A2:B2** (complete with a colon between the letter-number combos), and a right parenthesis. You then, of course, have to press Enter to make the entry stick.

When Excel isn't talking to you by popping up message boxes, it displays highly informative messages in the status bar at the bottom of the screen. This book renders many messages that you see on-screen like this:

```
=SUM(A2:B2)
```

Occasionally I may ask you to press a *key combination* in order to perform a certain task. Key combinations are written like this: Ctrl+S. That plus sign in between means that you should hold down both the Ctrl key and the S key at the same time before releasing them. This (sometimes cruel) type of finger aerobics may take some practice for you novices, but don't worry; you'll soon be a key-combo pro!

When you need to wade through one or more menus to get to the selection you want, I sometimes (though not often, mind you) use *command arrows* to lead you from the initial menu to the submenu and so on to the command you ultimately want. For example, if you need to first open the File menu to get to the Open command, I may write that instruction like this: File⇨Open.

Notice those underlined letters in the preceding paragraph? Those letters — given the racy name *hot keys* — represent commands that you can activate simply by first pressing the Alt key and then pressing the underlined keys in succession. In the example of File⇨Open, you'd press Alt, and then F, and then O.

Special icons

The following icons are strategically placed in the margins to point out stuff you may or may not want to read.

This icon alerts you to nerdy discussions that you may well want to skip (or read when no one else is around).

This icon alerts you to shortcuts or other valuable hints related to the topic at hand.

This icon alerts you to information to keep in mind if you want to meet with a modicum of success.

This icon alerts you to information to keep in mind if you want to avert complete disaster.

This icon alerts you to brand-new features never before seen until the release of Excel 97.

Where to Go from Here

If you've never worked with a computer spreadsheet, I suggest that, right after getting your chuckles with the cartoons, you go first to Chapter 1 and find out what you're dealing with. If you're already familiar with the ins and outs of electronic spreadsheets but don't know anything about creating worksheets with Excel, jump into Chapter 2, where you find out how to get started entering data and formulas. Then, as specific needs arise (like "How do I copy a formula?" or "How do I print just a particular section of my worksheet?"), you can go to the table of contents or the index to find the appropriate section and go right to that section for answers.

Part I

Getting In on the Ground Floor

The 5th Wave — By Rich Tennant

"I think the cursor's not moving, Mr. Dunt, because you've got your hand on the chalk board eraser and not the mouse."

In this part . . .

*O*ne look at the Excel 97 screen (with all its boxes, buttons, and tabs), and you realize that there's a whole lot of stuff going on here. This is no doubt due to the addition of the Windows 95 taskbar to the (already rather over-designed) Excel 97 screen and then throwing in the Office toolbar to boot! Well, not to worry: Chapter 1's only reason for being is to break down the parts of the Excel 97 screen and make some sense out of the rash of icons, buttons, and boxes that you're going to be facing day after day after day.

Of course, it's not enough to just sit back and have someone like me explain what's what on the screen. To get any good out of Excel, you've got to start learning how to use all these bells and whistles (or buttons and boxes, in this case). That's where Chapter 2 comes in, giving you the lowdown on how to use some of the screen's more prominent buttons and boxes to get your spreadsheet data entered. From this humble beginning, it's a quick trip to total screen mastery.

Chapter 1

What Is All This Stuff?

*J*ust because electronic spreadsheets like Excel 97 have become almost as commonplace on today's personal computers as word processors and games doesn't mean that they're either well understood or well used. In fact, I've encountered scads of users, even those who are reasonably well versed in the art of writing and editing in Microsoft Word, who have little or no idea of what they could or should do with Excel.

This is really a shame, especially in this day and age when Office 97 seems to be the only software found on the majority of machines (probably because together Windows 95 and Office 97 hog so much hard disk space, there's no room left to install anybody else's software). If you're one of the folks who has Office 97 on your computer but doesn't know a spreadsheet from a bedsheet, this means that Excel 97 is just sitting there taking up a lot of space. Well, it's high time to change all that.

What the Hell Would I Do with Excel?

Excel is a great organizer for all types of data, be they numeric, textual, or otherwise. Because the program has loads of built-in calculating capabilities, most people turn to Excel when they need to set up financial spreadsheets. These spreadsheets tend to be filled to the gills with formulas for computing stuff like total sales, net profits and losses, growth percentages, and that sort of thing.

Also popular are Excel's charting capabilities that enable you to create all types of charts and graphs from the numbers you crunch in your financial worksheets. Excel makes it really easy to turn columns and rows of boring, black-and-white numbers into colorful and snappy charts and graphs. You can then use these charts to add some pizzazz to written reports (like those created with Word 97) or to punch up overheads used in formal business presentations (like those created with Microsoft PowerPoint).

Now, even if your job doesn't involve creating worksheets with a lot of fancy-Dan financial calculations or la-di-da charts, you probably have plenty of things for which you could and should be using Excel. For instance, you may have to keep lists of information or maybe even put together tables of information for your job. Excel is a great list keeper (even though we tend to refer to such lists as *databases* in Excel) and one heck of a table maker. Therefore, you can use Excel anytime you need to keep track of the products you sell, clients you service, employees you oversee, or you name it.

Little boxes, little boxes . . .

There's a really good reason why Excel is such a whiz at doing financial calculations by formula and keeping lists and tables of information organized. Look at any blank Excel worksheet (the one in Figure 1-1 will do fine) and just what do you see? Boxes, lots of little boxes, that's what! These little boxes (and there are millions of them in each worksheet you encounter) are called *cells* in spreadsheet jargon. And each piece of information (like a name, address, monthly sales figure, even your Aunt Sally's birthdate) goes into its own box (cell) in the worksheet you're building.

If you're used to word processing, this idea of entering different types of information in little, bitty cells can be somewhat strange to get used to. If you're thinking in word-processing terms, you need to think of the process of building an Excel worksheet as being more like setting up a table of information in a Word document than writing a letter or report.

Why spreadsheet programs produce nothing but worksheets

Spreadsheet programs like Excel 97 refer to their electronic sheets as *worksheets* rather than *spreadsheets*. And, although it is perfectly acceptable (even preferable) to call one of its electronic sheets a worksheet, you never, never refer to Excel as a worksheet program — it is always called a spreadsheet program. So you can think of Excel as a spreadsheet program that produces worksheets, but *not* as a worksheet program that produces spreadsheets. (On the other hand, I often refer to worksheets as spreadsheets in this book — and so can you.)

Send it to my cell address

As you can see in Figure 1-1, the Excel worksheet contains a frame used to label the columns and rows. Columns are given letters of the alphabet, while the rows are numbered. The columns and rows must be labeled because the Excel worksheet is humongous (Figure 1-1 shows only a tiny part of the total worksheet). The column and row labels act like street signs in a city — they can help you identify your current location, even if they don't prevent you from becoming lost.

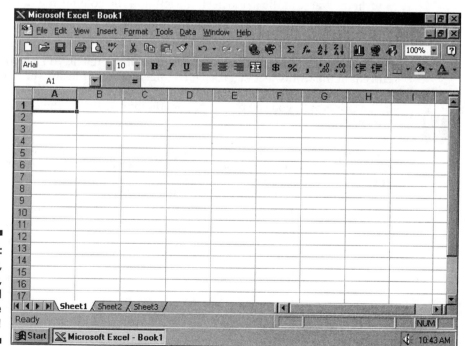

Figure 1-1:
Little boxes, little boxes, and they all look just the same!

Cells: the building blocks of all worksheets

The cells in an Excel worksheet are formed by the intersection of the column and row grid. Technically, such an arrangement is known as an *array*. An array keeps track of different pieces of information stored in it by referring to its row position and its column position (something you'll see more clearly when the subject of the R1C1 cell referencing system is discussed in the sidebar called "Cell A1 aka Cell R1C1" later in this chapter). This means that to display your worksheet data in its grid and tabular format, Excel just reads off the row and column position associated with the data you entered there.

As shown in Figure 1-2, Excel constantly shows you your current position in the worksheet in three different ways:

✔ Above the worksheet display at the beginning of what's called the *formula bar*, Excel lists the current cell location by its column and row reference as D5 when the cell at the intersection of column D and row 5 is current (the so-called *A1 cell reference system*).

✔ In the worksheet itself, the *cell pointer* (see the callout in Figure 1-2), shown by a heavy border, appears in the cell that's currently selected.

✔ In the frame of the worksheet, the letter of the column and the number of the row containing the cell pointer appear in bold and these parts of the frame have shadows, making them appear more sculpted.

You wonder why Excel makes such a big deal about telling you which cell is current in the worksheet? That's a good question, and the answer is important:

In the worksheet, you can only enter or edit information in the cell that's current.

The repercussions of this seemingly innocuous little statement are enormous. It means that if you're paying more attention to what you need to enter in your spreadsheet than to which cell is current, you can end up replacing something you've already entered. It also means that you'll never be able to edit a particular cell entry if you haven't first selected the cell to make it current.

Current cell reference   Cell pointer

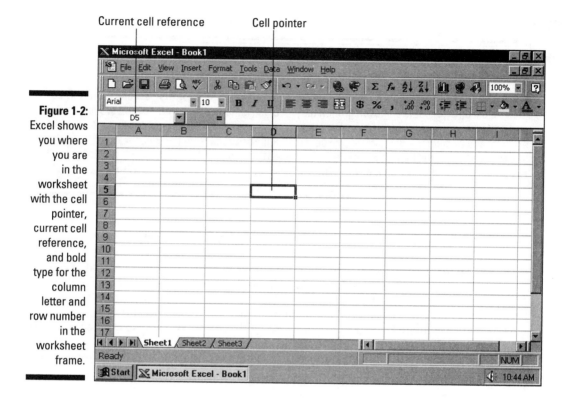

Figure 1-2:
Excel shows
you where
you are
in the
worksheet
with the cell
pointer,
current cell
reference,
and bold
type for the
column
letter and
row number
in the
worksheet
frame.

So just how many cells are we talking about here?

It's no exaggeration to say that each worksheet contains millions of cells, any of which can be filled with information. Each worksheet has 256 columns, of which only the first 10 or 11 (A through J or K) are normally visible in a new worksheet, and 65,536 rows, of which only the first 15 to 20 are normally visible in a new worksheet. If you multiply 256 by 65,536, you come up with a total of 16,777,216 empty cells in each worksheet you use (that's over 16 million of those suckers)!

And, as if that weren't enough, each new workbook that you start comes equipped with three of these worksheets, each with its own 16,777,216 blank cells. This gives you a grand total of 50,331,648 cells at your disposal in any one Excel file you happen to have open. And should that number prove to be too few (yeah, right!), you can add more worksheets (each with its 16,777,216 cells) to the workbook.

TECHNICAL STUFF

Cell A1 aka Cell R1C1

The A1 cell reference system is a holdover from the VisiCalc days (*VisiCalc* being the granddaddy of spreadsheet programs for personal computers). In addition to the A1 system, Excel 97 supports a much older, technically more correct system of cell references called the *R1C1 cell reference system*. In this system, both the columns and rows in the worksheet are numbered, and the row number precedes the column number. For example, in this system, cell A1 is called R1C1 (row 1, column 1); cell A2 is R2C1 (row 2, column 1); and cell B1 is R1C2 (row 1, column 2).

Assigning 26 letters to 256 columns

When it comes to labeling the 256 columns in a worksheet, our alphabet — with its measly 26 letters — is not up to the task. To make up the difference, Excel doubles up the cell letters in the column reference so that column AA immediately follows column Z. This is followed by column AB, AC, and so on to AZ. After column AZ, you find column BA, and then BB, BC, and so on. According to this system for doubling the column letters, the 256th (and last) column of the worksheet is column IV. This, in turn, gives the very last cell of any worksheet the cell reference IV65536.

What you should know about Excel at this point

Thus far, you know (or should know) the following things about Excel:

- ✔ Each Excel file is referred to as a *workbook*.

- ✔ Each new workbook you open contains three blank worksheets.

- ✔ Each worksheet in a workbook is divided into over 16 million cells (16,777,216 actually) made by the intersection of the 256 columns and 65,536 rows.

- ✔ Each worksheet is surrounded on the left and the top with a frame that labels the columns with letters of the alphabet and rows with numbers. Columns beyond column Z have a double-letter designation such as AA, AB, and so on.

More worksheet size trivia

If you were to produce the entire worksheet grid on paper, you would need a sheet that was approximately 21 feet wide by 1,365 feet long to do it! On a 14-inch computer screen, you can normally see no more than 10 or 11 complete columns and between 15 and 20 complete rows of the entire worksheet. With columns being about 1 inch wide and rows about 1/4 inch high, 10 columns represent a scant 3.9 percent of the total width of the worksheet, while 20 rows fill only about 0.03 percent of its total length. This should give you some idea of how little of the total worksheet is visible on the screen as well as just how much area is available.

- ✔ All spreadsheet information is stored in the individual cells of the worksheet. You can, however, only enter information into the cell that is current (that is, selected with the cell pointer).

- ✔ Excel indicates which of the over 16 million cells in the worksheet is the current (active) one by displaying its cell reference on the formula bar and displaying the cell pointer in the worksheet itself. (Refer to Figure 1-2.)

- ✔ The system for referencing cells in a worksheet — the so-called A1 cell reference system — combines the column letter (or letters) with the row number.

What you still need to know about Excel

Armed with the preceding information alone, however, you could easily get the mistaken idea that a spreadsheet program like Excel is little more than a quirky word processor with a gridlock that forces you to enter your information in tiny, individual cells instead of offering you the spaciousness of full pages.

Well, I'm here to say that Bill Gates didn't become a billionaire several times over by selling a quirky word processor (all you Microsoft Word users out there, please hold your tongues!). The big difference between the cell of a worksheet and the pages of a word processor is that each cell offers computing power along with text-editing and formatting capabilities. This computing power takes the form of formulas that you create in various cells of the worksheet.

Quite unlike a paper spreadsheet, which contains only values computed somewhere else, an electronic worksheet can store both the formulas and the computed values returned by these formulas. Even better, your formulas can use values stored in other cells of the worksheet, and, as explained later, Excel automatically updates the computed answer returned by such a formula anytime you change these values in the worksheet.

Excel's computational capabilities, combined with its editing and formatting capabilities, make the program perfect for generating any kind of document that uses textual and numeric entries and requires you to perform calculations on those values. Because you can make your formulas dynamic — so that their calculations are automatically updated when you change referenced values stored in other cells of the worksheet — you will find it much easier to keep the calculated values in a worksheet document both current and correct.

Getting the Darn Thing Started

If you're at all familiar with using Windows 95, it will come as no shock to find out that there are about a zillion ways to get Excel up and running once the program's been installed on your hard disk (actually, there are only about five, and I'm only going to talk about four of them). Suffice it to say at this point that all the various and sundry methods for starting Excel require that you have Windows 95 installed on your personal computer. After that, you have only to turn on the computer before you can use any of the following methods to get Excel 97 started.

Starting Excel 97 from the Office 97 shortcut bar

Starting Excel from the Office 97 shortcut bar is the easiest way to get the program up and running. The only problem with this method is that you can't use it unless you have the Office 97 shortcut bar installed on your computer and the Office toolbar (containing the Microsoft Excel button) selected. Supposing that both these preconditions are met, to start Excel 97, all you have to do is click the Microsoft Excel button on the Office toolbar to start the program (use Figure 1-3 to identify the Microsoft Excel button on this bar).

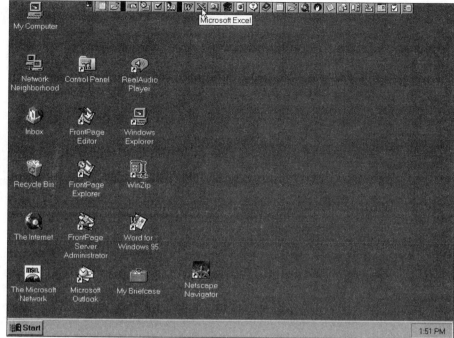

Figure 1-3:
To start
Excel 97
from the
Office
toolbar,
click the
Microsoft
Excel button
as shown in
the upper-
right corner.

Starting Excel 97 from the Windows 95 Start Menu

Even if you don't have the luxury of starting Excel from the Office 97 shortcut bar (because you don't have Office 97 or you didn't install the Office 97 short-cut bar), you can still start Excel 97 from the Windows 95 Start menu. (Hey, do you find dealing with these different years as confusing as I do?)

To start Excel 97 from the Start menu, follow these simple steps:

1. **Click the Start button on the Windows 95 taskbar to open the Windows 95 Start menu.**

2. **Select Programs at the top of the Start menu.**

3. **Select Microsoft Excel on the continuation menu.**

As soon as you get through step 3, Windows 95 opens Excel 97. As the program loads, you see the opening screen for Microsoft Excel 97. When Excel finishes loading, you are presented with a screen like the one shown in Figure 1-1 and Figure 1-2, containing a new workbook where you can begin working.

Starting Excel 97 from the Windows Explorer

Not content with just two ways for starting Excel 97? Well, here's another — this time using the Windows Explorer! The reason this start-up method is so valuable is that, with a slight variation, you can use it to open the Excel workbook you need to work on at the same time you launch the program.

First, here are the steps for starting Excel from the Explorer with a new, empty workbook:

1. **Open the Windows 95 Explorer.**

   Click the Start button on the taskbar, select Programs on the Start menu, and then click Windows Explorer.

2. **Locate the Microsoft Excel folder or the Microsoft Office folder in the All Folders list box of the Exploring - C:\ window.**

   Note that these folders are often located within the Programs folder on your hard disk. If you don't have Microsoft Office, go to step 3a; if you do have it, go to step 3b.

3a. **Click the Microsoft Excel folder icon in the All Folders list box, and then double-click the Excel program icon (appearing as the word "Excel" preceded by the XL icon) in the Contents of list box.**

3b. **Click the Office 97 folder icon in the All Folders list box, and then double-click the Excel folder icon in the Contents of list box before finally double-clicking the Excel program icon.**

Now this is a lot of stuff to go through if all you need to do is to start Excel 97 with a new workbook. But it's a great way to start the program if you happen to be using the Windows Explorer to find the Excel file you want to work with. In such a case, you have only to locate the Excel workbook file in the Contents of list box in the Exploring window and then double-click its file icon. Windows starts Excel 97 and then immediately opens the workbook file you just double-clicked.

Creating an Excel 97 shortcut

If you don't own Excel 97 as part of Office 97, and therefore don't have the option of starting the program with the Office shortcut, I highly recommend that you create a shortcut for Excel 97 so that you can start the program simply by double-clicking the shortcut icon on the desktop.

To create a shortcut bar for Excel 97, you follow these steps:

1. **Click the Start button on the taskbar.**

2. **Select Find on the Start menu and click Files or Folders on the Find continuation menu.**

3. **Type** excel.exe **in the Named edit box of the Find: All Files dialog box, and then press Enter or click the Find Now button.**

   Excel.exe is the filename of the program file that runs Excel 97.

4. **When Windows 95 finishes locating the file named Excel.exe on your hard disk, scroll down until you find a file named Excel (the .exe part of the filename normally remains hidden in a Windows 95 file listing) whose Type is listed as Application (this a dead giveaway that its real filename is Excel.exe and not just Excel).**

5. **Even if the Excel file icon's already selected, click it with the secondary mouse button (that is, right-click the file icon).**

   This opens its shortcut menu.

6. **Click Create Shortcut on the shortcut menu.**

   Windows 95 displays the alert dialog box warning you that Windows cannot create a shortcut in the Find dialog box and asking whether you want the shortcut placed on the desktop instead.

7. **Press Enter or click the Yes button.**

8. **Click the Close button (the one with the X) on the Find dialog box to get rid of it.**

   When Windows 95 closes the Find dialog box, you find a new icon on your desktop called "Shortcut to Excel." If you want, you can rename this icon to something a little less obvious like **Excel**, or words to that effect, by following step 9. Otherwise, if you're satisfied with the default shortcut name, you're done!

9. **Click the Shortcut to Excel icon with the secondary mouse button (that is, the right mouse button for most of you), and then click Rename on the shortcut menu.**

   You can then replace the original name by typing a new name (like Excel 97) beneath the icon and pressing Enter when you're finished.

To start Excel 97 with your new shortcut on the desktop, double-click the icon. Excel then opens with a new workbook as it does when you start the program from the Office 97 shortcut bar or the Start menu.

Automatically opening Excel every time you turn on your computer

This last technique for starting Excel 97 is only for those few of you who need to use Excel almost every single time you use your computer. If you fall into this class of Excel users, you can have Windows automatically start Excel 97 as soon as Windows 95 finishes loading, every time you turn on your computer. That way, all you have to do is turn on the power to your computer (you know where the computer's power switch is, don't you?), and in just a little while, you're set to get down to business in Excel 97.

To get Windows 95 to automatically start Excel every time you turn on the computer, you need to put a copy of the Excel 97 shortcut (described in the preceding section) in the Startup folder. You accomplish this little trick with these steps:

1. **Click the Start button on the taskbar, select Settings on the Start menu, and click Taskbar on the Settings continuation menu.**

2. **Click the Start Menu Programs tab in the Taskbar Properties dialog box.**

3. **Click the Advanced button (don't be afraid of the name) on the Start Menu Programs tab.**

4. **Click the little plus sign (+) in front of the Programs icon.**

   You can find the Programs icon beneath the Start Menu folder icon in the All Folders list box to open the Programs folder.

5. **Click Startup folder at the bottom of the All Folders list box.**

   When you click here, Windows displays the contents of the Startup folder in the Contents of list box on the right side of the Exploring window.

6. **If need be, drag the Exploring window and the Taskbar Properties dialog box out of the way (using their respective title bars) until you can see the Excel 97 shortcut on the desktop.**

7. **Hold down the Ctrl key, and then click and drag the Excel 97 shortcut icon from the desktop to the Contents of list box in the Exploring window.**

   When doing this step, be sure that you hold down the Ctrl key the whole time you drag (if you're doing it right, you should see a little plus sign in a box beneath your mouse pointer). Don't release the mouse button until you see that the outline of the Excel 97 shortcut icon appears in the Contents of list box. Then first release the mouse button before you let up on the Ctrl key. As soon as you release them, the Excel 97 shortcut icon will appear at the bottom of the Contents of list box in the Exploring window. If you don't see this shortcut icon, sorry, but you need to repeat steps 6 and 7 before proceeding to step 8.

8. **Click the Close button in the Exploring window to get rid of it.**

   The Close button is the one with an X.

9. **Click the OK button in the Taskbar Properties dialog box to close it.**

After placing a copy of the Excel 97 shortcut in the Startup folder, Excel 97 will now automatically open the next time you start Windows. You can test this setup by clicking the Start button and then clicking Sh<u>u</u>t Down on the Start menu. Next, click the <u>R</u>estart the computer radio button in the Shut Down windows dialog box before you click the <u>Y</u>es button or press Enter.

If you later decide that you don't want or need Excel staring you in the face each time you start your computer, you can stop all this automated start-up nonsense by removing the Excel 97 shortcut from the Startup folder. To do this, follow the first five steps of the preceding list and then switch to these steps:

6. **Click the Excel 97 shortcut icon in the Contents of 'Startup' list box.**

7. **Press the Delete key.**

8. **Click the <u>Y</u>es button.**

   Or you can press Enter in response to the message in the Confirm File Delete dialog box asking you if you are sure that you want to send 'Excel 97 Shortcut' to the Recycle Bin.

9. **Click the Close button in the Exploring window to get rid of it.**

   The Close button is the one with the X.

10. **Click the OK button or the Close button in the Taskbar Properties dialog box to close it.**

Mousing Around

Although most of Excel's capabilities are accessible from the keyboard, in most cases the mouse is the most efficient way to select a command or perform a particular procedure. For that reason alone, if you need to use Excel regularly in getting your work done, it is well worth your time to master the program's various mouse techniques.

Minding your mouse manners

Windows programs such as Excel use three basic mouse techniques to select and manipulate various objects in the program and workbook windows:

✔ **Clicking an object:** positioning the pointer on something and then pressing and immediately releasing the primary (left for right-handers or right for lefties) or, more rarely, the secondary (right for right-handers and left for southpaws) mouse button.

✔ **Double-clicking an object:** positioning the pointer on something and then pressing and immediately releasing the primary mouse button rapidly twice in a row.

✔ **Dragging an object:** positioning the pointer on something and then pressing and holding down the primary mouse button as you move the mouse in the direction you wish to drag the object. When you have positioned the object in the desired location on the screen, you then release the primary mouse button to place it.

When clicking an object to select it, you must make sure that the tip of the mouse pointer is touching the object you want to select before you click. To avoid moving the pointer slightly before you click, grasp the sides of the mouse between your thumb (on one side) and your ring and little fingers (on the other side), and then click the primary button with your index finger. If you run out of room on your desktop for moving the mouse, just pick up the mouse and reposition it on the desk (which does not move the pointer).

Getting your mouse pointer in shape

The shape of the mouse pointer is anything but static in the Excel program. As you move the mouse pointer to different parts of the Excel screen, the pointer changes shape to indicate a change in function. Table 1-1 shows you the various faces of the mouse pointer as well as the use of each shape.

Table 1-1	Minding the Shape of the Mouse Pointer in Excel
Mouse Pointer Shape	*What It Means*
⊕	This thick, white cross pointer appears as you move the pointer around the cells of the current worksheet. You use this pointer to select the cells you need to work with, which is then outlined by the cell pointer.
↖	The arrowhead pointer appears when you position the pointer on the toolbar, on the Excel menu bar, or on one of the edges of the block of cells that you've selected. You use the arrowhead pointer to choose Excel commands or to move or copy a cell selection with the drag-and-drop technique.

Mouse Pointer Shape	*What It Means*
I	The I-beam pointer appears when you click the entry in the formula bar, double-click a cell, or press F2 to edit a cell entry. You use this pointer to locate your place when editing a cell entry either in the cell itself or on the formula bar.
+	The fill handle (the thin, black cross) appears only when you position the pointer on the lower-right corner of the cell that contains the cell pointer. You use this pointer to create a series of sequential entries in a block or to copy an entry or formula in a block of cells.
▷?	The help pointer appears when you click the Help tool in the Standard toolbar. You use this pointer to click the menu command or tool on a toolbar for which you want help information.
↔	The double-headed arrow pointer appears when you've moved over the side of some object that can be sized. You use this pointer to increase or decrease the size of the object (be it a column, row, or text box).
⊣⊢	The split double-headed arrow pointer appears when you position the pointer over the horizontal or vertical split box or the tab split bar (see "Splitting the Difference" in Chapter 6). You use this pointer to split the workbook window into different panes or to increase or decrease the size of the horizontal scroll bar.
✛	The crossed double-headed arrow pointer appears when you choose Move on the workbook Control menu or press Ctrl+F7. You use this pointer to drag the workbook window into a new position in the area between the formula and status bar.

Don't confuse the mouse pointer with the cell pointer. The mouse pointer changes shape as you move it around the screen. The *cell pointer* always maintains its shape as an outline around the current cell or cell selection (whereupon it expands to include all the selected cells). The mouse pointer responds to any movement of your mouse on the desk and always moves independently of the cell pointer. You can use the mouse pointer to reposition the cell pointer, however. You do this by positioning the thick, white cross pointer in the cell that you want to hold the cell pointer and then clicking the primary mouse button.

So What Do All These Buttons Do?

Figure 1-4 identifies the different parts of the Excel program window that appear when you first start the program (assuming that you haven't selected an existing workbook to open at the same time the program starts and that you have the Office 97 shortcut bar open). As you can see, the Excel window, upon opening, is chock-full of all kinds of useful, though potentially confusing, stuff!

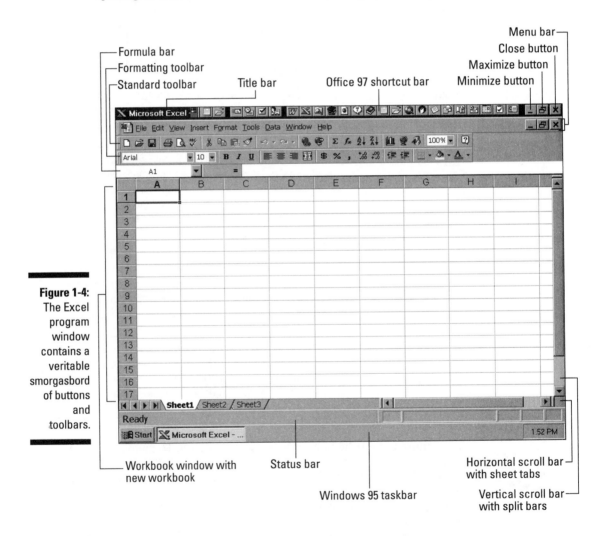

Figure 1-4: The Excel program window contains a veritable smorgasbord of buttons and toolbars.

Turning on to the title bar

The first bar in the Excel window is called the *title bar* because it shows you the name of the program that is running in the window (Microsoft Excel). When the workbook window is maxed out (as it is in Figure 1-4), the name of the workbook file follows Microsoft Excel, as in

```
Microsoft Excel - Book1
```

To the left of the program and filename on the title bar, you see the XL icon. If you click this icon, the program Control menu opens with all the commands that let you size and move the Excel program window. If you choose the Close command on this menu (or press the shortcut keys, Alt+F4), you exit from Excel and are returned to the desktop.

The buttons on the right side of the title bar are sizing buttons. If you click the Minimize button (the one with the underscore), the Excel window shrinks down to a button on the Windows 95 taskbar. If you click the Restore button (the one with the image of two smaller, tiled windows), the Excel window assumes a somewhat smaller size on the desktop, and the Restore button changes to the Maximize button (the one with a single, full-size window), which you can use to restore the window to its original full size. If you click the Close button (the one with an X), you exit Excel (just as though you had chosen Close on the Control menu or pressed Alt+F4).

Messing around with the menu bar

The second bar in the Excel window is the *menu bar*. This bar contains the Excel pull-down menus, File through Help, that you use to select the Excel commands you need to use (jump ahead to the section "Ordering Directly from the Menus" for more information on how to select commands).

To the left of the pull-down menus, you see an Excel file icon. If you click this icon, the file Control menu (much like the program Control menu) opens, showing all the commands that let you size and move the Excel workbook window (which fits within the Excel program window). If you choose the Close command on this menu (or press the shortcut keys, Ctrl+W or Ctrl+F4), you close the current Excel workbook without exiting the Excel program.

The sizing buttons on the right side of the menu bar do the same thing to the current workbook window as the sizing buttons on the title bar do to the Excel program window. If you click the Minimize button, the Excel workbook window shrinks down to a tiny workbook title bar at the bottom of the workbook area. If you click the Restore button, the current workbook window assumes a

Showing off a toolbar's screen tips

To display the name of a tool on any toolbar shown on the screen, simply position the mouse pointer on the button (WITHOUT clicking the button). Excel then displays the name of the button in a little box below the pointer and a brief description of what the tool does on the Status bar. (Microsoft refers to the indicators like this that appear next to the mouse pointer as *screentips*.)

somewhat smaller size on the workbook area; the XL workbook icon, filename, and file-sizing buttons move to the title bar of this somewhat smaller workbook window; and the Restore button changes to the Maximize button, which you can use to restore the window to its original full size. If you click the Close button (the one with the X), you close the current workbook file (just as though you had chosen Close on the file Control menu or pressed Ctrl+W or Ctrl+F4).

Scrutinizing the Standard toolbar

The Standard toolbar occupies the third bar of the Excel program window. Each button (more commonly called a *tool*) in this bar performs a particular function when you click it with the mouse. For example, you can use the first tool to open a new workbook, the second one to open an existing workbook file, the third one to save the current workbook, and the fourth one to print the workbook. Table 1-2 shows you the name and function of each tool on the Standard toolbar. Rest assured, you will come to know each one intimately as your experience with Excel grows.

Table 1-2	The Cool Tools on the Standard Toolbar	
Tool in Question	*Tool Name*	*What the Tool Does When You Click It*
🗋	New	Opens a new workbook with three blank worksheets
📂	Open	Opens an existing Excel workbook
💾	Save	Saves changes in the active workbook
🖨	Print	Prints the workbook

Tool in Question	Tool Name	What the Tool Does When You Click It
	Print Preview	Previews how the worksheet will appear when printed
	Spelling	Checks the spelling of text in your worksheet
	Cut	Cuts the current selection to the Clipboard
	Copy	Copies the current selection to the Clipboard
	Paste	Pastes the contents of the Clipboard in the current worksheet
	Format Painter	Applies all the formatting used in the current cell to any cell selection you choose
	Undo	Undoes your last action
	Redo	Repeats your last action
	Insert Hyperlink	Lets you insert a hypertext link to another file, Internet address (URL), or specific location in another document (see Chapter 10 for information on using hyperlinks)
	Web Toolbar	Displays and hides the Web Toolbar with the tools for publishing your worksheet on the World Wide Web (see Chapter 10 for information on using this toolbar)
	AutoSum	Adds a list of values with the SUM function
	Paste Function	Lets you use one of Excel's many built-in functions (see Chapter 2 for details)
	Sort Ascending	Sorts data in a cell selection in alphabetical and/or numerical order, depending upon the type of data in the cells

(continued)

Table 1-2 *(continued)*

Tool in Question	Tool Name	What the Tool Does When You Click It
	Sort Descending	Sorts data in a cell selection in reverse alphabetical and/or numerical order, depending upon the type of data in the cells
	ChartWizard	Steps you through the creation of a new chart in the active worksheet (see Chapter 8 for details)
	Map	Creates a map from worksheet data that analyzes the info by geographic region (see Chapter 8 for details)
	Drawing	Displays and hides the Drawing toolbar, which lets you draw various shapes and arrows (see Chapter 8 for details)
100%	Zoom	Changes the screen magnification to zoom in or out on your worksheet data
	Office Assistant	Activates the Office Assistant and lets you get tips on using Excel or ask him a question (see "Conferring with your Office Assistant" later in this chapter for details)

Finding your way around the Formatting toolbar

Beneath the Standard toolbar, you see the Formatting toolbar, so called because its buttons are mainly used to format cells in your worksheet. Table 1-3 shows you the name of each tool on this toolbar along with a brief description of its function.

Table 1-3   The Cool Tools on the Formatting Toolbar

Tool	Tool Name	What the Tool Does When You Click It
Arial	Font	Applies a new font to the entries in the cell selection
10	Font Size	Applies a new font size to the entries in the cell selection

Tool	Tool Name	What the Tool Does When You Click It
B	Bold	Applies bold to or removes bold from the cell selection
I	Italic	Applies italics to or removes italics from the cell selection
U	Underline	Underlines the *entries* in the cell selection (not the cells); if the entries are already underlined, clicking this tool removes the underlining
☰	Align Left	Left-aligns the entries in the cell selection
☰	Center	Centers the entries in the cell selection
☰	Align Right	Right-aligns the entries in the cell selection
⊞	Merge and Center	Centers the entry in the active cell across selected columns by merging their cells into one
$	Currency Style	Applies a Currency number format to the cell selection to display all values with a dollar sign, with commas between thousands, and two decimal places
%	Percent Style	Applies a Percentage number format to the cell selection; the values are multiplied by 100 and displayed with a percent sign and no decimal places
,	Comma Style	Applies a Comma number format to the cell selection to display commas separating thousands and adds two decimal places
.00	Increase Decimal	Adds one decimal place to the number format in the cell selection each time you click the tool; reverses direction and reduces the number of decimal places when you hold the Shift key as you click this tool
.00	Decrease Decimal	Reduces one decimal place from the number format in the cell selection each time you click the tool; reverses direction and adds one decimal place when you hold the Shift key as you click this tool

(continued)

Table 1-3 *(continued)*

Tool	Tool Name	What the Tool Does When You Click It
	Decrease Indent	Outdents the entry in the current cell to the left by one character width of the standard font
	Increase Indent	Indents the entry in the current cell to the right by one character width of the standard font
	Borders	Selects a border for the cell selection from the pop-up palette of border styles
	Fill Color	Selects a new color for the background of the cells in the cell selection from the pop-up color palette
	Font Color	Selects a new color for the text in the cells in the cell selection from the pop-up color palette

The Standard and Formatting toolbars contain the most commonly used tools and are the ones that are automatically displayed in the Excel window when you first start the program. Excel does, however, include several other toolbars that you can display as your work requires their special tools. As you soon discover, Excel's toolbars are a real boon to productivity because they make the program's standard routines so much more accessible than the pull-down menus.

Fumbling around the formula bar

The formula bar displays the cell address and the contents of the current cell. This bar is divided into three sections: the first, leftmost section (called the Name Box) contains the current cell address with a drop-down button to its right; the second, middle section is shaded and displays only a single button with an equal sign on it (called the Edit Formula button); and the third, rightmost section is the white area that takes up all the rest of the bar. If the current cell is empty, the third section of the formula bar is blank. As soon as you begin typing an entry or building a worksheet formula, the second and third sections of the formula bar come alive.

As soon as you press a key, the Cancel and Enter buttons appear in the second section (see Figure 1-5) between the drop-down button in the Name Box and the Edit Formula button. (See Chapter 2 for information on using these buttons.)

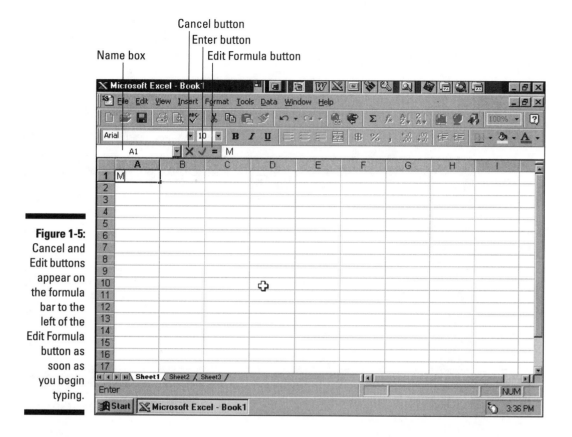

Cancel button
Enter button
Edit Formula button

Name box

Figure 1-5:
Cancel and
Edit buttons
appear on
the formula
bar to the
left of the
Edit Formula
button as
soon as
you begin
typing.

After this string of buttons, you see the characters that you've typed in the third section of the bar, mirroring the characters that appear in the worksheet cell itself. After you complete the entry in the cell — either by clicking the Enter button on the formula bar or by pressing Enter or an arrow key — Excel displays the entire entry or formula in the formula bar, and the string of buttons disappears from the center section of the formula bar. The contents of that cell thereafter appear in the formula bar whenever that cell contains the cell pointer.

Winding your way through the workbook window

A blank Excel workbook appears in a workbook window right below the formula bar when you first start the program (assuming that you don't start it by double-clicking an Excel workbook icon). As you can see in Figure 1-6, when the workbook window is less than full size and larger than a minimized workbook title bar, the window has its own Control menu (accessed by clicking the XL file

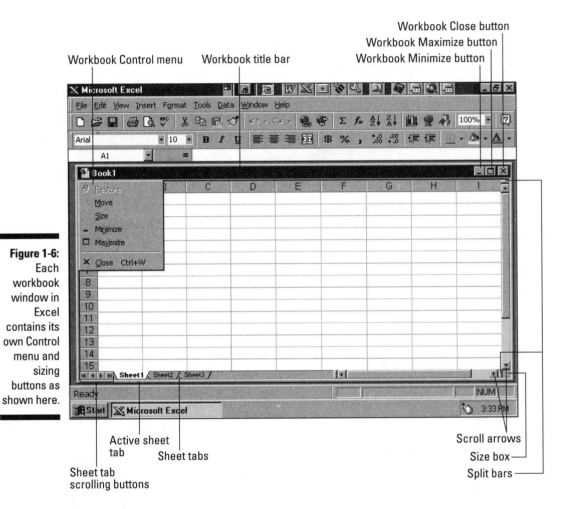

Workbook Close button
Workbook Maximize button
Workbook Minimize button

Workbook Control menu   Workbook title bar

Figure 1-6:
Each
workbook
window in
Excel
contains its
own Control
menu and
sizing
buttons as
shown here.

Sheet tab
scrolling buttons

Active sheet
tab

Sheet tabs

Scroll arrows
Size box
Split bars

icon), title bar, and sizing buttons. Its title bar also displays the workbook filename (this appears as a temporary filename like Book1, and then Book2 when you open your next new workbook, and so on, until you save the file the first time).

On the bottom of the workbook window, you see sheet tab scrolling buttons, then the sheet tabs for activating the various worksheets in your workbook (remember that there are three new sheets to start), followed by the horizontal scroll bar that you can use to bring new columns of the current worksheet into view. On the right side of the workbook window, you see a vertical scroll that you can use to bring new rows of the current worksheet into view (keeping in mind that you are only viewing a small percentage of the total columns and rows in each worksheet). At the intersection of the horizontal and vertical scroll bars, in the lower-right corner, you find a size box, which you can use to manually modify the size and shape of the less-than-maximized workbook window.

As soon as you start Excel, you can immediately begin creating a new spreadsheet in Sheet1 of the Book1 workbook that appears in the maximized workbook window. If you separate the workbook title bar, Control menu, and sizing buttons from the Excel menu bar, click the Restore button on the menu bar. Doing this will reduce the workbook window just enough to get all this stuff off the menu (as shown in Figure 1-6).

When a workbook sheet is not a worksheet

Worksheets are not the only type of sheet that you can have in an Excel workbook. In addition to worksheets, your workbook can contain *chart sheets,* which contain charts (see Chapter 8) created from data in one of the worksheets, and/or *macro sheets* (see Chapter 12), which in turn contain the code for macros that automate various tasks that you perform on your worksheets or charts.

Manually manipulating the workbook window

As I mentioned in the preceding section, when you're working with a less-than-maximized workbook window (like the one shown in Figure 1-6), you can manually size and move the window with the sizing box that appears in the lower-right corner at the intersection of the horizontal and vertical scroll bars.

To manipulate the size of a workbook window, position the mouse pointer on this sizing box, and then, when the mouse pointer changes shape to a double-headed arrow, drag the mouse as needed to adjust the size of the side or sides of the window. Note that the mouse pointer does not change to a double-headed arrow unless you position it on the edge of the window (that is, somewhere on the corner). While the pointer is positioned within the box, it retains its arrowhead shape.

- ✔ If you position the pointer on the bottom side of the window, and then drag the pointer straight up, the workbook window becomes shorter. If you drag the pointer straight down, the window becomes longer.

- ✔ If you position the pointer on the right side of the window, and then drag the pointer straight to the left, the workbook window becomes narrower; if you drag straight to the right, the window becomes wider.

- ✔ If you position the pointer on the lower-right corner of the window, and then drag the pointer diagonally toward the upper-left corner, the workbook window becomes both shorter and narrower; if you drag diagonally away from the upper-left corner, it becomes longer and wider.

When the outline of the workbook window reaches the desired size, you then release the primary mouse button and Excel redraws the workbook window to your new size.

After using the size button to change the size and shape of a workbook window, you must use the size button again and manually restore the window to its original shape and dimensions. There is, unfortunately, no magic Restore button available that you can click to automatically restore the workbook window that you changed back to its original shape and size.

Besides resizing workbook windows, you can also move them around within the area between the formula bar and status bar in the Excel program window. To move a workbook window

1. **Simply pick it up by the scruff of its neck — which, in this case, corresponds to the window's title bar.**

2. **After you've got it by the title bar, drag it to the desired position and release the primary mouse button.**

If you are experiencing any difficulty in dragging objects with the mouse, you can also move a workbook window by following these steps:

1. **Click the XL file icon on the workbook window's title bar to open its Control menu and then select the <u>M</u>ove command or press Ctrl+F7.**

   The mouse pointer will change shape from the normal thick, white-cross pointer to a pointer with crossed, double-headed arrows.

2. **Drag the window with the arrowheads' cross-hair pointer or press the arrow keys on the cursor keypad (←, ↑, →, or ↓) to move the workbook window into the desired position.**

3. **Press Enter to set the workbook window into position.**

   The mouse pointer returns to its normal thick, white-cross shape.

Slipping through the sheets

At the very bottom of the Excel workbook window that contains the horizontal scroll bar, you see the sheet tab scrolling buttons followed by the sheet tabs for the three worksheets in the workbook. Excel shows which worksheet is active by displaying its sheet tab on top in white as part of the displayed worksheet (rather than belonging to unseen worksheets below). To activate a new worksheet (thus bringing it to the top and displaying its information in the workbook window), you click its sheet tab.

If you add more sheet tabs to your workbook (see Chapter 12 for details on how to add more worksheets to your workbook) and the sheet tab for the worksheet you want to work with is not displayed, you can use the sheet tab scrolling buttons to bring the worksheet into view. Click the buttons with the triangles pointing left and right to scroll one worksheet at a time in either direction (left to scroll left and right to scroll right). Click the buttons with the triangles pointing left and right to the vertical lines to scroll the sheets so that the tabs for the very first or very last worksheets are displayed at the bottom.

Scoping out the status bar

The bar at the very bottom of the Excel program window is called the status bar because it displays information that keeps you informed of the current state of Excel. The left part of the status bar displays messages indicating the current activity you're undertaking or the current command you've selected from the Excel menu bar. When you first start Excel, the message Ready is displayed in this area (as shown in Figure 1-7), telling you that the program is ready to accept your next entry or command.

The right side of the status bar contains various boxes that display different indicators telling you when you've placed Excel in a particular state that somehow affects how you work with the program. For example, normally, when you first start Excel, the Num Lock indicator shows NUM in this part of the status bar.

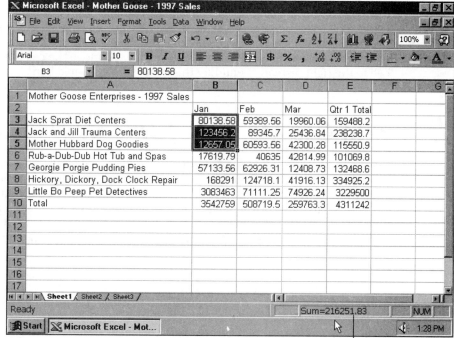

Figure 1-7:
The AutoCalculate indicator automatically displays the sum of the values in the selected (highlighted) cells in the worksheet.

AutoCalculate indicator

You AutoCalculate my totals

The widest box (the second one from the left) in the status bar contains the AutoCalculate indicator. You can use the AutoCalculate indicator to get a running total of any group of values in your worksheet (see the beginning of Chapter 3 if you need information on how to select groups of cells in a worksheet). For example, Figure 1-7 shows you a typical spreadsheet after selecting part of a column of cells, many of which contain values. The total of all the values in the cells that are currently selected in this worksheet automatically appears in the AutoCalculate indicator on the status bar.

Not only does the AutoCalculate indicator on the status bar give you the sum of the values in the cells you currently have selected, but it can also give you the count or the average of these values. To get the count of all the cells that contain values (cells containing text entries are not counted), you click the AutoCalculate indicator with the secondary mouse button and select Count on this indicator's shortcut menu. To get the average of the values in the current cell selection, you click the AutoCalculate indicator with the secondary mouse button and select Average on this indicator's shortcut menu. To return the AutoCalculate indicator to its normal totaling function, you click it with the secondary mouse button and choose SUM on the indicator's shortcut menu.

The Num Lock indicator and the numeric keypad

The NUM in the Num Lock indicator tells you that you can use the numbers on the numeric keypad to enter values in the worksheet. When you press the Num Lock key, NUM disappears from the Num Lock indicator. This is your signal that the cursor-movement functions that are also assigned to this keypad are now in effect. This means, for instance, that pressing 6 will move the cell pointer one cell to the right instead of entering this value in the formula bar!

You Gotta Get Me Out of This Cell!

Excel provides several methods for getting around each of the huge worksheets in your workbook. One the easiest ways is to click the tab for the sheet you want to work with, and then use the scroll bars in the workbook window to bring new parts of this worksheet into view. In addition, the program provides a wide range of keystrokes that you can use not only to move a new part of the worksheet into view but also to make a new cell active by placing the cell pointer in it.

The secrets of scrolling

To understand how scrolling works in Excel, imagine the worksheet as a humongous papyrus scroll attached to rollers on the left and right. To bring into view a new section of a papyrus worksheet that is hidden on the right, you crank the left roller until the section with the cells you want to see appears. Likewise, to scroll into view a new section of the worksheet that is hidden on the left, you would crank the right roller until the section of cells appears.

Calling up new columns with the horizontal scroll bar

You can use the *horizontal scroll bar* to scroll back and forth through the columns of a worksheet. To scroll new columns into view from the right, you click the right-arrow scroll button on the horizontal scroll bar. To scroll new columns into view from the left (anytime except when column A is the first column displayed), you click the left-arrow scroll button.

To scroll very quickly through columns in one direction or the other, you click the appropriate arrow scroll button in the scroll bar and *continue to hold down* the primary mouse button until the columns you want to see are displayed on the screen. As you scroll to the right in this manner, the *horizontal scroll box* (that big shaded box between the left- and right-arrow scroll buttons in the scroll bar) becomes increasingly smaller — it gets really teeny if you scroll really far right to columns in the hinterland such as BA. If you then click and hold down the left-arrow scroll button to scroll quickly back through columns to the left, you will notice that the horizontal scroll box becomes increasingly larger, until it takes up most of the scroll bar when you finally display column A again.

 You can use the scroll box in the horizontal scroll bar to make big jumps to the left and right in the columns of the worksheet. Simply drag the scroll box in the appropriate direction along the bar. As you drag, the letter of the column that would appear as the leftmost column in the worksheet (should you then release the mouse button) is displayed above the horizontal scroll bar (this feature of showing how far you've scrolled is known as *scroll tips*). You can use the column letter display in the horizontal scroll tips to gauge when to release the mouse button to stop the horizontal scrolling.

Raising up new rows with the vertical scroll bar

You can use the *vertical scroll bar* to scroll up and down through the rows of a worksheet. To scroll to new rows below those currently in view, you click the down-arrow scroll button on the vertical scroll bar. To scroll back up to rows above that are no longer in view (anytime except when row 1 is the first one displayed), you click the up-arrow scroll button.

To scroll very quickly through rows in one direction or the other, you click and hold down the appropriate arrow scroll button in the vertical scroll bar just as you do in the horizontal scroll bar. As you scroll down the rows with the down-arrow scroll button, the *vertical scroll box* (that big shaded box between the up- and down-arrow scroll buttons in the scroll bar) becomes increasingly smaller and smaller — it gets really teeny if you scroll way down to rows like 100 and higher. If you then click and hold down the up-arrow scroll button to scroll quickly back up through the rows, you will notice that the vertical scroll box becomes increasingly larger, until it takes up most of the scroll bar when you finally display row 1 again.

You can use the vertical scroll box to make big jumps up and down the rows of the worksheet by dragging the vertical scroll box in the appropriate direction along the bar. As you drag, the scroll tips shows you the number of the row that would appear at the very top of the worksheet area (should you release the mouse button at that very moment) is displayed to the left of the vertical scroll bar. You can use this row number display in the vertical scroll tips to tell when you should release the mouse button to stop the vertical scrolling.

Scrolling from screen to screen

You can also use the horizontal and vertical scroll bars to scroll through the columns and rows of your worksheet a screenful at a time. To do this, you click the light gray area of the scroll bar *not* occupied by the scroll box or the arrow scroll buttons. For example, to scroll to the right by a screenful of columns when the scroll box is snug against the left-arrow scroll button, you simply click the light gray area of the scroll bar behind the scroll box, between it and the right-arrow scroll button. Then, to scroll back to the left by a screenful of columns, you click the light gray area in front of the scroll box, between it and the left-arrow scroll button.

Likewise, to scroll up and down the rows of the worksheet a screenful at a time, you click the light gray area either above or below the vertical scroll box, between it and the appropriate arrow scroll button.

Scrolling with the IntelliMouse

Microsoft has developed a new type of mouse called the IntelliMouse, designed specifically for scrolling through Office 97 documents and lists of stuff in Windows 95. On the IntelliMouse, in between the normal left and right mouse buttons, you find a little wheel.

In Excel 97, you can use this wheel instead of the scroll bars to move to a new part of a worksheet as follows:

- Turn the wheel button up and down a notch to scroll up and down the rows of cells, three rows at a time. As you rotate the wheel down by notches, you scroll down the rows of the worksheet. As you rotate the wheel up by notches, you scroll up the rows of the worksheet.

- Click the wheel button to scroll in any of the four directions (up, down, left, or right). When you click the wheel button, the mouse pointer changes to a four-headed arrow shape. To then scroll in a particular direction, simply move the mouse (without clicking any of the mouse buttons) in the direction in which you wish to scroll the worksheet. When the part of the worksheet with the cells you want to use appears on the screen, click one of the cells in that area to stop the scrolling and return the mouse pointer to its normal white-cross shape.

Note that you can change how many rows up and down you scroll as you turn the wheel button and how far the mouse pointer moves when you move the mouse by following these steps:

1. **Open the Control Panel dialog box by clicking the Start button on the Windows 95 taskbar and then choosing Settings⇨Control Panel on the pop-up menus.**

2. **Open the Mouse Properties dialog box by double-clicking the Mouse icon in the Control Panel dialog box.**

3. **Click the Wheel tab in the Mouse Properties dialog box.**

4. **To change how many lines (rows) of the document (worksheet) you scroll each time you turn the wheel one notch, open the Settings for Wheel dialog box. Do this by clicking the Settings button in the Wheel section of the Wheel tab of the Mouse Properties dialog box. Replace 3 with a new value in the Scroll 3 lines at a time check box before you click the OK button or press Enter.**

   Performing this step closes the Settings for Wheel dialog box and brings you back to the Mouse Properties dialog box.

5. **To change how fast the mouse pointer scrolls when you click the Wheel button, open the Settings for Wheel Button dialog box. Do this by clicking the Settings button in the Wheel Button area on the Wheel tab of this dialog box. Drag the slider to adjust the speed with the ← and → key (press ← to go slower or → to go faster) before you click OK or press Enter.**

   Performing this step this closes the Settings for Wheel Button dialog box and brings you back to the Mouse Properties dialog box.

6. **Click the OK button in the Mouse Properties dialog box to close this dialog box.**

7. **Click the Close button in the Control Panel to close this dialog box.**

The keys to moving the cell pointer

The only disadvantage to using the scroll bars to move around is that the scroll bars only bring new parts of the worksheet into view — they don't actually change the position of the cell pointer. This means that, if you want to start making entries in the cells in a new area of the worksheet, you still have to remember to select the cell (by clicking it) or the group of cells (by dragging through them) where you want the data to appear before you begin entering the data.

Excel offers a wide variety of keystrokes for moving the cell pointer to a new cell. When you use one of these keystrokes, the program automatically scrolls a new part of the worksheet in view, if this is required in moving the cell pointer. Table 1-4 summarizes these keystrokes and how far each one moves the cell pointer from its starting position.

Note that, in the case of those keystrokes listed in Table 1-4 that use arrow keys, you must either use the arrows on the cursor keypad or else have the Num Lock disengaged on the numeric keypad of your keyboard. If you try to use these arrow keys to move around the worksheet when Num Lock is on (indicated by the appearance of NUM on the status bar), you'll either get numbers in the current cell or nothing will happen at all (and then you'll blame me)!

Table 1-4	Keystrokes for Moving the Cell Pointer
Keystroke in Question	*Where the Cell Pointer Moves*
→ or Tab	Cell to the immediate right
← or Shift+Tab	Cell to the immediate left
↑	Cell up one row
↓	Cell down one row
Home	Cell in Column A of the current row
Ctrl+Home	First cell (A1) of the worksheet
Ctrl+End or End, Home	Cell in the worksheet at the intersection of the last column that has any data in it and the last row that has any data in it (that is, the last cell of the so-called *active area* of the worksheet)
PgUp	Cell one screenful up in the same column
PgDn	Cell one screenful down in the same column
Ctrl+→ or End, →	First occupied cell to the right in the same row that is either preceded or followed by a blank cell
Ctrl+← or End, ←	First occupied cell to the left in the same row that is either preceded or followed by a blank cell
Ctrl+↑ or End, ↑	First occupied cell above in the same column that is either preceded or followed by a blank cell
Ctrl+↓ or End, ↓	First occupied cell below in the same column that is either preceded or followed by a blank cell
Ctrl+PgDn	Last occupied cell in the next worksheet of that workbook
Ctrl+PgUp	Last occupied cell in the previous worksheet of that workbook

Block moves

The keystrokes that combine the Ctrl or End key with an arrow key listed in Table 1-4 are among the most helpful for moving quickly from one edge to the other in large tables of cell entries or in moving from table to table in a section of the worksheet that contains many blocks of cells.

- ✔ If the cell pointer is positioned on a blank cell somewhere to the left of a table of cell entries that you want to view, pressing Ctrl+→ moves the cell pointer to the first cell entry at the leftmost edge of the table (in the same row, of course).

- ✔ When you then press Ctrl+→ a second time, the cell pointer moves to the last cell entry at the rightmost edge (assuming that there are no blank cells in that row of the table).

- ✔ If you switch direction and press Ctrl+↓, Excel moves right to the last cell entry at the bottom edge of the table (again assuming that there are no blank cells below in that column of the table).

- ✔ If, when the cell pointer is at the bottom of the table, you press Ctrl+↓ again, Excel moves the pointer to the first entry at the top of the next table located below (assuming that there are no other cell entries above this table in the same column).

- ✔ If you press Ctrl or End and arrow key combinations and there are no more occupied cells in the direction of the arrow key you selected, Excel advances the cell pointer right to the cell at the very edge of the worksheet in that direction.

- ✔ If the cell pointer is located in cell C15 and there are no more occupied cells in row 15, when you press Ctrl+→, Excel moves the cell pointer to cell IV at the rightmost edge of the worksheet.

- ✔ If you are in cell C15 and there are no more entries below in Column C and you press Ctrl+↓, Excel moves the pointer to cell C65536 at the very bottom edge of the worksheet.

When you use Ctrl and an arrow key to move from edge to edge in a table or between tables in a worksheet, you hold down Ctrl while you press one of the four arrow keys (indicated by the + symbol in keystrokes such as Ctrl+→).

When you use End and an arrow-key alternative, you must press and then release the End key *before* you press the arrow key (indicated by the comma in keystrokes such as End, →). Pressing and releasing the End key causes the END indicator to appear on the status bar. This is your sign that Excel is ready for you to press one of the four arrow keys.

Because you can keep the Ctrl key depressed as you press the different arrow keys you need to use, the Ctrl-plus-arrow-key method provides a more fluid method for navigating blocks of cells than the End-then-arrow-key method.

When you gotta go to that cell now!

Excel's Go To feature provides an easy method for moving directly to a distant cell in the worksheet. To use this feature, you display the Go To dialog box by selecting the Go To command on the Edit pull-down menu or by pressing Ctrl+G or the function key, F5. Then, in the Go To dialog box, you type the address of the cell you want to go to in the Reference edit box and select OK or press Enter. When typing in the cell address in the Reference text box, you can type the column letter or letters in upper- or lowercase letters.

When you use the Go To feature to move the cell pointer, Excel remembers the references of the last four cells that you visited. These cell references then appear in the Go To list box. Notice that the address of the cell you last came from is also listed in the Reference box. This makes it possible to move quickly from your present location to your previous location in a worksheet by pressing F5 and Enter (provided that you used the Go To feature to move to your present position).

Lotsa luck with Scroll Lock

You can use the Scroll Lock key to "freeze" the position of the cell pointer in the worksheet so that you can scroll new areas of the worksheet in view with keystrokes such as PgUp and PgDn without changing the cell pointer's original position (in essence, making these keystrokes work in the same manner as the scroll bars).

After engaging Scroll Lock, when you scroll the worksheet with the keyboard, Excel does not select a new cell as it brings a new section of the worksheet into view. To "unfreeze" the cell pointer when scrolling the worksheet via the keyboard, you just press the Scroll Lock key again.

Ordering Directly from the Menus

For those occasions when the Excel Standard and Formatting toolbars don't provide you with a ready-made tool for getting a particular task done, you have to turn to the program's system of menu commands. Excel exhibits a little bit of menu overkill in that, in addition to the regular pull-down menus found on the command bar of nearly all Windows applications, the program also offers a secondary system of *context* (or shortcut) *menus*.

Shortcut menus are so called because they offer fast access to just those menu commands normally used to manipulate the particular screen object that the menu is attached to (such as a toolbar, workbook window, or worksheet cell). As a result, shortcut menus often bring together commands that are otherwise found on several individual pull-down menus on the menu bar.

Penetrating the pull-down menus

As when moving the cell pointer in the worksheet, Excel offers you a choice of using the mouse or the keyboard to select commands from the command bar. To open a pull-down menu with the mouse, you simply click the menu name on the command bar. To open a pull-down menu with the keyboard, you hold down the Alt key as you type the letter that is underlined in the menu name (also known as the *command letter*). For instance, if you press Alt and, as you hold it down, then press E (abbreviated Alt+E), Excel opens the Edit menu because the *E* in "Edit" is underlined.

Alternately, you can press and release the Alt key or function key F10 to access the menu bar, and then press the → key until you highlight the menu you want to open. Then, to open the menu, you press the ↓ key.

After you've opened your pull-down menu, you can select any of its commands by clicking the command with the mouse, pressing the underlined letter in the command name, or by pressing the ↓ key until you highlight the command and then pressing the Enter key.

As you learn the Excel commands, you can combine the opening of a menu and selecting one of its menu commands. With the mouse, you click the menu, and then drag the pointer down the open menu until you highlight the desired command, whereupon you release the mouse button. You can accomplish the same thing with the keyboard by holding down the Alt key as you type the command letters for both the pull-down menu and its command. So that, to close the active workbook window by choosing the Close command on the File menu, you simply press Alt, and then type **FC**.

Some commands on the Excel pull-down menus have shortcut keystrokes assigned to them (shown after the command on the pull-down menu). You can use the shortcut keystrokes to select the desired command instead of having to access the pull-down menus. For example, to save changes to your workbook, you press the shortcut keys Ctrl+S instead of having to select the Save command from the File pull-down menu.

Many commands on the pull-down menus lead to the display of a dialog box, which contains further commands and options (see "Digging Those Dialog Boxes" later in this chapter). You can tell which commands on a pull-down menu lead to dialog boxes because the command name is followed by three periods (known as an *ellipsis*). For example, you know that selecting the File⇨Save As command on the pull-down menu opens a dialog box because the command is listed as Save As... on the File menu.

Also, note that pull-down menu commands are not always available to you. You can tell when a command is not currently available because the command name is in light gray (or *dimmed*) on the pull-down menu. A command on a pull-down menu remains dimmed until the conditions under which it operates exist in your document. For example, the Paste command on the Edit menu remains dimmed as long as the Clipboard is empty. But as soon as you move or copy some information into the Clipboard with the Cut or Copy commands on the Edit menu, the Paste option is no longer dimmed and appears in normal bold type when you open the Edit menu — indicating, of course, that this command is now available for your use.

A word to you Lotus 1-2-3 converts

If you ever used (or tried to use) Lotus 1-2-3 for DOS, you may remember that, in that spreadsheet program, you press the slash key (/ — the key that does double duty with the ? key) to activate the 1-2-3 menus. In deference to the millions of 1-2-3 users out there who have converted to Excel, this program also recognizes and responds appropriately (that is, it activates the menu bar) when you press the / key. It is only right that Excel borrows this keystroke from Lotus 1-2-3, since 1-2-3 borrowed it from its predecessor, VisiCalc, which actually originated its usage.

Because the slash key activates the menus, you can combine its use instead of that of the Alt key with the command letters when you wish to select Excel commands with the keyboard. For example, instead of pressing Alt+FS to save changes to the active document, you can just as well press /FS (almost takes you home, doesn't it?).

Parlez-vous 1-2-3?

If you're a Lotus 1-2-3 user who's just starting to use Excel with this current version, Excel 97, you'll be pleased to know that Excel also offers a couple of ways to make your transition from the 1-2-3 commands and keystroke shortcuts to the Excel commands and keystrokes a lot smoother:

 ✔ You can make it so that when you select the 1-2-3 command, Excel tells you what menu and menu commands you use to do the same thing in Excel (kind of like saying something in English and having the computer give you the French equivalent).

 ✔ Or you can set it up so that you select the 1-2-3 command and the program demonstrates what menu and menu commands you choose to do the same thing in Excel (kind of like saying something in English and having the computer actually translate it into French).

To set up Excel 97 so that the program shows or tells you what to do in Excel via the 1-2-3 equivalents, you follow these steps:

1. **Choose Tools⇨Options to open the Options dialog box.**

2. **Click the tab marked Transition in the Options dialog box.**

    This displays the options for changing the Transition settings.

3. Choose the Lotus 1-2-3 Help radio button.

4. Choose the OK button or press Enter.

After switching from the default Microsoft Excel Menus setting to Lotus 1-2-3 Help in the Options dialog box, whenever you type the almighty / key, instead of activating the Excel menu bar, the program displays the Help for Lotus 1-2-3 Users dialog box. This dialog box contains a Menu list box that shows all the old, familiar 1-2-3 menus (from Worksheet through Quit).

If you want the program to simply indicate the Excel command sequence when you finish selecting the 1-2-3 commands in the Menu list box, you select the Instructions radio button (under Help options on the right side). If you would prefer to have the program demonstrate the Excel command (meaning that the program will actually select the Excel commands and thereby make real changes to your worksheet), you choose the Demo radio button instead.

Then, to choose the 1-2-3 command you need Excel help on (either in instruction or demonstration form), you type the first letter of each menu command. For example, to learn how to format a range of cells with the Currency format in Excel, you type **RFC** to select the Range menu followed by the Format and Currency commands (just as you would normally do to select these commands within 1-2-3 itself).

If you have the Instruction radio button selected when you type **RFC**, Excel displays a small text box with the step-by-step instructions for selecting the Currency number format in Excel (something you can otherwise find out in Chapter 3). If you have the Demo radio button selected instead, Excel displays a dialog box asking you to select the number of decimal places you want the Currency format to show (two is the default, as in Lotus 1-2-3) as well as the range of cells to which this number format is to be applied. After selecting these settings and choosing OK, the program then demonstrates the procedure for opening the Format Cells dialog box by choosing Format⇨Cells on the pull-down menu and then selecting Currency as the format in the Category list box.

Those old-fashioned formulas

As one of the 1-2-3 faithful, you'll also be pleased to discover that although Excel prefers that you type an equal sign (=) to start a formula, it will accept the plus sign (+) that you're used to entering in Lotus 1-2-3 (by putting its equal sign in front of the plus sign).

The same goes when using a built-in function. Although Excel does not require anything other than the equal sign followed by the function name, the program will accept the @ symbol that 1-2-3 requires when using its functions. (So, for example, Excel will accept **@SUM** but will then convert it to the preferred =**SUM**).

Finally, although Excel uses a colon between the first and last cell address when designating a cell range, the program will accept the 1-2-3 method of placing two periods between the cell addresses (meaning that Excel will accept the range address **A1..A4** but convert it to the preferred **A1:A4**).

The program has also worked it all out so that 1-2-3 converts like yourself can have almost all of your old favorite navigation keys back the way Lotus intended them. For example, you know how the Tab and Shift+Tab in Excel only move the cell pointer one cell left or right, instead of scrolling the worksheet left or right by a screenful as they do in 1-2-3? Well, you can restore the so-called Big Right and Big Left scrolling functions (as well as moving to the first cell with Home key instead of to the beginning of the row) by choosing Options on the Tools menu, selecting the Transition tab, and then choosing the Transition navigation keys check box in the Settings area of the Options dialog box.

Comprehending shortcut menus

Unlike the pull-down menus, which you can access either with the mouse or the keyboard, you must use the mouse to open shortcut menus and select their commands. Because shortcut menus are attached to particular objects on the screen — like a workbook window, toolbar, or worksheet cell — Excel uses the *secondary* mouse button (that is, the right button for right-handers and the left button for lefties) to open shortcut menus. (Clicking a screen object, such as a cell, with whatever button is the *primary* button on your mouse simply selects that object).

Figure 1-8 shows you the shortcut menu attached to the Excel toolbars. To open this menu, you position the mouse pointer somewhere on the toolbar and click the secondary mouse button. Be sure that you don't click the primary button, or you will end up activating the tool that the pointer is on!

Once you open the Toolbar shortcut menu, you can use its commands to display or hide any of the built-in toolbars or to customize the toolbars (see Chapter 13 for details).

Figure 1-9 shows you the shortcut menu attached to any of the cells in a worksheet. To open this menu, you position the pointer on any one of the cells and click the secondary mouse button. Note that you can also open this shortcut menu and apply its commands to the group of cells that you have selected. (You find out how to make cell selections in Chapter 3.)

Because the commands on shortcut menus contain command letters, you can select one of their commands either by dragging down to the command and then clicking it either with the primary or secondary mouse button or by typing the underlined letter to select it. Otherwise, you can press the ↓ or ↑ key until you highlight the command and press Enter to select it.

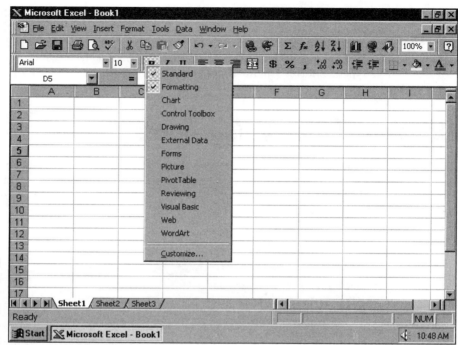

Figure 1-8:
The toolbar
shortcut
menu.

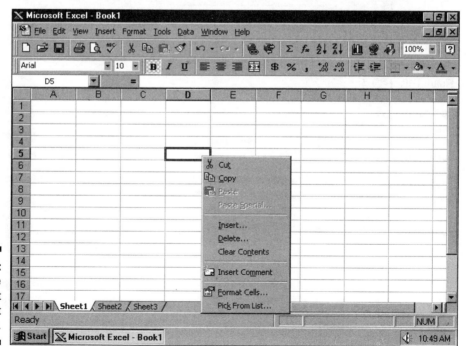

Figure 1-9:
The
worksheet
cell shortcut
menu.

The one shortcut menu that you can open with the keyboard is the shortcut menu attached to cells in a worksheet. To open this shortcut menu in the very upper-right corner of the workbook window, you press Shift+F10. Note that this keystroke works for any type of Excel sheet except a chart, which doesn't have this type of shortcut menu attached to it.

Digging Those Dialog Boxes

Many an Excel command is attached to a dialog box that presents you with a variety of options that you can apply to the command. Figures 1-10 and 1-11 show you the Save As and Options dialog boxes. Between these two dialog boxes, you can find almost all of the different types of buttons, tabs, and boxes used by Excel in Table 1-5.

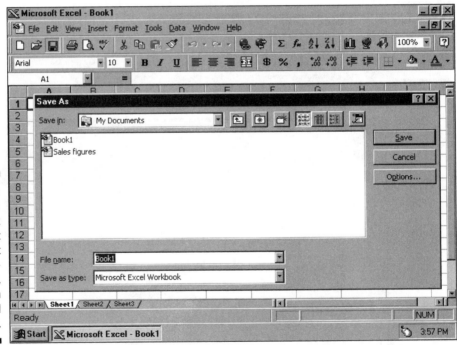

Figure 1-10:
The Save As dialog box contains edit boxes, list boxes, pop-up list boxes, along with command buttons.

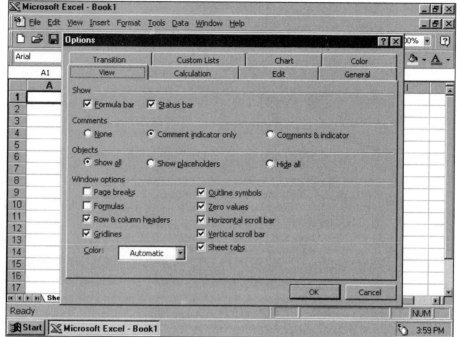

Figure 1-11:
The Options
dialog box
contains a
variety of
tabs, check
boxes, radio
buttons, and
command
buttons.

Table 1-5   The Parts of a Dialog Box

Button or Box in Question	What It's Good For
Tab	Provides a means of displaying a certain set of options in a complex dialog box like the Options dialog box (shown in Figure 1-11) bringing together a whole mess of different types of program settings that you can change.
Edit box (or Text box)	Provides a place for typing a new entry. Many edit boxes contain default entries that you can alter or replace entirely.
List box	Provides a list of options from which you choose. If the list box contains more options than can be displayed in its box, the list box contains a scroll bar that you can use to bring new options into view. Some list boxes are attached to a text box, allowing you to make a new entry in the text box either by typing it or by selecting it in the related list box.

(continued)

Table 1-5 *(continued)*

Button or Box in Question	What It's Good For
Pop-up (or Drop-down) list box	Provides a condensed version of a standard list box that, instead of displaying several options in its list, shows only the current option (which originally is also the default option). To open the list box and display the other options, you click the drop-down button that accompanies the box. Once the list is displayed, you can select a new option from it as you would in any standard list box.
Check box	Presents a dialog box option that you can turn on or off. When the check box is selected, you know that its option is selected. When a check box is blank, you know that its option is not selected.
Radio button	Presents items that have mutually exclusive options. The option button consists of a circle followed by the named option. Radio buttons are always arranged in groups and only one of the buttons in the group can be selected at one time. Excel lets you know which option is currently selected by placing a dot in the middle of its circle (when an option button is selected, it looks like a knob on an old-fashioned radio, thus the name radio button).
Spinner buttons	Spinner buttons appear as a pair of small boxes one on top of the other. The spinner button on the top has an upward-pointing arrowhead on it, whereas the spinner button on the bottom has a downward-pointing arrowhead on it. You use the spinner buttons to scroll up and down through a series of preset options as you select the one you want.
Command button	Initiates an action. The command button is rectangular in shape, and the name of the command is displayed within the button. If a name in a command button is followed by an ellipsis (. . .), Excel displays another dialog box containing even more options when you select the button.

Note: Although you can move a dialog box out of the way of some data in your worksheet, you cannot change the box's size or shape — these dimensions are permanently fixed by the program.

Many dialog boxes contain default options or entries that are automatically selected unless you make new choices before you close the dialog box.

> ✔ To close a dialog box and put your selections into effect, you click the OK button or the Close button (some boxes lack an OK button).
>
> ✔ If the OK button is surrounded by a dark border, which is very often the case, you can also press Enter to put your selections into effect.
>
> ✔ To close a dialog box without putting your selections into effect, you can either select the Cancel or Close button (the one with the X) in the dialog box, or simply press Esc.

Most dialog boxes group related options together as an item (often, this is done by placing a box around the options). When making selections in a dialog box with the mouse, you simply click the selection you want to use or, in the case of text entries, click the pointer in the entry to set the insertion point and then modify the entry.

When making selections with the keyboard, however, you must sometimes first activate the item before you can select any of its options.

> ✔ Press the Tab key until you activate one of the options in the item. (Shift+Tab activates the previous item.)
>
> ✔ When you press Tab (or Shift+Tab), Excel indicates which option is activated either by highlighting the default entry or placing a dotted line around the name of the option.
>
> ✔ After activating an option, you can change its setting either by pressing ↑ or ↓ (this works with sets of radio buttons or options in a list or drop-down list boxes), pressing the space bar (this works to select and deselect check boxes), or by typing a new entry (used in text boxes).

You can also select an option by pressing Alt and then typing the underlined (command) letter in the option or item name.

> ✔ By pressing Alt and typing the command letter of a text box option, you select the entry in that text box (which you can then replace by typing the new entry).
>
> ✔ By pressing Alt and typing the command letter of a check box option, you can turn the option on and off (by adding or removing its check mark).
>
> ✔ By pressing Alt and typing the command letter of a radio button, you can select the option while at the same time deselecting whatever radio button was previously current.

✔ By pressing Alt and typing the command letter of a command button, you either initiate the command or display another dialog box.

You can also select an item in the current list box option by typing the first few characters of its name — as soon as you begin typing, Excel opens an edit box to contain your characters and jumps to the first option in the list box whose name begins with the characters you enter.

In addition to the more elaborate dialog boxes shown in Figures 1-10 and 1-11, you also encounter a simpler type of dialog box used to display messages and warnings (these dialog boxes are appropriately known as *alert boxes*). Many dialog boxes of this type contain just an OK button that you must select to close the dialog box after reading the message.

Ogling the Online Help

You can get online help with Excel 97 anytime you need it while using the program. The only problem with the traditional online Help system is that it is only truly helpful when you are familiar with the Excel jargon. If you don't know what Excel calls a particular feature, you will have trouble locating it in the Help topics (just like trying to look up in a dictionary a word that you have no idea how to spell). To help alleviate this problem, Excel has added a new Office Assistant that lets you type in a question about how to do something in Excel in your own words. The Office Assistant then attempts to translate your question, phrased in perfectly good English, into its horrible Excel-technobabble so that it can then display the Help topics that give you the information you need.

Conferring with your Office Assistant

The Office Assistant personalizes the online Help system, while at the same time giving you the opportunity to ask questions about using Excel in plain English. When you first call upon the Office Assistant, he appears in the form of a rather animated paper clip named Clippit. To call upon Clippit and ask him a question about using Excel, you open the Office Assistant window by following these steps:

1. Click the Office Assistant button on the Standard toolbar (the very last one) or press the F1 function key.

Clippit appears in his own window with a question and answer balloon extending from the window that asks you what you would like to do (just like the one shown in Figure 1-12).

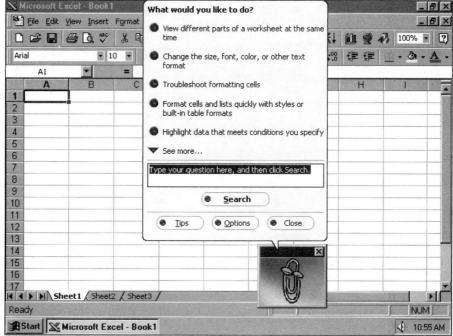

Figure 1-12:
Meet Clippit,
your
personal
Office
Assistant,
who is
ready to
answer your
every
question
about Excel.

2. **Type your question about using Excel in plain English, and then click the Search button or press Enter.**

As you type, Clippit pretends to be writing your question down in his notebook. After you select Search, Clippit searches for related Help topics and then displays the results as bulleted points in a new question and answer balloon that extends from the Office Assistant window.

3. **Click the Help topic that interests you the most in the list to open a new window containing the Help topic.**

When there are more related Help topics than will all fit into Clippit's question and answer balloon, a triangular button will appear at the end of the bulleted list (like you see in Figure 1-13). To see more Help topics, click this rectangle. When you locate the Help topic you want to read, click its bullet in the question and answer balloon.

4. **When you've finished reading or printing the Help topic, close the Help window by clicking the window's Close button or by pressing Ctrl+F4.**

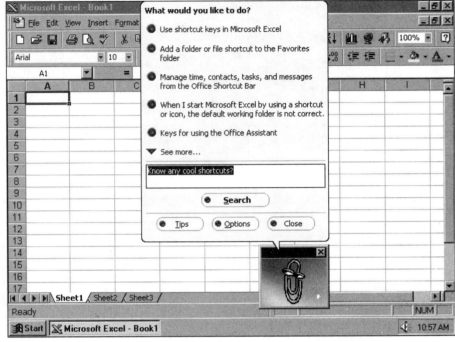

Figure 1-13:
Clippit's
response to
my question,
"Know any
cool
shortcuts?"

If you want to consult another one of the topics that Clippit displayed in response to your question, you simply need to click somewhere on the open the Office Assistant window to re-open the question and answer balloon (Clippit remembers your question until you replace it with a new one) and then click the Search button or press Enter to ask your question again. Clippit will then redisplay the same Help topics displayed in the question and answer balloon in response to your original question. To print a Help topic, click the Options button on the window's toolbar, and then click Print Topic on the pop-up menu that appears.

If the Office Assistant can't even figure out where to look for Help topics because you asked a completely zany question, at least as it relates to using Excel, such as "When will I win the lottery?," Excel beeps and then displays an alert box stating

```
Sorry, but I don't know what you mean. Please rephrase your
question.
```

which is the Office Assistant's way of saying "I don't have a clue as to what you're talking about!"

If the Office Assistant doesn't find any related topics, maybe because you asked a really ambiguous question, at least according to its limited, technical vocabulary, Excel beeps and then displays an alert box stating

```
There are several Help topics that may be related to your
request. If you don't see a topic that looks helpful, please
rephrase your question.
```

Most of the time, however, the Answer Wizard will fetch a bunch of Help topics (whether they're helpful or not) no matter how irrelevant or stupid your question. For example, I asked the Tip Wizard

```
Why is Excel so hard to use?
```

and its reply was to go and get a whole bunch of disparate Help topics, including tips on entering text, using Excel data in a mailing list, speeding up searches with the Find Fast feature, using Excel 97 files with previous versions of Excel or other programs, along with a bunch of unrelated topics like copying Excel data to Word or PowerPoint or how Excel calculates PivotTable data. When you think about it, I guess this screen is a pretty good answer to the question "Why is Excel so hard to use?"

To reduce the number of times that the Office Assistant gives you almost all the general Help topics at its disposal, you should try to get as much specific information in your question as possible. If you want to know whether Excel can figure compound interest on an investment, be sure to include key words such as *compound interest* and *investment* in the body of the question (unlike your grade school English teacher or Alex Trebek on *Jeopardy,* the Answer Wizard couldn't care less if your request is in the form of a question or demonstrates anything close to good grammar).

Sometimes you may think that the Help topics returned by the Answer Wizard have nothing to do with your question, only later to discover that the weird topics listed in the question and answer balloon were exactly what you needed to know. A lot of this is just the result of not yet being familiar with the bulk of Excel's technobabble.

After consulting the Office Assistant, you can close the question and answer balloon while leaving the Office Assistant window open. To close the balloon, just press the Esc key. To move the Office Assistant window out of the way as you work, drag the window by its title bar (which just happens to be completely empty).

If you later decide that you need to close the Office Assistant window altogether, you need to click its Close button (which just happens to be the only one that appears in the Office Assistant window).

Choosing a new persona for the Office Assistant

Clippit is just one of nine different "personalities" you can assign to the Office Assistant. In addition, you can choose between

- A bouncing ball with a smiley face (of all things) called The Dot, a three-dimensional Albert Einstein knockoff named (what else?) The Genius

- A vacuum cleaner-like robot (that only an R2D2 could love) called Hoverbot

- A spinning Microsoft Office Logo showing the four interlocking colors called Office Logo

- An animated planet Earth that turns into a flower and then back into a planet called Mother Nature

- A cartoon dog in a red cape called Power Pup

- An origami cat named Scribble

- A two-dimensional representation of the Bard of Avon himself called simply Will (the persona my editors all seem to be really wild about)

Each Office Assistant personality in the Gallery comes with its own animation and sounds (some make more noise than others). To select a new persona for your Office Assistant, you follow these steps:

1. **If you haven't already done so, click the Office Assistant button on the Standard toolbar or press F1 to open the Office Assistant window.**

2. **Click the Options button to open the Office Assistant dialog box.**

3. **Click the Gallery tab in the Office Assistant dialog box.**

4. **Click the Next button until you display the Office Assistant persona that you want to use.**

5. **Click the OK button to close the Office Assistant dialog box and replace Clippit with the new persona in the Office Assistant window.**

Note that if you find yourself getting bored with the same old staid antics from the Office Assistant, you can get him (or her, if you're using Mother Nature) to dance (or at least become a little more animated) by choosing the Animate! command in the Office Assistant's context menu (opened by clicking the window with the secondary mouse button).

Taking tips from the Office Assistant

As you go about building and editing your worksheets in Excel, the Office Assistant, like some spy in the background, is silently analyzing everything you do. As you select commands and push buttons, the Office Assistant is busy trying to amass a list of tips and tricks related to the tasks that you just did. You can always tell when the Office Assistant has come up with some new tips because a light bulb icon appears in the Office Assistant window along with the Office Assistant persona.

To see the tip that the Office Assistant has dug up for you, just click the light bulb in the Office Assistant window or click the Office Assistant window and click the Tips button in the question and answer balloon to open a tip balloon. To see earlier tips in the tip balloon, click the Back button. To return to later tips, click the Next button. When you're finished looking at the tips and want to put the tip balloon away, just click the Close button.

Carving out context-sensitive Help

You can get context-sensitive Help by choosing Help⇨What's This? on the pull-down menus or by pressing Shift+F1. When you do either of these, Excel changes the mouse pointer shape by adding a question mark to it. To get help on a particular command or a part of the Excel 97 window, you use this question-mark pointer to select it. For example, say that you want to refresh your memory on how you use the AutoSum button on the Standard toolbar to total a column of numbers. You simply click the AutoSum button with the arrowhead/question-mark Help pointer. When you do this, the program displays an AutoSum text box with a brief paragraph of information on using the AutoSum feature.

You can also use the context-sensitive Help to get information on any of the commands on the pull-down menus. Suppose, for instance, that you are curious about the purpose of the Full Screen command on the View pull-down menu. To obtain information on what this command does and how you use it, you choose Help⇨What's This? or press Shift+F1 and then click the View menu with the arrowhead/question-mark Help mouse pointer and, once this menu opens, click the Full Screen command. Doing this opens the Full Screen (View Menu) text box with a paragraph of information on using this command to display the maximum number of worksheet cells on the screen.

Tackling the Help topics

Beyond using the Office Assistant to get straight answers to your Excel questions or the context-sensitive Help to get quick information on using the toolbars and pull-down menus, you can, if all else fails, resort to using the Help Topics window to get even more online information on Excel. To open the Help Topics window, you choose Help⇨Contents and Index on the pull-down menus.

Doing this opens the Help Topics: Microsoft Excel window with three tabs: Contents, Index, and Find. Select the Contents tab to get information on performing essential techniques like creating, printing, or saving a worksheet. Select the Index tab to find information on a particular item or term such as *current cell, data entry,* or *fonts.* Select the Find tab to quickly find all kinds of related information about a particular topic such as worksheets, charts, or macros.

To select a topic on the Contents tab, click the topic to select it and then click the Open button (you can combine this by double-clicking the topic as well) to open its Help window. To locate and select a topic on the Index or Find tab, type the first few letters of the item or term you want help on in the first (edit) box. Then, in the Index tab, click the particular topic in the second (list) box before you click the Display button to open its Help window. In the Find tab, click the matching term in the second (list) box, and then click the topic you want to see in the third (list) box before you click the Open button (or press Enter) to open its Help window.

When reading a Help topic in the Help window, you may notice that certain terms are underlined (and in a different color on a color monitor).

- ✔ A term that is underlined with a solid underline is called a *jump term* because, when you click it, the Help system immediately "jumps" you to a related Help topic.

- ✔ A term that is underlined with a dotted line is a *glossary term,* meaning that it is attached to a brief definition. When you click a glossary term, the Help system displays the definition of that term in a small pop-up dialog box for as long as you hold down the mouse button.

If you come upon a Help topic that you want to print out, you can select the Print Topic command on the Options pull-down menu or the Help shortcut menu.

You can also copy information from an Excel Help topic to your word processor or even to an Excel document. To copy Help information, choose the Copy command on the Options pull-down menu or Help shortcut menu.

Once you've copied the Help topic in this manner, you can copy the Help information into a word-processing document or worksheet by starting the program and opening the document (if necessary) and then choosing the Paste command in the program's Edit menu.

After you've finished with the information in a Help window, you can return to the Help Topics: Microsoft Excel window by clicking the Help Topics button on the Help window's toolbar or you can close the Help window by clicking its Close button.

When It's Time to Make Your Exit

When you're ready to call it a day and quit Excel, you have several choices for shutting down the program:

 ✔ Click the Close button on the Excel program window.

 ✔ Choose File⇨Exit command in the pull-down menus.

 ✔ Double-click the Control menu button on the Excel program window (the one with the XL icon in the very upper-left corner of the screen).

 ✔ Press Alt+F4.

If you try to exit Excel after working on a workbook and you haven't saved your latest changes, the program beeps at you and displays an alert box asking you if want to save your changes. If you happen to have the Office Assistant open when you do this kind of exit, he (or she if you're using Mother Nature) goes through all kinds of convolutions when asking you in one of its question-and-answer balloons whether you want to save your changes. To save your changes before exiting, click the Yes command button (for detailed information on saving documents, see Chapter 2). If you've just been playing around in the worksheet and don't want to save your changes, you can abandon the document by choosing the No button.

Chapter 2

Creating a Spreadsheet from Scratch

● ●

In This Chapter

▶ Starting a new workbook

▶ Entering the three different types of data in a worksheet

▶ Getting Excel to put in your decimal point for you

▶ Creating simple formulas by hand

▶ Fixing your data-entry boo-boos

▶ Using the AutoCorrect feature

▶ Understanding the AutoComplete feature

▶ Using the AutoFill feature to complete a series of entries

▶ Restricting data entry to a particular group of cells

▶ Entering the same thing in a bunch of cells in one operation

▶ Entering built-in functions in your formulas with the Paste Function button

▶ Editing a formula with the Edit Formula button

▶ Totaling columns and rows of numbers with the AutoSum button

▶ Saving your precious work

● ●

*O*nce you know how to get into Excel 97, it's time to find out how to get yourself into trouble by actually using it! In this chapter, you're gonna find out how to put all kinds of information into all those little, blank worksheet cells described in Chapter 1. Here, you find out about the Excel AutoCorrect and AutoComplete features and how they can help cut down on errors and speed up your work. You also get some basic pointers on other smart ways to minimize the drudgery of data entry, such as filling out a series of entries with the AutoFill feature and entering the same thing in a bunch of cells all at the same time.

And after discovering how to fill up a worksheet with all this raw data, you find out what has to be the most important lesson of all: how to save all the information on disk so that you don't ever have to enter the stuff again!

So What Ya Gonna Put in That New Workbook of Yours?

When you start Excel without specifying a document to open, as happens if you start the program by clicking the Microsoft Excel button on the Office 97 shortcut bar (refer to Chapter 1), you get a blank workbook in a new workbook window. This workbook, temporarily named Book1, contains three blank worksheets (named Sheet1, Sheet2, and Sheet3). To begin to work on a new spreadsheet, you simply start entering information in the first sheet of the Book1 workbook window.

The ins and outs of data entry

Here are a few simple guidelines (a kind of data-entry etiquette, if you will) that you should keep in mind when you start creating a spreadsheet in Sheet1 of your new workbook:

- ✔ Whenever you can, organize your information in tables of data that use adjacent (neighboring) columns and rows. Start the tables in the upper-left corner of the worksheet and work your way down the sheet, rather than across the sheet, whenever possible. When it's practical, separate each table by no more than a single column or row.

- ✔ When you set up these tables, don't skip columns and rows just to "space out" the information. In Chapter 3, you see how to place as much white space as you want between information in adjacent columns and rows by widening columns, heightening rows, and changing the alignment.

- ✔ Reserve a single column at the left edge of the table for the table's row headings.

- ✔ Reserve a single row at the top of the table for the table's column headings.

- ✔ If your table requires a title, put the title in the row above the column headings. Put the title in the same column as the row headings. You see how to center this title across the columns of the entire table in Chapter 3.

You may wonder why, after making such a big stinking deal about how big each of the worksheets in a workbook is back in Chapter 1, I'm now on your case about not using that space to spread out the data you enter into it. After all, given all the real estate that comes with each and every Excel worksheet, you'd think conserving space would be one of the last things you'd have to worry about.

And you'd be 100 percent correct . . . except for one little, itty-bitty thing: Space conservation in the worksheet equals memory conservation. You see, as a table of data grows and expands into columns and rows in new areas of the worksheet, Excel decides that it had better reserve a certain amount of computer memory and hold it open just in case you might go crazy and fill that area full of cell entries. This means that if you skip columns and rows that you really don't need to skip (just to cut down on all that cluttered data), you end up wasting computer memory that could otherwise be used to store more information in the worksheet.

You must remember this . . .

So now you know: It's the amount of computer memory available to Excel that determines the ultimate size of the spreadsheet you can build, not the total number of cells in the worksheets of your workbook. When you run out of memory, you've effectively run out of space — no matter how many columns and rows are still left to fill. To maximize the information you can get into a worksheet, always adopt the "covered wagon" approach to worksheet design by keeping your data close together.

To check out how much computer memory is available to Excel at any given time, choose the About Microsoft Excel command from the Help menu, and then click the System Info button in the About Microsoft Excel dialog box. The Microsoft System Information dialog box then appears, displaying the Total memory as well as the Available Memory in *kilobytes* (thousands of bytes), along with a bunch of operating system factoids. When you finish viewing this information, click the Close button in both the Microsoft System Information and About Microsoft Excel dialog boxes.

Doing the Data-Entry Thing

Let's start by reciting (in unison) the basic rule of worksheet data entry. All together now:

> To enter data in a worksheet, position the cell pointer in the cell where you want the data, and then begin typing the entry.

Note that before you can position the cell pointer in the cell where you want the entry, Excel must be in Ready mode (as evidenced by the Ready indicator on the status bar). When you start typing the entry, however, Excel goes through a mode change from Ready to Enter mode (and "Enter" replaces "Ready" on the status bar).

If you're not in Ready mode, try pressing Esc.

As soon as you begin typing in Enter mode, the characters you type appear both in a cell in the worksheet area and on the formula bar near the top of the screen. Starting to type something that's ultimately destined to go into the current cell also triggers a change to the formula bar because two new boxes, Cancel and Enter, appear in between the Name Box (containing the address of the current cell) and the Edit Formula button.

As you continue to type, Excel displays your progress both on the formula bar and in the active cell in the worksheet (see Figure 2-1). However, the insertion point (the flashing vertical bar that acts as your cursor) is displayed only at the end of the characters displayed in the cell.

After you finish typing your cell entry, you still have to get it into the cell so that it stays put. In doing this, you also change the program from Enter mode back to Ready mode so that you can move the cell pointer to another cell and, perhaps, enter or edit the data there.

To complete your cell entry and, at the same time, get Excel out of Enter mode and back into Ready mode, you can click the Enter box on the formula bar, press Enter, or press one of the arrow keys like ↓, ↑, →,or ← to move to another cell.

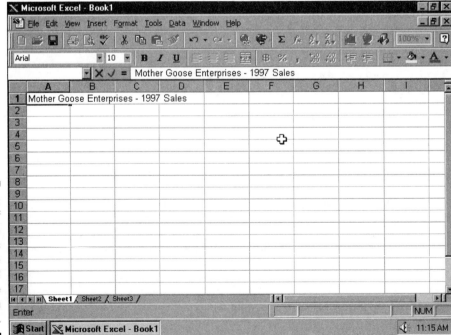

Figure 2-1: The stuff you type appears both in the current cell and on the Formula bar.

Now, even though each of these alternatives gets your text into the cell, each does something a little different afterwards, so please take note:

- ✔ If you click the Enter box on the formula bar, the text goes into the cell and the cell pointer just stays in the cell containing the brand new entry.

- ✔ If you press Enter, the text goes into the cell and the cell pointer moves down to the cell below in the next row.

- ✔ If you press one of the arrow keys, the text goes into the cell, and the cell pointer moves the next cell in the direction of the arrow. If you press ↓, the cell pointer moves below in the next row just as when you finish off a cell entry with the Enter key. However, if you press ↑, the cell pointer moves right to the cell in the next column; if you press ←, the cell pointer moves left to the cell in the previous column; and if you press ↑, the cell pointer moves up to the cell in the next row above.

No matter which of the methods you choose when putting an entry in its place, as soon as you complete your entry in the current cell, Excel deactivates the formula bar by removing the Cancel and Enter boxes. Thereafter, the data you entered continues to appear in the cell in the worksheet (with certain exceptions that I discuss later in this chapter), and every time you put the cell pointer into that cell, the data will reappear on the formula bar as well.

If, while still typing an entry or after finishing typing but prior to completing the entry, you realize that you're just about to stick it in the wrong cell, you can clear and deactivate the formula bar by clicking the Cancel box (the one with the X in it) or by pressing Esc. If, however, you don't realize that you had the wrong cell current until after you've entered your data there, you have to either move the entry to the correct cell (something you find out how to do in Chapter 4) or delete the entry (see Chapter 4) and then re-enter the data in the correct cell.

Getting the Enter key to put the cell pointer where you want it

Excel automatically advances the cell pointer to the next cell down in the column every time you press Enter to complete the cell entry. If you want to customize Excel so that pressing Enter doesn't move the cell pointer as the program enters your data, or to have it move the cell pointer to the next cell up, left, or right, choose Options on the Tools menu and select the Edit tab in the Options dialog box.

To prevent the cell pointer from moving at all, choose the Move Selection after Enter option to remove the check mark from its check box. To have the cell pointer move in another direction, choose the Direction pop-up list box right below the Move Selection after Enter check box and then select the new direction you want to use (Right, Up, or Left). When you're finished changing this setting, click the OK button or press Enter.

It Takes All Types

Unbeknownst to you as you go about happily entering data in your spreadsheet, Excel is constantly analyzing the stuff you type and classifying it into one of three possible data types: a piece of *text,* a *value,* or a *formula.*

If Excel finds that the entry is a formula, the program automatically calculates the formula and displays the computed result in the worksheet cell (you continue to see the formula itself, however, on the formula bar). If Excel is satisfied that the entry does not qualify as a formula (I give you the qualifications for an honest-to-goodness formula a little later in this chapter), the program then determines whether the entry should be classified as text or as a value.

Excel makes this distinction between text and values so that it knows how to align the entry in the worksheet. It aligns text entries with the left edge of the cell and values with the right edge. Also, because most formulas work properly only when they are fed values, by differentiating text from values, the program knows which will and will not work in the formulas you build. Suffice to say, you can foul up your formulas good if they refer to any cells containing text where Excel expects values to be.

The telltale signs of text

A text entry is simply an entry that Excel can't pigeonhole as either a formula or value. This makes text the catchall category of Excel data types. As a practical rule of thumb, most text entries (also known as *labels*) are a combination of letters and punctuation or letters and numbers. Text is used mostly for titles, headings, and notes in the worksheet.

You can tell right away whether Excel has accepted a cell entry as text because text entries are automatically aligned at the left edge of their cells. If the text entry is wider than the cell can display, the data spills over into the neighboring cell or cells on the right, *as long as those cells remain blank* (see Figure 2-2).

This means that if, sometime later, you enter information in a cell that contains spillover text from a cell to its left, Excel cuts off the spillover of the long text entry (see Figure 2-3). Not to worry: Excel doesn't actually lop these characters off the cell entry — it simply shaves the display to make room for the new entry. To redisplay the suddenly "missing" portion of the long text entry, you have to widen the column that contains the cell where the text is entered (to find out how to do this, skip ahead to Chapter 3).

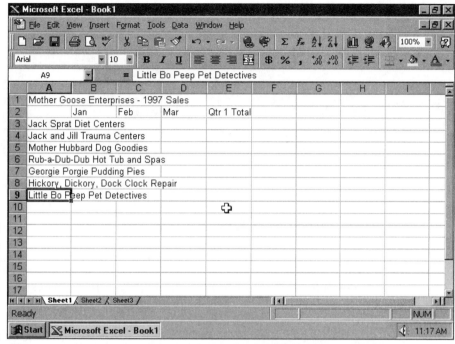

Figure 2-2:
Long text
entries spill
over into
neighboring
blank cells.

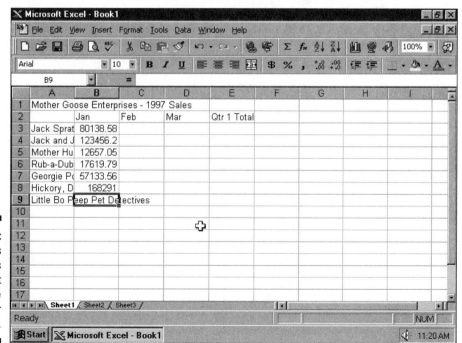

Figure 2-3:
Cell entries
in the cells
to the right
cut off the
spillover
text.

To Excel, text is nothing but a big zero

You can use the AutoCalculate indicator to prove to yourself that Excel gives all text entries the value of 0 (zero). Simply enter a number like 10 in one cell and then some stupid piece of text, like "Excel is like a box of chocolates," in the cell directly below. Then drag up so that both cells (the one with 10 and the one with the text) are highlighted. Then take a gander at the AutoCalculate indicator on the status bar, and you see that it reads SUM=10, proving that the text adds nothing to the total value of these two cells.

How Excel evaluates its values

Values are the building blocks of most of the formulas that you create in Excel. As such, they come in two flavors: numbers that represent quantities (such as 14 stores or $140,000 dollars) and numbers that represent dates (such as July 30, 1995) or times (such as 2:00 p.m.).

You can tell whether Excel has accepted your entry as a value because values are aligned at the right edge of their cells. If the value you enter is wider than the column containing the cell can display, Excel automatically converts the value to (of all things) *scientific notation* (for example, 6E+08 indicates that the 6 is followed by eight zeros for a grand total of 600 million!). To restore a value that's been converted into that weird scientific notation stuff back to a regular number, simply widen the column for that cell (Chapter 3 shows you how).

Making sure that Excel's got your number

In building a new worksheet, you'll probably spend a lot of your time entering numbers, representing all types of quantities from money you made (or lost) to the percentage of the office budget that went to coffee and donuts (you mean you don't get donuts?).

To enter a numeric value that represents a positive quantity, like the amount of money you made last year, just select a cell, type the numbers — for example, **459600** — and complete the entry in the cell by clicking the Enter box, pressing the Enter key, and so on. To enter a numeric value that represents a negative quantity, like the amount of money the office spent on coffee and donuts last year, begin the entry with the minus sign or hyphen (–) before typing the numbers — for example, **–175** (that's not too much to spend on coffee and donuts when you just made $459,600) — and then complete the entry.

If you're trained in Accounting, you can enclose the negative number (that's *expense* to you) in parentheses — **(175)**. Just note that, if you go to all the trouble to use parentheses for your negatives (expenses), Excel goes ahead and automatically converts the number so that it begins with a minus sign; meaning that if you enter **(175)** in the Coffee and Donut expense cell, Excel spits back **–175** (relax, you can find out how to get your beloved parentheses back for the expenses in your spreadsheet in Chapter 3).

With numeric values that represent dollar amounts, like the amount of money you made last year, you can include dollar signs ($) and commas (,) just as they appear in the printed or handwritten numbers you are working from. Just be aware that when you enter a number with commas, Excel assigns a number format to the value that matches your use of commas (for more information on number formats and how they are used, see Chapter 3). Likewise, when you preface a financial figure with a dollar sign, Excel assigns an appropriate dollar-number format to the value (one that automatically inserts commas between the thousands).

When entering numeric values with decimal places, use the period as the decimal point. When you enter decimal values, the program automatically adds a zero before the decimal point (Excel inserts **0.34** in a cell when you enter **.34**) and drops trailing zeros entered after the decimal point (Excel inserts **12.5** in a cell when you enter **12.50**).

If you don't know the decimal equivalent for a value that contains a fraction, you can just go ahead and enter the value with its fraction. For example, if you don't know that 2.1875 is the decimal equivalent for $2\,^3/_{16}$, just type **2 $^3/_{16}$** (making sure to add a space between the 2 and 3) in the cell. After completing the entry, when you put the cell pointer in that cell, you see $2\,^3/_{16}$ in the cell of the worksheet, but 2.1875 appears on the formula bar. As you see in Chapter 3, it's then a simple trick to format the display of $2\,^3/_{16}$ in the cell so that it matches the 2.1875 on the formula bar.

Note that, if you need to enter simple fractions such as $^3/_4$ or $^5/_8$, you must enter them as a mixed number preceded by zero; for example, enter **0 3/4** or **0 5/8** (be sure to include a space between the zero and the fraction). Otherwise, Excel gets mixed up and thinks that you're entering the dates March 4th (3/4) and May 8 (5/8).

When entering in a cell a numeric value that represents a percentage (so much out of a hundred), you have a choice:

✔ You can either divide the number by 100 and enter the decimal equivalent (by moving the decimal point two places to the left like your teacher taught you; for example, enter **.12** for 12 percent).

✔ You can enter the number with the percent sign (for example, enter **12%**).

Either way, Excel stores the decimal value in the cell (0.12 in this example). If you use the percent sign, Excel assigns a percentage-number format to the value in the worksheet so that it appears as 12%.

How to get your decimal places fixed (when you don't even know if they're broken)

If you find that you need to enter a whole slew of numbers that use the same number of decimal places, you can turn on Excel's Fixed Decimal setting and have the program enter the decimals for you. This feature really comes in handy when you have to enter hundreds of financial figures that all use two decimal places (for example, for the number of cents).

To *fix* the number of decimal places in a numeric entry, follow these steps:

1. **Choose Tools⇨Options on the menu bar.**

   The Options dialog box appears.

2. **Choose the Edit tab in the Options dialog box.**

3. **Choose Fixed Decimal in the Settings section to select its check box.**

   By default, Excel fixes the decimal place two places to the left of the last number you type. To change the default Places setting, go to step 4, otherwise move to step 5.

4. **Type a new number in the Places edit box or use the spinner buttons to change the value.**

   For example, you could change the Places setting to 3 to enter numbers with the following decimal placement: 00.000.

5. **Click OK or press Enter.**

   Excel displays the FIX status indicator on the status bar to let you know that the Fixed Decimal feature is active.

After fixing the decimal place in numeric values, Excel automatically adds the decimal point to any numeric value you enter — all you do is type the digits and complete the entry in the cell. For example, to enter the numeric value 100.99 in a cell after fixing the decimal point to 2 places, type the digits **10099**. When you complete the cell entry, Excel automatically inserts a decimal point two places from the right in the number you typed, leaving 100.99 in the cell.

Don't get in a fix over your decimal places!

While the Fixed Decimal setting is turned on, Excel adds a decimal point to all the numeric values you enter. However, if you want to enter a number without a decimal point, or one with a decimal point in a position different from the one called for by this feature, you have to remember to type the decimal point (period) yourself. For example, to enter the number 1099 instead of 10.99 when the decimal point is fixed at 2 places, type **1099.** in the cell.

And, for heaven's sake, please don't forget to turn off the Fixed Decimal feature before you start work on another worksheet or exit Excel. Otherwise, when you intend to enter values like 20, you'll end up with 0.2 instead, and you won't have a clue what's going on!

When you're ready to return to normal data entry for numerical values (where you enter any decimal points yourself), open the Options dialog box, choose the Edit tab again, deselect the Fixed Decimal check box, and click OK or press Enter. Excel removes the FIX indicator from the status bar.

Tapping on the old ten-key

You can make the Fixed Decimal feature work even better by selecting the block of the cells where you want to enter the numbers (see "Entries all around the block," later in this chapter) and then pressing Num Lock so that you can do all the data entry for this cell selection from the numeric keypad (à la ten-key adding machine).

Using this approach, all you have to do to enter the range of values in each cell is type the number's digits and press Enter on the numeric keypad — Excel inserts the decimal point in the proper place as it moves the cell pointer down to the next cell. Even better, when you finish entering the last value in a column, pressing Enter automatically moves the cell pointer to the cell at the top of the next column in the selection.

Figures 2-4 and 2-5 illustrate how you can make the ten-key method work for you. In Figure 2-4, the Fixed Decimal feature has been turned on (using the default of two decimal places), and the block of cells from B3 through D9 has been selected. You also see that six entries have already been made in cells B3 through B8 and a seventh, 30834.63, is about to be completed in cell B9. To make this entry when the Fixed Decimal feature is turned on, you simply type **3083463** from the numeric keypad.

Figure 2-5 shows you what happens when you press Enter (either on the regular keyboard or the numeric keypad). As you can see, not only does Excel automatically add the decimal point to the value in cell B9, but it also moves the cell pointer up and over to cell C3 where you can continue entering the values for this column.

Entering dates with no debate

At first look, it may strike you as a bit odd that dates and times are entered as values in the cells of a worksheet rather than as text. The reason for this is simple, really: Dates and times entered as values can be used in formula calculations, whereas dates and times entered as text cannot. For example, if you enter two dates as values, you can then set up a formula that subtracts the more recent date from the older date and returns the number of days between them. This kind of thing just couldn't happen if you were to enter the two dates as text entries.

Excel determines whether the date or time you type is entered as a value or as text by the format you follow. If you follow one of Excel's built-in date and time formats, the program recognizes the date or time as a value. If you don't follow one of the built-in formats, the program enters the date or time as a text entry — it's as simple as that.

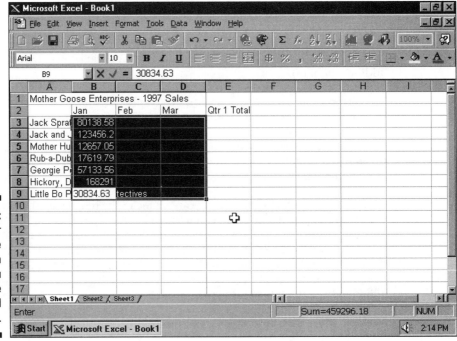

Figure 2-4:
To enter the value 30834.63 in cell B9, you simply type **3083463** and press Enter.

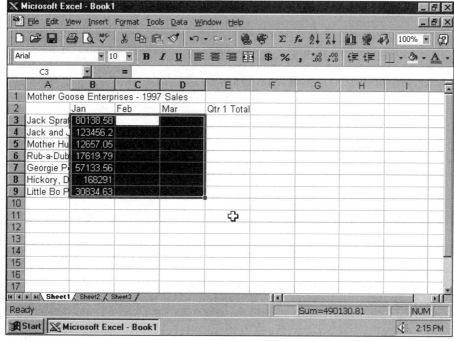

Figure 2-5:
When you press Enter to enter 30834.63 in cell B9, the program automatically moves the cell pointer to cell C3.

Excel recognizes the following time formats:

3:21 PM

3:21:04 PM

15:21

15:21:04

The dating game

Dates are stored as serial numbers that indicate how many days have elapsed from a particular starting date; times are stored as decimal fractions indicating the elapsed part of the 24-hour period. Excel supports two date systems: the 1900 date system used by Excel on Windows, where January 1, 1900 is the starting date (serial number 1) and the 1904 system used by Excel for the Macintosh, where January 2, 1904 is the starting date.

If you ever get a hold of a workbook created with Excel for the Macintosh that contains dates that seem all screwed up when you open the file, you can rectify this problem by choosing Options from the Tools menu, selecting the Calculation tab in the Options dialog box, and then selecting the 1904 date system check box under Workbook options before you click OK.

Excel knows the following date formats (Note that month abbreviations always use the first three letters of the name of the month, as in Jan, Feb . . .):

November 24, 1997 or November 24, 97

11/24/97 or 11-24-97

25-Nov-97

25-Nov

Nov-97

Fabricating those fabulous formulas!

As entries go in Excel, formulas are the real workhorses of the worksheet. If you set up a formula properly, it computes the right answer when you first enter it into a cell. From then on, it keeps itself up-to-date, recalculating the results whenever you change any of the values that the formula uses.

You let Excel know that you're about to enter a formula, rather than some text or a value, in the current cell by starting the formula with the equal sign (=). Most simple formulas follow the equal sign with a built-in function such as SUM or AVERAGE (see "Inserting a function into a formula with the Paste Function and the Formula Palette" later in this chapter, for more information on using functions in formulas). Other simple formulas use a series of values or cell references that contain values separated by one or more of the following mathematical operators:

+ (plus sign) for addition

– (minus sign or hyphen) for subtraction

* (asterisk) for multiplication

/ (slash) for division

^ (caret) for raising a number to a power

For example, to create a formula in cell C2 that multiplies a value entered in cell A2 by a value in cell B2, enter the following formula in cell C2:

```
=A2*B2
```

To enter this formula in cell C2, follow these steps:

1. **Select cell C2**.

2. **Type the entire formula** =A2*B2 **in the cell.**

3. Press Enter.

Or

1. Select Cell C2.

2. Type = (equal sign).

3. Select cell A2 in the worksheet by using the mouse or the keyboard.

This action places the cell reference A2 in the formula in the cell (as shown in Figure 2-6).

4. Type *.

The asterisk is used for multiplication rather than the x you used in school.

5. Select cell B2 in the worksheet by using the mouse or the keyboard.

This action places the cell reference B2 in the formula (as shown in Figure 2-7).

6. Click the Enter box to complete the formula entry, while at the same time keeping the cell pointer in cell C2.

Excel displays the calculated answer in cell C2 and the formula =A2*B2 in the formula bar (as shown in Figure 2-8).

When you're finished entering the formula =A2*B2 in cell C2 of the worksheet, Excel displays the calculated result depending on the values currently entered in cells A2 and B2. The major strength of the electronic spreadsheet is the capability of formulas to automatically change their calculated results to match changes in the cells referenced by the formulas.

Now comes the fun part: After creating a formula like the preceding one that refers to the values in certain cells (rather than containing those values itself), you can change the values in those cells, and Excel automatically recalculates the formula, using these new values and displaying the updated answer in the worksheet! Using the example shown in Figure 2-8, say that you change the value in cell B2 from 100 to 50. The moment you complete this change in cell B2, Excel recalculates the formula and displays the new answer, 1000, in cell C2.

If you want it, just point it out

The method of selecting the cells you use in a formula, rather than typing their cell references, is known as *pointing*. Pointing is not only quicker than typing cell references, it also reduces the risk that you might type the wrong cell reference. When you type a cell reference, you can easily type the wrong column letter or row number and not realize your mistake just by looking at the calculated result returned in the cell.

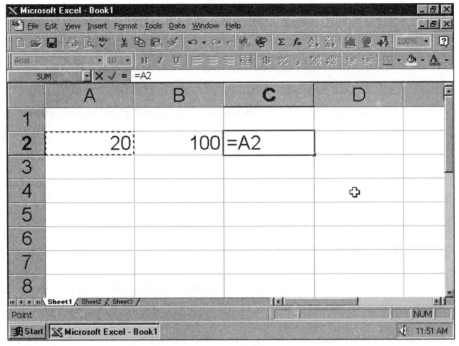

Figure 2-6:
To start the
formula,
type = and
then select
cell A2.

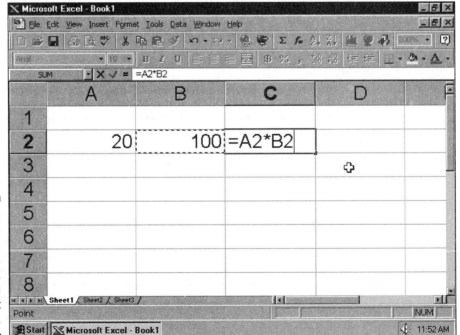

Figure 2-7:
To complete
the second
part of the
formula,
type * and
select
cell B2.

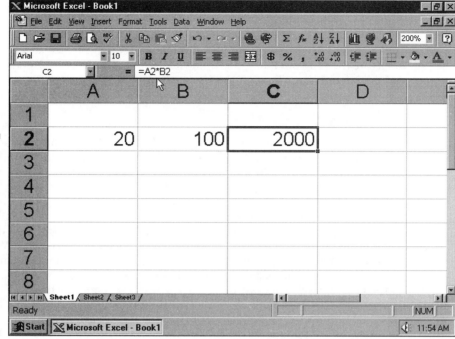

Figure 2-8:
When you
click the
Enter box,
Excel
displays the
answer in
cell C2 while
the formula
appears in
the formula
bar above.

If you select the cell you want to use in a formula, either by clicking it or moving the cell pointer to it, there is less chance that you'll enter the wrong cell reference.

Altering the natural order of operations

Many formulas you create perform more than one mathematical operation. Excel performs each operation, moving from left to right, according to a strict pecking order (the natural order of arithmetic operations). In this order, multiplication and division pull more weight than addition and subtraction and are, therefore, performed first, even if these operations don't come first in the formula (when reading from left to right).

Consider the series of operations in the following formula:

```
=A2+B2*C2
```

If cell A2 contains the number 5, B2 contains the number 10, and C2 contains the number 2, Excel evaluates the following formula:

```
=5+10*2
```

In this formula, Excel multiplies 10 times 2 to equal 20 and then adds this result to 5 to produce the result 25.

If you want Excel to perform the addition between the values in cells A2 and B2 before the program multiplies the result by the value in cell C2, enclose the addition operation in parentheses as follows:

```
=(A2+B2)*C2
```

The parentheses around the addition tell Excel that you want this operation performed before the multiplication. If cell A2 contains the number 5, B2 contains the number 10, and C2 contains the number 2, Excel adds 5 and 10 to equal 15 and then multiplies this result by 2 to produce the result 30.

In fancier formulas, you may need to add more than one set of parentheses, one within another (like the wooden Russian dolls that nest within each other) to indicate the order in which you want the calculations to take place. When nesting parentheses, Excel first performs the calculation contained in the most inside pair of parentheses and then uses that result in further calculations as the program works its way outward. For example, consider the following formula:

```
=(A4+(B4-C4))*D4
```

Excel first subtracts the value in cell C4 from the value in cell B4, then adds the difference to the value in cell A4, and finally multiplies that sum by the value in D4.

Without the additions of the two sets of nested parentheses, left to its own devices, Excel would first multiply the value in cell C4 by that in D4, add the value in A4 to that in B4, and then perform the subtraction.

When nesting parentheses in a formula, pair them properly so that you have a right parenthesis for every left parenthesis in the formula. If you do not include a right parenthesis for every left one, Excel displays an alert dialog box with the message "Parentheses do not match" or "Error in Formula" when you try to enter the formula. After you close this dialog box, Excel goes right back to the formula bar, where you can insert the missing parenthesis and press Enter to correct the unbalanced condition. By the way, Excel tries to show you where the unbalanced condition exists by highlighting the closest cell reference.

Formula flub-ups

Under certain circumstances, even the best formulas can appear to have freaked out once you get them in your worksheet. You can tell right away that a formula's gone haywire because instead of the nice calculated value you expected to see in the cell, you get a strange, incomprehensible message in all uppercase letters beginning with the number sign (#) and ending with an exclamation point (!) or, in one case, a question mark (?). This weirdness is known, in the parlance of spreadsheets, as an *error value*. Its purpose is to let you know that some element — either in the formula itself or in a cell referred to by the formula — is preventing Excel from returning the anticipated calculated value.

The worst thing about error values is that they can contaminate other formulas in the worksheet. If a formula returns an error value to a cell and a second formula in another cell refers to the value calculated by the first formula, the second formula returns the same error value and so on down the line.

After an error value shows up in a cell, you have to discover what caused the error and edit the formula in the worksheet. Table 2-1 lists some error values that you might run into in a worksheet and explains the most common causes.

Table 2-1   Error Values That You Can Encounter from Faulty Formulas

What Shows Up in the Cell	What's Going On Here?
#DIV/0!	Appears when the formula calls for division by a cell that either contains the value 0 or, as is more often the case, is empty. Division by zero is a no-no according to our math.
#NAME?	Appears when the formula refers to a *range name* (see Chapter 6 for info on naming ranges) that doesn't exist in the worksheet. This error value appears when you type the wrong range name or fail to enclose in quotation marks some text used in the formula, causing Excel to think that the text refers to a range name.
#NULL!	Appears most often when you insert a space (where you should have used a comma) to separate cell references used as arguments for functions.
#NUM!	Appears when Excel encounters a problem with a number in the formula, such as the wrong type of argument in an Excel function or a calculation that produces a number too large or too small to be represented in the worksheet.
#REF!	Appears when Excel encounters an invalid cell reference, such as when you delete a cell referred to in a formula or paste cells over the cells referred to in a formula.
#VALUE!	Appears when you use the wrong type of argument or operator in a function, or when you call for a mathematical operation that refers to cells that contain text entries.

Fixing Up Those Data Entry Flub-ups

We all wish we were perfect, but alas, because so few of us are, we are best off preparing for those inevitable times when we mess up. When entering vast quantities of data, it's really easy for those nasty little typos to creep into your work. In your pursuit of the perfect spreadsheet, there are things you can do: First, get Excel to automatically correct certain typos right as they happen with its AutoCorrect feature; second, manually correct any of the disgusting little errors that get through, either while you're still in the process of making the entry in the cell or after the entry has gone in.

You really AutoCorrect that for me

The AutoCorrect feature is a godsend for those of us who tend to make the same stupid typos over and over again. With AutoCorrect, you can alert Excel 97 to your own particular typing gaffes and tell the program how it should automatically fix them for you.

When you first install Excel, the AutoCorrect feature already knows to automatically correct two initial capital letters in an entry (by lowercasing the second capital letter), capitalize the name of the days of the week, and to replace a set number of text entries and typos with particular substitute text.

You can add to the list of text replacements at any time when using Excel. These text replacements can be of two types: typos that you routinely make along with the correct spellings, and abbreviations or acronyms that you type all the time along with their full forms. To add to the replacements

1. **Choose Tools⇨AutoCorrect on the menu bar to open the AutoCorrect dialog box.**

2. **Enter the typo or abbreviation in the Replace edit box.**

3. **Enter the correction or full form in the With edit box.**

4. **Click the Add button or press Enter to add the new typo or abbreviation to the AutoCorrect list.**

5. **Click the OK button to close the AutoCorrect dialog box.**

Figure 2-9 shows the AutoCorrect dialog box after I entered "mge" in the Replace edit box and "Mother Goose Enterprises" in the With edit box. After clicking the Add button to add this abbreviation to the AutoCorrect list and closing the AutoCorrect dialog box, I no longer have to take the time to spell out Mother Goose Enterprises in any of the spreadsheets that I create because AutoCorrect will be there, ready to convert my "mge" to "Mother Goose Enterprises" as soon as I type it.

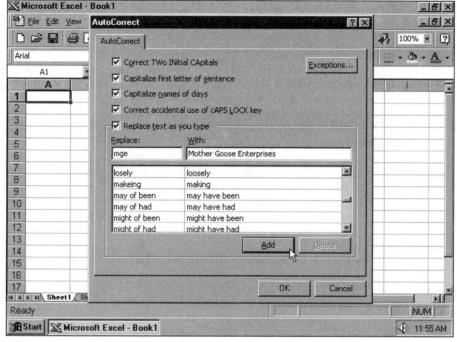

Figure 2-9:
Entering my
favorite
acronym
and the
automatic
correction
that Excel is
to replace
it with.

Cell editing etiquette

Despite the help of AutoCorrect, some mistakes are bound to get you. How you correct them really depends upon whether you notice before or after you complete the cell entry.

✔ If you catch the mistake before you complete an entry, you can delete it by pressing Backspace (the key immediately above the Enter key) until you remove all the incorrect characters from the cell. Then you can retype the rest of the entry or the formula before you complete the entry in the cell.

✔ If you don't discover the mistake until after you've completed the cell entry, you have a choice of replacing the whole thing or editing just the mistakes.

✔ When dealing with short entries, you'll probably want to go the replacement route. To replace a cell entry, you have only to position the cell pointer in that cell, type your replacement entry, and then complete the replacement entry by clicking the Enter box or pressing Enter or one of the arrow keys.

✔ When the error in an entry is relatively easy to fix and the entry is on the long side, you'll probably want to edit the cell entry rather than replace it. To edit the entry in the cell, simply double-click the cell or select the cell and then press F2.

✔ Doing either one reactivates the formula bar by once again displaying the Enter and Cancel boxes, while at the same time placing the insertion point in the cell entry in the worksheet (if you double-click, the insertion point is positioned wherever you click; if you press F2, the insertion point is positioned after the last character in the entry).

✔ Notice also that the mode indicator changes to Edit. While in this mode, you can use the mouse or the arrow keys to position the insertion point at the place in the cell entry that needs fixing.

Table 2-2 lists the keystrokes you can use to reposition the insertion point in the cell entry and delete unwanted characters. If you want to insert new characters at the insertion point, simply start typing. If you want to delete existing characters at the insertion point as you type new ones, press Ins to switch from the normal insert mode to overtype mode. To return to normal insert mode, press Ins a second time. When you finish making corrections to the cell entry, you must re-enter the edited entry before Excel updates the contents of the cell.

While Excel is in Edit mode, you must re-enter the edited cell contents by either clicking the Enter box or pressing Enter. You can use the arrow keys as a way to complete an entry only when the program is in Enter mode. When the program is in Edit mode, the arrow keys move the insertion point only through the entry that you're editing, not to a new cell.

Table 2-2	**Keystrokes for Fixing Those Cell Entry Flub-Ups**
Keystroke	*What the Keystroke Does*
Del	Deletes the character to the right of the insertion point
Backspace	Deletes the character to the left of the insertion point
→	Positions the insertion point one character to the right
←	Positions the insertion point one character to the left
↑	Positions the insertion point, when it is at the end of the cell entry, to its preceding position to the left
End or ↓	Moves the insertion point after the last character in the cell entry
Home	Moves the insertion point in front of the first character of the cell entry
Ctrl+→	Positions the insertion point in front of the next word in the cell entry
Ctrl+←	Positions the insertion point in front of the preceding word in the cell entry
Ins	Switches between insert and overtype mode

The Tale of Two Edits: Cell versus formula bar editing

Excel gives you a choice between editing a cell's contents either in the cell (as discussed earlier) or on the formula bar. Whereas, most of the time, editing right in the cell is just fine, when dealing with really, really long entries (like humongous formulas that seem to go on forever or text entries that take up paragraphs and paragraphs), you may prefer to do your editing on the formula bar. This is because Excel expands the formula bar to as many rows as

are necessary to display the entire cell contents; whereas, in the worksheet display, the cell contents may be running right off the screen.

To edit the contents in the formula bar rather than in the cell itself, you must position the cell pointer in the cell and then double-click somewhere (probably the first place that needs changing) in the cell contents on the formula bar.

Taking the Drudgery Out of Data Entry

Before leaving the topic of data entry, I feel duty bound to cover some of the shortcuts that really help to cut down on the drudgery of this task. These data-entry tips include using the AutoComplete and AutoFill features as well as doing data entry in a preselected block of cells and entering the same things in a bunch of cells all at the same time.

I'm just not complete without you

The AutoComplete feature in Excel 97 is not something you can do anything about; it's just something to be aware of as you enter your data. In an attempt to cut down on your typing load, our friendly software engineers at Microsoft came up with the AutoComplete feature.

AutoComplete is kinda like a moronic mind reader who anticipates what you might want to enter next based upon what you just entered earlier. This feature comes into play only when you're entering a column of text entries (it does not come into play when entering values or formulas or when entering a row of text entries). When entering a column of text entries, AutoComplete looks at the kinds of entries you make in that column and automatically duplicates them in subsequent rows whenever you start a new entry that begins with the same letter as an existing entry.

For example, say I enter **Jack Sprat Diet Centers** (one of the companies owned and operated by Mother Goose Enterprises) in cell A3 and then move the cell pointer down to cell A4 in the row below and press J (lowercase or uppercase, it doesn't matter), AutoComplete immediately inserts "ack Sprat Diet Centers" in this cell after the J, as shown in Figure 2-10.

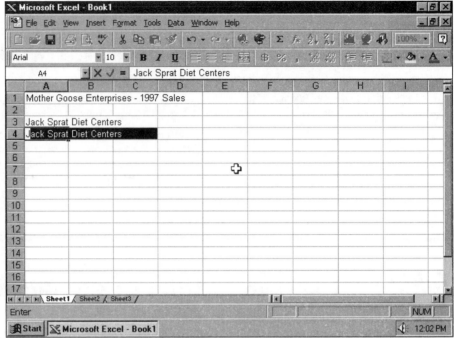

Figure 2-10:
AutoComplete
duplicates a
previous
entry if you
start a new
entry in
the same
column that
begins with
the same
letter.

Now this is great if I happen to need Jack Sprat Diet Centers as the row heading in both cells A3 and A4. Anticipating that I might be typing a different entry that just happens to start with the same letter as the one above, AutoComplete automatically selects everything after the first letter in the duplicated entry it inserted (from "ack" on, in this example). This enables me to replace the duplicate supplied by AutoComplete just by continuing to type (which is what I did after shooting Figure 2-10 because I needed to enter Jack and Jill Trauma Centers — another of Mother's companies — in cell A4).

If you override a duplicate supplied by AutoComplete in a column by typing one of your own (as in my example with changing Jack Sprat Diet Centers to Jack and Jill Trauma Centers in cell A4), you effectively shut down its ability to supply any more duplicates for that particular letter. So, for instance, in my example, after changing Jack Sprat Diet Centers to Jack and Jill Trauma Centers in cell A4, AutoComplete doesn't do anything if I then type **J** in cell A5. In other words, you're on your own if you don't continue to accept AutoComplete's typing suggestions.

Fill 'er up with AutoFill

Many of the worksheets you create with Excel require the entry of a series of sequential dates or numbers. For example, a worksheet may require you to title the columns with the 12 months, from January through December, or to number the rows from 1 to 100.

Excel's AutoFill feature makes short work of this kind of repetitive task. All you have to enter is the starting values for the series. In most cases, AutoFill is smart enough to figure out how to extend the series for you when you drag the fill handle to the right (to take the series across columns to the right) or down (to extend the series to the rows below).

Remember that the AutoFill handle looks like this + and appears only when you position the mouse pointer on the lower-right corner of the cell (or the last cell, when you've selected a block of cells). Keep in mind that if you drag a cell selection with the white-cross mouse pointer rather than the AutoFill handle, Excel simply extends the cell selection to those cells you drag through (see Chapter 3). If you drag a cell selection with the arrowhead pointer, Excel moves the cell selection (see Chapter 4).

When creating a series with the fill handle, you can drag only in one direction at a time. For example, you can extend the series or fill the range to the left or right of the cell range that contains the initial values, or you can extend the series or fill the range above or below the cell range that contains the initial values. You can't, however, extend the series or fill the range in two directions at the same time (such as down and to the right by dragging the fill handle diagonally).

As you drag the mouse, the program keeps you informed of whatever entry would be entered into the last cell selected in the range by displaying that entry next to the mouse pointer (as a kind of AutoFill tips, if you will). When you release the mouse button after extending the range with the fill handle, Excel either creates a series in all of the cells you selected or fills the entire range with the initial value.

Figures 2-11 and 2-12 illustrate how to use AutoFill to enter a row of months, starting with January in cell B2 and ending with June in cell G2. To do this, you simply enter **January** in cell B2 and then position the mouse pointer on the fill handle in the lower-right corner of this cell before you drag through to cell G2 on the right (as shown in Figure 2-11). When you release the mouse button, Excel fills in the names of the rest of the months (February through June) in the selected cells (as shown in Figure 2-12). Note that Excel keeps the cells with the series of months selected, giving you another chance to modify the series (if you went too far, you can drag the fill handle to the left to cut back on the list of months; if you didn't go far enough, you can drag it to the right to extend the list of months further).

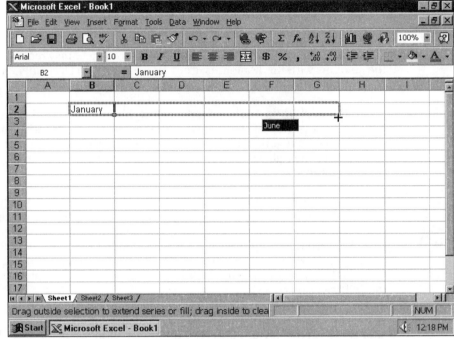

Figure 2-11:
To create a
series of
months, type
January in
the first cell
and then
use the fill
handle to
select the
range of
cells where
the months
will be
entered.

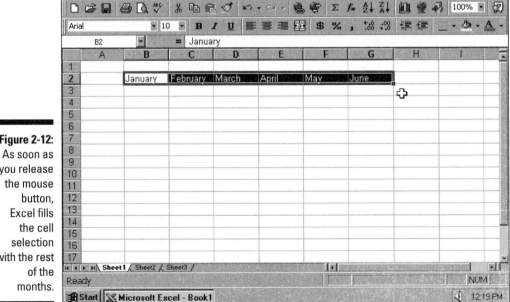

Figure 2-12:
As soon as
you release
the mouse
button,
Excel fills
the cell
selection
with the rest
of the
months.

Table 2-3 shows some of the different initial values that AutoFill can use and the types of series that Excel can create from them.

Working with a spaced series

AutoFill uses the initial value you select (date, time, day, year, and so on) to "design" the series. All of the sample series shown in Table 2-3 change by a factor of one (one day, one month, or one number). You can tell AutoFill to create a series that changes by some other value: Enter two sample values in neighboring cells that describe the amount of change you want between each value in the series. Make these two values the initial selection that you extend with the fill handle.

For example, to start a series with Saturday and enter every other day across a row, enter **Saturday** in the first cell and **Monday** in the cell next door. After selecting both cells, drag the fill handle across the cells to the right as far you need to extend the series. When you release the mouse button, Excel follows the example set in the first two cells by entering every other day (Wednesday to the right of Monday, Friday to the right of Wednesday, and so on).

Table 2-3   Samples of Series You Can Create with AutoFill

Value Entered in First Cell	*Extended Series Created by AutoFill in the Next Three Cells*
June	July, August, September
Jun	Jul, Aug, Sep
Tuesday	Wednesday, Thursday, Friday
Tue	Wed, Thu, Fri
4/1/97	4/2/97, 4/3/97, 4/4/97
Jan-97	Feb-97, Mar-97, Apr-97
15-Feb	16-Feb, 17-Feb, 18-Feb
10:00 PM	11:00 PM, 12:00 AM, 1:00 AM
8:01	9:01, 10:01, 11:01
Quarter 1	Quarter 2, Quarter 3, Quarter 4
Qtr2	Qtr3, Qtr4, Qtr1
Q3	Q4, Q1, Q2
Product 1	Product 2, Product 3, Product 4
1st Product	2nd Product, 3rd Product, 4th Product

Copying with AutoFill

You can use AutoFill to copy a text entry throughout a cell range (rather than fill in a series of related entries). To copy a text entry to a cell range, you must hold down the Ctrl key as you click and drag the fill handle. When you hold down the Ctrl key as you click the fill handle, a plus sign appears to the right of the fill handle — your sign that AutoFill will *copy* the entry in the active cell instead of creating a series using it (you can also tell because the entry that appears as the AutoFill tip next to the mouse pointer as you drag contains the same text as the original cell).

Although holding down Ctrl as you drag the fill handle copies a text entry, just the opposite is true when it comes to values! If you enter a number like 17 in a cell and then drag the fill handle across the row, Excel just copies the number 17 in all the cells you select. If, however, you hold down Ctrl as you drag the fill handle, Excel then fills out the series (17, 18, 19, and so on).

Creating custom lists for AutoFill

In addition to varying the increment in a series created with AutoFill, you can also create your own custom series. For example, in the bosom of Mother Goose Enterprises, you will find the following companies:

- Jack Sprat Diet Centers
- Jack and Jill Trauma Centers
- Mother Hubbard Dog Goodies
- Rub-a-Dub-Dub Hot Tubs and Spas
- Georgie Porgie Pudding Pies
- Hickory, Dickory, Dock Clock Repair
- Little Bo Peep Pet Detectives

Rather than have to type this list of companies in the cells of each new worksheet (or even copy them from an existing worksheet), you can create a custom series that will produce the whole list of companies simply by entering Jack Sprat Diet Centers in the first cell and then dragging the fill handle to the blank cells where the rest of the companies should appear.

To create this kind of custom series, follow these steps:

1. **Choose Tools⇨Options on the menu bar to open the Options dialog box.**

2. **Choose the Custom Lists tab to display the Custom lists and List entries boxes.**

If you've already gone to the time and trouble of typing the custom list in a range of cells, go to step 3a. If you haven't yet typed the series in an open worksheet, go to step 3b instead.

3a. Click in the Import List from the cells edit box and then drag the dialog box out of the way so that you can see your list and select the range of cells (see Chapter 3 for details). After selecting the cells, click the Import button to copy this list into the List entries list box and skip to step 5 (as shown in Figure 2-13).

3b. Choose the List entries list box and then type each entry (in the desired order), being sure to press Enter after typing each one.

When all of the entries in the custom list appear in the List entries list box in the order you're going to want them, proceed to step 4.

4. Choose the Add button to add the list of entries to the Custom lists box.

Finish creating all the custom lists you need, using the preceding steps. When you are done, move on to step 5.

5. Choose OK or press Enter to close the Options dialog box and return to the current worksheet in the active workbook.

After adding a custom list to Excel, from then on you need only enter the first entry in a cell and then use the fill handle to extend it to the cells below or to the right.

If you don't even want to bother with typing the first entry, use the AutoCorrect feature — refer to "You really AutoCorrect that for me" earlier in this chapter — to create an entry that will fill in as soon as you type your favorite acronym for it (such as "jsdc" for "Jack Sprat Diet Centers").

Entries all around the block

When you want to enter a table of information in a new worksheet, you can simplify the job of entering the data if you select all the empty cells in which you want to make entries before you begin entering any information. Just position the cell pointer in the first cell of what is to become the data table and then select all the cells in the subsequent columns and rows (for information on the ways to select a range of cells, see Chapter 3). After you select the block of cells, you can begin entering the first entry.

When you select a block of cells (also known as a *range*) before you start entering information, Excel restricts data entry to that range as follows:

✔ The program automatically advances the cell pointer to the next cell in the range when you click the Enter box or press Enter to complete each cell entry.

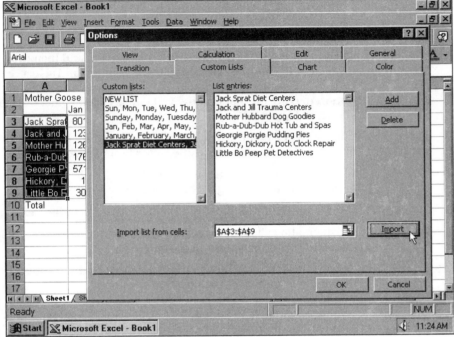

Figure 2-13:
Creating a
custom
company
list from
existing
worksheet
entries.

✔ In a cell range that contains several different rows and columns, Excel advances the cell pointer down each row of the column as you make your entries. When the cell pointer reaches the cell in the last row of the column, the cell pointer advances to the first selected row in the next column to the right. If the cell range uses only one row, Excel advances the cell pointer from left to right across the row.

✔ When you finish entering information in the last cell in the selected range, Excel positions the cell pointer in the first cell of the now-completed data table. To deselect the cell range, click the mouse pointer on one of the cells in the worksheet (inside or outside the selected range — it doesn't matter) or press one of the arrow keys.

Be sure that you don't press one of the arrow keys to complete a cell entry within a preselected cell range instead of clicking the Enter box or pressing Enter. Pressing an arrow key deselects the range of cells when Excel moves the cell pointer. To move the cell pointer around a cell range without deselecting the range, try these methods:

✔ Press Enter to advance to the next cell down each row and then across each column in the range. Press Shift+Enter to move up to the previous cell.

✔ Press Tab to advance to the next cell in the column on the right and then down each row of the range. Press Shift+Tab to move left to the previous cell.

✔ Press Ctrl+. (period) to move from one corner of the range to another.

Data entry express

You can save a lot of time and energy when you want the same entry (text, value, or formula) to appear in many cells of the worksheet; you can enter the information in all the cells in one operation. You first select the cell ranges to hold the information (Excel lets you select more than one cell range for this kind of thing — see Chapter 3 for details). Then you construct the entry on the formula bar and press Ctrl+Enter to put the entry into all the selected ranges.

The key to making this operation a success is to hold the Ctrl key as you press Enter so that Excel inserts the entry on the formula bar into all the selected cells. If you forget to hold Ctrl and you just press Enter, Excel only places the entry in the first cell of the selected cell range.

How to Make Your Formulas Function Even Better

Earlier in this chapter, I showed you how to create formulas that perform a series of simple mathematical operations such as addition, subtraction, multiplication, and division. Instead of creating more complex formulas from scratch out of an intricate combination of these operations, you can find an Excel function to get the job done.

A *function* is a predefined formula that performs a particular type of computation. All you have to do to use a function is supply the values that the function uses when performing its calculations (in the parlance of the Spreadsheet Guru, such values are known as the *arguments of the function*). As with simple formulas, you can enter the arguments for most functions either as a numerical value (for example, **22** or **–4.56**) or, as is more common, as a cell reference (for example, **B10**) or as a cell range (for example, **C3:F3**).

Just as with a formula you build yourself, each function you use must start with an equal sign (=) so that Excel knows to enter the function as a formula rather than as text. Following the equal sign, you enter the name of the function (in uppercase or lowercase — it doesn't matter, as long as you don't misspell the name). Following the name of the function, you enter the arguments required to perform the calculations. All function arguments are enclosed in a pair of parentheses.

If you type the function directly in a cell, remember not to insert spaces between the equal sign, function name, and the arguments enclosed in parentheses. Some functions use more than one value when performing their designated calculations. When this is the case, you separate each function with a comma (not a space).

After you type the equal sign, function name, and the left parenthesis that marks the beginning of the arguments for the function, you can point to any cell or cell range you want to use as the first argument instead of typing the cell references. When the function uses more than one argument, you can point to the cells or cell ranges you want to use for the second argument right after you type the , (comma) to complete the first argument.

After you finish entering the last argument, type a right parenthesis to mark the end of the argument list and then click the Enter box or press Enter or an arrow key to insert the function in the cell and have Excel calculate the answer.

Inserting a function into a formula with the Paste Function and the Formula Palette

Although you can enter a function by typing it directly in a cell, Excel provides a Paste Function button on the Standard toolbar that displays the Paste Function dialog box from which you select the function to use. After you select your function, Excel opens the Formula Palette right below the formula bar. This Formula Palette allows you to specify the function arguments. The real boon comes when you're fooling with an unfamiliar function or one that's kind of complex (some of these puppies can be really hairy) and you open the Formula Palette when the Office Assistant is open (refer to "Conferring with your Office Assistant" in Chapter 1). Under those conditions, the Office Assistant is ready to give you loads of help in completing the argument edit boxes that the Formula Palette presents to you by keeping track of all the arguments you need to use and sees to it that you don't mess up on your parentheses or commas separating the argument list.

To open the Paste Function dialog box, you select the cell that needs the formula and then click the Paste Function button (the one marked *fx*) on the Standard toolbar. When you click the Paste Function button, the Paste Function dialog box appears, similar to the one shown in Figure 2-14.

The Paste Function dialog box contains two list boxes: Function <u>c</u>ategory and Function <u>n</u>ame. When you open this dialog box, Excel automatically selects Most Recently Used as the category in the Function <u>c</u>ategory list box and displays the functions you usually use in the Function <u>n</u>ame list box.

If your function isn't among the most recently used, you must then select the appropriate category of your function in the Function <u>c</u>ategory list box (if you

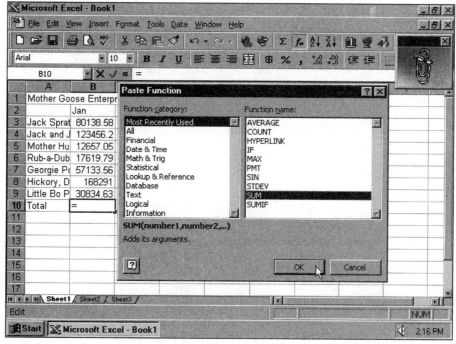

Figure 2-14:
Select the function you want to use in the Paste Function dialog box.

don't know the category, choose All). After that, of course, you still need to choose the particular function in the Function name list box.

When you select a function in the Function name list box, Excel displays the required arguments for the function at the bottom of this dialog box and inserts the function name (along with the obligatory parentheses) in the current cell. For example, suppose that you select the SUM function (the "crown jewel" of the Most Recently Used function category) in the Function name list box. As soon as you do, the program puts an equal sign into the cell (and on the formula bar) and shows the arguments as

```
SUM(number1,number2,...)
```

at the bottom of the first Paste Function dialog box.

To continue and fill in the number arguments for the SUM function, you then click the OK button or press Enter. As soon as you do, Excel inserts

```
SUM()
```

in the current cell and on the formula bar (following the equal sign) and the Formula Palette with the SUM arguments appears below the formula bar (as shown in Figure 2-15). This is where you add the arguments for the SUM function.

Formula Palette

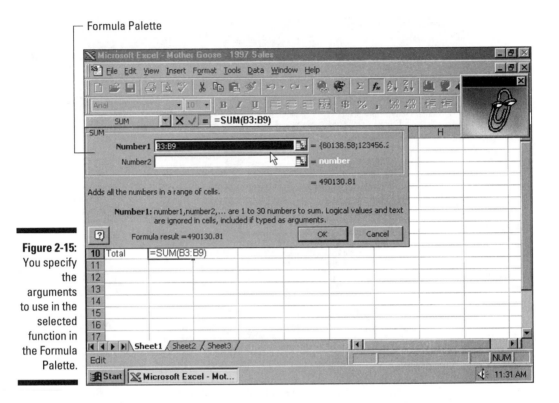

Figure 2-15:
You specify
the
arguments
to use in the
selected
function in
the Formula
Palette.

As the Formula Palette in Figure 2-15 points out, you can select up to 30 numbers to be summed. What it doesn't tell you, however (there's always some trick, huh?), is that these numbers don't have to be in single cells. In fact, most of the time you will be selecting a whole slew of numbers in nearby cells (in a multiple cell selection — that range thing) that you want to total.

To select your first number argument in the dialog box, you click the cell (or drag through the block of cells) in the worksheet while the insertion point is in the Number1 edit box. Excel then displays the cell address (or range address) in the Number1 edit box while, at the same time, showing the value in the cell (or values, if you've selected a bunch of cells) in the box to the right. Excel displays the total so far near the bottom of the Formula Palette after the words "Formula result=."

Keep in mind, when selecting cells, that you can minimize this arguments dialog box down to just the contents of the Number1 edit box and a maximize button by clicking the minimize button on the right of the Number1 edit box. After minimizing the arguments dialog box so that you can select the cells to be used as the first argument, you can expand it again by clicking the maximize button (the only button displayed on the far right). Instead of minimizing the dialog box, you can also temporarily move it out of the way by clicking on any part and then dragging the dialog box to its new destination on the screen.

If you're adding more than one cell (or bunch of cells) in a worksheet, you press the Tab key or click the Number2 edit box to move the insertion point there (Excel responds by extending the argument list with a Number3 edit box). Here is where you specify the second cell (or cell range) that is to be added to the one now showing in the Number1 edit box. After you click the cell or drag through the second cell range, the program displays the cell address(es), with the numbers in the cell(s) to the right and the running total near the bottom of the Formula Palette after the words "Formula result=" (as shown in Figure 2-16). Note that you can minimize the entire arguments dialog box down to just the contents of the argument edit box you're dealing with (Number2, Number3, and so on) and a maximize button by clicking its particular minimize button if the dialog box obscures the cells that you need to select.

When you've finished pointing out the cells or bunches of cells to be summed, you then click the OK button to close the Formula Palette and put the SUM function in the current cell.

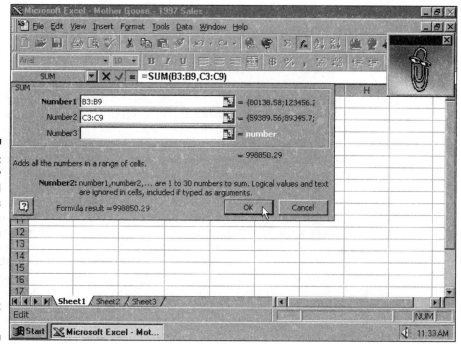

Figure 2-16:
To specify additional arguments for a function in the Formula Palette, press Tab to expand the argument list.

Editing a function with the Edit Formula button

Excel 97's new Edit Formula button lets you edit formulas (especially those with functions) right from the formula bar. To use it, you select the cell with the formula to be edited before you click the Edit Formula button (the one sporting the equal sign that appears immediately in front of the current cell entry on the formula bar).

As soon as you click the Edit Formula button, Excel responds in these two ways:

✔ The contents of the Name Box at the beginning of the formula bar displays the function at the top of the list of Most Recently Used functions instead of the address of the current cell. When you click the drop-down button to the right of the Name Box, Excel displays a pop-up list containing all of functions on the Most Recently Used function list.

✔ The Formula Palette showing the result of the formula in the current cell appears in the upper-left corner of the workbook window. If this formula uses a function, this palette shows the current arguments of the function (similar to the ones shown earlier in Figure 2-15 and 2-16).

You can then edit the formula as required. If you want to replace a function that's used in the formula, select (by highlighting) the function's name on the formula bar, then click the drop-down button on the Name Box, and select the new function in the list that's to replace the one you've highlighted (to have access to more functions than those in the Most Recently Used category, click More Functions at the bottom of the list box and Excel will display the Paste Function dialog box like the one shown earlier in Figure 2-14).

To edit just the arguments of a function, select the cell references in the appropriate argument's edit box (marked Number1, Number2, Number3, and so on) and then make whatever changes are required to the cell addresses or select a new range of cells. Keep in mind that Excel will automatically add any cell or cell range that you highlight in the worksheet to the current argument. If you want to replace the current argument, you need to highlight it and then get rid of its cell addresses by pressing the Delete key before you highlight the new cell or cell range to be used as the argument (remember that you can always minimize this dialog box or move it to a new location if it obscures the cells you need to select).

When you've finished editing the formula, click the OK button or press Enter in the Formula Palette to put it away, update the formula, and return the Name Box on the formula bar to normal (so that the Name Box once again displays the address of the current cell instead of the name of the function at the top of the Most Recently Used list).

I'd be totally lost without AutoSum

Before leaving this fascinating discussion on entering functions, I want you to get to the AutoSum tool on the Standard toolbar (the one with the Σ). This little tool is worth its weight in gold, as it not only enters the SUM function but also selects the most likely range of cells in the current column or row that you want totaled and automatically enters them as the function's argument. And nine times out of ten, Excel selects (by highlighting) the correct cell range to be totaled. For that tenth case, you can manually correct the range by simply dragging the cell pointer through the block of cells that need to be summed.

Figure 2-17 shows how to use the AutoSum tool to total the sales of Jack Sprat Diet Centers in row 3. To total the sales in this row, position the cell pointer in cell E3, where the first-quarter total is to appear, and click the AutoSum tool. Excel inserts the SUM function (equal sign and all) onto the formula bar; places a *marquee* (the moving dotted line) around the cells B3, C3, and D3; and uses the cell range B3:D3 as the argument of the SUM function.

Figure 2-18 shows the worksheet after you insert the function in cell E3. The calculated total appears in cell E3 while the following SUM formula appears in the formula bar:

```
=SUM(B3:D3)
```

After entering the function to total the sales of Jack Sprat Diet Centers, you can copy this formula to total sales for the rest of the companies by dragging the fill handle down column E until the cell range E3:E9 is highlighted.

Figure 2-19 illustrates how you can use the AutoSum tool to total the January sales for all the Mother Goose Enterprises in column B. Position the cell pointer in cell B10 where you want the total to appear. When you click the AutoSum tool, Excel places the marquee around cells B3 through B9 and correctly enters the cell range B3:B9 as the argument of the SUM function.

Figure 2-20 shows the worksheet after inserting the function in cell B10 and using the AutoFill feature to copy the formula to cells C10, D10, and E10 to the right. (To use AutoFill, drag the fill handle through the cells to the right until you reach cell E10 before you release the mouse button.)

Making Sure the Data's Safe and Sound

All the work you do in any of the worksheets in your workbook is at risk until you save the workbook as a disk file. Should you lose power or should your computer crash for any reason before you save the workbook, you're out of luck. You have to re-create each and every keystroke — a painful task, made all

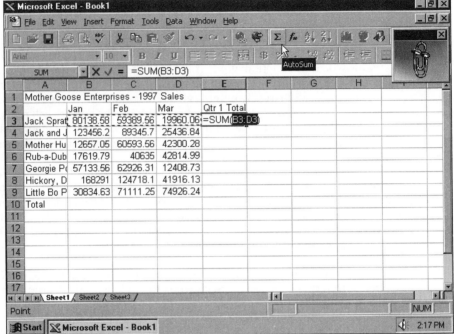

Figure 2-17:
Using the
AutoSum
button to
total the
sales of
Jack Sprat
Diet Centers
in row 3.

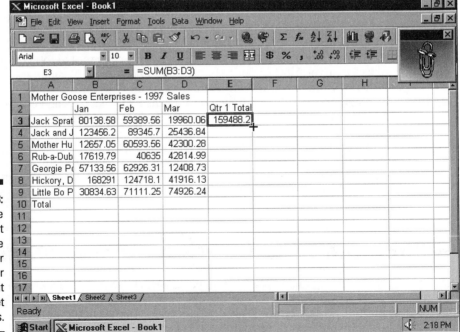

Figure 2-18:
The
worksheet
with the
first-quarter
total for
Jack Sprat
Diet
Centers.

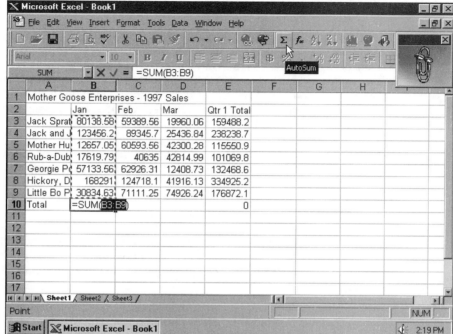

Figure 2-19:
Using the
AutoSum
button to
add the
January
sales in
column B.

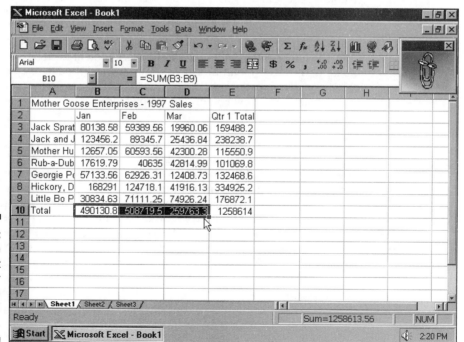

Figure 2-20:
The
worksheet
after
copying the
SUM
formulas.

the worse because it's so unnecessary. To avoid this unpleasantness altogether, adopt this rule of thumb: Save your work anytime you've entered more informa- tion than you could possibly bear to lose.

To encourage frequent saving on your part, Excel even provides you with a Save button on the Standard toolbar (the one with the picture of the disk, third from the left). You don't even have to take the time and trouble to choose the Save command from the File menu (or even press Ctrl+S); you can simply click this tool whenever you want to save new work on disk.

The first time you click the Save tool, Excel displays the Save As dialog box (similar to the one shown in Figure 2-21). You can use this dialog box to replace the temporary document name (Book1, Book2, and the like) with a more descriptive filename and to select a new drive and folder before you save the workbook as a disk file. It's just this easy:

✔ To rename the workbook, type the filename in the File name edit box. When you first open the Save As dialog box, the suggested Book1-type filename is selected; you can just start typing the new filename to replace it.

✔ To change the drive on which the workbook is stored, click the Save in drop-down button and then click the appropriate drive name, such as Hard disk (C:) or 3 $^1/_2$ Floppy (A:) in the drop-down list box.

✔ To change the folder in which the workbook is saved, select the drive if necessary (as described previously) and then click the desired folder. If you want to save the workbook in a folder that's inside one of the folders shown in the list box, just double-click that folder. When all is said and done, the name of the folder where the workbook file will be saved should appear in the Save in edit box. If you want to save the file in a brand-new folder, click the Create New Folder button (see Figure 2-21) and enter the folder name in the New Folder dialog box before choosing OK or pressing Enter.

Remember that, under Windows 95, your filenames can contain spaces and be a maximum of 255 characters long (you do want to name your file with an entire paragraph, don't you?). This is great news, especially if you were a DOS or Windows 3.1 user who suffered under that eight-dot-three filename restriction for so long. Just be aware when naming your workbooks that if you transfer it to a machine that doesn't use Windows 95, the Excel filenames will appear severely abbreviated, and they will all be followed with the .XLS Excel filename extension (which, by the way, is stuck onto workbook files created in Excel 97: It's just that Windows 95 has enough sense to hide this filename extension from you).

When you finish making changes in the Save As dialog box, click the Save button or press Enter to have Excel 97 save your work. When Excel saves your workbook file, the program saves all the information in every worksheet in your workbook (including the last position of the cell pointer) in the designated folder and disk. You don't have to fool with the Save As dialog box again unless you want to rename the workbook or save a copy of it in a different directory. If you want to do either of these things, you must choose the Save As command from the File menu rather than click the Save tool or press Ctrl+S.

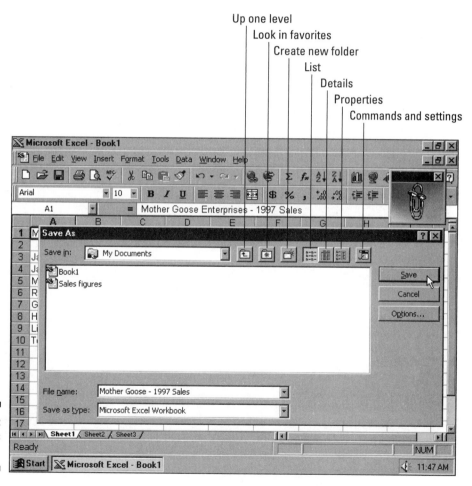

Up one level
Look in favorites
Create new folder
List
Details
Properties
Commands and settings

Figure 2-21:
The Save As
dialog box.

Part II
Editing without Tears

In this part . . .

The business world wouldn't be half bad if it just weren't for the fact that right around the time you master your job, somebody goes and changes it on you. When your life must always be flexible, changing gears and "going with the flow" can really grate on a person! The sad truth is that a big part of the work that you do with Excel 97 is changing the stuff you slaved so hard to enter into the spreadsheet in the first place.

Part II breaks this editing stuff down into three phases: formatting the raw data, rearranging the formatting data and/or in some cases deleting it, and, finally, spitting the final formatted and edited data out in printed form. Take it from me, once you know your way around editing your spreadsheets (as presented in this part of the book), you're more than half way home with Excel 97.

Chapter 3

Making It All Look Pretty

In This Chapter

▶ Selecting the cells to be formatted

▶ Formatting a table of data with AutoFormat

▶ Using number formats on cells containing values

▶ Creating custom number formats for your worksheet

▶ Adjusting the widths of columns in a worksheet

▶ Adjusting the height of rows in a worksheet

▶ Hiding columns and rows in the worksheet

▶ Changing the font and font size

▶ Changing the alignment of the entries in a cell selection

▶ Adding borders, shading, and colors to a cell selection

▶ Formatting cells with styles

▶ Formatting cells with Conditional Formatting

*I*n spreadsheet programs like Excel, you don't normally worry about how the stuff looks until after you've entered all the data in the worksheets of your workbook and saved it all safe and sound (see Chapters 1 and 2). Only then is it time to pretty up the information so that it's clearer and easy to read.

After you decide on the types of formatting you want to apply to a portion of the worksheet, you select all the cells to be beautified and then click the appropriate tool or choose the menu command to apply those formats to the cells. This means that before you find out about all the fabulous formatting features you can use to dress up cells, you first need to know how to pick out the group of cells that you want to apply the formatting to — a process formally known as *selecting the cells* or, alternately, *making a cell selection*.

Be aware, also, that entering data into a cell and formatting that data are two completely different things in Excel. Because they're separate, you can change the entry in a formatted cell, and the new entry will assume the cell's formatting.

This enables you to format blank cells in a worksheet, knowing that when you get around to making entries in those cells, those entries will automatically assume the formatting assigned to those cells.

Choosing a Select Group of Cells

Given the monotonously rectangular nature of the worksheet and its components, it shouldn't come as a surprise to find that all the cell selections you make in the worksheet have the same kind of cubist feel to them. After all, worksheets are just blocks of cells of varying numbers of columns and rows.

A *cell selection* (also known as a *cell range*) is whatever collection of neighboring cells you pick out for formatting or editing. The smallest possible cell selection in a worksheet is just one cell (the so-called *active cell;* the cell with the cell pointer is really just a single cell selection). The largest possible cell selection in a worksheet is all of the cells in that worksheet (the whole enchilada, so to speak). Most of the cell selections you need for formatting a worksheet will probably be somewhere in between, consisting of cells in several adjacent columns and rows.

Excel shows a cell selection in the worksheet by highlighting the block. (Figure 3-1 shows several cell selections of different sizes and shapes.)

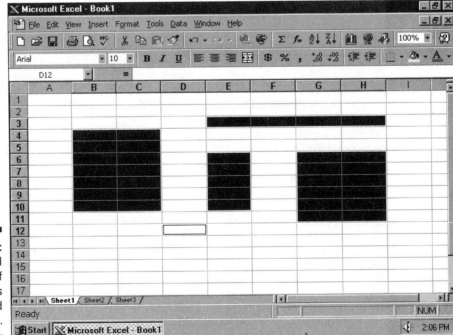

Figure 3-1: Several cell selections of various shapes and sizes.

In Excel, you can select more than one cell range at a time (a phenomenon somewhat ingloriously called a *discontiguous* or *nonadjacent selection*). In fact, although I billed Figure 3-1 as having several cell selections, it is really just one big, nonadjacent cell selection with cell D12 (the active one) as the cell that was selected last.

Point-and-click cell selections

The mouse is a natural for selecting a range of cells. Just position the mouse pointer (in its thick, white-cross form) on the first cell and drag in the direction that you want to extend the selection.

- To extend the cell selection to columns to the right, drag right, highlighting neighboring cells as you go.
- To extend the selection to rows to the bottom, drag down.
- To extend the selection down and to the right at the same time, drag diagonally toward the cell in the lower-right corner of the block you are highlighting.

Shifty cell selections

To speed up the old cell-selection procedure, you can use the old Shift+click method, which goes as follows:

1. **Click the first cell in the selection.**

   This selects that cell.

2. **Position the mouse pointer in the last cell in the selection.**

   This would be kitty-corner from the first cell if you're selecting a rectangular block.

3. **Press the Shift key and hold it down as you click the mouse button again.**

   When you click the mouse button the second time, Excel selects all the cells in the columns and rows between the first cell and last cell.

The Shift key works with the mouse like an *extend* key to extend a selection from the first object you select through to, and including, the second object you select (see "Extend that cell selection," later in this chapter). Shift enables you to select the first and last cells as well as all the intervening cells in a worksheet or all the document names in a dialog list box.

If, when making a cell selection with the mouse, you notice that you have included the wrong cells before you release the mouse button, you can deselect the cells and resize the selection by moving the pointer in the opposite direction.

If you've already released the mouse button, click the first cell in the high-lighted range to select just that cell (and deselect all the others) and then start the whole selection process again.

Nonadjacent cell selections

To select a nonadjacent cell selection made up of more than one discontiguous block of cells, drag through the first cell range and then hold down the Ctrl key as you click the first cell of the second range and drag the pointer through the cells in this range. As long as you hold down Ctrl while you select the subsequent ranges, Excel doesn't deselect any of the previously selected cell ranges.

The Ctrl key works with the mouse like an *add* key to include non-neighboring objects in Excel (see "Nonadjacent cell selections with the keyboard," later in this chapter). With Ctrl, you can add to the selection of cells in a worksheet or to the document names in a dialog list box without having to deselect those already selected.

Going for the "big" cell selections

You can select the cells in entire columns or rows or even all the cells in the worksheet by applying the following clicking-and-dragging techniques to the worksheet frame:

- ✔ To select every single cell in a particular column, click its column letter on the frame at the top of the worksheet document window.

- ✔ To select every cell in a particular row, click its row number on the frame at the left edge of the document window.

- ✔ To select a range of entire columns or rows, drag through the column letters or row numbers on the frame surrounding the workbook.

- ✔ To select more than entire columns or rows that are not right next to each other (that old discontiguous stuff, again), press and hold down the Ctrl key while you click the column letters or row numbers of the columns and rows that you want to add to the selection.

- ✔ To select each and every cell in the worksheet, click the unmarked button in the upper-left corner of the workbook frame formed by the intersection of the row with the column letters and the column with the row numbers.

Selecting the cells in a table of data, courtesy of AutoSelect

Excel provides a really quick way (called AutoSelect) to select all the cells in a table of data entered as a solid block. (Don't try this when you need to select empty cells or on a table of data that has blanks in the first column or top row.) To use AutoSelect, simply follow these steps:

1. **Click the first cell of the table to select it.**

   That's the one in the table's upper-left corner.

2. **Hold down the Shift key as you double-click either the right or bottom edge of the selected cell with the arrowhead mouse pointer (see Figure 3-2).**

   If you double-click the bottom edge of the cell, the cell selection expands to that cell in the last row of the first column (as shown in Figure 3-3). If you double-click the right edge of the cell, the cell selection expands to the cell in the last column of the first row.

3a. **Double-click somewhere on the right edge of the cell selection (see Figure 3-3) if the cell selection now consists of the first column of the table.**

   This selects all the remaining rows of the table of data (as shown in Figure 3-4).

3b. **Double-click somewhere on the bottom edge of the current cell selection if the cell selection now consists of the first row of the table.**

   This selects all the rest of the rows in the table.

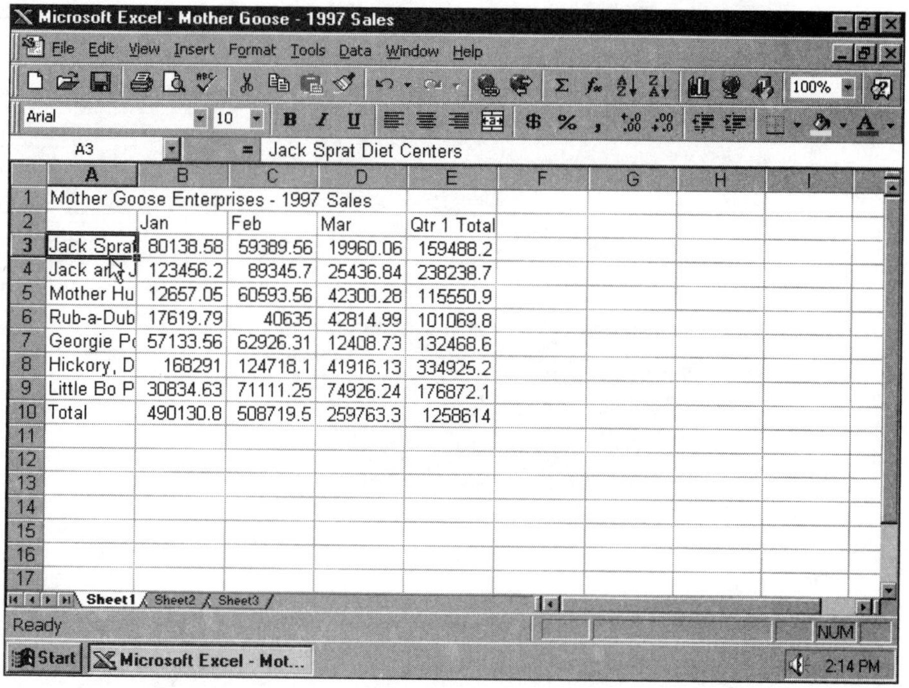

Figure 3-2:
Position the
mouse
pointer on
the bottom
edge of the
first cell to
select the
cells in the
first column
of the data
table with
AutoSelect.

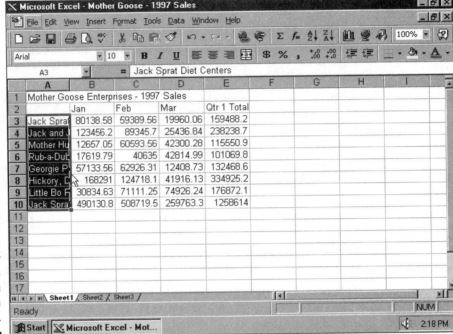

Figure 3-3:
Double-clicking the bottom edge of the selected cells while holding down the Shift key selects the first column of the data table.

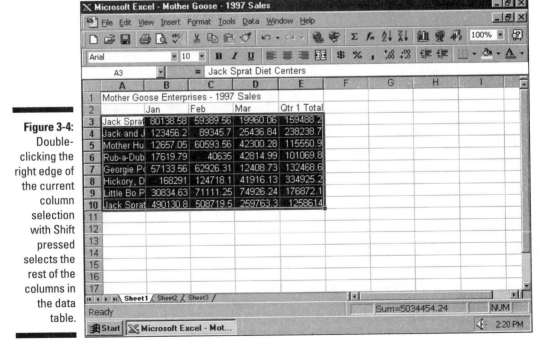

Figure 3-4:
Double-clicking the right edge of the current column selection with Shift pressed selects the rest of the columns in the data table.

Although the preceding steps make it sound like you have to select the first cell of the table when you use AutoSelect, you can actually select any of the cells in the four corners of the table. Then, when expanding the cell selection in the table with the Shift key depressed, you can choose whatever direction you like (left by clicking the left edge, right by clicking the right edge, up by clicking the top edge, or down by clicking the bottom edge) to select either the first or last row of the table or the first or last column. After expanding the cell selection to include either the first or last row or first or last column, you need to click whichever edge of that current cell selection will expand it so that it includes all the remaining table rows or columns.

Keyboard cell selections

If you're not really keen on using the mouse, you can use the keyboard to select the cells you want. In keeping with the Shift+click method of selecting cells, the easiest way to select cells with the keyboard is to combine the Shift key with other keystrokes that move the cell pointer. (Chapter 1 lists these keystrokes.)

Start by positioning the cell pointer in the first cell of the selection and then hold the Shift key as you press the appropriate cell-pointer movement keys. When you hold the Shift key as you press direction keys, such as the arrow keys ($\uparrow$, $\leftarrow$, $\downarrow$, $\rightarrow$), PgUp, or PgDn, Excel anchors the selection on the current cell and not only moves the cell pointer as usual but also highlights cells as it goes.

When making a cell selection this way, you can continue to alter the size and shape of the cell range with the cell-pointer movement keys as long as you don't release the Shift key. After you let up on the Shift key, pressing any of the cell-pointer movement keys immediately collapses the selection, reducing it to just the cell with the cell pointer.

Extend that cell selection

If holding the Shift key as you move the cell pointer is too tiring, you can place Excel in Extend mode by pressing (and promptly releasing) F8 before you press any cell-pointer movement key. Excel displays the EXT (for extend) indicator on the status bar — your sign that the program will select all the cells that you move the cell pointer through (just as though you were holding down the Shift key).

When you've highlighted all the cells you want in the cell range, press F8 again to turn off Extend mode. The EXT indicator disappears from the status bar, and then you can once again move the cell pointer with the keyboard without highlighting everything in your path.

AutoSelect keyboard style

For the keyboard equivalent of AutoSelect with the mouse (refer to "Selecting the cells in a table of data, courtesy of AutoSelect" earlier in this chapter), you combine the use of the F8 (Extend key) or the Shift key with the Ctrl+arrow keys or End+arrow keys to zip the cell pointer from one end of a block to the other, merrily selecting all the cells in its path as it goes.

To select an entire table of data with a keyboard version of AutoSelect, you follow these steps:

1. **Position the cell pointer in the first cell.**

   That's the one in the upper-left corner of the table.

2. **Press F8 (or hold the Shift key) and then press Ctrl+→ (or End, → if you prefer) to extend the cell selection to the cells in the columns on the right.**

3. **Then press Ctrl+↓ (or End, ↓ if you prefer) to extend the selection to the cells in the rows below.**

Keep in mind that the directions in the above steps are arbitrary — you can just as well press Ctrl+↓ (or End, ↓) before you press Ctrl+→ (or End, →). Just be sure (if you're using the Shift key instead of F8) that you don't let up on the Shift key until after you finish performing these two directional maneuvers. Also, if you pressed F8 to get the program into Extend mode, don't forget to press this key again to get out of Extend mode after the table cells are all selected (or you'll end up selecting cells that you don't want included when you next move the cell pointer).

Nonadjacent cell selections with the keyboard

Selecting more than one cell range is a little more complicated with the keyboard than it is with the mouse. When using the keyboard, you alternate between anchoring the cell pointer and moving the cell pointer to select the cell range, unanchoring the cell pointer and repositioning it at the beginning of the next range. To unanchor the cell pointer so that you can move it into position for selecting another range, press Shift+F8. This puts you in Add mode, in which you can move to the first cell of the next range without selecting any more cells. Excel lets you know that the cell pointer is unanchored by displaying the ADD indicator on the status bar.

To select more than one cell range using the keyboard, you follow these general steps:

1. **Move the cell pointer to the first cell of the first cell range you want to select.**

2. Press F8 to get into Extend mode.

Move the cell pointer to select all the cells in the first cell range. Alternatively, hold the Shift key as you move the cell pointer.

3. Press Shift+F8 to switch to Add mode.

The ADD indicator appears in the status bar.

4. Move the cell pointer to the first cell of the next nonadjacent range you want to select.

5. Press F8 again to get back into Extend mode and then move the cell pointer to select all the cells in this new range.

6. If you still have other nonadjacent ranges to select, repeat Steps 3, 4, and 5 until you have selected and added all the cell ranges you want to use.

Cell selections à la Go To

If you want to select a really big cell range that would take a long time to select by pressing various cell-pointer movement keys, use the Go To feature to extend the range to a far distant cell. All you gotta do is follow this pair of steps:

1. Start by positioning the cell pointer in the first cell of the range; then press F8 to anchor the cell pointer and get Excel into Extend mode.

2. Press F5 to open the Go To dialog box, type the address of the last cell in the range (the cell kitty-corner from the first cell), and then press Enter.

Because Excel is in Extend mode at the time you use Go To to jump to another cell, the program not only moves the cell pointer to the designated cell address but selects all the intervening cells as well. After selecting the range of cells with the Go To feature, don't forget to press F8 (the Extend key) again to prevent the program from messing up your selection by adding on more cells the next time you move the cell pointer.

Trimming Your Tables with AutoFormat

Here's a formatting technique that doesn't require you to do any prior cell selecting. (Kinda figures, doesn't it?) In fact, the AutoFormat feature is so automatic that, to use it, the cell pointer just has to be somewhere within the table of data prior to your choosing the AutoFormat command on the Format pull-down menu.

As soon as you open the AutoFormat dialog box, Excel automatically selects all the cells in the table. (You get a rude message in an alert box if you choose the command when the cell pointer isn't within the confines of the table or in one of the cells directly bordering the table.)

You can make short work of formatting a table of data by choosing one of the 16 built-in table formats. Here's how:

1. **Choose Format⇨AutoFormat to open the AutoFormat dialog box.**

2. **Click a format in the Table format list box to see a preview of its formats in the Sample area.**

   This sample should give you an idea of what kind of formatting is included in a particular table format and how it makes the table look. (Unfortunately, Excel can't display a miniature of your table in the Sample area.)

3. **Continue selecting formats from the list box in this manner to preview other table formats until you find the one you want to use.**

4. **Click the OK button or press Enter to close the AutoFormat dialog box and apply the selected format to the table in the worksheet.**

When you're familiar enough with the table formats to know which one you want to use, you can save time by double-clicking the desired format in the Table format list box to both close the AutoFormat dialog box and apply the formatting to the selected table.

If you ever goof up and select a table format that you just absolutely hate after you see it in the worksheet, choose the Edit⇨Undo AutoFormat on the menu bar (or press Ctrl+Z) before you do anything else; Excel restores the table to its previous state. (For more on getting yourself out of a jam with the Undo feature, see Chapter 4.) If you decide later on that you don't want any of the automatic table formatting, you can get rid of all of it (even when it's too late to use Undo) by opening the AutoFormat dialog box and choosing None in the Table format list box (located at the very bottom of the list) before you click OK or press Enter.

Each of the built-in table formats offered by AutoFormat is nothing more than a particular combination of various kinds of cell and data formatting that Excel applies to the cell selection in a single operation. (Boy, does this ever save time!) Each one enhances the headings and values in the table in a slightly different way.

Figure 3-5 shows the first quarter 1997 sales table for Mother Goose Enterprises (introduced in Chapter 2) just before the Simple table format is selected in the AutoFormat dialog box. Figure 3-6 shows the sales table with the Simple table format applied to it. Notice that not only did AutoFormat bold the worksheet title and headings in rows 1 and 2 and draw borderlines to separate these headings from the rest of the table data, but it also centered the title *Mother Goose Enterprises – 1997 Sales* over columns A through E and the headings in cells B2 through E2. Note, however, that the Simple table format does nothing to spruce up the dollar amounts in the table.

Figure 3-7 shows the table after reopening the AutoFormat dialog box and, this time, choosing the 3D Effects 2 table format for the same cell range. As you can see, after selecting this table format, Excel increased the width of column A to contain the entire worksheet title, *Mother Goose Enterprises – 1997 Sales* in cell A1. This kind of column sizing is known as *best-fit* (somewhat misapplied in this case) and is accomplished with the AutoFit feature. To rectify this little boo-boo, you simply narrow column A until it's just wide enough to display all of the company names in rows 3 through 9 of column A and let the worksheet title in cell A1 once again overhang columns B through E as it naturally wants to do. (For information on how to widen and narrow columns, both manually and with the AutoFit feature, see "Calibrating Columns," later in this chapter.)

The 3D Effects 2 AutoFormat is not the only table format that uses AutoFit to apply this type of *best-fit* to all the selected columns (and therefore can give you a really wide first column if your table has a long title in the first cell like the ones shown in Figure 3-5 through 3-7). You also get this best-fit-which-is-not situation — shown in Figure 3-7 — if you choose the Classic 2; Financial 1, 2, or 3; Accounting 1; Colorful 3; List 1 or 2; or 3D Effects 1 table formats. All the others prefer to center long titles in the first cell across all the columns in the table (which can give you the problem illustrated in Figure 3-6!).

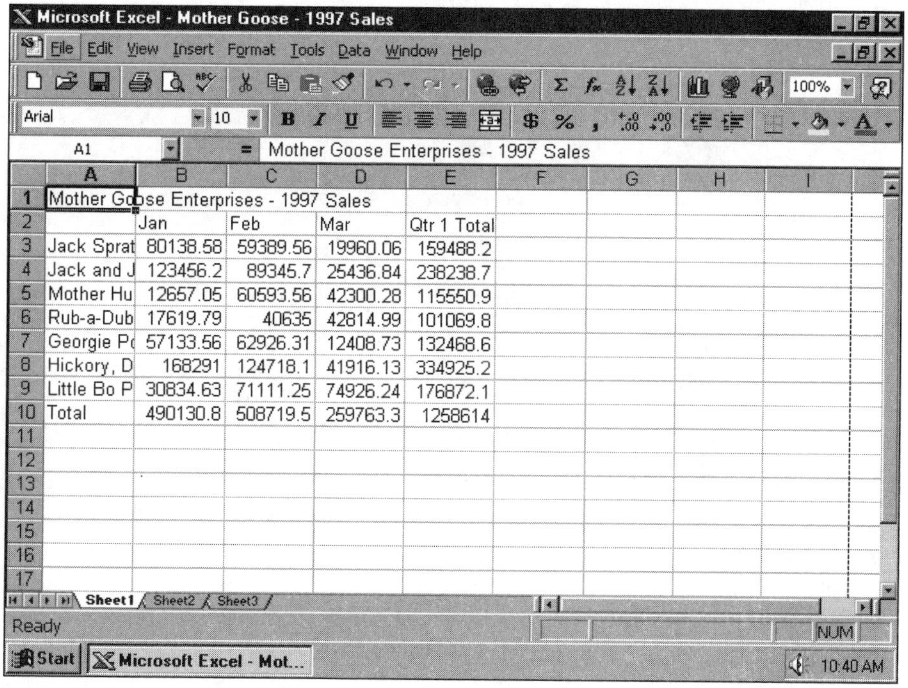

Figure 3-5:
Using
AutoFormat
to select
and format
the Mother
Goose
Enterprises
first quarter
sales table.

	A	B	C	D	E
1	Mother Goose Enterprises - 1997 Sales				
2		Jan	Feb	Mar	Qtr 1 Total
3	Jack Sprat	80138.58	59389.56	19960.06	159488.2
4	Jack and J	123456.2	89345.7	25436.84	238238.7
5	Mother Hu	12657.05	60593.56	42300.28	115550.9
6	Rub-a-Dub	17619.79	40635	42814.99	101069.8
7	Georgie P(	57133.56	62926.31	12408.73	132468.6
8	Hickory, D	168291	124718.1	41916.13	334925.2
9	Little Bo P	30834.63	71111.25	74926.24	176872.1
10	Total	490130.8	508719.5	259763.3	1258614

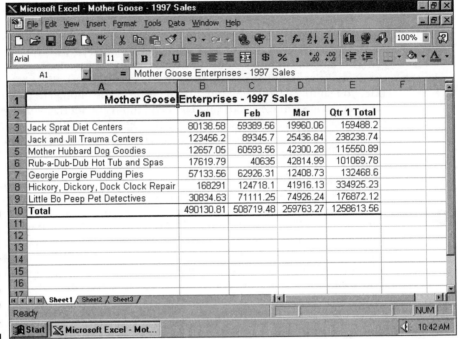

Figure 3-6:
Mother's first quarter sales table in the Simple table format.

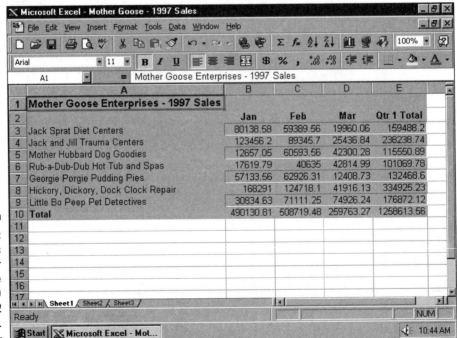

Figure 3-7:
Mother's first quarter sales table in the 3D Effects 2 table format.

Festooning Your Cells with the Formatting Toolbar

Some worksheets require a lighter touch than the AutoFormat feature offers. For example, you may have a table where the only emphasis you want to add is to make the column headings bold at the top of the table and to underline the row of totals at the bottom (done by drawing a borderline along the bottom of the cells).

With the tools on the Formatting toolbar, which appears right below the Standard toolbar, you can accomplish most data and cell formatting without ever venturing into the shortcut menus, let alone (heaven forbid) opening up the pull-down menus.

You can use the tools on the Formatting toolbar to assign new fonts and number formats to cells; to change the alignment of their contents; or to add borders, patterns, and colors to them. (Refer to Table 1-3 in Chapter 1 for a complete rundown on the use of each of these tools.)

Transient toolbars

Normally, the Standard and Formatting toolbars appear at the top of the Excel 97 program window (right below the menu bar) in a stationary position politely referred to as being in a *docked* position (*beached* is more like it). Although Excel automatically docks these toolbars at the top of the screen, you are free to move them (as well as any other toolbars that you open — see Chapter 13 for details on using and customizing other toolbars) around by dragging them (kicking and screaming) into new positions.

When you drag the Standard or Formatting toolbar down from its perch and into the work area containing the open workbook, the toolbar then appears in a separate little window like the one containing the Formatting toolbar shown in Figure 3-8. Such toolbars-in-a-window are referred to as *floating toolbars* because they float like clouds above the open workbook below (how poetic!). And not only can you move these little dears, but you can resize them as well:

- You can move a floating toolbar into new positions over the worksheet document by dragging it by its tiny title bar.

- You can resize a floating toolbar by dragging any one of its sides (wait until the mouse pointer changes to a double-headed arrow before you start dragging).

- As you drag a side of the floating toolbar, the outline of the toolbar assumes a new shape to accommodate the tools in a prescribed tool arrangement. When the toolbar outline assumes the shape you want, release the mouse button, and Excel redraws the toolbar.

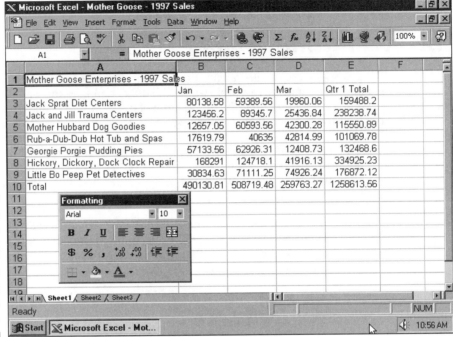

Microsoft Excel - Mother Goose - 1997 Sales

	A	B	C	D	E	F
1	Mother Goose Enterprises - 1997 Sales					
2		Jan	Feb	Mar	Qtr 1 Total	
3	Jack Sprat Diet Centers	80138.58	59389.56	19960.06	159488.2	
4	Jack and Jill Trauma Centers	123456.2	89345.7	25436.84	238238.74	
5	Mother Hubbard Dog Goodies	12657.05	60593.56	42300.28	115550.89	
6	Rub-a-Dub-Dub Hot Tub and Spas	17619.79	40635	42814.99	101069.78	
7	Georgie Porgie Pudding Pies	57133.56	62926.31	12408.73	132468.6	
8	Hickory, Dickory, Dock Clock Repair	168291	124718.1	41916.13	334925.23	
9	Little Bo Peep Pet Detectives	30834.63	71111.25	74926.24	176872.12	
10	Total	490130.81	508719.48	259763.27	1258613.56	

Figure 3-8:
The Formatting toolbar peacefully floating above the worksheet.

✔ To close a floating toolbar when you no longer want it in the document window, click the close box (the small box in the upper-left corner of the toolbar window).

To drag a toolbar to a new position on the screen, click on the double bar (| |) displayed at the very beginning of the toolbar. To restore a floating toolbar to its original docked position on the screen, just double-click the toolbar's title bar.

Floating the menu bar

Toolbars like the Standard and Formatting toolbar are not the only things that float in Excel 97. In this version of the program, you can even float the menu bar containing all of the pull-down menus (thus, the reason for the double bar that now appears at the very beginning of the menu bar when it's docked at the top of the screen right below the Excel window's title bar). When you select a menu on a floating menu bar, its commands may appear above the bar next to the menu's name rather than below the bar (as is normal), depending upon how much room there is between the floating bar and the bottom of the screen.

Toolbar docking maneuvers

Let's face it, sometimes a floating toolbar can be a real pain because you're constantly having to move it out of the way as you add to and edit your worksheet data. To get a toolbar out of the way so that it no longer obscures any of the worksheet cells, you can simply dock it.

There are four docking stations in Excel: the top of the screen above the formula bar, the very left edge of the screen, the very right edge of the screen, or the bottom of the screen right above the status bar. Figure 3-9 shows the Formatting toolbar after docking it at the bottom of the work area.

To dock a floating toolbar in one of these four areas, drag it by the title bar as far to the side of the window as possible and release the mouse button when the outline of the bar assumes a shape that accommodates a single column (when docking left or right) or a single row (when docking top or bottom). Toolbars you dock on the left or right of the document window reorient their tools so that they run vertically down the toolbar.

Excel won't let you dock the Standard or Formatting toolbar on the left or right side of the screen because both of these toolbars contain drop-down list boxes that can't be reoriented with the toolbar (so that their contents pop out to the

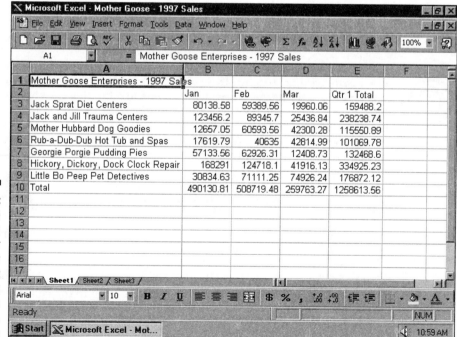

Figure 3-9: The Formatting toolbar safely docked at the bottom of the work area.

left or right of the tool). This restriction on docking on the left or right side of the screen also applies to the Drawing, Chart, and WorkGroup toolbars due to their inclusion of tools that use drop-down list boxes.

Sometimes, after a toolbar is docked, the active document window loses one or the other of the scroll bars. To get the missing scroll bar back, click the document Maximize button to max out the current document. If you're working with an empty workbook (like Book1), you can properly size the document window and restore the scroll bars by closing the workbook with the File⇨Close command on the menu bar and then opening a new workbook in its place by clicking on the New tool on the Standard toolbar (the very first tool). When Excel opens the new workbook (Book2), the document window fits nicely (with all the scroll bars intact) and reflects your current toolbar-docking arrangement.

Using the Format Cells Dialog Box

Excel's Format⇨Cells command on the menu bar (Ctrl+1 for short) makes it a snap to apply a whole rash of different kinds of formatting to a cell selection. The Format Cells dialog box that this command calls up contains six tabs: Number, Alignment, Font, Border, Patterns, and Protection. In this chapter, I show you how to use the Number, Alignment, Font, Border, and Patterns tabs in the Format Cells dialog box to assign new number formats and fonts to your cells as well as to change their alignment, borders, and patterns. For information on how and when to use the options on the Protection tab, see Chapter 6.

The keystroke shortcut — Ctrl+1 — that opens the Format Cells dialog box is one worth learning. (Many of you will be doing almost as much formatting as you do data entry in a worksheet.) Just keep in mind that the shortcut is Ctrl plus the number 1 and not the function key F1. Further, you must use the 1 key on the top row of the regular typewriter keyboard, not the 1 located on your numeric keypad. Pressing Ctrl plus the 1 on the numeric keypad doesn't work any better than pressing Ctrl+F1.

Getting to know the number formats

As Chapter 2 explains, how you enter values into a worksheet determines the type of number format they get. Here are some examples:

 ✔ If you enter a financial value complete with the dollar sign and two decimal places, Excel assigns a Currency number format to the cell along with the entry.

✔ If you enter a value representing a percentage as a whole number followed by the percent sign without any decimal places, Excel assigns to the cell the Percentage number format that follows this pattern along with the entry.

✔ If you enter a date (remember that dates are values, too) that follows one of the built-in Excel number formats like 02/19/97 or 19-Feb-97, the program assigns a Date number format that follows the pattern of the date along with a special value representing the date.

Although it's fine to format values in this manner as you go along (and even necessary in the case of dates), you don't have to do it this way. You can always assign a number format to a group of values before or after you enter them. And, in fact, formatting numbers after you enter them is often the most efficient way to go because it's just a two-step procedure:

1. **Select all the cells containing the values that need dressing up.**

2. **Select the number format you want to use either from the Formatting toolbar or the Format Cells dialog box.**

   Many times, you can use one of the tools on the Formatting toolbar — if not, you can select a number format from the Number tab in the Format Cells dialog box (Ctrl+1).

Even if you're a really good typist and prefer (thank you very much) to enter each value exactly as you want it to appear in the worksheet, you'll still have to resort to using number formats to make the values that are calculated by formulas match the others you've entered. This is because Excel applies a General number format (which the Format Cells dialog box explains as "General format cells have no specific number format.") to all the values it calculates as well as any you enter that don't exactly follow one of the other Excel number formats. The biggest problem with the General format is that it has the nasty habit of dropping all leading and trailing zeros from the entries. This makes it very hard to line up numbers in a column on their decimal points.

Figure 3-10 shows this sad state of affairs. The figure shows a sample worksheet with the first-quarter 1997 sales figures for Mother Goose Enterprises before any of the values have been formatted. Notice how the columns of monthly sales figures zig and zag? This is the fault of Excel's General number format; the only cure is to format the values with another more uniform number format.

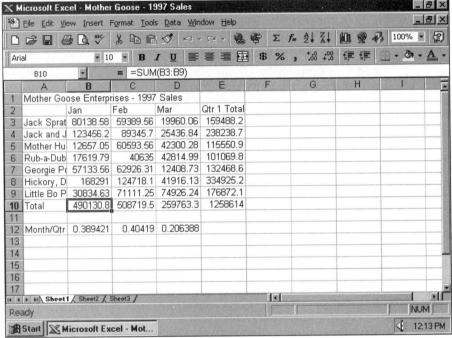

Figure 3-10:
First quarter
sales
zigging and
zagging in
columns B
through E.

Currying your cells with the Currency Style

Given the financial nature of most worksheets, you probably use the Currency
format more than any other. This is a really easy format to apply because the
Formatting toolbar contains a Currency Style tool that adds a dollar sign,
commas between thousands of dollars, and two decimal places to any values in
a selected range. If any of the values in the cell selection are negative, this
Currency format displays them in parentheses (the way accountants like them)
and displays them in red on a color monitor (the way governments like them).

In Figure 3-11, only the cells containing totals are selected for the Currency
format (cell ranges E3:E10 and B10:D10). This cell selection was then formatted
with the Currency format by simply clicking the Currency Style button on the
Formatting toolbar (the one with the $ icon, naturally).

Note: Although you could put all the figures in the table into the Currency
format to line up the decimal points, this would result in a superabundance of
dollar signs in a fairly small table. In this example, I've decided that only the
monthly and quarterly totals should be formatted à la Currency.

Microsoft Excel - Mother Goose - 1997 Sales

	A	B	C	D	E	F	G	H
1	Mother Goose Enterprises - 1997 Sales							
2		Jan	Feb	Mar	Qtr 1 Total			
3	Jack Sprat	80138.58	59389.56	19960.06	$ 159,488.20			
4	Jack and J	123456.2	89345.7	25436.84	$ 238,238.74			
5	Mother Hu	12657.05	60593.56	42300.28	$ 115,550.89			
6	Rub-a-Dub	17619.79	40635	42814.99	$ 101,069.78			
7	Georgie Pc	57133.56	62926.31	12408.73	$ 132,468.60			
8	Hickory, D	168291	124718.1	41916.13	$ 334,925.23			
9	Little Bo P	30834.63	71111.25	74926.24	$ 176,872.12			
10	Total	$ 490,130.81	$ 508,719.48	$ 259,763.27	$ 1,258,613.56			
11								
12	Month/Qtr	0.389421206	0.40419037	0.206388425				

E3 = =SUM(B3:D3)

Currency Style

Sum= $3,775,840.68   NUM

Start   Microsoft Excel - Mot...   12:17 PM

Figure 3-11:
The totals in the Mother Goose sales table after clicking the Currency Style button on the Formatting toolbar.

"Look, Ma, no more format overflow!"

When I applied the Currency number format to the selection in the cell ranges of E3:E10 and B10:D10 in the sales table shown in Figure 3-11, Excel 97 not only added dollar signs, commas between the thousands, a decimal point, and two decimal places to the highlighted values, but also, at the same time, automatically widened columns B, C, D, and E just enough to display all this new formatting. In earlier versions of Excel, you would have had to widen these columns yourself, and instead of the perfectly aligned numbers, you would have been confronted with columns of #######s in cell ranges E3:E10 and B10:D10. Such pound signs where nicely formatted dollar totals should be serve as overflow indicators, declaring that whatever formatting you've added to the value in that cell has added so much to the value's display that Excel can no longer display it within the current column width.

Fortunately, Excel 97 eliminates the format overflow indicators when you're formatting the values in your cells by automatically widening their columns. The only time you'll ever run across these dreaded #######s in your cells will be when you take it upon yourself to manually narrow a worksheet column (see "Calibrating Columns," later in this chapter) to such an extent that Excel can no longer display all the characters in its cells with formatted values.

Currying your cells with the Comma Style

The Comma format offers a good alternative to the Currency format. Like Currency, the Comma format inserts commas in larger numbers to separate thousands, hundred thousands, millions, and, well, you get the idea.

This format also displays two decimal places and puts negative values in parentheses and in red (on a color monitor). What it doesn't display is dollar signs. This makes it perfect for formatting tables where it's obvious that you're dealing with dollars and cents or for larger values that have nothing to do with money.

The Comma format also works well for the bulk of the values in the sample first-quarter sales worksheet. Figure 3-12 shows this table after the cells containing the monthly sales for each Mother Goose company were formatted with the Comma format. To do this, select the cell range B3:D9 and click the Comma Style button (the one with the , [comma] icon, of course) on the Formatting toolbar.

Figure 3-12 shows how the Comma format takes care of the earlier alignment problem in the quarterly sales figures. Moreover, notice how the Comma-formatted monthly sales figures align perfectly with the Currency-formatted monthly totals in row 10. If you look really closely (you might need a magnifying glass for this one), you see that these formatted values no longer abut the right edges of their cells; they've moved slightly to the left. The gap on the right between the last digit and the cell border is there to accommodate the right parenthesis in negative values, ensuring that they, too, align precisely on the decimal point.

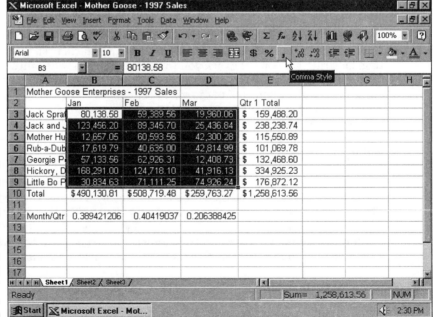

Figure 3-12:
Monthly
sales figures
after
formatting
them with
the Comma
number
format.

Playing Around with the Percent Style

Many worksheets use percentages in the form of interest rates, growth rates, inflation rates, and so on. To insert a percentage in a cell, place the percent sign (%) after the number. To indicate an interest rate of 12 percent, for example, you enter **12%** in the cell. When you do this, Excel assigns a Percent number format and, at the same time, divides the value by 100 (that's what makes it a percentage) and places the result in the cell (0.12 in this example).

Not all percentages in a worksheet are entered by hand in this manner. Some may be calculated by a formula and returned to their cells as raw decimal values. In such cases, you should add a Percent format to convert the calculated decimal values to percentages (done by multiplying the decimal value by 100 and adding a percent sign).

The sample first-quarter sales worksheet just happens to have some percentages calculated by formulas in row 12 that need formatting (these formulas indicate what percentage each monthly total is of the first-quarter total in cell E10). Figure 3-13 shows these values after they have been formatted with a Percent format. To accomplish this feat, you simply select the cells and click the Percent Style button on the Formatting toolbar. (Need I point out that it's the tool with % sign?)

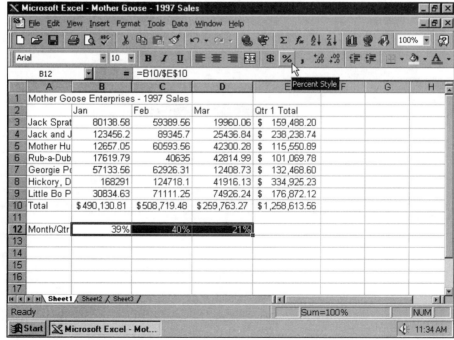

Figure 3-13: Monthly-to-quarterly sales percentages formatted with the Percent number format.

Deciding how many decimal places

You can increase or decrease the number of decimal places used in a number entered with the Currency Style, Comma Style, or Percent Style tool on the Formatting toolbar simply by clicking the Increase Decimal tool or the Decrease Decimal tool also located on this toolbar. (Remember to click these tools while the cell range you just formatted is still selected.)

Each time you click the Increase Decimal tool (the one with the arrow pointing left), Excel adds another decimal place to the number format you applied. Figure 3-14 shows percentages in the cell range B12:D12 after I increased the number of decimal places in the Percent format from none to two. (The Percent Style doesn't use any decimal places.) I accomplished this by clicking the Increase Decimal tool twice in a row.

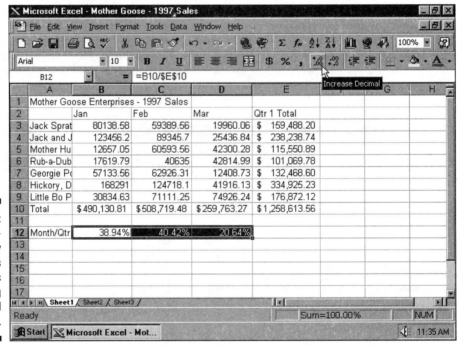

Figure 3-14:
Monthly-to-
quarterly
sales
percentages
after adding
two decimal
places.

The values behind the formatting

Make no mistake about it: All that these fancy number formats do is spiff up the presentation of the values in the worksheet. Like a good illusionist, a particular number format sometimes appears to transform some entries magically, but in reality, the entries are the same old numbers you started with. For example, suppose that a formula returns the following value:

```
25.6456
```

Now suppose that you format the cell containing this value with the Currency Style tool. The value now appears as follows:

```
$25.65
```

This change may lead you to believe that Excel rounded the value up to two decimal places. In fact, the program has rounded up only the *display* of the calculated value — the cell still contains the same old value of 25.6456. If you use this cell in another worksheet formula, keep in mind that Excel uses the behind-the-scenes value in its calculation, not the spiffed-up one shown in the cell.

But what if you want the values to match their formatted appearance in the worksheet? Well, Excel can do that in a single step. Be forewarned, however, that this is a one-way trip. You can convert all underlying values to the way they are displayed by selecting a single check box, but you can't return them to their previous state by deselecting the check box.

Well, because you insist on knowing this little trick anyway, here goes (just don't write and try to tell me that you weren't warned):

1. **Make sure that all the values in your worksheet are formatted with the right number of decimal places.**

   You must do this step before you convert the precision of all values in the worksheet to their displayed form.

2. **Choose Tools⇨Options on the menu bar.**

3. **Click the Calculation tab to bring up the calculation options.**

4. **Choose the Precision as Displayed option under Workbook Options to put a check mark in its check box and click the OK button.**

   Excel displays the Data will permanently lose accuracy alert dialog box (or in a question-and-answer balloon if the Office Assistant is open).

5. **Go ahead (live dangerously) and click the OK button or press Enter to convert all values to match their display.**

After converting all the values in a worksheet with the Precision as Displayed option, as described in the preceding steps, you may be wise to select the Save As command on the File pull-down menu and edit the filename in the File name edit box (maybe, by appending "as Displayed" to the current filename) before you click the Save button or press Enter. That way, you'll still have a disk copy of the original workbook file with the values as entered and calculated by Excel that can act as a backup to your new "as Displayed" version.

Ogling the other number formats

Excel supports a whole bunch more number formats than just the Currency, Comma, and Percent formats. To use them, select the cell range (or ranges) to be formatted and select Format Cells on the cell shortcut menu (click the secondary mouse button somewhere in the cell selection) or the Cells command on the Format menu (Ctrl+1) to open the Format Cells dialog box.

After the Format Cells dialog box is open, you then choose the Number tab and select the desired format from the Category list box. Some Number format categories — such as Date, Time, Fraction, and Special — give you further formatting choices in a Type list box. Other number formats, such as Number and Currency, have their own particular boxes that give you options for refining their formats. As you click the different formats in these list boxes, Excel shows what effect this would have on the first of the values in the current cell selection in the Sample area above. When the sample has the format you want to apply to the current cell selection, you just click the OK button or press Enter to apply the new number format.

Sorting through the Special number formats

Excel contains a nifty category of number formats called Special. The Special category contains the following four number formats that may be of interest to you:

- ✔ **Zip Code:** Retains any leading zeros in the value (important in zip codes and of absolutely no importance in arithmetic computations) as in 00123.

- ✔ **Zip Code + 4:** Automatically separates the last four digits from the first five digits and retains any leading zeros as in 00123-5555.

- ✔ **Phone Number:** Automatically encloses the first three digits of the number in parentheses and separates the last four digits from the previous three with a dash as in (999) 555-1111.

- ✔ **Social Security Number:** Automatically puts dashes in the value to separate its digits into groups of three, two, and four as in 666-00-9999.

These Special number formats really come in handy when creating databases in Excel, which often deal with stuff like zip codes, telephone numbers, and sometimes even Social Security numbers (see Chapter 9 for more on creating databases).

Creating custom number formats

If none of the predefined number formats of the various types in the different categories fit your bill, you can always resort to creating a custom number of your very own design. To create custom number format, you must choose Custom as the Category in the Format Cells dialog box and then select the number format code that is closest to what you want from the Type list box and then, most often, edit this number format code in the Type edit box.

There's only one problem with doing this: Excel wasn't lying when it called them number format *codes*. All you see in the Type list box when Custom is the Category is a bunch of weird-looking codes composed of lots of #s, 0s, ?s, Ds, Ms, and Ys. Rather than work yourself into a lather (or, heaven forbid, do something nerdy like trying to decipher this gibberish), make life easier and focus your attention on the Sample area above the Type edit box as you select various formats from the Format Codes list box. There, Excel shows how the value in the active cell of the selected range will look in the selected format. As soon as you see what you like, go for it by clicking the OK button or pressing Enter.

In addition to choosing built-in formats by their number format codes, you can create your own custom codes by doing a little creative editing. Although you do have to use these junky number format codes (ugh) when performing this editing, you really don't have to be a rocket scientist to figure out how to do it. (Not that being a rocket scientist would hurt!)

Rather than bore you with a lot of examples of custom number formats that even a computer nerd would have trouble staying awake through, I just want to introduce you to a custom number format you might actually find quite handy in your worksheets — one that hides the display of any cell entry in the worksheet (you can continue to see the entry on the formula bar when the cell pointer is in its cell). You can then use your custom hidden format to tempo-rarily hide certain cell ranges that you don't want printed out or visible in your worksheet on-screen.

To build the custom hidden number format, open the Format Cells dialog box (Ctrl+1), click Custom in the Category list box in the Number tab of the Format Cells dialog box, and then select General in the Type list box and replace this text with the following number format codes:

```
;;;
```

Decoding those darned number format codes

If you just have to know what some of these number format codes mean, here goes. Each number format can control how positive numbers, negative numbers, and everything else looks. These parts are divided by semicolons (any format not so divided covers all the other types of entries). The 0 is a placeholder for a digit and is filled by a zero if the value lacks a digit in that place. The # sign is a placeholder for a digit not to be filled if the value lacks a digit for that place. Ms are used for months in dates or minutes in time, Ds for days, Ys for years, Hs for hours, and Ss for seconds.

The custom hidden number format just consists of three semicolons in a row (with no spaces between them). Odd as this looks, these three semicolons tell Excel that it should display nothing for positive values, nothing for negative values, and, while you're at it, nothing for anything else in the cell.

After entering the codes in the Type edit box, click the OK button or press Enter to apply the custom format to the current cell selection. Custom formats are saved as part of the worksheet the next time you save the workbook file. (Remember, don't neglect that Save tool on the Standard toolbar!)

When you apply this hidden format to cells, the cell display disappears in the worksheet (the contents still show up on the formula bar when you select the cell). To make hidden entries reappear, simply select the hidden cells, open the Format Cells dialog box, and select one of the other visible number formats (the General format, for example) and apply it to cells.

Note that the custom number formats that you create are added to the bottom of the Type list box. This means that when you next open the Format Cells dialog box and select Custom in the Category list box of the Number tab, you may have to scroll through the Type list box all the way to the bottom before you can locate and select the number format codes that you're responsible for adding.

Calibrating Columns

For those times when Excel 97 doesn't automatically adjust the width of your columns to your complete satisfaction, the program makes your changing the column widths a breeze. The easiest way to adjust a column is to do a *best-fit,* using the AutoFit feature. With this method, Excel automatically determines how much to widen or narrow the column to fit the longest entry currently in the column.

Here's how to use AutoFit to get the best-fit for a column:

1. **Position the mouse pointer on the column frame, on the right border of the column that needs adjusting.**

   The mouse pointer changes to a double-headed arrow pointing left and right.

2. **Double-click the mouse button.**

   Excel widens or narrows the column width to suit the longest entry.

You can do a best-fit for more than one column at a time. Simply select all the columns that need adjusting (if the columns neighbor one another, drag through their column letters on the frame; if they don't, hold Ctrl as you click the individual column letters). After the columns are selected, double-click any of the right borders on the frame.

As I pointed out earlier in this chapter, best-fit à la AutoFit doesn't always produce the expected results. All you have to do is AutoFit a column with a table title to become acquainted with this fact (as the 3D Effects 2 table format did in Figure 3-7). A long title that spills into several columns to the right produces an awfully wide column when you use best-fit.

When AutoFit's best-fit won't do, drag the right border of the column (on the frame) until it's the size you need instead of double-clicking it. This manual technique for calibrating the column width also works when more than one column is selected. Just be aware that all selected columns assume whatever size you make the one that you're actually dragging.

You can also set the widths of columns from the Column Width dialog box. When you use the dialog box, you enter the number of characters you want for the column width. To open this dialog box, choose the Column Width command from the column shortcut menu (which you open by clicking on any selected column or column letter with the secondary mouse button), or choose Format⇨Column⇨Width on the menu bar.

The Column width edit box in the Column Width dialog box shows how many characters are in the standard column width in the worksheet or in the current column width if you previously adjusted it. To change the widths of all the columns you've selected in the worksheet (except those already adjusted manually or with AutoFit), enter a new value in the Column width edit box and click the OK button.

If you want Excel to size the column to best-fit, using the pull-down menus, choose Format⇨Column⇨AutoFit Selection on the menu bar. Note that you can use this AutoFit Selection command to apply best-fit to a column based on just some of the cell entries. For example, say that you wanted to use best-fit to make a column just wide enough for a range of headings but not including the worksheet title (that spills over several blank columns to the right). All you have to do is select just the cells in that column that contain the headings on which the new column width should be based before you choose Format⇨ Column⇨AutoFit Selection.

If you want to return a column selection to the standard (default) column width using the pull-down menus, you simply choose Format⇨Column⇨Standard Width on the menu bar. This opens the Standard Width dialog box containing the value 8.43 in the Standard column width edit box (this happens to be the default width of all columns in a new worksheet). To return all the selected columns to this standard width, click the OK button in this dialog box or simply press Enter.

Rambling rows

The story with adjusting the heights of rows is pretty much the same as that with adjusting columns, except that you do a lot less row adjusting than you do column adjusting. That's because Excel automatically changes the height of the rows to accommodate changes to their entries (such as selecting a larger font size or wrapping text in a cell — both of these techniques are coming right up). Most row-height adjustments come about when you want to increase the amount of space between a table title and the table or between a row of column headings and the table of information without actually adding a blank row. (See "From top to bottom" later in this chapter for details.)

To increase the height of a row, drag the bottom border of the row frame down until the row is high enough and then release the mouse button. To shorten a row, reverse this process and drag the bottom row-frame border up. To use AutoFit to create a best-fit for the entries in a row, you double-click the bottom row frame border.

As with columns, you can also adjust the height of selected rows with a dialog box. To open the Row Height dialog box, choose the Row Height command from the row shortcut menu (opened by clicking on any selected row or row number with the secondary mouse button) or choose Format⇨Row⇨Height on the menu bar. To set a new row height for the selected row (or rows), enter the number of characters in the Row height edit box and click OK (the default row height is 12.75 characters, in case you care). To return to the best-fit for a particular row, choose Format⇨Row⇨AutoFit on the menu bar.

Now you see it, now you don't

A funny thing about narrowing columns and rows: You can get too carried away and make a column so narrow or a row so short that it actually disappears from the worksheet! This can actually come in handy for those times when you don't want part of the worksheet visible. For example, you may have a worksheet that contains a column listing employee salaries — required in calculating the departmental budget figures, but that you would prefer to leave off most printed reports. Rather than waste time moving the column of salary figures outside the area to be printed, you can just hide the column until after you print the report.

Hiding columns and rows, courtesy of the pull-down and shortcut menus

Although you can hide worksheet columns and rows by just adjusting them out of existence, Excel does offer an easier method of hiding them via the Format pull-down menu or column or row shortcut menus. Suppose that you need to hide column B in the worksheet because it contains some irrelevant or sensitive information that you don't want printed. To hide this column, you could follow these steps:

1. **Click the letter B on the frame to select the column.**

2. **Choose Format⇨Column⇨Hide on the menu bar.**

That's all there is to it — column B goes *poof!* All the information in the column disappears from the worksheet. When you hide column B, notice that the row of column letters in the frame now reads A, C, D, E, F, and so forth.

Note that you could just as well have hidden column B by clicking its column letter on the frame with the secondary mouse button and then clicking the Hide command on the column's shortcut menu.

So now, suppose that you've printed the worksheet and need to make a change to one of the entries in column B. To unhide the column, follow these steps:

1. **Position the mouse pointer on column letter A in the frame and drag the pointer right to select both columns A and C.**

   You must drag from A to C to include hidden column B as part of the column selection — don't click with the Ctrl key or you won't get B.

2. **Choose Format⇨Column⇨Unhide on the menu bar.**

Excel brings back the hidden B column and all three columns (A, B, and C) are selected. You can then click the mouse pointer on any cell in the worksheet to deselect the columns.

Note that you could also unhide column B by selecting columns A and C and then clicking either one of them with the secondary mouse button and clicking the Unhide command on the column shortcut menu.

Hiding columns and rows with the mouse

I won't lie to you — hiding and redisplaying columns with the mouse can be *very* tricky (just ask my assistant, Robert!). It requires a degree of precision that you may not possess (especially if you've just recently started using the rodent). However, if you consider yourself a real mouse master, you can hide and unhide columns solely by dragging the mouse pointer as follows:

- To hide a column with the mouse, drag the column's right edge to the left until it's on top of the left edge and then release the mouse button.
- To hide a row with the mouse, drag the row's bottom border up until it's on top of the upper border.

As you drag a border, Excel displays a screen tip with the current column width or row height measurement in a box near the mouse pointer (just like with the screen tips that appear when using the scroll bars or with the fill handle when using AutoFill to extend a series as explained in Chapter 1). When this Width or Height indicator reaches 0.00, you know that it's time to release the mouse button.

Unhiding a column or row with the mouse is a reversal of the hiding process. This time, you drag the column or row border in between the nonsequential columns or rows in the opposite direction (right for columns and down for rows). The only trick to this is that you must position the mouse pointer just right on the column or row border so that the pointer doesn't just change to a double-headed arrow but changes to a double-headed arrow split in the middle. (Contrast the shapes of the split double-headed arrow pointer with the regular, old double-headed arrow pointer in Table 1-1.)

If you ever manually hide a column or row only to find that you just can't get that blasted split-bar pointer to appear so that you can drag it back into existence, don't get frantic. With columns, just drag through the first and last column or row between those that are hidden and then choose the Unhide command on the columns or rows shortcut menu (see the preceding section)!

Futzing with the Fonts

When you start a new worksheet, Excel assigns a uniform font and type size to all the cell entries you make. This font varies according to the printer you use — for a laser printer like the HP LaserJet or Apple LaserWriter, Excel uses a font called *Arial* in a 10-point size. Although this font is fine for normal entries, you may want to use something with a little more zing for titles and headings in the worksheet.

If you don't especially care for the standard font that Excel uses, modify it by choosing Tools➪Options on the menu bar and then selecting the General tab. When you do this, you see an option called Standard font near the bottom of the Options dialog box. Select the new standard font from its drop-down list. If you want a different type size, choose the Size option as well and either enter the new point size for the standard font or select it from this option's drop-down list.

With the tools on the Formatting toolbar, you can make most font changes (including selecting a new font style or new font size) without having to resort to the settings on the Font tab in the Format Cells dialog box (Ctrl+1).

✔ To select a new font for a cell selection, click the drop-down button next to the Font drop-down edit box on the Formatting toolbar; then select the name of the font you want to use from the list box.

✔ If you want to change the font size, click the drop-down button next to the Font Size drop-down edit box on the Formatting toolbar; then select the new font size.

You can also add the attributes of bold, italics, underlining, or strikeout to the font you're using. The Formatting toolbar contains the Bold, Italic, and Underline buttons, which not only add these attributes to a cell selection but remove them as well. After you click one of these attribute tools, notice that the tool changes by losing the shading around its right and bottom edge and becoming a lighter shade of gray. Excel does this to make it appear as though a tool button is pushed in. When you click a "pushed-in" button to remove an attribute, Excel changes the button back to its original form so that it no longer appears pushed in.

Although you'll probably make most font changes with the toolbars, on rare occasions you may find it more convenient to make these changes from the Font tab in the Format Cells dialog box (Ctrl+1).

As you can see in Figure 3-15, this Font tab in the Format Cells dialog box brings together under one roof fonts, font styles such as bold and italics, effects like underlining and strikeout, as well as color changes. When you want to make a lot of font-related changes to a cell selection, the Font tab may be your best bet. One of the nice things about using this tab is that it contains a Preview box that shows you how your font changes appear (on-screen at least).

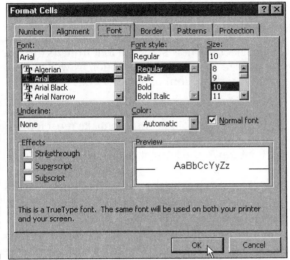

Figure 3-15:
Use the Font
tab in the
Format Cells
dialog box to
make lots
of font
changes at
one time.

If you change font colors with the Color option on the Font tab in the Format
Cells dialog box or with the Font Color button on the Formatting toolbar (the
very last button) and then print the worksheet with a black-and-white printer,
Excel renders the colors as shades of gray. The Automatic choice in the Font
tab Color drop-down list box picks up the color assigned in Windows as the
window text color. This color is black unless you changed it on the Appearance
tab of the Display Properties dialog box in Windows 95. (For help on this
subject, please see *Windows 95 For Dummies,* by Andy Rathbone, from
IDG Books Worldwide, Inc. — and tell Andy that Greg sent ya!).

Altering the Alignment

The alignment assigned to cell entries when you first make them is simply a
function of the type of entry it is: All text entries are left-aligned, and all values
are right-aligned. You can, however, alter this standard arrangement anytime it
suits you.

The Formatting toolbar contains three normal alignment tools: the Align Left,
Center, and Align Right buttons. These buttons align the current cell selection
exactly as you expect them to. After the Right Align button, you find a special
alignment tool called Merge and Center.

Despite its rather strange name, you'll want to get to know this button. You can use it to center a worksheet title across the entire width of a table in seconds (or faster, depending upon your machine). Figures 3-16 and 3-17 show how you can use this tool. In Figure 3-16, notice that the title for the 1997 sales worksheet is entered in cell A1. Because it's a long text entry, it spills over to the empty cell to the right (B1). To center this title over the table (which extends from column A through E), select the cell range A1:E1 (the width of the table) and then click the Merge and Center button on the Formatting toolbar. Figure 3-17 shows the result: The cells in row 1 of columns A through E are merged into one cell, and now the title is properly centered in this supercell and consequently over the entire table.

If you ever need to split up a supercell that you've merged with the Merge and Center back into its original, individual cells, you can do this by selecting the cell, opening the Format Cells dialog box (Ctrl+1), clicking the Alignment tab, and then deselecting the <u>M</u>erge cells check box at the bottom before you click OK or press Enter.

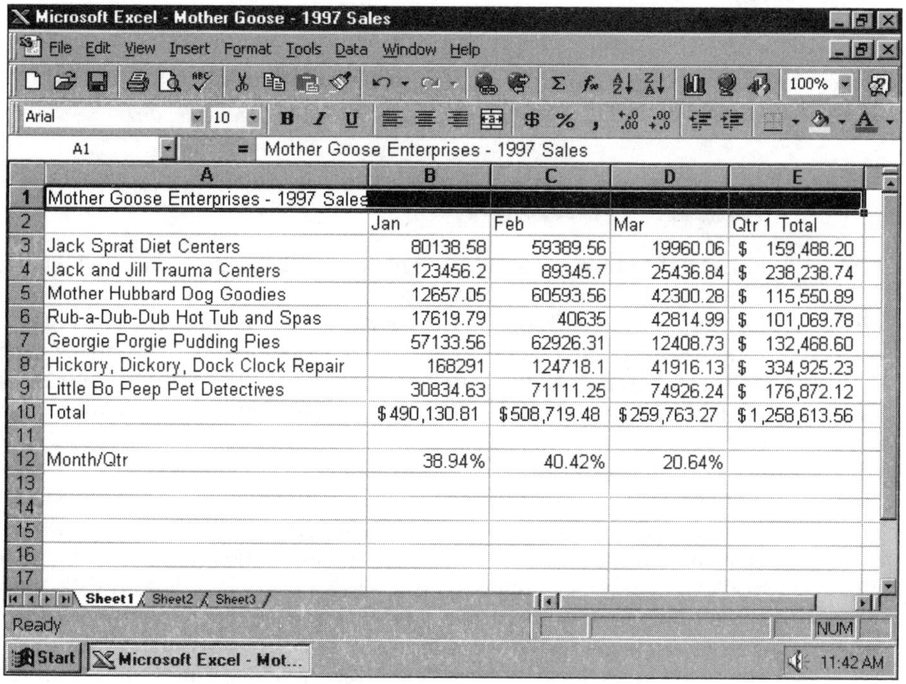

Figure 3-16:
Centering the worksheet title over a table width with the Merge and Center button.

	A	B	C	D	E
1	Mother Goose Enterprises - 1997 Sales				
2		Jan	Feb	Mar	Qtr 1 Total
3	Jack Sprat Diet Centers	80138.58	59389.56	19960.06	$ 159,488.20
4	Jack and Jill Trauma Centers	123456.2	89345.7	25436.84	$ 238,238.74
5	Mother Hubbard Dog Goodies	12657.05	60593.56	42300.28	$ 115,550.89
6	Rub-a-Dub-Dub Hot Tub and Spas	17619.79	40635	42814.99	$ 101,069.78
7	Georgie Porgie Pudding Pies	57133.56	62926.31	12408.73	$ 132,468.60
8	Hickory, Dickory, Dock Clock Repair	168291	124718.1	41916.13	$ 334,925.23
9	Little Bo Peep Pet Detectives	30834.63	71111.25	74926.24	$ 176,872.12
10	Total	$ 490,130.81	$508,719.48	$ 259,763.27	$1,258,613.56
11					
12	Month/Qtr	38.94%	40.42%	20.64%	
13					
14					
15					
16					
17					

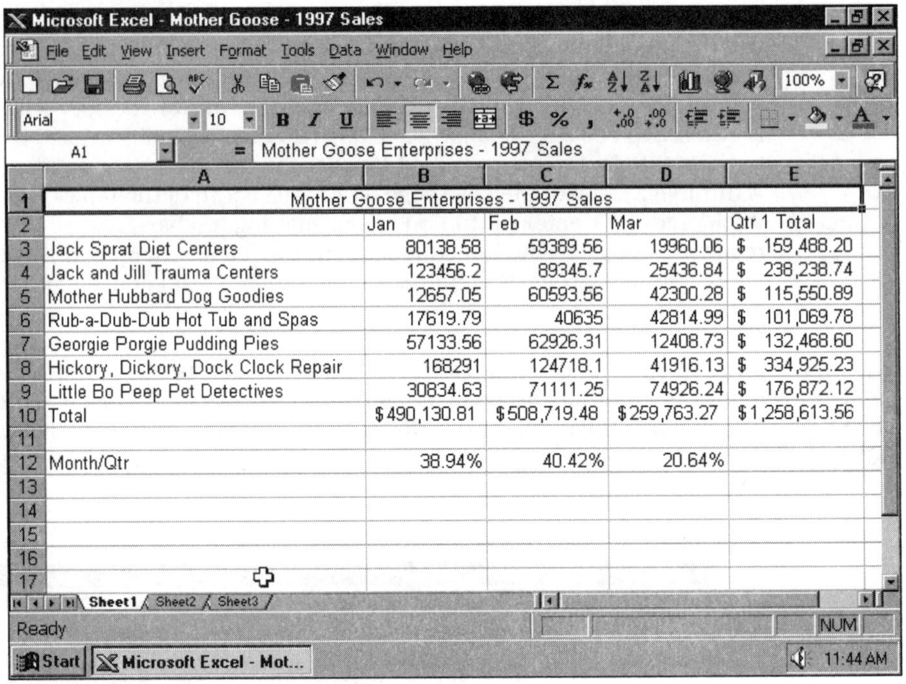

X Microsoft Excel - Mother Goose - 1997 Sales					_ |`| X

File   Edit   View   Insert   Format   Tools   Data   Window   Help

Arial   10   **B** *I* U $ % ,   100%

A1   =   Mother Goose Enterprises - 1997 Sales

	A	B	C	D	E
1	Mother Goose Enterprises - 1997 Sales				
2		Jan	Feb	Mar	Qtr 1 Total
3	Jack Sprat Diet Centers	80138.58	59389.56	19960.06	$ 159,488.20
4	Jack and Jill Trauma Centers	123456.2	89345.7	25436.84	$ 238,238.74
5	Mother Hubbard Dog Goodies	12657.05	60593.56	42300.28	$ 115,550.89
6	Rub-a-Dub-Dub Hot Tub and Spas	17619.79	40635	42814.99	$ 101,069.78
7	Georgie Porgie Pudding Pies	57133.56	62926.31	12408.73	$ 132,468.60
8	Hickory, Dickory, Dock Clock Repair	168291	124718.1	41916.13	$ 334,925.23
9	Little Bo Peep Pet Detectives	30834.63	71111.25	74926.24	$ 176,872.12
10	Total	$490,130.81	$508,719.48	$259,763.27	$1,258,613.56
11					
12	Month/Qtr	38.94%	40.42%	20.64%	
13					
14					
15					
16					
17					

Sheet1 / Sheet2 / Sheet3 /

Ready   NUM

Start   Microsoft Excel - Mot...   11:44 AM

Figure 3-17:
The
worksheet
title after
centering it
across
columns A
through E.

Intent on Indents

In Excel 97, you can indent the entries in a cell selection by clicking the Increase Indent button on the Standard toolbar (the button immediately to the left of the Borders button with the picture of the arrow pushing the lines of text to the right). Each time you click this button, Excel indents the entries in the current cell selection to the right by one character width of the standard font. (See "Futzing with the Fonts" earlier in this chapter if you don't know what a standard font is or how to change it.)

Note that you can remove an indent by clicking the Decrease Indent button on the Standard toolbar (the button immediately to the left of the Increase Indent button with the picture of the arrow pushing the lines of text to the left). Also, you can change how many characters an entry is indented with the Increase Indent button or outdented with the Decrease Indent button by opening the Format Cells dialog box (Ctrl+1), selecting the Alignment tab, and then altering the value in the Indent edit box (either by typing a new value in this edit box or by dialing up a new value with its spinner buttons).

From top to bottom

Left, right, and *center* alignment all refer to the placement of a text entry in relation to the left and right cell borders (that is, horizontally). You can also align entries in relation to the top and bottom borders of their cells (that is, vertically). Normally, all entries are vertically aligned with the bottom of the cells (as though they were resting on the very bottom of the cell). You can also vertically center an entry in its cell or align it with the top of its cell.

To change the vertical alignment of a cell selection, open the Format Cells dialog box (Ctrl+1) and then choose the Alignment tab (shown in Figure 3-18) and select Top, Center, Bottom, or Justify in the Vertical drop-down list box.

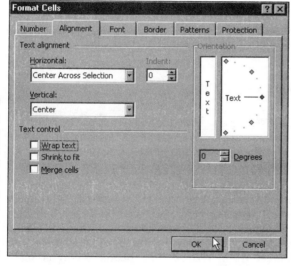

Figure 3-18:
Changing
the vertical
alignment
by selecting
Center on
the Vertical
pop-up
menu.

Figure 3-19 shows the title for the 1997 Mother Goose Enterprises sales worksheet after it was centered vertically in its cell. (This text entry was previously centered across the cell range A1:E1; the height of row 1 was increased from the normal 12.75 characters to 33.75 characters.)

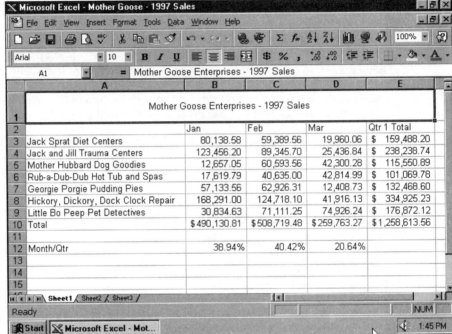

Figure 3-19:
The
worksheet
title after
centering it
vertically
between the
top and
bottom of
row 1.

Tampering with how the text wraps

Traditionally, column headings in worksheet tables have been a problem because you either had to keep them really short or abbreviate them if you wanted to avoid widening all the columns more than the data warranted. You can get around this problem in Excel by using the Wrap text feature. Figure 3-20 shows a new worksheet in which the column headings containing the various Mother Goose companies use the Wrap text feature to avoid widening the columns as much as these long company names would otherwise require.

To create the effect shown in Figure 3-20, select the cells with the column headings (the cell range B2:H2) and then select the Wrap text check box in the Alignment tab in the Format Cells dialog box to turn on text wrap. (You can see this check box in Figure 3-18.)

Text wrap breaks up the long text entries in the selection (that either spill over or are cut off) into separate lines. To accommodate more than one line in a cell, the program automatically expands the row height so that the entire wrapped-text entry is visible.

Figure 3-20:
A new
worksheet
with the
column
headings
containing
the Mother
Goose
company
names
formatted
with Wrap
Text option.

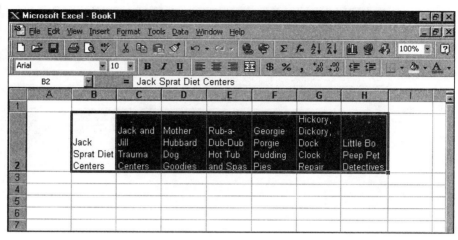

When you turn on Wrap text, Excel continues to use the horizontal and vertical alignment you specified for the cell. Note that you can use any of the Horizontal alignment options including Left (indent), Center, Right, Justify, or Center Across Selection. You can't, however, use the Fill option. Select the Fill option on the Horizontal pop-up menu only when you want Excel to repeat the entry across the entire width of the cell.

If you want to wrap a text entry in its cell and have Excel justify the text with both the left and right borders of the cell, select the Justify Fill option on the Horizontal pop-up menu in the Alignment tab in the Format Cells dialog box.

You can break a long text entry into separate lines by positioning the insertion point in the cell entry (or on the formula bar) at the place where you want the new line to start and pressing Alt+Enter. Excel expands the row containing the cell (and the formula bar above) when it starts a new line. When you press Enter to complete the entry or edit, Excel automatically wraps the text in the cell, according to the cell's column width and the position of the line break.

Reordering the orientation

Instead of wrapping text entries in cells, you may find it more beneficial to change the orientation of the text. Figure 3-21 shows a situation where changing the orientation of the wrapped column headings works much better than just wrapping them in their normal orientation in the cells.

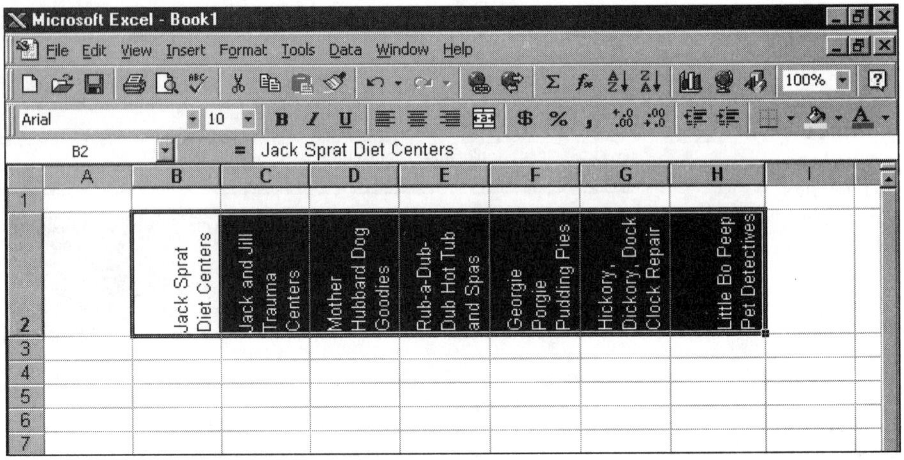

Figure 3-21:
Worksheet
after
rotating the
company
column
headings in
row 2 up 90
degrees.

This example shows the same order form introduced in Figure 3-20 after switching the orientation of the column headings with the various Mother Goose companies. Notice that switching the text orientation allows their columns to be narrower than when displayed in the normal orientation.

To make this switch, you select the cell range B2:H2 and then, in the Alignment tab of the Format cells dialog box, click the diamond in the Text Orientation section at the top (at twelve o'clock, so to speak, in the diagram) so that the word "Text" is running up and 90 degrees appears in the Degrees edit box below (you can change the orientation of the entries in your cell selection by entering the number of degrees in this box if you don't want to fool around with the diamonds in the diagram in this dialog box). Note that the Wrap edit box is still selected so that the text is both rotated and wrapped (thus avoiding really long, skinny columns).

Figure 3-22 shows the same company headings after using the Text Orientation option on the Alignment tab of the Format Cells dialog box to rotate the company column headings up just 45 degrees from their horizontal orientation. To accomplish this, I clicked the diamond in between the one at the top of the diagram (at twelve o'clock) and the one in the middle of the diagram (at three o'clock). Note that I could have done the same thing just as well by entering **45** in the Degrees edit box below the the diagram in the Orientation section.

You can set any amount of text rotation from 90 degrees up from horizontal (90 in the Degrees edit box) all the way to 90 degrees down from horizontal (-90 in the Degrees edit box) either by entering the number of degrees in the Degrees edit box, clicking the appropriate place on the semicircular diagram, or by dragging the line extending from the word "Text" in the diagram to the desired angle. To set the text vertically so that each letter is above the other in a single column, click the area of the diagram that shows the word "Text" arranged in this manner (to the immediate left of the diagram that allows you to rotate the text up or down from normal horizontal).

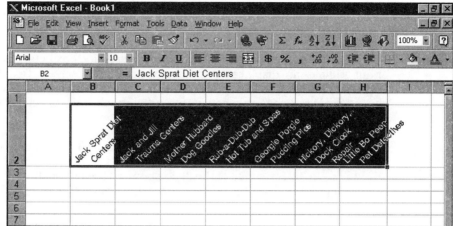

Figure 3-22:
Worksheet
after
rotating the
company
column
headings in
row 2 up
45 degrees.

Shrink to fit

For those times when you need to prevent Excel from widening the column to fit its cell entries (as might be the case when you need to display an entire table of data on a single screen or printed page), you can use the new Shrink to fit Text control option on the Alignment tab of the Format Cells dialog box. When you select the Shrink to fit check box, Excel reduces the font size of the entries to the selected cells so that they don't require changing the current column width. Just be aware when using this Text control option that, depending the length of the entries and width of the column, you can end up with some text entries that are so small as to be completely illegible to the human eye!

Bring on the borders!

The gridlines normally displayed in the worksheet to separate the columns and rows are just guidelines to help you keep your place as you build your spread-sheet. You can choose to print them with your data or not. To emphasize sections of the worksheet or parts of a particular table, you can add borderlines or shading to certain cells. Don't confuse the *borderlines* you add to accent a particular cell selection with the *gridlines* normally used to define cell borders in the worksheet — borders you add are printed whether or not you print the worksheet gridlines.

To better see the borders you add to the cells in a worksheet, remove the gridlines normally displayed in the worksheet as follows:

1. **Choose the Tools⇨Options command on the menu bar and then select the View tab.**

2. Select the Gridlines option to remove the check mark from its check box.

3. Click OK or press Enter.

Note that the Gridlines check box in the Options dialog box determines whether or not gridlines are displayed in the worksheet on your screen. To determine whether or not gridlines are printed as part of the worksheet printout, you choose the File⇨Page Setup command and then select the Sheet tab and select or deselect the Gridlines check box under Print.

To add borders to a cell selection, open the Format Cells dialog box (Ctrl+1) and then choose the Border tab (shown in Figure 3-23). Select the type of line you want to use in the Style area of the dialog box and then select from the Border section of the dialog box the edge or edges you want this line applied to.

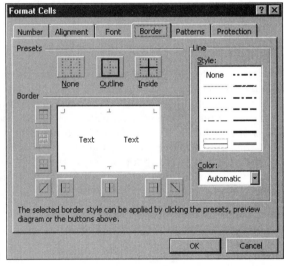

Figure 3-23:
Selecting borders for a cell selection with the Border tab in the Format Cells dialog box.

When selecting where you want the borderlines drawn, keep these things in mind:

- To have Excel draw borders around only the outside edges of the entire selection, click the Outline button in the Presets section.

- If you want borderlines to appear around all four edges of each cell in the selection, select the Inside button in the Presets section instead.

When you want to add borderlines to a single cell or around the outer edge of a cell selection, you don't even have to open the Border dialog box; you can simply select the cell or cell range and then click the Borders button drop-down list button on the Formatting toolbar and select which type of borderlines to use in the border palette that appears.

To get rid of borders, you must select the cell or cells that presently contain them, open the Format Cells dialog box (Ctrl+1), select the None button in the Presets section. Note that you can also do the same thing by clicking the first button in the Borders pop-up menu (the one showing only dotted lines around and within the rectangle).

Putting on new patterns

You can also add emphasis to particular sections of the worksheet or one of its tables by changing the color and/or pattern of its cells. If you're using a black-and-white printer (as all but a fortunate few of us are), you will want to restrict your color choices to light gray in the color palette. Also, you will want to restrict your use of patterns to only the very open ones with few dots when enhancing a cell selection that contains any kind of entries (otherwise, the entries will be almost impossible to read when printed).

To choose a new color and/or pattern for part of the worksheet, select the cells you want to pretty up and then open the Format Cells dialog box (Ctrl+1) and choose the Patterns tab (shown in Figure 3-24). To change the color of the cells, click the desired color in the Color palette shown under the Cell shading heading. To change the pattern of the cells (in addition or instead), click the Pattern's drop-down list box to open an expanded color palette that contains a number of black-and-white patterns to choose from. Click the desired pattern in this expanded palette. Excel shows what your creation will look like in the worksheet in the Sample box of the Patterns tab of the Format Cells dialog box.

To remove a shading pattern from cells, select the cell range, open the Format Cells dialog box (Ctrl+1) and select the Patterns tab; then choose the No Color option at the top of the Color palette.

Figure 3-24:
Selecting
new colors
and patterns
with the
Patterns tab
in the
Format Cells
dialog box.

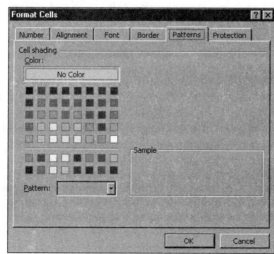

Using those fantastic floating border palettes

Just as you can add certain borders with the Borders palette attached to the Borders button on the Formatting toolbar, you can remove borders using this palette as well. To remove the borderlines from a cell selection with this button, choose the first border box in the Borders palette. Remember, too, that you can tear the Borders palette (like the Fill Color and Font Color palettes) off of the Formatting toolbar by dragging it completely off the toolbar, thus making it a floating palette that remains open as you work. Then, to close the floating palette later on, you click its Close button in the upper-right corner of its little-bitty window.

You can assign new colors (but not new patterns) to your cell selection from the Fill Color palette opened with the Fill Color button (the button with the paint bucket, second from the end) on the Formatting toolbar. Simply select the cells to be colored, click the Fill Color tool's drop-down list button, and choose the desired color in the color palette that appears. (Remember, too, that the Fill Color palette is one of those that you can tear off and have floating in the worksheet area.)

Although you can't select new patterns (only colors) with the Fill Color tool, you can remove both colors and patterns assigned to a cell selection by selecting the cells and then clicking on the Fill Color tool's button and choosing No Fill at the top of the Fill Color palette that appears.

If you want the text in a cell range to be a different color from the background you assign, you can change the text color from the Font Color palette by clicking the Font Color button on the Formatting toolbar (the very last one). Change the color of the cells' background by choosing a new color from the Font Color palette by clicking the Font Color button on the Formatting toolbar. To return the text to black in a cell range, select the cells and then choose Automatic at the top of the Font Color palette.

Showing Off in Styles

Cell styles are Excel's way of bringing together under one roof a whole lot of different kinds of formatting (including the number format, font, alignment, borders, patterns, and protection status). Excel includes six built-in cell styles that you can use in any worksheet: Comma, Comma [0], Currency, Currency [0], Normal, and Percent. And when you add hyperlinks (as described in Chapter 10), Excel adds two more built-in styles: Hyperlink and Followed Hyperlink.

The most common of these styles is the Normal style. This is the one automatically used in formatting all cells in a new worksheet. The styles Comma, Comma [0], Currency, Currency [0], and Percent are used to format cell selections with different number formats. (The Followed Hyperlink and Hyperlink styles are used to format hypertext links in the worksheet as described in Chapter 10.)

To apply any of these built-in cell styles (or any others you create on your own) to the current cell selection, simply choose Format⇨Style on the menu bar and then select a new style from the Style name drop-down list box.

Creating new cell styles for a worksheet is as simple as falling off a log. All you do is format one of the cell entries in the worksheet to use all the formatting you want to include in the new style (including the number format, font, alignment, borders, patterns, and protection status — see Chapter 6, if you don't have a clue what that last one is or does).

Then, with the cell pointer located in the sample formatted cell, open the Style dialog box (by choosing Format⇨Style), choose the Style name edit box, type in the name for your new style before you click the Add button, and click OK or press Enter.

The next time you save the workbook, Excel saves the new style as part of the document. To apply the new style to other cells in a worksheet, simply select the cells and then open the Style dialog box and select the style name from the Style name drop-down list box.

Styles are a great way to make custom number formats a lot easier to use in a workbook. For example, you could create a Hidden number style to use the custom number format discussed earlier in this chapter that hides all types of entries. After creating this custom number format (refer back to "Creating custom number formats" in this chapter for details on how to go about doing this), apply it to a sample cell in the worksheet and then create a new style named *Hidden* in the Style dialog box and add it to the worksheet. After saving the workbook with this new style, you can thereafter apply it to other cell ranges in the worksheet right from the Style dialog box.

Follow these steps if you want to merge styles that were created for other workbooks saved on disks into the workbook you're currently creating:

1. **Open the workbook that contains the styles you want copied into the current workbook.**

2. **Choose the Window command and select the workbook that is to receive these styles.**

3. **Choose Format⇨Style on the menu bar to open the Style dialog box in the workbook that is to receive a copy of the styles from the other workbook.**

4. **Click the Merge button to open the Merge Styles dialog box, and double-click the name of the workbook from which to copy the styles in the Merge Styles From list box.**

If the workbook you're currently working on contains styles (other than the standard six that are part of every new workbook) with the same names as some of those in the workbook whose styles you're copying, Excel displays an alert dialog box asking you if you want it to go ahead and merge styles that have the same name. To overwrite the styles in the current workbook whose names are the same, click the Yes button. To merge only the styles with different names, click the No button. To abandon the whole bloody merger of styles, click the Cancel button.

Fooling Around with the Format Painter

Using styles to format worksheet cells is certainly the way to go when you have to apply the formatting over and over again in the workbooks you create. However, there may be times when you simply want to reuse a particular cell format and apply it to select groups of cells in a single workbook without ever bothering to create an actual style for it.

For those occasions when you feel the urge to format on the fly (so to speak), you use the Format Painter tool on the Standard toolbar (the one with the paintbrush icon right next to the Paste tool). This wonderful little tool enables you to take the formatting from a particular cell that you've fancied up and apply its formatting to other cells in the worksheet simply by selecting those cells.

To use the Format Painter to copy a cell's formatting to other worksheet cells, just follow these easy steps:

1. **Format an example cell or cell range in your workbook, selecting whatever fonts, alignment, borders, patterns, and color you want it to have.**

2. **With the cell pointer in one of the cells you just fancied up, click the Format Painter button in the Standard toolbar.**

   The mouse pointer changes from the standard thick, white cross to a thick, white cross with an animated paintbrush by its side, and you see a marquee around the selected cell whose formatting is to be used by the Format Painter.

3. Drag the white-cross-plus-animated-paintbrush pointer (the Format Painter pointer for short) through all of the cells you want to format in the same manner as the example cell you first selected.

As soon as you release the mouse button, Excel applies all of the formatting used in the example cell to all of the cells you just selected!

To keep the Format Painter selected so that you can format a bunch of different cell ranges with the Format Painter pointer, double-click the Format Painter button after you select the sample cell with the desired formatting. To stop formatting cells with the Format Painter pointer, you simply click the Format Painter button (it remains depressed when you double-click it) again to restore the button to its undepressed state and return the mouse pointer to its normal thick, white-cross shape.

Note that you can use the Format Painter to restore a cell range that you've gussied all up back to its boring default (General) cell format. To do this, you click an empty, previously unformatted cell in the worksheet before you click the Format Painter button and then use the Format Painter pointer to drag through the cells you want returned to the default General format.

Conditional Formatting

Excel 97 introduces the concept of conditional cell formatting, which is formatting that is only done when a cell contains a particular value. For example, you can create a conditional format that displays a cell's contents in 14 point, bold type (instead of the normal 10 point, regular type) only when the cell contains a certain value (such as 150,000) or a value that falls into a definite range (between 50,000 and 100,000). You could also have a cell display its contents in red when its value is negative (less than 0).

Figure 3-25 shows an example of conditional formatting in the Jack Sprat Diet Centers - Projected Income for 1998 in the Net earnings (loss) cell (B28). This cell contains the formula that calculates the projected net earnings (or loss, as the case may be).

In this example, I wanted to use the Conditional Formatting feature to display this cell's contents in bold black text on a light gray cell background when the projected net earnings are $500,000 or greater and in bold red text on a black cell background whenever the projected earnings are less than $500,000. In order to make this happen, I followed these steps:

1. Select cell B28 where the conditional formatting is to take place.

Prior to using Conditional Formatting, you must select the cells or cell ranges to which this formatting is to be applied.

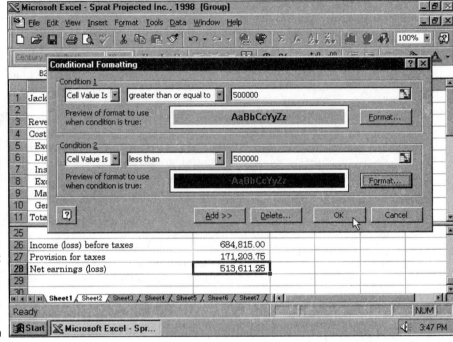

Figure 3-25:
Formatting
the Net
earnings
(loss) cell
in the
Projected
Income
statement
in the
Conditional
Formatting
dialog box.

2. **Choose Format⇨Conditional Formatting on the pull-down menus to open the Conditional Formatting dialog box.**

3. **Check to make sure that the Cell Value Is option is selected rather than the Formula Is option in the first edit box in the Condition1 area.**

   When creating a conditional format, you can either specify that the cells be formatted when they contain a particular value or range of values (in which case, you use the Cell Value Is option) or when a formula that you specify in the Conditional Formatting is TRUE (in which case, you use the Formula Is option).

4. **Change between in the second edit box to greater than or equal to in the second edit box.**

   When using the Cell Value Is option, you can set this second edit box to between, not between, equal to, not equal to, greater than, less than, greater than or equal to, or less than or equal to, as suits the situation.

5. **Enter 500000 in the third edit box.**

6. **Select the Format button in the Condition 1 area to open the Format Cells dialog box, where you specify format settings for the selected cells.**

   This Format Cells dialog box contains just three tabs: Font, Border, and Patterns, which you can use to format the selected cells when they meet the first condition.

7. **Choose the format settings for the first condition on the Font and Pattern tabs of the Format Cells dialog box; then click the OK button to close the Format Cells dialog box and return to the Conditional Formatting dialog box.**

   For the cell formatting when the value is greater than or equal to $500,000, I chose Bold as the Font style and Automatic as the Color on the Font tab and light gray as Cell Shading Color on the Patterns tab.

8. **Select the Add>> to button at the bottom of the Conditional Formatting dialog box to expand the dialog box with a second condition.**

   When using the Conditional Formatting feature, you can set up as many conditions as you need to cover all the circumstances that may arise. In this example, I only need to set up two formatting conditions: one where the value is 500,000 or greater and another where the value is less than 500,000.

9. **Enter the particulars for the second condition in the second set of edit boxes.**

   For the second condition, I kept the Cell Value Is option in the first edit box, selected less than for the second edit box, and entered 500000 in the third edit box (as shown back in Figure 3-25).

10. **Select the Format button in the Condition 2 area and use the options that appear on the Font, Border, and Patterns tab of the Format Cells dialog box to set up the formatting for the second condition.**

    For the formatting for the second condition, I set the Font Style to Bold and the Color to red on the Font tab and the Cell Shading Color to black on the Patterns tab.

11. **After setting up the formatting for the second condition, click OK in the Format Cells dialog box to close it; then click the OK button in the Conditional Formatting dialog box to close it and apply the conditional formatting to the selected cell.**

Figure 3-26 shows you what happens after closing the Conditional Formatting dialog box and applying the formatting to the Net earnings (loss) cell (B28). Because the current value is greater than $500,000, Excel formats it with the formatting for the first condition (bold, black text on a gray cell background). Figure 3-27 shows what happens when you change the values in the projected income statement such that the value in the Net earnings (loss) cell (B28) falls below $500,000. When this happens, Excel chooses the formatting for the second condition (bold, red text on a black cell background) and applies it to the Net earnings (loss) cell.

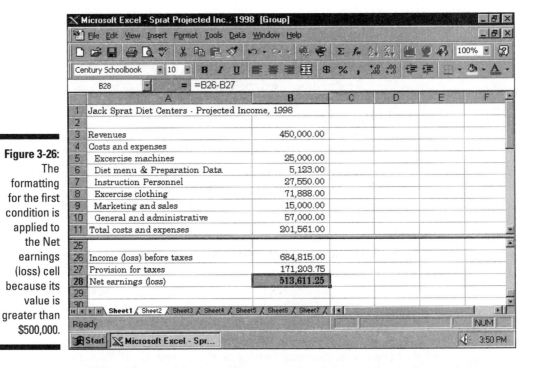

Figure 3-26: The formatting for the first condition is applied to the Net earnings (loss) cell because its value is greater than $500,000.

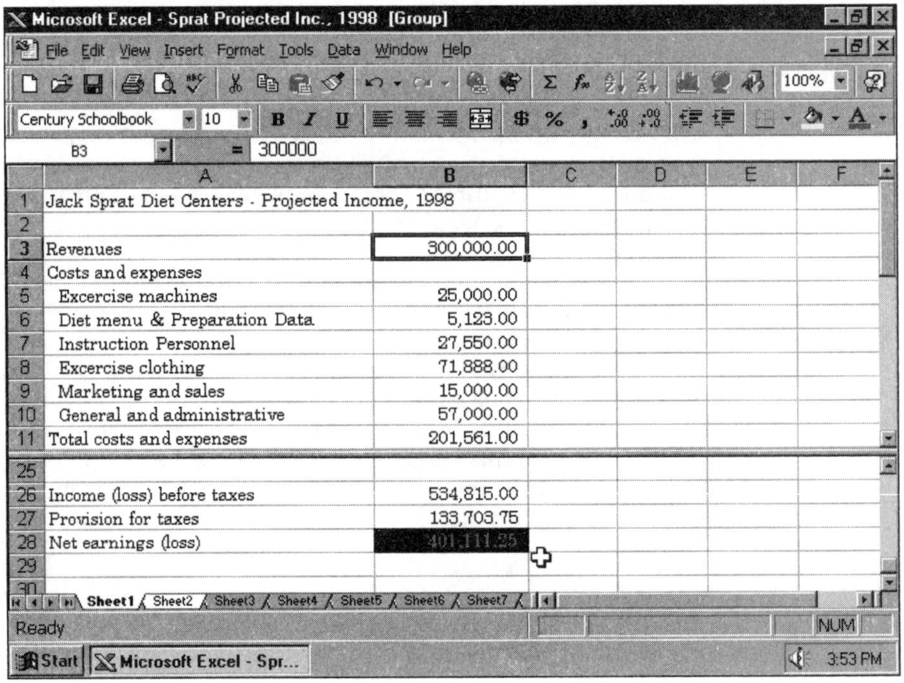

Figure 3-27: The formatting for the second condition is applied to the Net earnings (loss) cell because its value is now less than $500,000.

Chapter 4

Going through Changes

In This Chapter

▶ Opening workbook files for editing

▶ Undoing your boo-boos

▶ Moving and copying with drag and drop

▶ Copying formulas

▶ Moving and copying with Cut, Copy, and Paste

▶ Deleting cell entries

▶ Deleting columns and rows from the worksheet

▶ Inserting new columns and rows in the worksheet

▶ Spell checking the worksheet

*P*icture this: You've just finished creating, formatting, and printing a major project with Excel — a workbook with your department's budget for the next fiscal year. Because you finally understand a little bit about how this thing works, you finished the job in crack time. You're actually ahead of schedule.

You turned the workbook over to your boss so that she can check the numbers. There's plenty of time for making those inevitable last-minute corrections — you're feeling on top of this situation.

Then comes the reality check — your boss brings the document back, and she's plainly agitated. "We forgot to include the estimates for the temps and our overtime hours. They've got to go right here. While you're adding them, can you move these rows of figures up and those columns over?"

As she continues to suggest improvements, your heart begins to sink. These modifications are in a different league from "Let's change these column headings from bold to italics and add shading to that row of totals." Clearly, you're looking at a lot more work on this baby than you had contemplated. Even worse, you're looking at making structural changes that threaten to unravel the very fabric of your beautiful worksheet.

As the preceding fable points out, editing a worksheet in a workbook can occur on different levels:

- You can make changes that affect the contents of the cells, such as copying a row of column headings or moving a table to a new area in a particular worksheet.

- You can make changes that affect the structure of a worksheet itself, such as inserting new columns or rows (so that you can enter new data originally left out) or deleting unnecessary columns or rows from an existing table so that you don't leave any gaps.

- You can even make changes to the number of worksheets in a workbook (either by adding or deleting sheets).

In this chapter, you discover how to safely make all these types of changes to a workbook. As you see, the mechanics of copying and moving data or inserting and deleting rows are simple to master. It's the impact that such actions have on the worksheet that takes a little more effort to understand. Not to worry! You always have the Undo feature to fall back on for those (hopefully rare) times when you make a little tiny change that throws an entire worksheet into complete and utter chaos.

Opening the Darned Thing Up for Editing

Before you can do any damage — I mean, make any changes — to a workbook, you have to open it up in Excel. To open a workbook, you can click the Open tool on the Standard toolbar (the one second from the left with the picture of a file folder opening up), you can choose File⇨Open on the menu bar, or you can even press the keystroke shortcut Ctrl+O (or, if you prefer function keys: Ctrl+F12).

Any way you open it, Excel displays the Open dialog box similar to the one shown in Figure 4-1. Then you select the workbook file you want to work on in the list box in the middle of the Open dialog box. After clicking the filename in this list box, you can open it by choosing the Open button or pressing the Enter key. If you're handy with the mouse, double-click the workbook's filename in the list box to open it.

Opening more than one workbook at a time

If you know that you're going to edit more than one of the workbook files' sheets shown in the list box of the Open dialog box, you can select multiple files in the list box and Excel will then open all of them (in the order they're listed) when you click the Open button or press Enter.

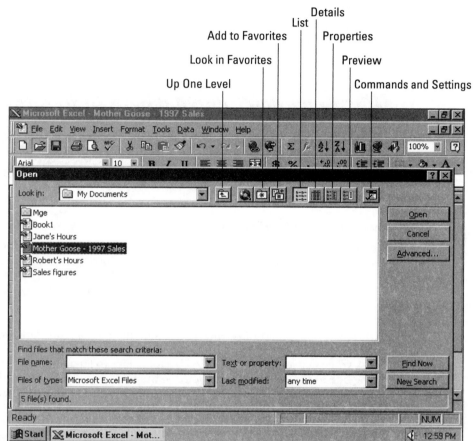

Figure 4-1:
The Open
dialog box.

Remember that in order to select multiple files all listed sequentially in the list box, you click the first filename and then hold down the Shift key as you click the last filename. To select files that are not listed sequentially, you need to hold down the Ctrl key as you click the various filenames.

After the workbook files are open in Excel, you can then switch documents by selecting their filenames from the Window pull-down menu (see Chapter 7 for detailed information on working on more than one worksheet at a time).

Opening recently edited workbooks from the File menu

If you know that the workbook you need to edit is one of those that you've had open recently, you don't even have to fool around with the Open dialog box. Just open the File pull-down menu and select the filename from the bottom of the File menu (Excel keeps a running list of the last four files you opened in the program). If the workbook you want to work with is one of those shown at the bottom of the File menu, you can open it by clicking its filename in the menu or typing its number (1, 2, 3, or 4).

When you don't know where to find them

The only problem you can encounter in opening a document from the Open dialog box is locating the filename. Everything's hunky-dory as long as you can see the workbook filename listed in its list box. But what about those times when a file seems to have mysteriously migrated and is now nowhere to be found in the list?

Searching the wide disk over

When you can't find the filename you're looking for in the list box, the first thing you need to do is check to make sure that you're looking in the right folder — because if you're not, you're never going to find the missing file. To tell which folder is currently open, you check the Look in drop-down list box at the top of the Open dialog box (refer back to Figure 4-1).

If the folder that is currently open is not the one that has the workbook file you need to use, you then need to open the folder that does contain the file. In Excel, you can use the Up One Level button (refer to Figure 4-1) in the Open dialog box to change levels until you see the folder you want to open in the list box. To open the new folder, click its icon in the list box and then click the Open button or press Enter (or you can just double-click its icon).

If the workbook file you want is on another disk, click the Up One Level button until My Computer appears in the Look in drop-down list box. You can then switch disks by clicking the drive icon in the list box and then choosing the Open button or pressing Enter (or you can just double-click the drive icon).

When you locate the file you want to use in the list box in the Open dialog box, you can open it by clicking its file icon and then clicking the Open button or pressing Enter (or by double-clicking the file icon).

Playing favorites

Assuming that you are successful in locating your file by going up and down the disk hierarchy as described in the preceding section, you can save yourself all this work the next time you need to open this folder to find a workbook by adding the folder to the My Favorites folder. That way, you can select and open the folder right away simply by clicking the Look in Favorites button (refer to Figure 4-1) and then selecting it from My Favorites.

To add a folder (or a particular file) to the My Favorites folder, you follow these steps:

1. **Select the folder or file icon (as described in the previous section) in the Open dialog box.**

2. **Click the Add to Favorites button (see Figure 4-1).**

3. **Choose the Add Selected Item to Favorites command in the pop-up menu that's attached to the Add to Favorites button.**

   This adds the folder or file that's selected in the Open dialog list box.

After you've added a folder or a file to the My Favorites folder, you can open it in the Open dialog box by clicking the Look in Favorites button and then either double-clicking its folder or file icon or selecting it and then clicking the Open button or pressing Enter.

File hide-and-seek

The Open dialog box now has a Find feature built into it that you can always use to locate a particular file within the open folder. This feature enables you to reduce your search in the Open dialog list box to just those files that fall into a specific category (like those files you modified today or sometime this week) or just those files that contain a certain phrase or property (like they were done by a particular author or they contain a particular keyword).

When using the Find feature in the Open dialog box, you can tell Excel exactly how you want it to conduct its search.

- ✔ To have Excel restrict the files in the Open dialog list box to just those whose filenames contain certain text, select the File name drop-down list box and enter that text in its edit box.

- ✔ To have Excel include certain files with a type different from Microsoft Excel files, open the Files of type drop-down list box and select that type from the list.

- ✔ To have Excel restrict the files displayed in the Open list box to just those that contain a certain text or property such as title, author, or keywords entered into a file summary, choose the Text or property drop-down list box and enter the text or property in its edit box. (To create a file summary with keywords that you can search and all sorts of facts about the workbook, you select the file in the Open dialog box, then click the Commands and Settings button on the toolbar, choose Properties on the pull-down menu, and click the Summary tab in the file's Properties dialog box.)

- ✔ To have Excel restrict the files displayed in the Open list box to just those that have been modified within a certain time frame, open the Last modified drop-down list box and select the time (today, last week, this week, last month, this month, or anytime).

Advanced hide-and-seek

As if the four Find drop-down list boxes for finding files by filename, file type, text or property, or date last modified weren't enough, Excel offers more searching possibilities when you click the Advanced button in the Open dialog box. Figure 4-2 shows you the Advanced Find dialog box. When you open this dialog box, you notice that whatever criteria you set up in the Open dialog box is now displayed in the Find files that match these criteria list box.

You can then use the other settings in the Define more criteria section of the Advanced Find dialog box to add more search criteria.

> ✔ Normally, your advanced search criteria are added onto the original criteria so that all of them must be true in order for Excel to match a file (because the And radio button is selected). If, instead, you want Excel to match a file if it meets either the original criteria *or* the new criteria you're setting up, click the Or radio button.

> ✔ Often, Excel searches the filename and makes its matches according to its contents. If you want to have Excel match other properties (like the Author, Contents, Creation Date, and so on), open the Property drop-down list box and then choose the desired property in its list box.

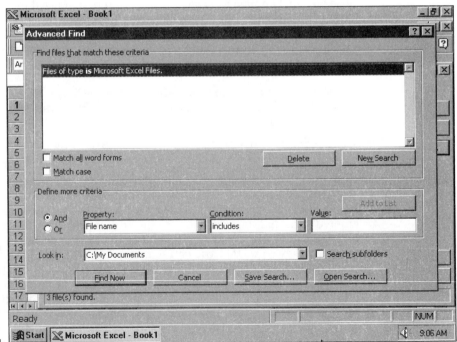

Figure 4-2:
The
Advanced
Find dialog
box.

✔ In general, Excel just looks to see if a certain value or piece of text is included in the designated property (be it the File name, Author, or whatever). If you would rather have the program match files only when their property begins or ends with that value or text, open the Condition drop-down list box and select the begins with or the ends with option.

✔ Enter the value or text that should be matched in the Value edit box. For example, if you want to find all the files where the Contents includes the text "Jack Sprat," you enter **Jack Sprat** in this edit box. If, on the other hand, you want to find all the files where the Contents includes the number "1,250,750," you enter **1250750** in the Value edit box.

When you're finished setting up your advanced criteria in the Define more criteria area, you can add them to the Find files that match these criteria list box by choosing the Add to List button. If you want the search to distinguish between uppercase and lowercase (when it involves text), you need to select the Match case check box to put a check mark in it.

Normally, Excel just conducts the file search in the folder that's currently listed in the Look in drop-down list box at the bottom of the Advanced Find dialog box. If you want, you can change which folders Excel will search by opening the Look in drop-down list box and selecting a different level in the file hierarchy. If you want Excel to search all folders that are contained within the folder listed in the Look in drop-down edit box, you need to select the Search subfolders check box, which puts a check mark in it. For example, if you want Excel to search the whole hard disk including all the folders (and folders within folders) on this disk, you select Hard disk (C:) in the Look in drop-down list box and then select the Search subfolders check box as well.

When you have added all the advanced criteria you can think of for your search, click the Find Now button to set Excel off hunting for the files that match all your conditions. During the search, Excel closes the Advanced File dialog box, leaving open only the Open dialog box. When the program completes the file search, it displays the results (hopefully including the workbook files you want to use) in the list box of the Open dialog box. If your search includes a lot of folders (all the folders on the hard disk or something like that), you may even have to scroll to go through all the file icons that are displayed.

Making a positive ID

Normally, Excel displays the folders and files in the Open dialog box's list box as a simple list showing the folder or file icon.

To switch the way the files are displayed in the Open dialog box's list box, you simply click any of the following buttons on the Open dialog box toolbar (refer to Figure 4-1):

✔ Click the Details button to display the file size in kilobytes, type of file, and date the file was last modified along with the file icon and filename (as shown in Figure 4-3).

✓ Click the Properties button to display the file summary information next to the file icon and filename when you select each file in the list (as shown in Figure 4-4). (To create the file summary for a file, you select the file in the Open dialog box, then click the Commands and Settings button on the toolbar, choose Properties on the pull-down menu, and click the Summary tab in the file's Properties dialog box.)

✓ Click the Preview button to display a miniature preview showing the upper-left corner of the first worksheet in the workbook file next to the file icon and filename when you select each file in the list (as shown in Figure 4-5).

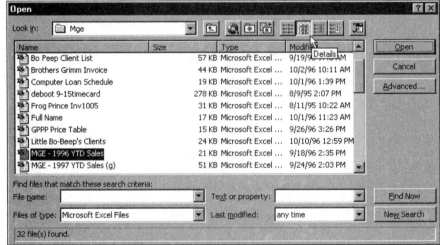

Figure 4-3:
The Open dialog box after switching the file view to Details.

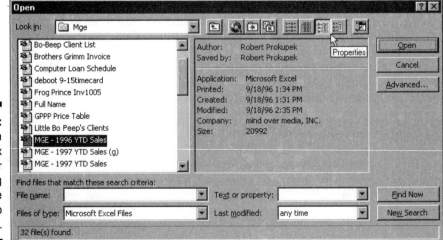

Figure 4-4:
The Open dialog box after switching the file view to Properties.

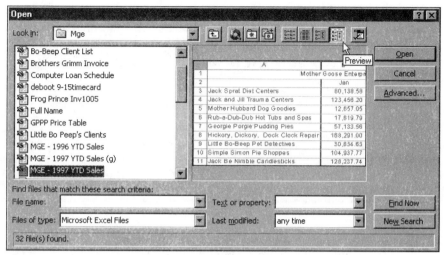

Figure 4-5:
The Open
dialog box
after
switching
the file view
to Preview.

Doing stuff besides opening files

The last button on the Open dialog box toolbar is the Commands and Settings button (identified in Figure 4-1). Clicking this button (with the primary mouse button, by the way) opens the menu shown in Figure 4-6. The following commands on this menu let you make some changes to the file list in the Open dialog box as well as do stuff besides just open the selected files:

- **Open Read Only:** This command opens the files that are selected in the Open dialog box's list box in a read-only state, which means that you can look but you can't touch (actually, you can touch, you just can't save your changes). To save changes in a read-only file, you must use the Save As command on the Excel File menu and give the workbook file a new filename. (Refer to the section "Making Sure the Data's Safe and Sound" in Chapter 2.)

- **Open As Copy:** This command opens a copy of the files that are selected in the Open dialog box. That way, if you mess up the copies, you always have the originals to fall back on.

- **Print:** This command sends the files that are selected in the Open dialog box's list box to whatever printer is selected in Windows 95. This command enables you to print a whole bunch of files without having to first open them in Excel (the way you normally print — see Chapter 5).

- **Properties:** This command opens the Properties dialog box for the first folder or file that is selected in the Open dialog box's list box. This enables you to change or add summary information for the file as well as look at a bunch of boring statistics about the folder or file.

Save search criteria for another day

You can save the search criteria that you've gone to all of that trouble to set up so that you can reuse it later on. To save the search criteria listed in the Find files that match these criteria list box of the Advanced Find dialog box, select the <u>S</u>ave Search button, type in a descriptive name for your search ("All files on C: with keywords 'For Eyes Only,'" or something like that), and click OK. To reuse the search criteria later to find files in the Open dialog box, click the Commands and Settings button on the Open dialog box toolbar, select the S<u>a</u>ved Searches command and select the name of the search from its cascading menu.

✔ **Sorting:** This command enables you to sort the folders and files in the Open dialog box's list box. Normally, folders and files (with folders preceding files) are alphabetically sorted by name in ascending order. You can use this command to sort the folders and files by their size, type, and the date last modified in either ascending or descending order as well.

✔ **Searc<u>h</u> Subfolders:** This command acts like the Searc<u>h</u> subfolders check box (refer to "Advanced hide-and-seek," earlier in this chapter) in the Advanced Find dialog box. The Advanced Find dialog box includes all folders nested within the folder that's currently shown in the Look <u>i</u>n drop-down list box during any file search that you conduct from the Open dialog box.

✔ **<u>G</u>roup files by folder:** This command groups together by folder all files that meet your search criteria in the Open dialog box's list box.

✔ **Map <u>N</u>etwork Drive:** This command only works if you are using Excel on some kind of LAN (Local Area Network). It enables you (if you know what you're doing) to log onto somebody else's computer and have fun with all their precious files!

✔ **Add/Modify <u>F</u>TP Locations:** This command lets you define or modify an FTP (File Transfer Protocol) site, either one maintained on your company's intranet or one that's out there somewhere on the Internet (for more information on FTP and what it means to thee, see *Internet For Dummies*, 3rd Edition, written by Levine and Baroudi and published by IDG Books Worldwide, Inc.).

✔ **S<u>a</u>ved Searches:** This command enables you to select a search using the search criteria that you saved with its own name in the Advanced Find dialog box (see the sidebar, "Save search criteria for another day").

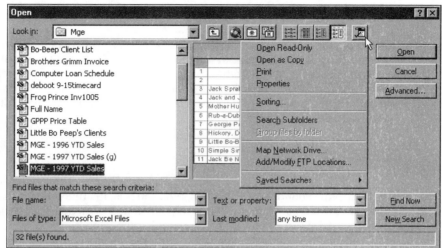

Figure 4-6:
The Open
dialog box
showing
the menu
attached
to the
Commands
and Settings
button.

Much Ado about Undo

Before you start tearing into the workbook that you just opened, you should get to know the Undo feature and how it can put right many of the things that you could inadvertently mess up. The Undo command on the Edit menu is a regular chameleon command. If you delete the contents of a cell selection with the Clear command on this same menu, Undo changes to Undo Clear. If you move some entries to a new part of the worksheet with the Cut and Paste commands (again, found on the Edit menu), the Undo command changes to Undo Paste.

In addition to choosing Undo (in whatever guise it appears) from the Edit menu, you can also choose this command by pressing Ctrl+Z (perhaps for *unZap*) or you can click the Undo tool on the Standard toolbar (the one with the arrow curving to the left).

The Undo command on the Edit menu changes in response to whatever action you just took. Because it keeps changing after each action, if you forget to strike when the iron is hot, so to speak, by using the Undo feature to restore the worksheet to its previous state *before* you choose another command, you then need to consult the pop-up menu on the Undo button on the Standard toolbar to select the previous action that you want undone. To open this menu, you click the drop-down button that appears to the right of the Undo icon (the curved arrow pointing to the left). After the Undo pop-up menu is open, click the action on this menu that you want undone. Excel will then undo this action and all actions that precede it in the list (which are automatically selected).

Undo is Redo the second time around

After choosing the Undo command (by whatever means you find most convenient), Excel 97 adds a new Redo command to the Edit menu. If you delete an entry from a cell with Edit⇨Clear⇨All on the menu bar and then choose Edit⇨Undo Clear (or press Ctrl+Z or click the Undo tool on the toolbar), the next time you open the Edit menu, you see the following command at the top of the menu beneath Undo:

```
Redo Clear Ctrl+Y
```

When you choose the Redo command, Excel redoes the thing you just undid. Actually, this sounds more complicated than it is. It simply means that you use Undo to switch back and forth between the result of an action and the state of the worksheet just before that action until you decide how you want the worksheet (or until they turn off the lights and lock up the building).

Note that you may find it a heck of a lot easier to just click the Undo and the Redo buttons on the Standard toolbar rather than go through all the rigmarole of choosing their respective commands on the Edit pull-down menu. The Undo button is the one with the picture of the arrow curving to the left; the Redo button is the one with the picture of the arrow curving to the right. Note that you can redo multiple actions in a workbook by clicking the drop-down button to the right of the Redo button's icon (the curved arrow pointing to the right) and clicking the action on the menu that you want redone. Excel then redoes the action that you select as well as all the actions that precede it on the menu.

What ya gonna do when you can't Undo?

Just when you think it is safe to begin gutting the company's most important workbook, I really feel I've got to tell you that (yikes!) Undo doesn't work all the time! Although you can undo your latest erroneous cell deletion, bad move, or unwise copy, you can't undo your latest imprudent save. (You know, like when you meant to choose Save As from the File menu to save the edited worksheet under a different document name but instead chose Save and ended up saving the changes as part of the current document.)

Unfortunately, Excel doesn't let you know when you are about to take a step from which there is no return — until it's too late. After you've gone and done the un-undoable and you open the Edit menu right where you expect the Undo *blah, blah* command to be, it now says

```
Can't Undo
```

To add insult to injury, this extremely unhelpful command appears dimmed to indicate that you can't choose it — as though being able to choose it would change anything!

There is one exception to this rule — a time when the program gives you advance warning (which you should heed). When you choose a command that is normally undoable but currently — because you're low on memory, or the change will affect so much of the worksheet, or both — Excel knows that it can't undo the change if it goes through with it, the program displays an alert box telling you that there isn't enough memory to undo this action and asking whether you want to go ahead anyway. If you click the Yes button and complete the edit, just realize that you do so without any possibility of pardon. If you find out, too late, that you deleted a row of essential formulas (that you forgot about because you couldn't see them), you can't bring them back with Undo. In such a case, you would have to close the file (File➪Close) and *NOT save your changes.*

Doing the Old Drag-and-Drop Thing

The first editing technique you need to learn is called *drag and drop*. As the name implies, it's a mouse technique that you can use to pick up a cell selection and drop it into a new place on the worksheet. Although drag and drop is primarily a technique for moving cell entries around a worksheet, you can adapt it to copy a cell selection as well.

To use drag and drop to move a range of cell entries (you can only move one cell range at a time), follow these steps:

1. **Select the range as you normally would.**

2. **Position the mouse pointer on one edge of the selected range.**

   Your signal that you can start dragging the cell range to its new position in the worksheet is when the pointer changes to the arrowhead.

3. **Drag.**

   You drag by depressing and holding down the primary mouse button — usually the left one — while moving the mouse.

   As you drag, you actually move only the outline of the cell range, and Excel keeps you informed of what the new cell range address would be (as a kind of drag-and-drop tooltips) if you release the mouse button. Drag the outline until it's positioned on the new cells in the worksheet where you want the entries to appear (as evidenced by the cell range in the drag-and-drop tooltip).

4. Release the mouse button.

The cell entries within that range reappear in the new location as soon as you release the mouse button.

Figures 4-7 and 4-8 show how you can drag and drop to move a cell range. In Figure 4-7, the cell range A10:E10 (containing the quarterly totals) is selected and is about to be moved to row 12 to make room for sales figures for two new companies: Simple Simon Pie Shoppes and Jack Be Nimble Candlesticks, which hadn't been acquired when this workbook was first created. In Figure 4-8, you see the Mother Goose Enterprises 1997 sales worksheet right after making this move and then selecting cell B12.

Notice in Figure 4-8 that the argument for the SUM function in cell B12 has not kept pace with the change — it continues to sum only the range B3:B9. Eventually, this range must be expanded to include cells B10 and B11, the first-quarter sales figures for the new Simple Simon Pie Shoppes and Jack Be Nimble Candlesticks (you can find out how to do this in the upcoming section, "Formulas on AutoFill").

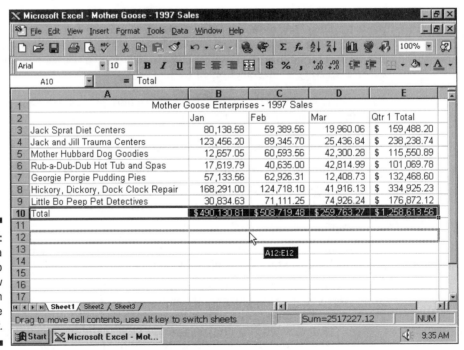

Figure 4-7:
Dragging a selection to its new position in the worksheet.

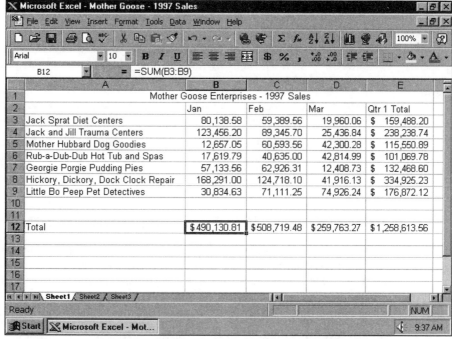

Figure 4-8:
The
worksheet
after the
drag-and-
drop
operation.

Copies drag-and-drop style

Okay, so the preceding section explained moving a cell range with drag and drop. But what if you want to copy a cell range instead? For example, you need to start a new table in rows further down the worksheet, and you want to copy the cell range with the formatted title and column headings for the new table. To copy the formatted title range in the sample worksheet, follow these steps:

1. **Select the cell range.**

   In the case of Figures 4-7 and 4-8, that's cell range B2:E2.

2. **Hold the Ctrl key as you position the mouse pointer on an edge of the selection.**

   The pointer changes from a thick, shaded cross to an arrowhead with a + (plus) sign to the right of it with the drag-and-drop screen tips right beside it. Keep in mind that the plus sign next to the pointer is your signal that drag and drop will *copy* the selection rather than *move* it.

3. Drag the cell-selection outline to the place where you want the copy to appear and release the mouse button.

If, when using drag and drop to move or copy, you position the outline of the selection so that it overlaps any part of cells that already contain entries, Excel displays an alert box with the following question:

```
Do you want to replace contents of the destination cells?
```

To avoid replacing existing entries and to abort the entire drag-and-drop mission, click Cancel in this alert box. To go ahead and exterminate the little darlings, click OK or press Enter.

Insertions courtesy of drag and drop

Like the Klingons of Star Trek fame, spreadsheets such as Excel never take prisoners. When you place or move a new entry into an occupied cell, the new entry completely replaces the old as though the old entry never existed in that cell.

To insert the cell range you're moving or copying within a populated region of the worksheet without wiping out existing entries, hold the Shift key as you drag the selection (if you're copying, you have to get really ambitious and hold down both the Shift and Ctrl keys at the same time!). With the Shift key depressed as you drag, instead of a rectangular outline of the cell range, you get an I-beam shape that shows where the selection will be inserted along with the address of the cell range (as a kind of Insertion screen tips) indicating where it would be inserted if you release the mouse button. As you move the I-beam shape, notice that it gloms on to the column and row borders as you move it. When you position the I-beam shape at the column or row border where you want the cell range to be inserted, release the mouse button. Excel inserts the cell range and repatriates the existing entries to neighboring blank cells (out of harm's way).

When inserting cells with drag and drop, it might be helpful to think of the I-beam shape as a pry bar that pulls apart the columns or rows along the axis of the I. Figures 4-9 and 4-10 show how to use the I-beam to move the quarterly totals in column E of the Mother Goose Enterprises 1997 Sales worksheet to column B. When you drag the cell range E2:E10 to the cell range B2:B10, you can be sure that Excel will insert these totals while moving the existing columns of sales entries to the right.

Figure 4-9 shows the worksheet after I selected the cell range of quarterly totals (E2:E10), depressed *and held down* the Shift key, and dragged the I-beam shape until it rested on the border between columns A and B (between column A listing the individual Mother Goose companies and column B listing the January sales).

Notice the orientation of the I-beam shape in Figure 4-9, how the long part of the I runs with the column border. Getting the I-beam selection indicator to assume this orientation can be tricky. To prepare to drag the cell selection, position the mouse pointer on one of the long edges (either the left or right) of the selection. When you drag the selection, position the mouse pointer slightly in front of the column border (not on it).

Also, keep in mind that sometimes after moving a range to a new place in the worksheet, instead of the data appearing, you will see only #######s in the cells (Excel 97 doesn't automatically widen the new columns for the incoming data as it does when formatting the data). Remember that the way to get rid of the #######s in the cells is by widening their column enough to display all the data-plus-formatting, and the easiest way to do this kind of widening is by double-clicking the right border of the column.

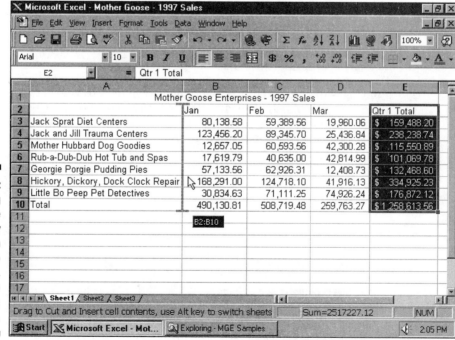

Figure 4-9: Dragging the quarterly totals from column E to column B, replacing no existing entries.

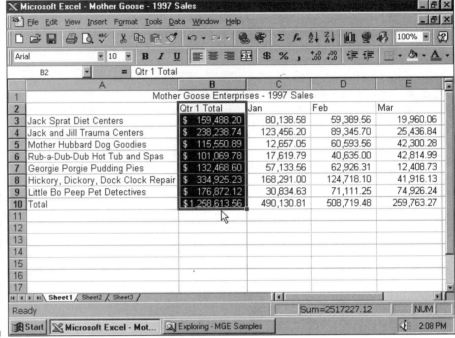

Figure 4-10:
The
worksheet
after Excel
inserted the
quarterly
total range
in column B.

Formulas on AutoFill

Copying with drag and drop (by holding down the Ctrl key) is useful when you need to copy a bunch of neighboring cells to a new part of the worksheet. Frequently, however, you just need to copy a single formula you've just created to a bunch of neighboring cells that need to perform the same type of calculation (such as totaling columns of figures). This type of formula copy, although quite common, can't be done with drag and drop. Instead, use the AutoFill feature (introduced in Chapter 2) or the Copy and Paste commands (see "Cut and Paste, digital style," later in this chapter).

But I held down the Shift key just like you said . . .

Drag and drop in insert mode is one of Excel's most finicky features. Sometimes, you do everything just right and you still get the alert box indicating that Excel is about to replace existing entries instead of pushing them aside (always click the Cancel button). Fortunately, you can insert things with the Cut and Insert Paste commands (see "Cut and Paste, digital style," later in this chapter) without worrying about which way the I-beam selection goes.

Figures 4-11 and 4-12 show how you can use AutoFill to copy one formula to a range of cells. Figure 4-11 shows the Mother Goose Enterprises 1997 Sales worksheet after the Simple Simon Pie Shoppes and Jack Be Nimble Candlesticks were added to the list. Remember that these companies were missing from the original worksheet, so I made room for them by moving the Totals down to row 12 (you can see this back in Figure 4-8).

Unfortunately, Excel doesn't update the sum formulas to include the new rows (the SUM function still uses B3:B9 when it should be extended to include rows 10 and 11). To make the SUM function include all the rows, position the cell pointer in cell B12 and click the AutoSum tool on the Standard toolbar. Excel suggests the new range B3:B11 for the SUM function.

Figure 4-11 shows the worksheet after I re-created the SUM formula in cell B12 with the AutoSum tool to include the expanded range. I dragged the fill handle to select the cell range C12:E12 (where this formula should be copied). Notice that I deleted the original formulas from the cell range C12:E12 in this figure to make it easier to see what's going on; normally, you just copy over the original outdated formulas and replace them with new correct copies.

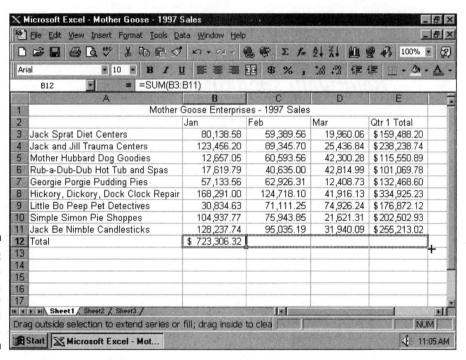

Figure 4-11:
Copying a
formula to a
cell range
with
AutoFill.

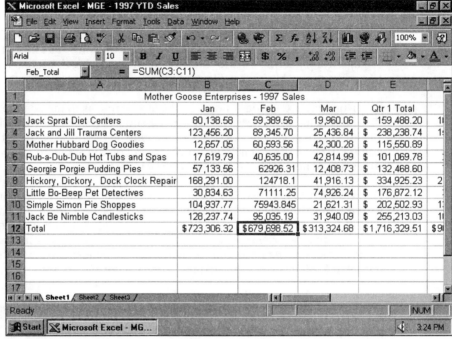

Figure 4-12:
The
worksheet
after I
copied the
formula for
totaling the
monthly
sales.

Relatively speaking

Refer to Figure 4-12 to see the worksheet after the formula in a cell is copied to the cell range C12:E12 and cell C12 is active. Notice how Excel handles the copying of formulas. The original formula in cell B12 is as follows:

```
=SUM(B3:B11)
```

When the original formula is copied next door to cell C12, Excel changes the formula slightly so that it looks like this:

```
=SUM(C3:C11)
```

Excel adjusts the column reference, changing it from B to C, because I copied from left to right across the rows.

When you copy a formula to a cell range that extends down the rows, Excel adjusts the row numbers in the copied formulas rather than the column letters to suit the position of each copy. For example, cell E3 in the Mother Goose Enterprises 1997 Sales worksheet contains the following formula:

```
=SUM(B3:D3)
```

When you copy this formula down to cell E4, Excel changes the copy of the formula to the following:

```
=SUM(B4:D4)
```

Excel adjusts the row reference to keep current with the new row 4 position. Because Excel adjusts the cell references in copies of a formula relative to the direction of the copying, the cell references are known as *relative cell references*.

Some things are absolutes!

All new formulas you create naturally contain relative cell references unless you say otherwise. Because most copies you make of formulas require adjustments of their cell references, you rarely have to give this arrangement a second thought. Then, every once in a while, you come across an exception that calls for limiting when and how cell references are adjusted in copies.

One of the most common of these exceptions is when you want to compare a range of different values to a single value. This happens most often when you want to compute what percentage each part is to the total. For example, in the Mother Goose Enterprises 1997 Sales worksheet, you encounter this situation in creating and copying a formula that calculates what percentage each monthly total (in the cell range B14:D14) is of the quarterly total in cell E12.

Suppose that you want to enter these formulas in row 14 of the Mother Goose Enterprises 1997 Sales worksheet, starting in cell B14. The formula in cell B14 for calculating the percentage of the January-sales-to-first-quarter-total is very straightforward:

```
=B12/E12
```

This formula divides the January sales total in cell B12 by the quarterly total in E12 (what could be easier?). Look, however, at what would happen if you dragged the fill handle one cell to the right to copy this formula to cell C14:

```
=C12/F12
```

The adjustment of the first cell reference from B12 to C12 is just what the doctor ordered. However, the adjustment of the second cell reference from E12 to F12 is a disaster. Not only do you not calculate what percentage the February sales in cell C12 are of the first quarter sales in E12, but you also end up with one of those horrible #DIV/0! error things in cell C14.

To stop Excel from adjusting a cell reference in a formula in any copies you make, convert the cell reference from relative to absolute. You can do this by pressing the function key F4. Excel indicates that you've made the cell reference absolute by placing dollar signs in front of the column letter and row number. For example, look at Figure 4-13. Cell B14 in this figure contains the correct formula to copy to the cell range C14:D14:

```
=B12/$E$12
```

Figure 4-14 shows the worksheet after this formula is copied to the range C14:D14 with the fill handle and cell C14 selected. Notice that the formula bar shows that this cell contains the following formula:

```
=C12/$E$12
```

Because E12 was changed to $E$12 in the original formula, all the copies have this same absolute (nonchanging) reference.

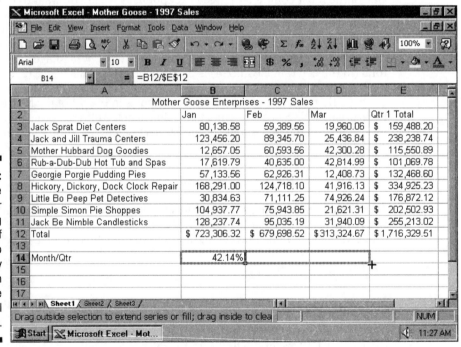

Figure 4-13: Copying the formula for computing the ratio of monthly to quarterly sales with an absolute cell reference.

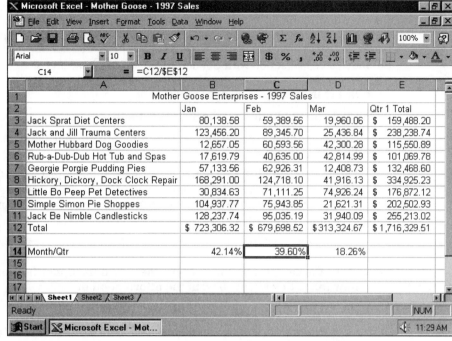

Figure 4-14: The worksheet after copying the formula with the absolute cell reference.

If you goof up and copy a formula where one or more of the cell references should have been absolute but you left them all relative, edit the original formula as follows:

1. **Double-click the cell with the formula and click the Edit Formula button on the formula bar or press F2 to edit it.**

2. **Position the insertion point somewhere on the reference you want to convert to absolute.**

3. **Press F4.**

4. **When you finish editing, click the Enter button on the formula bar and then copy the formula to the messed-up cell range with the fill handle.**

Cut and Paste, digital style

Instead of drag and drop or AutoFill, you can use the old standby Cut, Copy, and Paste commands to move or copy information in a worksheet. These commands use the Clipboard as a kind of electronic halfway house where the information you cut or copy remains until you decide to paste it somewhere.

Because of this Clipboard arrangement, you can use these commands to move or copy information to any other worksheet open in Excel or even to other programs running in Windows (like a Word for Windows 95 document).

To move a cell selection with Cut and Paste, follow these steps:

1. **Select the cells you want to move.**

2. **Click the Cut button on the Standard toolbar.**

   Or, if you prefer, you can choose Cut from the cell shortcut menu or Edit⇨Cut from the menu bar.

   You can cut out all of this button-and-menu stuff and just press Ctrl+X. Whenever you choose the Cut command in Excel, the program surrounds the cell selection with a *marquee* (a dotted line that travels around the cells' outline) and displays the following message on the status bar:

   > Select destination and press ENTER or choose Paste

3. **Move the cell pointer to, or select, the cell in the upper-left corner of the new range to which you want the information moved.**

4. **Press Enter to complete the move operation.**

   Or, if you're feeling really ambitious, click the Paste button on the Standard toolbar, or choose Paste from the cell shortcut menu, or choose Edit⇨Paste on the menu bar, or press Ctrl+V (do you think there are enough pasting alternatives in Excel?).

Notice that, when you indicate the destination range, you don't have to select a range of blank cells that matches the shape and size of the cell selection you're moving. Excel only needs to know the location of the cell in the upper-left corner of the destination range to figure out where to put the rest of the cells.

In fact, you can mess yourself up if you select more than the first cell of the destination range and the selected range doesn't exactly match the size and shape of the selection you're moving. When you press Enter, Excel displays an alert box with the following message:

> Cut and paste areas are different shapes

If you click OK to get rid of this dialog box, you have to correct the size of the destination range to successfully complete the move operation.

Copying a cell selection with the Copy and Paste commands follows an identical procedure to the one you use with the Cut and Paste commands. After selecting the range to copy, you have even more choices about how to get the information into the Clipboard. Instead of clicking the Copy button on the Standard toolbar or choosing Copy from the cell shortcut menu or Copy from the Edit menu, you can press Ctrl+C.

Paste it again, Sam . . .

When copying a selection with the Copy and Paste commands and the Clipboard, you can copy the information multiple times. Just make sure that instead of pressing Enter to complete the first copy operation, you click the Paste button on the Standard toolbar or choose the Paste command (from the cell shortcut menu or the Edit menu) or press Ctrl+V.

When you use the Paste command to complete a copy operation, Excel copies the selection to the range you designated without removing the marquee from the original selection. This is your signal that you can select another destination range (either in the same or a different document).

After selecting the first cell of the next range where you want the selection copied, choose the Paste command again. You can continue in this manner, pasting the same selection to your heart's content. When you make the last copy, press Enter instead of choosing the Paste command. If you forget and choose Paste, get rid of the marquee around the original cell range by pressing the Esc key.

Note that you can do multiple pasting jobs with the Paste command only after copying stuff to the Clipboard and not after cutting stuff. This means that anytime you use the Cut and Paste commands to move something in the worksheet, you might as well press Enter to paste because you don't accrue any more pasting benefits from choosing the Paste command.

So what's so special about Paste Special?

Normally, Excel copies all the information in the range of cells you selected: formatting as well the formulas, text, and other values you entered. If you want, you can specify that only the entries be copied (without the formatting) or that just the formatting be copied (without the entries). You can even have Excel copy only values in a cell selection, which means that Excel copies all text entries and values entered in a cell selection but does *not* include formulas or formatting. When you paste values, all formulas in the cell selection are discarded and only the calculated values are retained — these values appear in the new cell range just as though you entered them manually.

To paste particular parts of a cell selection while discarding others, you choose the Paste Special command on the cell shortcut menu or on the Edit pull-down menu rather than the standard Paste command (meaning that you don't get the benefit of clicking the Paste button on the Standard toolbar or using the nifty Ctrl+V keyboard shortcut). When you choose Paste Special over Paste, Excel displays the Paste Special dialog box shown in Figure 4-15. Here, you can specify which parts of the current cell selection to use by choosing the appropriate Paste radio button as follows:

✔ Normally, Excel chooses the All radio button in the Paste section to paste all the stuff in the cell selection (formulas, formatting, you name it).

✔ Click the Formulas radio button in the Paste section to paste all the text, numbers, and formulas in the current cell selection while at the same time omitting all of the current formatting applied to their cells.

✔ Click the Values radio button in the Paste section to convert formulas in the current cell selection to their calculated values.

✔ Click the Formats radio button in the Paste section to paste only the formatting from the current cell selection and leave the cell entries in the dust.

✔ Click the Comments radio button in the Paste section to paste only the notes that you've attached to their cells (kinda like electronic sticky notes — see Chapter 6 for details).

✔ Click the Validation radio button in the Paste section to paste only the data validation rules into the cell range that you've set up with the new Data⇨Validation command (for details on using this command, you'll have to get a hold of my *MORE Excel 97 For Windows For Dummies*).

✔ Click the All except borders radio button in the Paste section to paste all the stuff in the cell selection except any borders used there.

✔ Normally, the None radio button in the Operation section of the Paste Special dialog box is selected, indicating that Excel will perform no operation between the data entries you've cut or copied to the Clipboard and the data entries in the cell range where you paste.

✔ Click the Add radio button in the Operation section to add the data you've cut or copied to the Clipboard and the data entries in the cell range where you paste.

✔ Click the Subtract radio button in the Operation section to subtract the data you've cut or copied to the Clipboard from the data entries in the cell range where you paste.

✔ Click the Multiply radio button in the Operation section to multiply the data you've cut or copied to the Clipboard by the data entries in the cell range where you paste.

✔ Click the Divide radio button in the Operation section to divide the data you've cut or copied to the Clipboard by the data entries in the cell range where you paste.

✔ Choose the Skip Blanks check box when you want Excel to paste every-where except for any empty cells in the incoming range. In other words, a blank cell cannot overwrite your current cell entries.

✔ Choose the Transpose check box when you want Excel to change the orientation of the pasted entries (for example, if the original cells' entries ran down the rows of a single column of the worksheet, the transposed pasted entries will run across the columns of a single row).

✔ Click the Paste Link button when you're copying cell entries and you want to establish a link between copies you're pasting and the original entries so that changes to the original cells are automatically updated in the pasted copies.

Figure 4-15:
The Paste
Special
dialog box.

Let's Be Clear about Deleting Stuff

No discussion about editing in Excel would be complete without a section on getting rid of the stuff you put into cells. You can perform two kinds of deletions in a worksheet.

✔ **Clearing a cell:** Just deletes or empties the cell's contents without removing the cell from the worksheet, which would alter the layout of the surrounding cells.

✔ **Deleting a cell:** Gets rid of the whole kit and caboodle — cell structure along with all its contents and formatting. When you delete a cell, Excel has to shuffle the position of entries in the surrounding cells to plug up any gaps made by the demise.

Sounding the all clear!

To get rid of just the contents of a cell selection rather than delete the cells along with their contents, select the range of cells to be cleared and press Delete or choose Edit⇨Clear⇨Contents on the menu bar.

If you want to get rid of more than just the contents of a cell selection, choose Edit⊏⊐Clear and then choose from among the cascading menu commands:

- ✔ Choose All to get rid of all formatting and notes as well as entries in the cell selection.
- ✔ Choose Formats to delete only the formatting from the current cell selection without touching anything else.
- ✔ Choose Comments if you only want to remove the notes in the cell selection but leave everything else behind.
- ✔ Choose Hyperlinks to get rid of the hypertext links in the cell selection without getting rid of the contents (see Chapter 10 for the lowdown on hyperlinks).

Get these cells outta here!

To delete the cell selection rather than just clear out its contents, select the cell range and choose Delete from the cell shortcut menu or Edit⊏⊐Delete from the menu bar. Excel displays the Delete dialog box shown in Figure 4-16. You use the radio button options in this dialog box to indicate how Excel should shift the cells left behind to fill in the gaps when the cells currently selected are blotted out of existence:

- ✔ Normally, the Shift cells left radio button is selected, meaning that Excel moves entries from neighboring columns on the right to the left to fill in gaps created when you delete the cell selection by clicking OK or pressing Enter.
- ✔ If you want Excel to move entries up from neighboring rows below, click the Shift cells up radio button.
- ✔ If you decide to remove all the rows in the current cell selection, click the Entire row radio button in the Delete dialog box.
- ✔ If you decide to delete all the columns in the current cell selection, click the Entire column radio button.

Figure 4-16:
The Delete
dialog box.

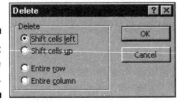

If you know ahead of time that you want to delete an entire column or row from the worksheet, you can select the column or row on the workbook window frame and then choose Delete from the column or row shortcut menu or choose Edit➪Delete from the menu. You can remove more than one column or row at a time provided that they all neighbor one another and that you select them by dragging through their column letters or row numbers (Excel can't delete nonadjacent selections).

 Deleting entire columns and rows from a worksheet is risky business unless you are sure that the columns and rows in question contain nothing of value. Remember, when you delete an entire row from the worksheet, you delete *all information from column A through IV* in that row (and you can see only a very few columns in this row). Likewise, when you delete an entire column from the worksheet, you delete *all information from row 1 through 65,536* in that column.

Kindly Step Aside . . .

For those inevitable times when you need to squeeze new entries into an already populated region of the worksheet, you can insert new cells in the area rather than go through all the trouble of moving and rearranging several individual cell ranges. To insert a new cell range, select the cells (many of which are already occupied) where you want the new cells to appear and then choose Insert on the cell shortcut menu or the Insert➪Cells command on the menu bar. Doing either of these displays the Insert dialog box with the following radio button options:

- ✔ Click the Shift cells right radio button to shift existing cells to the right to make room for the ones you want to add before choosing OK or pressing Enter.

- ✔ To instruct the program to shift existing entries down instead, use the default Shift cells down radio button before choosing OK or pressing Enter.

- ✔ As when you delete cells, when you insert cells with the Insert dialog box, you can insert complete rows or columns in the cell range by clicking either the Entire row or the Entire column radio button. You can also select the row number or column letter on the frame before you choose the Insert command.

Note that you can also insert entire columns and rows in a worksheet by choosing the Columns or Rows command on the Insert menu without having to open the Insert dialog box.

Keep in mind that just as when you delete whole columns and rows, inserting entire columns and rows affects the entire worksheet, not just the part you see. If you don't know what's out in the hinterlands of the worksheet, you can't be sure how the insertion will impact — perhaps even sabotage — stuff (especially formulas) in the other unseen areas. I suggest that you scroll all the way out in both directions to make sure that nothing's out there.

Stamping Out Your Spelling Errors

If you're as good a speller as I am, you'll be really relieved to learn that Excel 97 has a built-in spell checker that can catch and get rid of all those embarrassing little spelling errors. With this in mind, you no longer have any excuse for putting out worksheets with typos in the titles or headings.

To check the spelling in a worksheet, choose Tools➪Spelling on the menu bar or click the Spelling button (the one with a check mark under ABC) on the Standard toolbar or press F7.

Any way you do it, Excel begins checking the spelling of all text entries in the worksheet. When the program comes across an unknown word, it displays the Spelling dialog box, similar to the one shown in Figure 4-17.

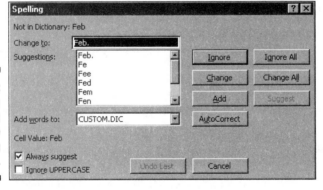

Figure 4-17:
Checking
your spelling
in the
Spelling
dialog box.

Excel suggests replacements for the unknown word, with a likely replacement in the Suggestions list box appearing in the Change to list box of the Spelling dialog box. If that replacement is incorrect, you can scroll through the Suggestions list and click the correct replacement. Use the Spelling dialog box options as follows:

- ✔ To replace the word listed after the Not in Dictionary prompt with the word listed in the Change to list box, click the Change button.
- ✔ To change all occurrences of this misspelled word in the worksheet to the word listed in the Change to list box, click the Change All button.

✔ If you want to add the unknown word (such as your name) to a custom dictionary so that it won't be flagged when you check the spelling in the worksheet later on, click the Add button.

✔ If you want Excel from then on to automatically correct this spelling error with the suggestion shown in the Change to edit box (by adding the misspelling and suggestion to the AutoCorrect dialog box — refer to "You really AutoCorrect that for me" in Chapter 2), click the AutoCorrect button.

✔ If you think that the word is fine as-is, then click the Ignore button (or the Ignore All button if you don't want the spell checker to bother you with this word again).

Notice that the Excel spell checker not only flags words not found in its built-in or custom dictionary but also flags occurrences of double words in a cell entry (such as *total total*) or words with unusual capitalization (such as *NEw York* instead of *New York*).

Keep in mind that you can check the spelling of just a particular group of entries by selecting the cells before you choose Tools⇨Spelling on the menu bar, click the Spelling button on the Standard toolbar, or press F7.

Chapter 5
Printing the Masterpiece

● ●

In This Chapter

▶ Previewing pages before printing

▶ Using the Print button on the Standard toolbar to print the current worksheet

▶ Printing all the worksheets in a workbook

▶ Printing just some of the cells in a worksheet

▶ Changing the orientation of the printing

▶ Printing the whole worksheet on a single page

▶ Changing the margins for a report

▶ Adding a header and footer to a report

▶ Printing column and row headings as print titles on every page of a report

▶ Inserting page breaks in a report

▶ Printing the formulas in your worksheet

● ●

*W*hen all is said and done, for most people, getting the data down on paper is really what spreadsheets are all about (all the talk about the "paperless" office to the contrary). All the data entry, all the formatting, all the formula checking, all the things you do to get a spreadsheet ready are really just preparation for printing its information.

In this chapter, you find out just how easy it is to print reports with Excel 97. And you discover that just by following a few simple guidelines, you can produce top-notch reports the first time you send the document to the printer (instead of the second or even the third time around).

The only trick to printing a worksheet is getting used to the paging scheme and learning how to control it. Many of the worksheets you create with Excel are not only longer than one printed page but also wider. Unlike a word processor, such as Word 97, which only pages the document vertically (because it won't let you create a document wider than the page size you're using), spreadsheet programs like Excel 97 often have to break up pages both vertically and horizontally to print a worksheet document (a kind of tiling of the print job, if you will).

When breaking a worksheet into pages, Excel first pages the document vertically down the rows in the first columns of the print area (just like a word processor). After paging the first columns, the program pages down the rows of the second set of columns in the print area. Excel pages down and then over until all the document included in the print area (which can include the entire worksheet or just sections) is paged.

When paging the worksheet, keep in mind that Excel does not break up the information within a row or column. If all the information in a row won't fit at the bottom of the page, the program moves the entire row to the following page. So, too, if all the information in a column won't fit at the right edge of the page, the program moves the entire column to a new page. (Because Excel pages down and then over, chances are that the column will not appear on the next page of the report.)

There are several ways to deal with such paging problems — and, in this chapter, you're going to be exposed to them all! After you have these page problems under control, printing, as you shortly see, is a proverbial piece of cake.

Starting the Show with Print Preview

Do the world a favor and save a forest or two by using the Print Preview feature before you print any worksheet, section of worksheet, or entire workbook. Because of the peculiarities in paging worksheet data, you should check the page breaks for any report that requires more than one page. Print Preview mode not only shows you exactly how the worksheet data will be paged when printed but also enables you to modify the margins, change the page settings, and even go ahead and print the report when everything looks okay.

To switch to Print Preview mode, click the Print Preview button on the Standard toolbar (it's the one with the magnifying glass on the page, right next to the Print button) or choose File⇨Print Preview on the menu bar. Excel displays all the information on the first page of the report in a separate window with its own toolbar. The mouse pointer becomes a magnifying glass. Figure 5-1 shows the Print Preview window with the first page of a three-page sample report.

When Excel displays a full page in the Print Preview window, you can barely read its contents; increase the view to actual size if you need to verify some of the information. You can zoom up to 100 percent by clicking the previewed page with the magnifying-glass mouse pointer or by clicking the Zoom button at the top of the Print Preview window. Figure 5-2 shows the first page of the three-page report after you zoom in by clicking the Zoom pointer (with the magnifying-glass icon) on the top central portion of the page.

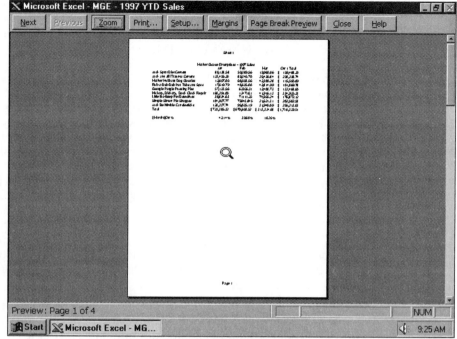

Figure 5-1:
The first
page of a
three-page
report,
shown in
Print
Preview
mode.

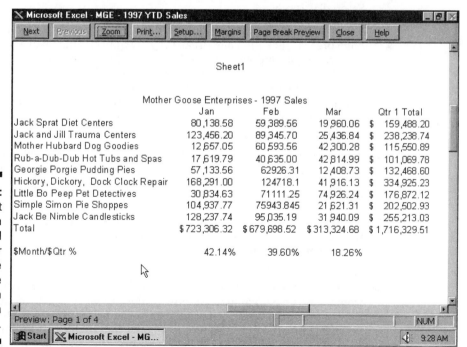

Figure 5-2:
The first
page of a
previewed
report after
clicking the
top of the
page with
the Zoom
tool.

After a page is enlarged to actual size, use the scroll bars to bring new parts of the page into view in the Print Preview window. If you prefer to use the keyboard, press the ↑ and ↓ keys or PgUp and PgDn to scroll up or down the page; press ← and → or Ctrl+PgUp and Ctrl+PgDn to scroll left and right.

To return to the full-page view, click the mouse pointer (in its arrowhead form) anywhere on the page or click the Zoom button on the Print Preview toolbar a second time. Excel indicates the number of pages in a report on the status bar of the Print Preview window. If your report has more than one page, you can view pages that follow the one you are previewing by clicking on the Next command button at the top of the window. To review a page you've already seen, back up a page by clicking the Previous button. You can also advance to the next page by pressing the PgDn or ↓ key or move back to the previous page by pressing the PgUp or ↑ key when the page view is full-page rather than actual size.

When you finish previewing the report, you have the following options:

- ✔ If the pages look okay, you can click the Print button to display the Print dialog box and start printing the report from there (see "Printing it your way" later in this chapter).

- ✔ If you notice some paging problems that you can solve by choosing a new paper size, page order, orientation, or margins, or if you notice a problem with the header or footer in the top or bottom margin of the pages, you can click the Setup button and take care of these problems in the Page Setup dialog box.

- ✔ If you notice some paging problems that you can solve by modifying the page breaks, click the Page Break Preview button. This takes you back to the workbook window with a reduced view of the worksheet where you can change the page breaks by dragging the borders with the mouse. After you've got the borders adjusted the way you want them, return to the normal view by choosing View⇨Normal on the Excel menu bar. You can then print the report by choosing File⇨Print on the menu bar or by clicking the Print button on the Standard toolbar.

- ✔ If you notice some problems with the margins or with the column widths and you want to adjust them in Print Preview mode, you can click the Margins button and drag the margin markers into place (see "Massaging the margins" later in this chapter for details).

- ✔ If you notice any other kind of problem, such as a typo in a heading or a wrong value in a cell, click the Close button and return to the normal worksheet document window; you cannot make any text editing changes in the Print Preview window.

- ✔ After you make corrections to the worksheet, you can print the report from the normal document window by choosing File⇨Print on the menu bar (or pressing Ctrl+P). Alternatively, you can switch back to Print Preview mode to make a last-minute check and click the Print button, or use the Print button on the Standard toolbar (fourth from left with the printer icon on it).

The Page Stops Here . . .

Excel automatically displays the page breaks in the normal document window after you preview the document. Page breaks appear on-screen as dotted lines between the columns and rows that will print out on different pages.

To get rid of page breaks in the document window, choose Tools⇨Options on the menu bar, choose the View tab, clear the check mark from the Page breaks check box, and click OK or press Enter.

Printing it right away

As long as you want to use Excel's default print settings to print all of the cells in the current worksheet, printing in Excel 97 is a breeze. Simply click the Print button on the Standard toolbar (the fourth tool from the left, with the printer icon). The program then prints one copy of all the information in the current worksheet, including any charts and graphics — but not including comments you added to cells. (See Chapter 6 for details about adding comments to your worksheet and Chapter 8 for details about charts and graphics.)

After you click the Print tool, Excel routes the print job to the Windows 95 print queue, which acts like a middleman to send the job to the printer. While Excel is sending the print job to the print queue, Excel displays a Printing dialog box to keep you informed of its progress (such as Printing Page 2 of 3). After this dialog box disappears, you are free to go back to work in Excel (be aware, however, that Excel will probably move like a slug until the job is actually printed). To abort the print job while it's being sent to the print queue, click the Cancel button in the Printing dialog box.

If you don't realize that you want to cancel the print job until after Excel finishes shipping it to the print queue (that is, while the Printing dialog box appears on-screen), you must open the dialog box for your printer and cancel printing from there. To cancel a print job from this dialog box, follow these steps:

1. **Click the printer icon at the far right of the Windows 95 taskbar (to the immediate left of the current time) with the secondary mouse button to open its shortcut menu.**

   This printer icon displays the screen tip, 1 document(s) pending for *so-and-so* (for example, when I'm printing, this message will say "1 document[s] pending for Greg) when you position the mouse pointer over it.

2. **Choose the Open Active Printers command on the printer icon's shortcut menu.**

   This opens the dialog box for the printer with the Excel print job in its queue (as described under the Document heading in the list box).

3. **Select the Excel print job that you want to cancel in the list box of your printer's dialog box.**

4. **Choose Document⇨Cancel Printing on the menu bar.**

5. **Wait for the print job to disappear from the queue in the printer's dialog box and then click the Close button to get rid of it and return to Excel.**

Printing it your way

Printing with the Print tool on the Standard toolbar is fine, provided that all you want is a single copy of all the information in the current worksheet. If you want more copies, more or less data (such as all the worksheets in the workbook or just a cell selection within a particular worksheet), or you need to change some of the page settings (like the size of the page or the orientation of the printing on the page), then you need to print from the Print dialog box (shown in Figure 5-3).

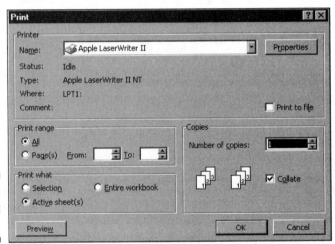

Figure 5-3:
The Print
dialog box.

Excel provides a number of ways to open the Print dialog box:

- ✔ Press Ctrl+P.
- ✔ Choose the File⇨Print command on the menu bar.
- ✔ Press Ctrl+Shift+F12.

Printing in particular

Within the Print dialog box are the Print range and Print what areas, where you can select how much of the information is printed, and the Copies area, where you can change the number of copies printed. Here's how you use these areas:

✔ **All:** When the All radio button in the Page range section is selected, all of the pages in your document will print. Because this is the default choice, you only need to select it after you have printed only a portion of the document, using the Page(s) radio button.

✔ **Page(s):** Normally, Excel prints all of the pages required to produce the information in the areas of the workbook that you want printed. Sometimes, however, you may need to reprint only a page or range of pages that you've modified within this section. To reprint a single page, enter its page number in both the From and To edit boxes in the Page Range section or select these page numbers with the spinner buttons. To reprint a range of pages, put the first page number in the From edit box and the last page number in the To edit box. (Excel automatically deselects the All radio button and selects the Page[s] radio button in the Page Range section as soon as you start typing in the From or To edit boxes.)

✔ **Selection:** Select this radio button in the Print what section to have Excel print just the cells that are currently selected in your workbook. (Yes, you must remember to select these cells before opening the Print dialog box and choosing this radio button!)

✔ **Active sheet(s):** Excel automatically displays and selects this radio button and prints all of the information in whatever worksheets are active in your workbook. Normally, this means printing just the data in the current worksheet. To print other worksheets in the workbook when this radio button is chosen, hold down Ctrl as you click the sheet's tab. To include all the sheets between two sheet tabs, click the first one and then hold Shift as you click the second tab (Excel selects all the tabs in between).

✔ **Entire workbook:** Select this radio button in the Print what section to have Excel print all the data in each of the worksheets in your workbook.

✔ **Number of copies:** To print more than one copy of the report, enter the number of copies you want to print in the Number of copies edit box in the Copies section — or use the spinner buttons to select the required number.

✔ **Collate:** When you *collate* pages, you simply make separate stacks of each complete report, rather than print all copies of page one, and then all copies of page two, and so on. To have Excel collate each copy of the report for you, select the Collate check box in the Copies section to put a check mark in it.

After you finish choosing new print options, you can send the job to the printer by choosing OK or pressing Enter. To use another printer that's been installed for Windows 95 (Excel lists the current printer in the Name edit box and all printers installed for Windows 95 on the Name pop-up menu), select the new printer on the Name pop-up menu in the Printer section at the top of the dialog box before you start printing.

Setting and clearing the Print Area

Excel 97 includes a special printing feature called the *Print Area*. You can use the File⇨Print Area⇨Set Print Area command to define any cell selection on a worksheet as the Print Area. After the Print Area is defined, Excel 97 will then print this cell selection anytime you print the worksheet (either with the Print button on the Standard toolbar or from the Print dialog box, using the File⇨Print command or one of its shortcuts). Whenever you fool with the Print Area, you need to keep in mind that once defined, its cell range is the only one you can print (regardless of what options you select in the Print dialog box) until you clear the Print Area.

To clear the Print Area (and therefore go back to the printing defaults established in the Print dialog box — see "Printing in particular," which immediately precedes this section, for details), you just have to select File⇨Print Area⇨Clear Print Area on the menu bar.

You can also define and clear the Print Area from the Sheet tab of the Page Setup dialog box (see the next section). To define the Print Area from this dialog box, insert the cursor in the Print area edit box on the Sheet tab and then select the cell range or ranges in the worksheet (remembering that you can reduce the Page Setup dialog box to just this edit box by clicking its minimize box). To clear the Print Area from this dialog box, select the cell addresses in the Print area edit box and press the Delete key.

My Page Was Setup!

As I said at the beginning of this chapter, about the only thing the slightest bit complex in printing a worksheet is figuring out how to get the pages right. Fortunately, the options in the Page Setup dialog box give you a great deal of control over what goes on which page. To open the Page Setup dialog box, choose File⇨Page Setup on the menu bar or click the Setup button if the Print Preview window is open. The Page Setup dialog box contains four tabs: Page, Margins, Header/Footer, and Sheet.

The particular options offered in the Page tab of the Page Setup dialog box may vary slightly with the type of printer you use. Figure 5-4 shows the Page Setup dialog box when the Apple LaserWriter is the current printer (all the options you see here are also present when using other laser printers such as the HP LaserJet printer).

For most types of printers, the Page tab of the Page Setup dialog box includes options for changing the orientation, scaling the printing, and choosing a new paper size and print quality:

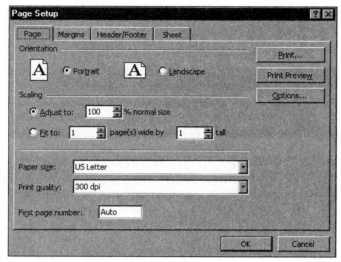

✔ **Orientation:** Portrait positions the paper so that the short side is on the top and bottom. Landscape positions the printing with the long side of the paper on top and bottom (see "Getting the lay of the landscape," which follows).

✔ **Adjust to:** Lets you increase or decrease the size of the print by a set percentage (much like using the Zoom feature to zoom in and out on worksheet data on-screen). When entering values in the Adjust to edit box, keep in mind that 100 percent represents normal size and that any percentage below that reduces the size of the print (and puts more on each page), whereas any percentage above increases the size of the print (and puts less on each page).

✔ **Fit to:** Lets you fit all of the printing on a single page (by default) or on a set number of pages wide by a set number of pages tall (see "Packing it all on one page," later in this chapter).

✔ **Paper size:** Lets you switch to a new paper size by selecting a new size in the drop-down list box (this list contains only those paper sizes that your printer can accommodate).

✔ **Print quality:** Some printers (like dot-matrix printers) let you change the quality of the printing depending upon whether you're producing a first rough draft or a final printout.

✔ **First page number:** Lets you change the starting page number when you want the first number to be higher than 1. You use this numbering option only when you're printing page numbers in the header or footer (see "From header to footer," later in this chapter).

✔ **Options:** Opens a Properties dialog box for the specific printer you have selected. This dialog box may have tabs such as Paper, Graphics, Device Options, and PostScript, depending upon the model and type of printer you're using. The options on these tabs let you fine-tune settings such as the paper tray to use, the graphics quality, the PostScript output format, and the like.

Getting the lay of the landscape

For many printers (including most of the dot-matrix, laser, or ink-jet persuasion), the Page tab of the Page Setup dialog box includes an Orientation section for changing the printing from the more normal *portrait* (where the printing runs parallel to the short edge of the paper) to *landscape* (where the printing runs parallel to the long edge of the paper). With these types of printers, you can usually use the Adjust to or Fit to options (see "Packing it all on one page," which follows) to scale the size of the printing, making it possible to enlarge or reduce the printing by a particular percentage or to force all the information on a single page or a set number of pages.

Because many worksheets are far wider than they are tall (like budgets or sales tables that track expenditures over all 12 months), if your printer supports changing the orientation of the page, you may find that such worksheets look better if you switch the orientation from the normal portrait mode (which accommodates fewer columns on a page because the printing runs parallel to the short edge of the page) to landscape mode.

Figure 5-5 shows the Print Preview window with the first page of a report in landscape mode. For this report, Excel can get three more columns of information on this page in landscape mode than it can in portrait mode. However, because this page orientation accommodates fewer rows, the total page count for this report is increased from two pages in portrait mode to four pages in landscape mode.

Packing it all on one page

If your printer supports scaling options, you're in luck. You can always get a worksheet to fit on a single page simply by clicking the Fit to radio button. When you click this radio button, Excel figures out how much to reduce the size of the information you're printing to get it all on one page.

If you preview this one page and find that the printing is just too small to read comfortably, reopen the Page tab of the Page Setup dialog box and try changing the number of pages in the page(s) wide by tall edit boxes (to the immediate

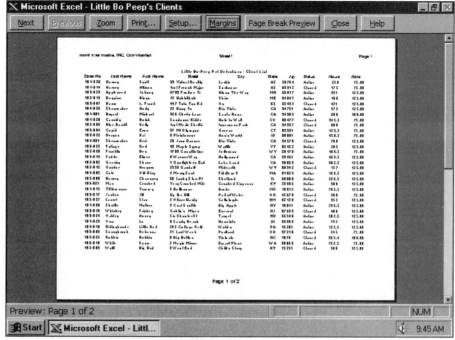

Figure 5-5:
A report shown in landscape mode in the Print Preview window.

right of the Fit to radio button). For example, instead of trying to stuff everything on one page, check out how it looks to fit the worksheet on two pages across: Enter **2** in the page(s) wide edit box and leave 1 in the pages tall edit box. Alternatively, see how the worksheet looks on two pages down: Leave the 1 in the page(s) wide edit box and enter **2** in the pages tall edit box.

After using the Fit to option, you may find that you don't want to scale the printing. Cancel scaling by clicking the Adjust to radio button right above the Fit to button and enter **100** in the % normal size edit box (or select 100 with its spinner buttons).

Massaging the margins

Excel uses a standard top and bottom margin of 1 inch on each page of the report and a standard left and right margin of $3/4$ inch.

Frequently, you find that you can squeeze the last column or the last few rows of the worksheet data you're printing on a page just by adjusting the margins for the report. To get more columns on a page, try reducing the left and right margins. To get more rows on a page, try reducing the top and bottom margins.

You can change the margins in two ways:

  ✔ Open the Page Setup dialog box (either by choosing File⫸Page Setup on the menu bar or by clicking the Setup button in the Print Preview window) and then select the Margins tab (see Figure 5-6) and enter the new settings in the Top, Bottom, Left, and Right edit boxes — or select the new margin settings with their respective spinner buttons.

  ✔ Open the Print Preview window, click the Margins button, and drag the margin markers to their new positions (see Figure 5-7).

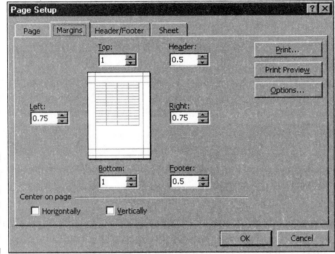

Figure 5-6: The Margins tab in the Page Setup dialog box.

You can use the Center on page options in the Margins tab of the Page Setup dialog box to center a selection of data (that takes up less than a full page) between the current margin settings. Select the Horizontally check box to center the data between the left and right margin. Select the Vertically check box to center the data between the top and bottom margins.

If you use the Margins button in the Print Preview window to change the margin settings, you can modify the column widths as well as the margins. (Figure 5-7 shows the margin and column markers that appear when you click the Margins button in the Print Preview window.) To change one of the margins, position the mouse pointer on the desired margin marker (the pointer shape changes to a double-headed arrow) and drag the marker in the appropriate direction. When you release the mouse button, Excel redraws the page using the new margin setting. You may gain or lose columns or rows, depending on what kind of adjustment you make. Changing the column widths is the same story: Drag the column marker to the left or right to decrease or increase the width of a particular column.

Header margin marker   Column markers

Top margin marker   Right margin markers

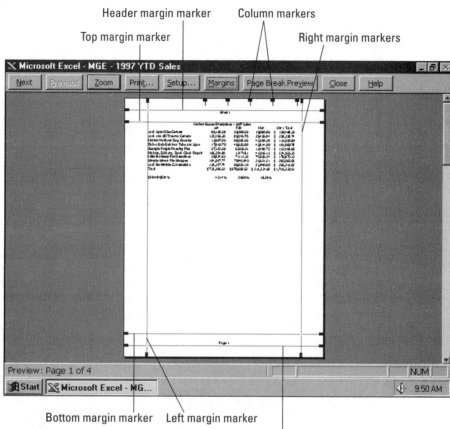

Figure 5-7:
The Print
Preview
window
after
clicking the
Margins
button.

Bottom margin marker   Left margin marker

Footer margin marker

From header to footer

Headers and footers are simply standard text that appears on every page of the report. The header prints in the top margin of the page, and the footer prints — you guessed it — in the bottom margin. Both are centered vertically in the margins. Unless you specify otherwise, Excel automatically adds a header that shows the name of the worksheet you are printing (as shown on its sheet tab) and a footer that shows the current page number.

You can use a header and footer in a report to identify the document used to produce the report and display the page numbers and the date and time of printing.

Getting a standard job

To modify the headers or footers in some way, open the Header/Footer tab in the Page Setup dialog box and make your changes in the He<u>a</u>der and/or <u>F</u>ooter drop-down list box found there (see Figure 5-8). Both the He<u>a</u>der and <u>F</u>ooter drop-down list boxes in this tab contain a wide number of stock pieces of information for your header and footer, including the name of the worksheet (picked up from the sheet tab — see Chapter 6 to learn how to rename a sheet tab), who prepared the worksheet (picked up from the User <u>N</u>ame option in the General tab of the Options dialog box — see Chapter 12), the page number, the current date, the name of the workbook document, or various combinations of these pieces of information.

Figure 5-8 shows the Header/Footer tab of the Page Setup dialog box after choosing

```
mind over media Confidential, Sheet1, Page 1
```

in the He<u>a</u>der drop-down list box (mind over media is the company to which Excel is registered [this name is the same as the one listed as the registered user on the About Microsoft Excel dialog box], 1997 Sales is the name of the worksheet, and Page 1 is, of course, the current page number) and also choosing

```
Page 1 of ?
```

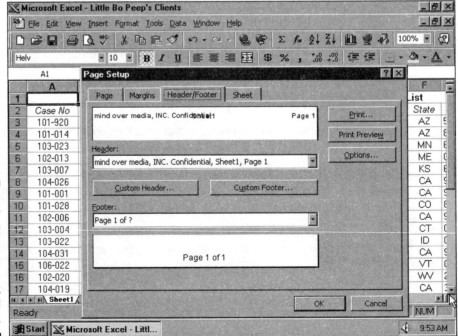

Figure 5-8:
The Header/
Footer tab of
the Page
Setup dialog
box with a
stock
header and
footer.

in the Footer drop-down list box (which puts in the current page number, along with the total number of pages, in the report). You can select this paging option in either the Header or Footer drop-down list box.

Figure 5-9 shows the first page of the report in Print Preview mode. Here, you can see the header and footer as they will print (fortunately, you can verify in the Print Preview window that the header information won't all print on top of each other as it appears in the header preview area in the Page Setup dialog box). You can also see how the Page 1 of ? works in the footer: On the first page, you see the centered footer, Page 1 of 2; on the second page, you would see the centered footer, Page 2 of 2.

If you don't want a header or footer printed in your report, you simply open the Header/Footer tab in the Page Setup dialog box and then select the (none) option at the very top of the Header and Footer drop-down list box.

Getting a custom job

Most of the time, the stock headers and footers available in the Header and Footer drop-down list boxes are sufficient for your report needs. Every once in a while, however, you may want to insert information not available in these list boxes or in an arrangement not offered in the stock headers and footers. For those times, you need to turn to the Custom Header and Custom Footer buttons in the Header/Footer tab of the Page Setup dialog box and go about creating your header or footer by inserting your own information.

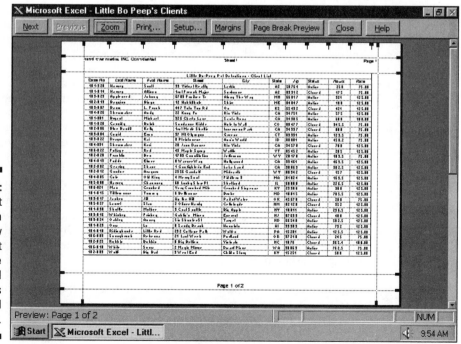

Figure 5-9:
The first page of a preview report showing the header and footer as they will print.

Figure 5-10 shows the Header dialog box that appears when you click the Custom Header button after selecting the stock header shown in Figure 5-8.

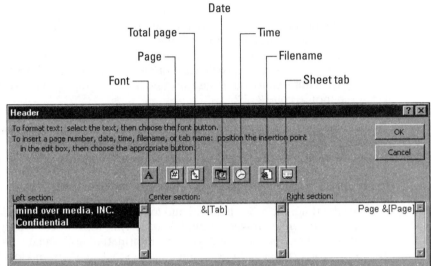

Figure 5-10:
Creating a
custom
header in
the Header
dialog box.

Notice that in the custom Header dialog box, the header is divided into three sections: Left section, Center section, and Right section. All header text you enter in the Left section of this dialog box is justified with the left margin of the report. All header text you enter in the Center section box is centered between the left and right margins, and (you guessed it) all text you enter in the Right section box is justified with the right margin of the report.

You can use the Tab key to advance from section to section in the header and to select the contents of that section, or you can press Alt plus the mnemonic letter (Alt+L for the Left section, Alt+C for the Center section, and Alt+R for the Right section). If you want to break the header text in one of the sections, press Enter to start a new line. If you want to clear the contents of a section, select the items and press Delete.

As Figure 5-10 shows, Excel puts some pretty weird codes with lots of ampersands (&[Tab] and Page &[Page]) in the center and right sections of this stock header. When creating a custom header (or footer), you too can mix weird ampersand codes with the standard text (like "For Eyes Only" and such). To insert the weird ampersand codes in a section of the header (or footer), you click the appropriate button:

✔ **Page button:** inserts the &[Page] code that puts in the current page number.

✔ **Total page button:** inserts the &[Pages] code that puts in the total number of pages. Thus, you can have Excel display the Page 1 of 4 kind of thing by typing the word **Page** and pressing the spacebar, clicking the Page button, pressing the spacebar again, typing **of**, pressing the spacebar a third time, and, finally, pressing the Total Page button to insert Page &[Page] of &[Pages] in the custom header (or footer).

✔ **Date button:** inserts the &[Date] code that puts in the current date.

✔ **Time button:** inserts the &[Time] code that puts in the current time.

✔ **Filename button:** inserts the name of the workbook file.

✔ **Sheet tab button:** inserts the &[Tab] code that puts in the name of the worksheet as shown on the sheet tab.

In addition to inserting ampersand codes in the custom header (or footer), you can select a new font, font size, or font attribute for any of its sections by clicking the Font button. When you click the Font button, Excel opens the Font dialog box where you can select a new font, font style, font size, or special effects (like strikethrough, superscript, or subscript).

When you're finished creating your custom header (or footer), click the OK button to close the Header (or Footer) dialog box and return to the Header/ Footer tab of the Page Setup dialog box (where you can see the fruits of your labor in the sample boxes).

Sorting out the sheet settings

The Sheet tab of the Page Setup dialog box (similar to the one shown in the following section in Figure 5-11) contains a variety of printing options that may come in handy from time to time:

✔ **Print area:** This edit box shows you the cell range of the current print area that you've selected with the File⇨Print Area⇨Set Print Area command on the menu bar. Use this edit box to make changes to the range of cells that you want to print. To change the print area range, select this edit box, and then drag through the cell range in the worksheet or type in the cell references or range names (as explained in Chapter 6). Separate individual cell ranges with a comma (as in A1:G72, K50:M75) when designating nonadjacent areas. If, in selecting the cell range, you find that you need to, you can reduce the Page Setup dialog box to just the Print area edit box by clicking its minimize button.

Use the Print area option when your workbook contains a section that you routinely need to print so that you don't have to keep selecting the range and then choosing the Selection radio button in the Print dialog box every blasted time you print it.

✔ **Rows to repeat at top:** Use this option to designate rows of a worksheet as *print titles* to be printed across the top of each page of the report (see "Putting out the print titles," which follows this section). Select this edit box and then drag down the rows or enter the row references (such as 2:3). If, in selecting the rows to use as print titles, you find it necessary, you can reduce the Page Setup dialog box to just the Rows to repeat at top edit box by clicking its minimize button.

✔ **Columns to repeat at left:** Use this option to designate columns of a worksheet as print titles to be printed at the left edge of each page of the report (see "Putting out the print titles," which follows this section). Select this edit box and then drag across the columns or enter the column references (such as A:B). If, in selecting the columns to use as print titles, you find you need to, you can reduce the Page Setup dialog box to just the Columns to repeat at left edit box by clicking its minimize button.

✔ **Gridlines:** Hides or shows the cell gridlines in the printed report. (Refer to Figure 5-5 to see the page of a report in Print Preview after removing the check mark from the Gridlines check box.)

✔ **Black and white:** When you select this check box, Excel prints the different colors assigned to cell ranges in black and white. Select this option when you've used colors for text and graphics in a workbook on a color monitor but want to print them in monochrome on a black-and-white printer (otherwise, they become shades of gray on a black-and-white printer).

✔ **Draft quality:** When you select this check box, Excel doesn't print cell gridlines (regardless of the status of the Gridlines check box) and omits some graphics from the printout. Select this option when you want to get a fast and dirty copy of the report and are only concerned with checking the text and numbers.

✔ **Row and column headings:** When you select this check box, Excel includes the worksheet frame with the column letters and row numbers on each page of the report. Select this option when you want to be able to identify the location of the printed information (see "Letting Your Formulas All Hang Out," later in this chapter, for an example).

✔ **Comments:** When you select the At end of sheet or As displayed on sheet options on the Comments pop-up menu, Excel prints the text of comments attached to cells that are included in the report. When you select the At end of sheet option, the program prints the notes in a series all together at the end of the report. When you select the As displayed on sheet, the program prints only the notes that are currently displayed in the worksheet (see "Electronic Sticky Notes" in Chapter 6 for details).

✔ **Down, then over:** Normally, Excel selects this radio button, which tells the program to number and page a multipage report by proceeding down the rows and then across the columns to be printed.

✔ **Over, then down:** Select this radio button to alter the way a multipage report is numbered and paged. When you select this option, Excel proceeds to number and page across the columns and then down the rows to be printed.

Putting out the print titles

The Print titles section of the Sheet tab of the Page Setup dialog box enables you to print particular row and column headings on each page of the report. Excel refers to such row and column headings in a printed report as *print titles*. Don't confuse print titles with the header of a report. Even though both are printed on each page, header information is printed in the top margin of the report; print titles always appear in the body of the report — at the top, in the case of rows used as print titles, and on the left, in the case of columns.

To designate print titles for a report, follow these steps:

1. **Open the Page Setup dialog box by choosing File⇨Page Setup on the menu bar.**

   The Page Setup dialog box appears, as shown in Figure 5-11.

2. **Select the Sheet tab.**

   To designate worksheet rows as print titles, go to step 3a. To designate worksheet columns as print titles, go to step 3b.

3a. **Select the Rows to repeat at top edit box and then drag through the rows whose information is to appear at the top of each page in the worksheet below. If, in selecting the rows, you find it necessary, you can reduce the Page Setup dialog box to just the Rows to repeat at top edit box by clicking the edit box's minimize button.**

   In the example shown in Figure 5-11, I clicked the minimize button associated with the Rows to repeat at top edit box and then dragged through rows 1 and 2 in column A of the Bo Peep Pet Detectives — Client List worksheet, and the program entered the row range $1:$2 in the Rows to repeat at top edit box.

   Note that Excel indicates the print-title rows in the worksheet by placing a dotted line (that moves like a marquee) on the border between the titles and the information in the body of the report.

3b. **Select the Columns to repeat at left and then drag through the range of columns whose information is to appear at the left edge of each page of the printed report in the worksheet below. If, in selecting the columns, you find it necessary, you can reduce the Page Setup dialog box to just the Columns to repeat at left edit box by clicking its minimize button.**

   Note that Excel indicates the print-title columns in the worksheet by placing a dotted line (that moves like a marquee) on the border between the titles and the information in the body of the report.

4. **Click OK or press Enter.**

   After you close the Page Setup dialog box, the dotted line showing the border of the row and/or column titles disappears from the worksheet.

In Figure 5-11, rows 1 and 2 containing the worksheet title and column headings for the BoPeep Pet Detectives clients database are designated as the print titles for the report. Figure 5-12 shows the Print Preview window with the second page of the report. In this figure, you can see how these print titles appear on all pages of the report.

To clear print titles from a report if you no longer need them, open the Sheet tab of the Page Setup dialog box and then delete the row and column ranges from the Rows to repeat at top and the Columns to repeat at left edit boxes before you click OK or press Enter.

When Ya Gonna Give Your Page a Break?

Sometimes, as you preview a report, you see that Excel split onto different pages information that you know should always appear together on the same page. If, after trying other approaches (such as changing the page size, orientation, or margins), you still can't remedy the bad page break, you can use the new Page Break Preview feature to adjust the pages in your report. To switch to Page Break Preview mode when you're in the regular workbook window, choose View⇨Page Break Preview on the menu bar. To switch to Page Break Preview mode when you're in the Page Preview window, click the Page Break Preview button on the toolbar.

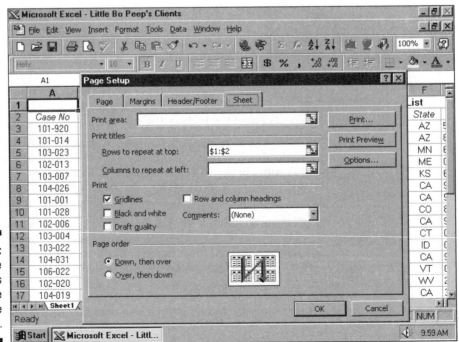

Figure 5-11:
Setting the
print titles
for the
sample
report.

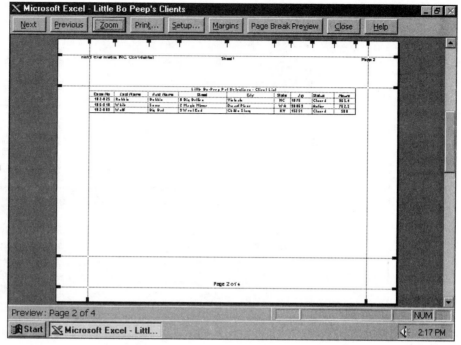

Figure 5-12:
The second preview page of the sample report showing the print titles defined in Figure 5-11.

Figure 5-13 shows a worksheet in Page Break Preview with an example of a bad vertical page break that you can remedy by adjusting the location of the page break between Page 2 and Page 3. Given the page size, orientation, and margin settings for this report, Excel breaks the page between columns L and M. This break separates the sales figures for July, August, and September in columns J, K, and L from the Quarter 3 Totals in column M.

To keep all the third-quarter figures on the same page, you need to move the page break to the left so that the break between Page 2 and Page 3 occurs between columns I and J. That way, all the third quarter sales (for July, August, and September) will be printed together with the Quarter 3 totals on Page 3 of the report. Figure 5-13 shows how you can create the vertical page break in Page Break Preview mode by following these steps:

1. Choose View⇨Page Break Preview on the menu bar.

This takes you into a page break preview window that shows your worksheet data at a reduced magnification (60 percent of normal in Figure 5-13) with the page numbers displayed in large light type and the page breaks shown by heavy lines between the columns and rows of the worksheet.

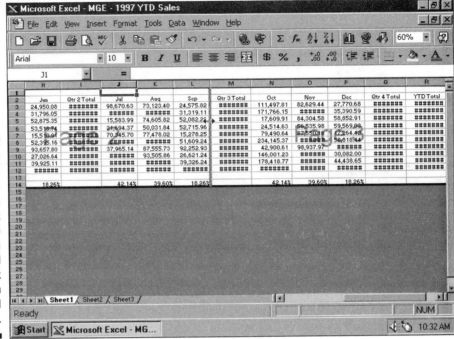

Figure 5-13:
Choosing
the
Insert⇨Page
Break
command to
insert a
manual
page break
between
columns I
and J.

2. **Click OK or press Enter to get rid of the Welcome to Page Break Preview alert dialog box that is displayed when you first get into page break preview.**

3. **Position the mouse pointer somewhere on the page break indicator (one of the heavy lines surrounding the representation of the page) that you need to adjust; when the pointer changes to a double-headed arrow, drag the page indicator to the desired column or row and release the mouse button.**

   For the example shown in Figure 5-13, I drag the page break indicator between Page 2 and Page 3 to the left so that it's between columns I and J. Excel then inserts a new page break between columns Q and R (which adds a Page 4 to the report). I then drag this page break indicator to the left so that it's between columns M and N (so that all the fourth quarter sales are together on the fourth page with the fourth quarter and year-to-date totals, as shown in Figure 5-14).

4. **After you've finished adjusting the page breaks in Page Break Preview (and, presumably, printing the report), choose View⇨Normal on the menu bar to return the worksheet to its regular view of the data.**

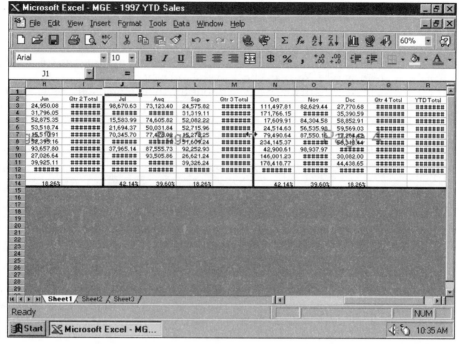

Figure 5-14:
The
worksheet
after
inserting the
manual
page break
between
columns I
and J.

Keep in mind that you can also modify the page breaks with the Insert⇨Page Break command on the menu bar in the regular worksheet. When inserting a manual page break with this command, you use the top and left edges of the cell pointer to determine where the manual page break is placed. The top edge of the cell pointer determines where the page break occurs horizontally; the left edge of the cell pointer determines where the page break occurs vertically. Then, after placing the cell pointer, you choose the Insert⇨Page Break command and Excel inserts dotted lines between the columns and rows that indicate the limits of the new page break.

To remove a manual page break from a worksheet, position the cell pointer somewhere in the row below a horizontal page break or somewhere in the column to the right of a vertical page break. (Manual page breaks are indicated in the worksheet by dotted lines that are indistinguishable from automatic page breaks.) Then choose Insert⇨Remove Page Break on the menu bar. (The Page Break command changes to the Remove Page Break command on the Insert menu, depending on where you place the cell pointer.) If you inserted both a vertical and a horizontal page break at the same time, you must position the cell pointer in the same cell you used to create the two page breaks in order to get rid of them both in a single operation.

Letting Your Formulas All Hang Out

One more basic printing technique you may need every once in a while is how to print the formulas in a worksheet instead of printing the calculated results of the formulas. You can check over a printout of the formulas in your worksheet to make sure that you haven't done anything stupid (like replace a formula with a number or use the wrong cell references in a formula) before you distribute the worksheet company-wide — which can be really embarrassing.

Before you can print a worksheet's formulas, you have to display the formulas, rather than their results, in the cells.

1. **Choose Tools⇨Options on the menu bar.**

2. **Select the View tab.**

3. **Select the Formulas check box to put a check mark in it.**

4. **Click the OK button or press Enter.**

When you follow these steps, Excel displays the contents of each cell in the worksheet as they normally appear only in the formula bar or when you're editing them in the cell. Notice that value entries lose their number formatting, formulas appear in their cells (Excel widens the columns with best-fit so that the formulas appear in their entirety), and long text entries no longer spill over into neighboring blank cells.

Excel allows you to toggle between the normal cell display and the formula cell display by pressing Ctrl+~, (that is, press Ctrl and the tilde key). The tilde key is the one (usually found in the upper-left corner of your keyboard) that does double-duty above the weird backward accent key, `, which is not to be confused with the apostrophe that appears on a key below the quotation mark.

After Excel displays the formulas in the worksheet, you are ready to print it as you would any other report. You can include the worksheet column letters and row numbers as headings in the printout so that, if you *do* spot an error, you can pinpoint the cell reference right away. To include the row and column headings in the printout, click the Row and column headings check box in the Sheet tab of the Page Setup dialog box before you send the report to the printer.

After you print the worksheet with the formulas, return the worksheet to normal by opening the Page Setup dialog box and selecting the View tab and then deselecting the Formulas check box before clicking OK, or pressing Enter, or just choosing Ctrl+~.

Part III
Getting Organized and Staying That Way

The 5th Wave   **By Rich Tennant**

In the end, it was Edward Scissorhand's cousin, Jonathan Hammerhead who brought the group to a consensus on a worksheet design.

In this part . . .

*I*n today's business world, we all know how vital it is to stay organized — as well as how difficult it is. Needless to say, keeping straight the spreadsheets you create in Excel 97 is no less important and, in some cases, no less arduous.

Part III helps you tackle this conundrum by giving you the inside track on how to keep on top of all the stuff in every single worksheet you create or edit. Not only do you discover in Chapter 6 how to keep track of the information in one worksheet, but also, in Chapter 7, how to juggle the information from one worksheet to another and even from one workbook to another.

Chapter 6

Oh, What a Tangled Worksheet We Weave!

• •

In This Chapter

▶ Zooming in and out on a worksheet

▶ Splitting up the workbook window into two or four panes

▶ Freezing columns and rows on-screen for worksheet titles

▶ Attaching comments to cells

▶ Naming your cells

▶ Finding and replacing stuff in your worksheet

▶ Controlling when a worksheet is recalculated

▶ Protecting your worksheets

• •

*Y*ou already know that each Excel worksheet offers an awfully big place in which to store information (and that each workbook you open offers you three of these babies). Because your computer monitor lets you see only a tiny bit of any of the worksheets in a workbook at any one time, the issue of keeping on top of information is not a small one (pun intended).

Although the Excel worksheet employs a coherent cell-coordinate system you can use to get anywhere in the great big worksheet, you've got to admit that this A1, B2 stuff — although highly logical — remains fairly alien to human thinking. (I mean, saying "Go to cell IV88" just doesn't have anywhere near the same impact as saying "Go to the corner of Hollywood and Vine.") Consider for a moment how hard it is to come up with a meaningful association between the 1996 depreciation schedule and its location in the cell range AC50:AN75 so that you can remember where to find it.

In this chapter, you learn some of the more effective techniques for keeping on top of information. You learn how to change the perspective on a worksheet by zooming in and out on the information, how to split the document window into separate panes so that you can display different sections of the worksheet at the same time, and how to keep particular rows and columns on the screen at all times.

And, as if that weren't enough, you also see how to add comments to cells, assign descriptive, English-type names to cell ranges (like Hollywood_and_Vine!), and use the Find and Replace commands to locate and, if necessary, replace entries anywhere in the worksheet. Finally, you see how to control when Excel recalculates the worksheet and how to limit where changes can be made.

Zeroing In with Zoom

So what are you gonna do now that the boss won't spring for that 21-inch monitor for your computer? All day long, it seems that you're either straining your eyes to read all the information in those little, tiny cells, or you're scrolling like mad trying to locate a table you can't seem to find today. Never fear, the Zoom feature is here. You can use Zoom like a magnifying glass to blow up part of the worksheet or shrink it down to size.

Figure 6-1 shows a blowup of an employee-roster worksheet after increasing it to 200-percent magnification (twice normal size). To blow up a worksheet like this, click the 200% option at the top of the Zoom button's pop-up menu — the button second from the end on the Standard toolbar. (You can also do this by choosing View➪Zoom on the menu bar and then selecting the 200% radio button in the Zoom dialog box, if you really want to go to all that trouble.) One thing's for sure, you don't have to go after your glasses to read the names in those cells! The only problem with 200-percent magnification is that you can see only a few cells at one time.

Figure 6-2 shows the same worksheet, this time at 25-percent magnification (roughly one-quarter normal size). To reduce the display to this magnification, you click the 25% setting on the Zoom button's pop-up menu on the Standard toolbar (unless you're just dying to open the Zoom dialog box so that you can accomplish this via its 25% radio button).

Whew! At 25 percent of normal screen size, the only thing you can be sure of is that you can't read a thing! However, notice that with this bird's-eye view, you can see at a glance how far over and down the data in this worksheet extends.

The Zoom pop-up menu and dialog box offers five precise magnification settings (200%, 100% [normal screen magnification], 75%, 50%, and 25%). To use other percentages besides these, you have the following options:

✔ If you want to use other precise percentages in between the five preset percentages (such as 150% or 85%) or settings greater or less than the highest or lowest (such as 400% or 10%), select the Zoom button's edit box on the Standard toolbar, type the new percentage, and press Enter. (You can also do this by opening the Zoom dialog box and entering the percentage in its Custom edit box.)

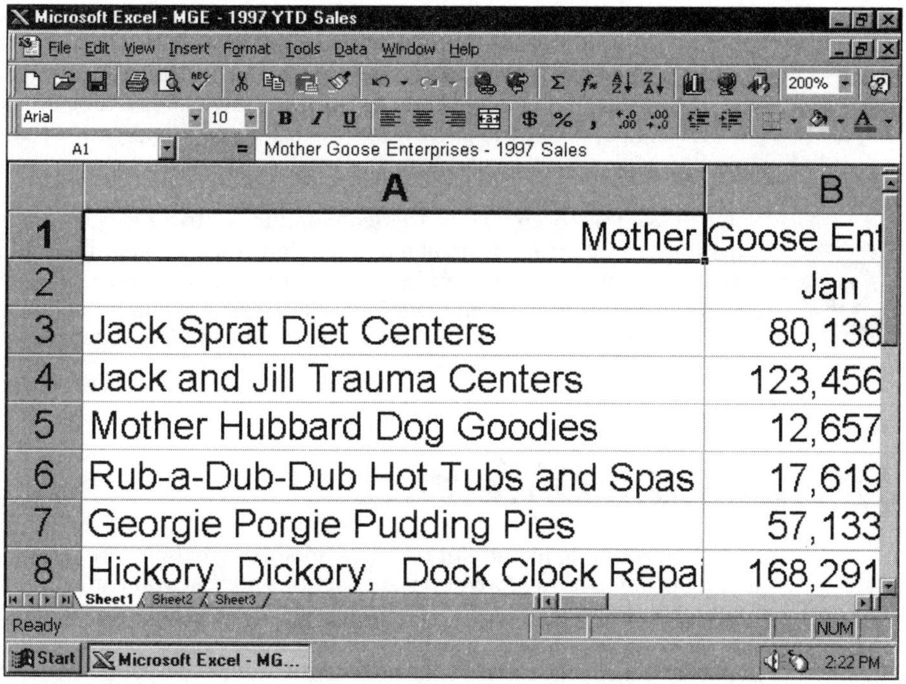

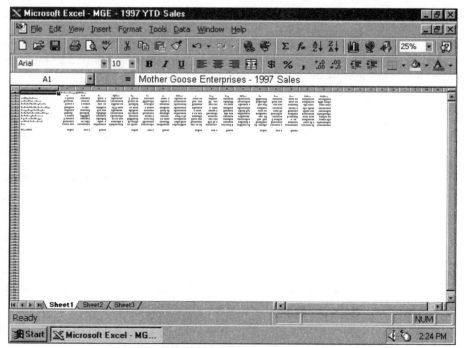

Figure 6-1:
Zooming in:
a sample
worksheet
at 200-
percent
magnification.

Figure 6-2:
Zooming
out: a
sample
worksheet
at 25-
percent
magnification.

> ✔ If you don't know what percentage to enter in order to display a particular
> cell range on the screen, select the range, choose Selection at the very
> bottom of the Zoom button's pop-up menu or open the Zoom dialog box,
> select the Fit Selection radio button, and then click OK or press Enter.
> Excel figures out the percentage necessary to fill up your screen with just
> the selected cell range.

You can use the Zoom feature to locate and move to a new cell range in the
worksheet. First, select a small magnification, such as 50%. Then locate the cell
range you want to move to and select one of its cells. Finally, use the Zoom
feature to return the screen magnification to 100% again. When Excel returns
the display to normal size, the cell you selected and its surrounding range
appear on-screen.

Splitting the Difference

Although zooming in and out on the worksheet can help you get your bearings,
it can't bring together two separate sections so that you can compare their data
on the screen (at least not at a normal size where you can actually read the
information). To manage this kind of trick, split the document window into
separate panes and then scroll the worksheet in each pane so that they display
the parts you want to compare.

Splitting the window is easy. Figure 6-3 shows a projected income statement for
the Jack Sprat Diet Centers after splitting its worksheet window horizontally
into two panes and scrolling up rows 12 through 17 in the second pane. Each
pane has its own vertical scroll bar, which enables you to scroll different parts
of the worksheet into view.

To split a worksheet into two (upper and lower) horizontal panes, you can drag
the *split bar,* located right above the scroll arrow at the very top of the vertical
scroll bar, down until the window is divided as you want it. Use the following
steps:

1. **Click the vertical split bar and hold down the primary mouse button.**

   The mouse pointer changes to a double-headed arrow with a split in its
   middle (like the one used to display hidden rows).

2. **Drag downward until you reach the row at which you want the document window divided.**

   A gray dividing line appears in the workbook document window as you
   drag down, indicating where the document window will be split.

3. **Release the mouse button.**

   Excel divides the window into horizontal panes at the pointer's location
   and adds a vertical scroll bar to the new pane.

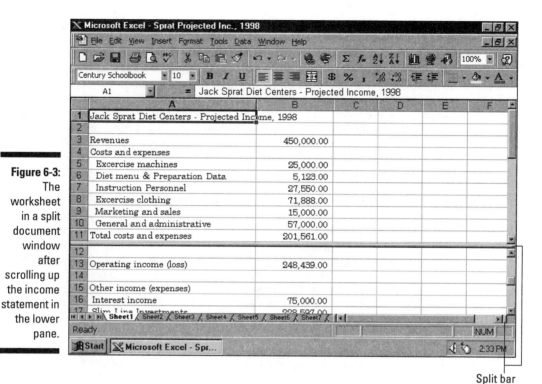

Figure 6-3:
The
worksheet
in a split
document
window
after
scrolling up
the income
statement in
the lower
pane.

Split bar

You can also split the document window into two vertical (left and right) panes by following these steps:

1. **Click the split bar located at the right edge of the horizontal scroll bar.**

2. **Drag to the left until you reach the column at which you want the document window divided.**

3. **Release the mouse button.**

   Excel splits the window at that column and adds a second horizontal scroll bar to the new pane.

Don't confuse the tab split bar to the left of the horizontal scroll bar with the horizontal split bar at its right. You drag the tab split bar to increase or decrease the number of sheet tabs displayed at the bottom of the workbook window; you use the horizontal split bar to divide the workbook window into two vertical panes.

Note that you can make the panes in a workbook window disappear by double-clicking anywhere on the split bar that divides the window rather than having to drag the split bar all the way to one of the edges of the window to get rid of it.

Instead of dragging split bars, you can divide a document window with the Window⇨Split command on the menu bar. When you choose this command, Excel uses the position of the cell pointer to determine where to split the window into panes. The program splits the window vertically at the left edge of the pointer and horizontally along the top edge. If you want the workbook window split into just two horizontal panes, do this: Using the top of the cell pointer as the dividing line, position the cell pointer in the first column of the desired row that is displayed on your screen. If you want the workbook window split into just two vertical windows, do this: Using the left edge of the cell pointer as the dividing line, position the cell pointer in the first row of the desired column that's displayed on your screen.

When the left edge of the cell pointer is right up against the left edge of the workbook window (as it is when the pointer is in any cell in the very first column shown on-screen), the program doesn't split the window vertically — it splits the window horizontally along the top edge of the cell pointer. When the top edge of the pointer is right up against the top edge of the document window (as it is when the pointer is in a cell in the very first row displayed on-screen), the program doesn't split the window horizontally — it splits the window vertically along the left edge of the cell pointer.

If you position the cell pointer somewhere in the midst of the cells displayed on-screen when you choose the Window⇨Split command, Excel splits the window into four panes along the top and left edge of the cell pointer. For example, if you position the cell pointer in cell C6 of the Mother Goose Enterprises 1997 Sales worksheet and then choose Window⇨Split, the window splits into four panes: A horizontal split occurs between rows 5 and 6, and a vertical split occurs between columns B and C (as shown in Figure 6-4).

After the window is split into panes, you can move the cell pointer into a particular pane either by clicking one of its cells or by pressing Shift+F6 (which moves the pointer to the last occupied cell or the top-left cell in each pane in the workbook window in a counterclockwise direction). To remove the panes from a window, choose Window⇨Remove Split on the menu bar.

Fixed Headings Courtesy of Freeze Panes

Window panes are great for viewing different parts of the same worksheet that normally can't be seen together. You can also use window panes to freeze headings in the top rows and first columns so that the headings stay in view at all times, no matter how you scroll through the worksheet. Frozen headings are especially helpful when you work with a table that contains information that extends beyond the rows and columns shown on-screen.

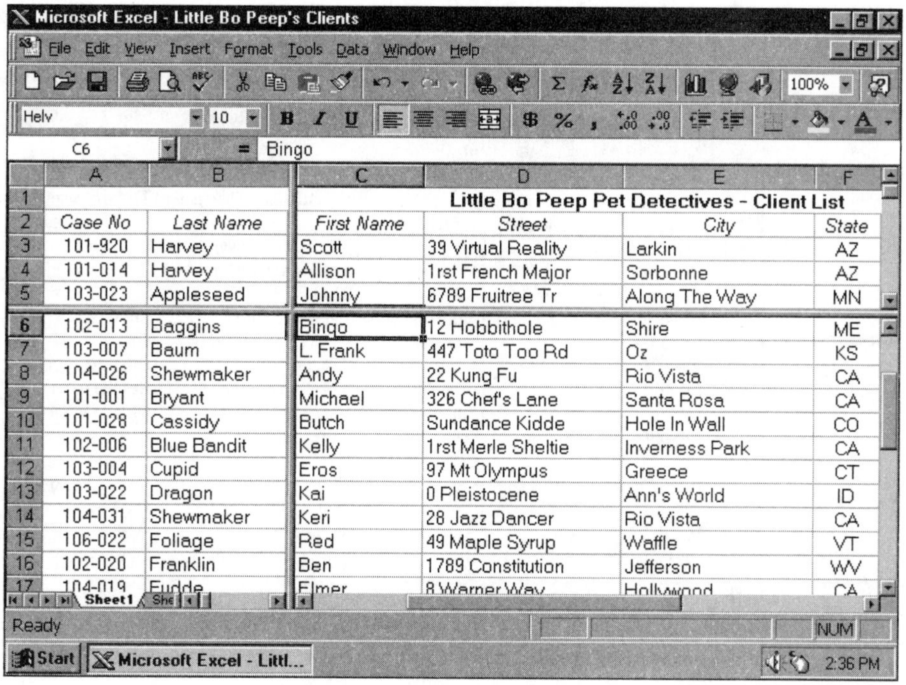

Figure 6-4:
The
worksheet
window split
into four
panes with
the cell
pointer in
cell C6.

Figure 6-5 shows just such a table. The client-list worksheet contains many more rows than you can see at one time (unless you decrease the magnification to 25% with Zoom, which makes the data too small to read). As a matter of fact, this worksheet continues down to row 34.

By splitting the document window into two horizontal panes between rows 2 and 3 and then freezing the top pane, you can keep the column headings in row 2 that identify each column of information on the screen as you scroll the worksheet up and down to review information on different employees. If you further split the window into vertical panes between columns B and C, you can keep the case numbers and last names on the screen as you scroll the worksheet left and right.

Figure 6-5 shows the employee roster after splitting the window into four panes and freezing them. To create and freeze these panes, follow these steps:

1. **Position the cell pointer in cell C3.**

2. **Choose Window➪Freeze Panes on the menu bar.**

   In this example, Excel freezes the top and left window pane above row 3 and left of column C.

When Excel sets up the frozen panes, the borders of frozen panes are represented by a single line rather than a thin bar, as is the case with unfrozen panes.

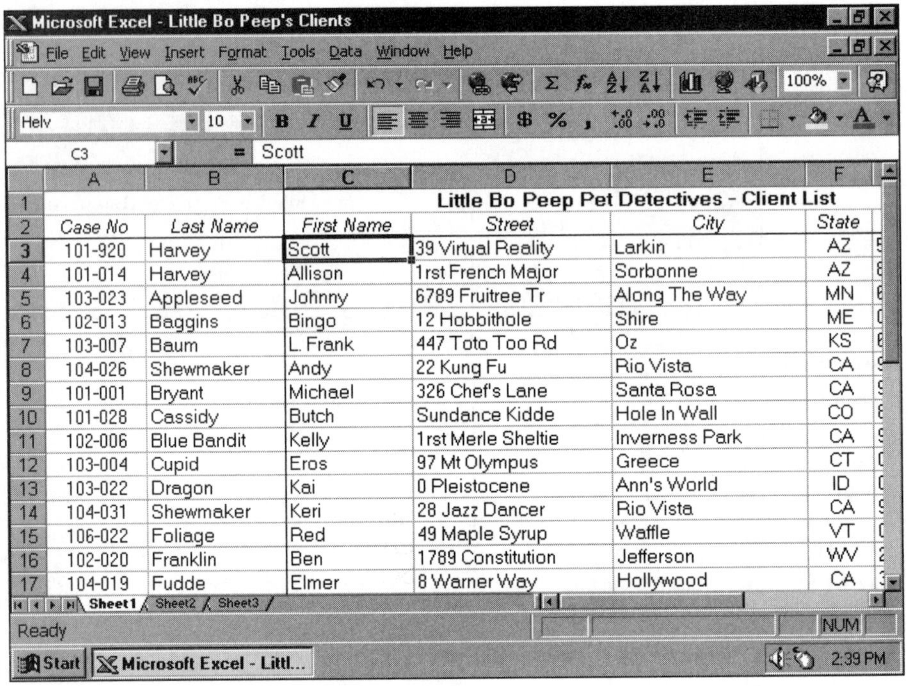

Figure 6-5:
Frozen
panes to
keep the
column
headings
and last
names on
the screen
at all times.

Figure 6-6 shows what happens when you scroll the worksheet up after freezing the window panes. In this figure, I scrolled the worksheet up so that rows 24 through 34 appear under rows 1 and 2. Because the vertical pane with the worksheet title and column headings is frozen, it remains on-screen. (Normally, rows 1 and 2 would have been the first to disappear as you scrolled the worksheet up.)

Figure 6-7 shows what happens when you scroll the worksheet to the left. In this figure, I scrolled the worksheet so that columns G through L appear after columns A and B. Because the first two columns are frozen, they remain on-screen, helping you identify who belongs to what information.

To unfreeze the window panes in a worksheet, choose Window⇨Unfreeze Panes. Choosing this command removes the window panes, indicating that Excel has unfrozen them.

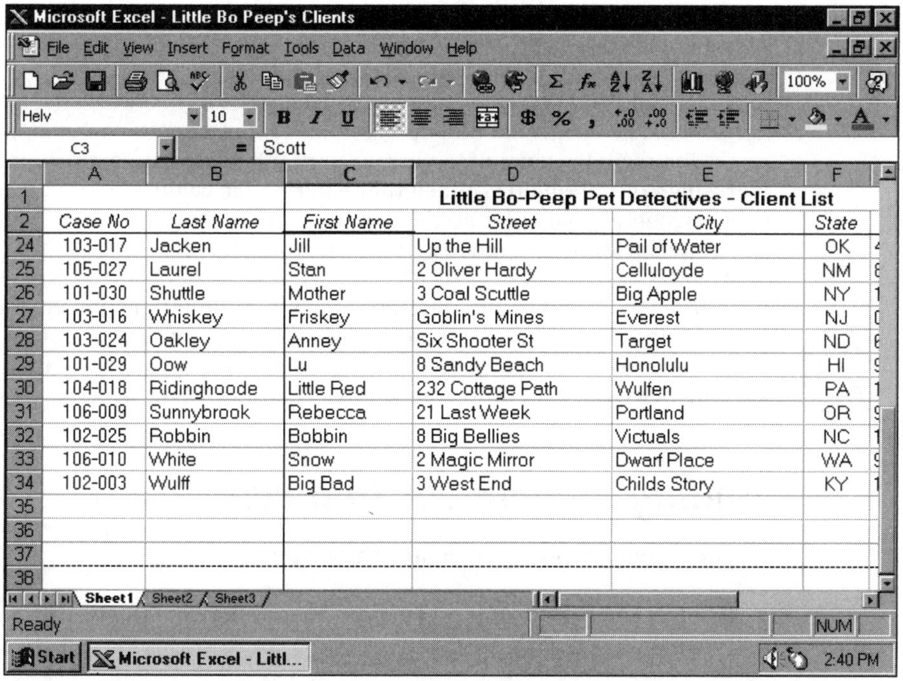

	A	B	C	D	E	F
2	Case No	Last Name	First Name	Street	City	State
24	103-017	Jacken	Jill	Up the Hill	Pail of Water	OK
25	105-027	Laurel	Stan	2 Oliver Hardy	Celluloyde	NM
26	101-030	Shuttle	Mother	3 Coal Scuttle	Big Apple	NY
27	103-016	Whiskey	Friskey	Goblin's Mines	Everest	NJ
28	103-024	Oakley	Anney	Six Shooter St	Target	ND
29	101-029	Oow	Lu	8 Sandy Beach	Honolulu	HI
30	104-018	Ridinghoode	Little Red	232 Cottage Path	Wulfen	PA
31	106-009	Sunnybrook	Rebecca	21 Last Week	Portland	OR
32	102-025	Robbin	Bobbin	8 Big Bellies	Victuals	NC
33	106-010	White	Snow	2 Magic Mirror	Dwarf Place	WA
34	102-003	Wulff	Big Bad	3 West End	Childs Story	KY

Figure 6-6: The Bo Peep clients list scrolled up to display the last rows in the database.

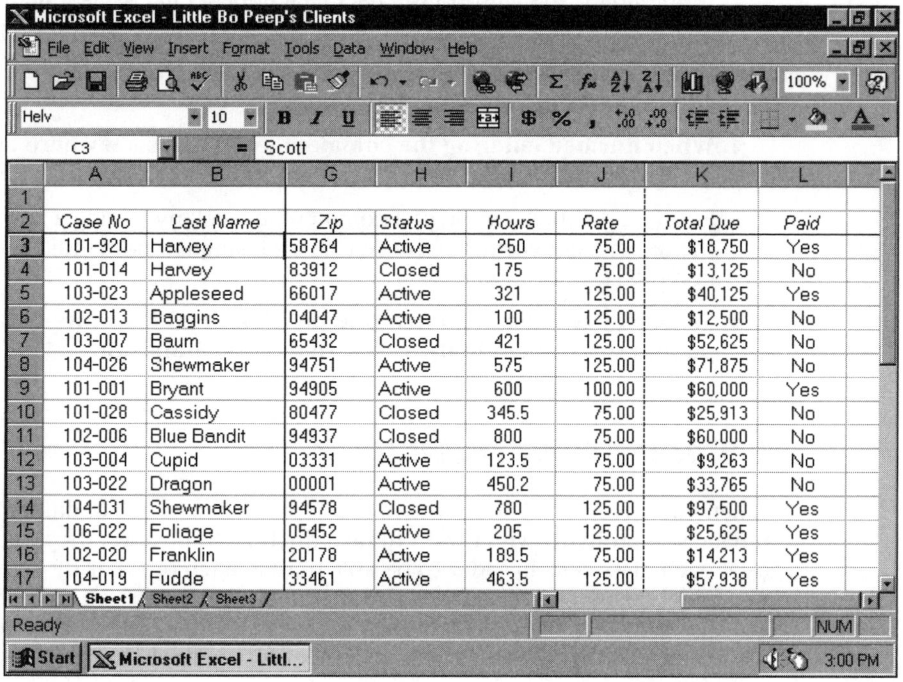

	A	B	G	H	I	J	K	L
2	Case No	Last Name	Zip	Status	Hours	Rate	Total Due	Paid
3	101-920	Harvey	58764	Active	250	75.00	$18,750	Yes
4	101-014	Harvey	83912	Closed	175	75.00	$13,125	No
5	103-023	Appleseed	66017	Active	321	125.00	$40,125	Yes
6	102-013	Baggins	04047	Active	100	125.00	$12,500	No
7	103-007	Baum	65432	Closed	421	125.00	$52,625	No
8	104-026	Shewmaker	94751	Active	575	125.00	$71,875	No
9	101-001	Bryant	94905	Active	600	100.00	$60,000	Yes
10	101-028	Cassidy	80477	Closed	345.5	75.00	$25,913	No
11	102-006	Blue Bandit	94937	Closed	800	75.00	$60,000	No
12	103-004	Cupid	03331	Active	123.5	75.00	$9,263	No
13	103-022	Dragon	00001	Active	450.2	75.00	$33,765	No
14	104-031	Shewmaker	94578	Closed	780	125.00	$97,500	Yes
15	106-022	Foliage	05452	Active	205	125.00	$25,625	Yes
16	102-020	Franklin	20178	Active	189.5	75.00	$14,213	Yes
17	104-019	Fudde	33461	Active	463.5	125.00	$57,938	Yes

Figure 6-7: The Bo Peep clients list scrolled left to display columns G through L.

Electronic Sticky Notes

Excel lets you add text comments to particular cells in a worksheet. *Comments* act kind of like electronic pop-up versions of sticky notes. For example, you can add a comment to yourself to verify a particular figure before printing the worksheet or to remind yourself that a particular value is only an estimate (or even to remind yourself that it's your anniversary and to pick up a little something special for your spouse on the way home!).

In addition to using notes to remind yourself of something you've done or that still remains to be done, you can also use a note to mark your current place in a large worksheet. You can then use the note's location to quickly find your starting place the next time you work with that worksheet.

Adding a comment to a cell

To add a comment to a cell, follow these steps:

1. **Select the cell to which you want to add the comment.**

2. **Choose Insert⇨Comment on the menu bar.**

   A new text box appears (similar to the one shown in Figure 6-8). This text box contains the name of the user as it appears in the User name edit box on the General tab of the Options dialog box) and the insertion point located at the beginning of a new line right below the user name.

3. **Type the text of your comment in the text box.**

4. **When finished entering the comment text, click somewhere outside of the text box.**

   Excel marks the location of a comment in a cell by adding a tiny triangle in the upper-right corner of the cell. (This triangular note indicator appears in red on a color monitor.)

5. **To display the comment in a cell, position the thick white-cross mouse pointer somewhere in the cell with the note indicator.**

Comments in review

When you have a workbook whose sheets contain a bunch of different comments, you probably won't want to take the time to position the mouse pointer over each of its cells in order to be able to read each one. For those times, you need to choose View⇨Comments on the menu bar. When you choose this command, Excels displays all of the comments in the workbook while at the same time displaying the Reviewing toolbar (shown in Figure 6-9).

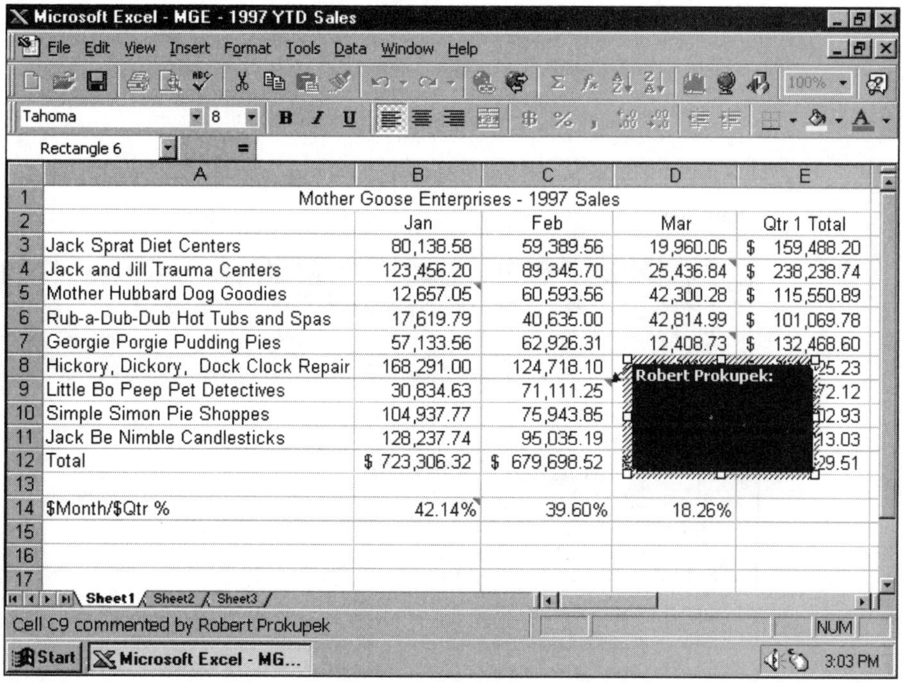

Figure 6-8:
Adding a
comment to
a cell in a
new text
box.

With the Reviewing toolbar open, you can then move back and forth from comment to comment by clicking its Next Comment and Previous Comment buttons. When you reach the last comment in the workbook, you will receive an alert box asking you if you want to continue reviewing the comments from the beginning (which you can do by simply choosing the OK button). After you're finished reviewing the comments in your workbook, you can hide their display by clicking the Show All Comments buttons on the Reviewing toolbar (or by again choosing View⇨Comments on the menu bar, if the Reviewing toolbar is no longer open).

Editing the comments in a worksheet

There are a couple of different methods for editing the contents of a comment, depending upon whether or not the comment is already displayed on the screen. If the comment is displayed in the worksheet, you can edit its contents by clicking the I-beam mouse pointer in its text box. Clicking the I-beam pointer locates the insertion point, while at the same time selecting the comment's text box (indicated by the appearance of a thick cross-hatched line with sizing handles around the text box). After making your editing changes, just click somewhere outside the comment's text box to deselect the comment.

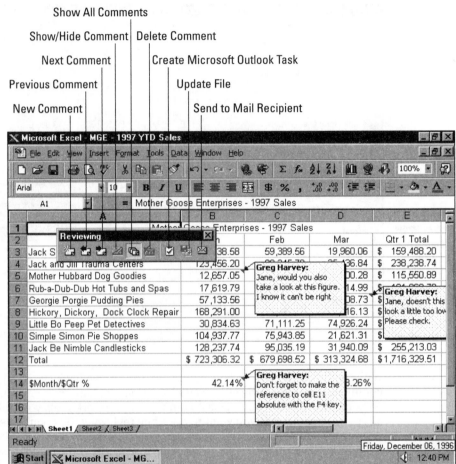

Figure 6-9:
The Reviewing toolbar.

If the comment is not displayed in the worksheet, you need to select its cell. After the cell pointer is in the cell whose comment needs editing, you can choose Insert⇪Edit Comment on the menu bar or Edit Comment on the cell's shortcut menu (opened by clicking the cell with the secondary mouse button).

To change the placement of a comment, you select the comment by clicking somewhere on it and then position the mouse pointer on one of the edges of its text box. When a four-headed arrow appears at the tip of the mouse pointer, you can drag the text box to a new place in the worksheet. Note that when you release the mouse button, Excel redraws the arrow connecting the comment's text box to the note indicator in the upper-right corner of the cell.

To change the size of a comment's text box, you select the comment and then position the mouse pointer on one of its sizing handles and then drag in the appropriate direction (away from the center of the box to increase its size or toward the center to decrease its size). When you release the mouse button, Excel redraws the comment's text box with the new shape and size. However, when changing the size and shape of a comment's text box, keep in mind that the program does *not* change the way that the comment text wraps within the text box (meaning that it's possible to obscure some of the text of your comment when resizing its text box).

To change the font of the comment text, you need to click the comment with the secondary mouse button and choose Format⇨Comment on the menu bar (or you can press Ctrl+1 like you do to open the Format Cells dialog box). When you do, Excel will open the Format Comment dialog box that contains a lone Font tab (with the same options as the Font tab of the Format Cells dialog box shown back in Figure 3-15). You can then use the options on the Font tab to change the font, font style, font size, or color of the text displayed in the selected comment.

To delete a comment, you need to select its cell in the worksheet and then choose Edit⇨Clear⇨Comments on the menu bar or choose Delete Comment on the cell's shortcut menu. Excel removes the comment along with the note indicator from the selected cell.

Note that you can change the background color of a comment's text box or select a new shape or shading for the text box by using the buttons on the Drawing toolbar. For information on how to identify and use its buttons, see "Telling all with a text box" in Chapter 8.

Getting your comments in print

When printing a worksheet, you can print the comments along with the selected worksheet data by selecting the Comments check box in the Sheet tab of the Page Setup dialog box. (Refer to "Sorting out the sheet settings" in Chapter 5 for details on choosing between the At end of sheet and As displayed on sheet settings.)

The Cell Name Game

By assigning descriptive names to cells and cell ranges, you can go a long way toward keeping on top of the location of important information in a worksheet. Rather than trying to associate random cell coordinates with specific information, you just have to remember a name. And, best of all, after you name a cell or cell range, you can use this name with the Go To feature.

If I only had a name . . .

When assigning range names to a cell or cell range, you need to follow a few guidelines:

- ✔ Range names must begin with a letter of the alphabet, not a number. For example, instead of *97Profit*, use *Profit97*.

- ✔ Range names cannot contain spaces. Instead of a space, use the underscore (Shift+hyphen) to tie the parts of the name together. For example, instead of *Profit 97*, use *Profit_97*.

- ✔ Range names cannot correspond to cell coordinates in the worksheet. For example, you can't name a cell *Q1* because this is a valid cell coordinate. Instead, use something like *Q1_sales*.

To name a cell or cell range in a worksheet:

1. **Select the cell or cell range that you want to name.**

2. **Click the cell address in the Name Box on the formula bar.**

   Excel selects the cell address in the Name Box.

3. **Type the name for the selected cell or cell range in the Name Box.**

   When typing the range name, you must follow Excel's naming conventions: Refer to the bulleted list of cell-name dos and don'ts, earlier in this section for details.

4. **Press the Enter key.**

To select a named cell or range in a worksheet, click the range name on the Name Box pop-up menu. To open this pop-up menu, click the pop-up button that appears to the right of the cell address on the formula bar.

Note that you can also accomplish the same thing by pressing F5 or choosing Edit⇨Go To on the menu bar. The Go To dialog box appears (see Figure 6-10). Double-click the desired range name in the Go to list box (alternatively, select the name and click OK or press Enter). Excel moves the cell pointer directly to the named cell. If you selected a cell range, all the cells in that range are selected.

Name that formula!

Cell names are not only a great way to identify and find cells and cell ranges in your spreadsheet but also a great way to make out the purpose of your formulas. For example, say that you have a simple formula in cell K3 that calculates the total due by multiplying the hours you worked for the client (in cell I3) by the client's hourly rate (in cell J3). Normally, this formula would be entered in cell K3 as

```
=I3*J3
```

However, if you assign the name Hours to cell I3 and the name Rate to cell J3, you could then enter the formula as

```
=Hours*Rate
```

in cell K3. I don't think there's anyone who would dispute that the formula =Hours*Rate is much easier to understand than =I3*J3.

To enter a formula using cell names rather than cell references, follow these steps (see Chapter 2 if you need to brush up on how to create formulas):

1. **Name your cells as described earlier in this section.**

   For this example, give the name Hours to cell I3 and the name Rate to cell J3.

2. **Place the cell pointer in the cell where the formula is to appear.**

   For this example, put the cell pointer in cell K3.

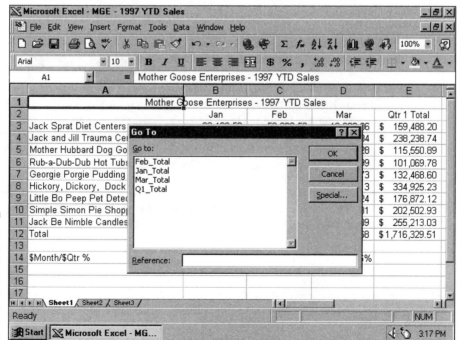

Figure 6-10:
Selecting a cell by choosing its range name in the Go To dialog box.

3. **Type = (equal sign) to start the formula.**

4. **Select the first cell referenced in the formula by selecting its cell name on the formula bar drop-down list (as described in the previous section).**

   For this example, you select cell I3 by selecting its cell name, Hours, on the drop-down list.

5. **Type the arithmetic operator used in the formula.**

   For this example, you would type * (asterisk) for multiplication. (Refer to Chapter 2 for a list of the other arithmetic operators.)

6. **Select the second cell referenced in the formula by selecting its cell name on the formula bar drop-down list (as described in the previous section).**

   For this example, you select cell J3 by selecting its cell name, Rate, on the drop-down list.

7. **Click the Enter box or press Enter to complete the formula.**

   In this example, Excel enters the formula =Hours*Rate in cell K3.

Note that you can't use the fill handle to copy a formula that uses cell names, rather than cell addresses, to other cells in a column or row that perform the same function (see "Formulas on AutoFill" in Chapter 4). When you copy an original formula that uses names rather than addresses, Excel copies the original formula without adjusting its cell references to the new rows and columns.

Naming formulas with data table headings

In Excel 97, when working with a traditional data table that contains row and columns headings (like the one shown in Figure 6-11), you can use the table's row and column headings in place of cell addresses to identify the cells used in your formulas. This feature not only eliminates the need for assigning range names to the cells but also ensures that these row- and column-heading labels appear in the copies you make of the original formula!

Figures 6-11 and 6-12 illustrate how easy it is to create a descriptive formula using the row and column headings from the data table and then copy that formula (and its use of the row and column headings) to other cells in the table.

Figure 6-11 shows a simple data table that computes the sales price for a number of pies sold by the Georgie Porgie Pudding Pies company. The first column of the table contains the row headings that identify each type of pie that is to be put on sale. The second column contains the retail prices for each type of pie, and the third column contains discount percentages. The fourth column of this data table contains the sale prices of each type of pie. To compute the sales price of each type of pie, you need to create a formula that subtracts the discount amount (calculated by multiplying the retail price of the pie by the discount percentage) from the retail price.

To create the first sale price formula in cell D5 using the row and column headings, I had to type in the entire formula (there's no way you can point to the labels in the data table — you only succeed in selecting cell addresses). In place of the address of the cell containing the retail price value (cell B5 in this example) and the cell with the discount percentage (C5), I entered the column heading followed by the row heading for each cell, as in:

```
=Retail Price Berry Pie-(Retail Price Berry Pie*Discount
Berry Pie)
```

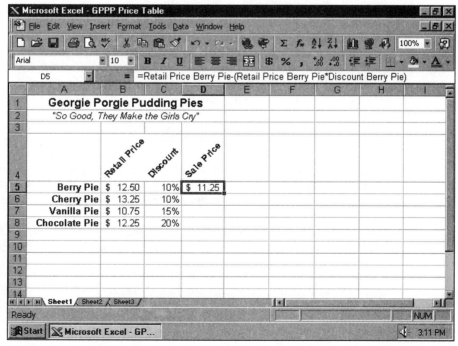

Figure 6-11: Creating a formula that uses the row and column headings in the data table.

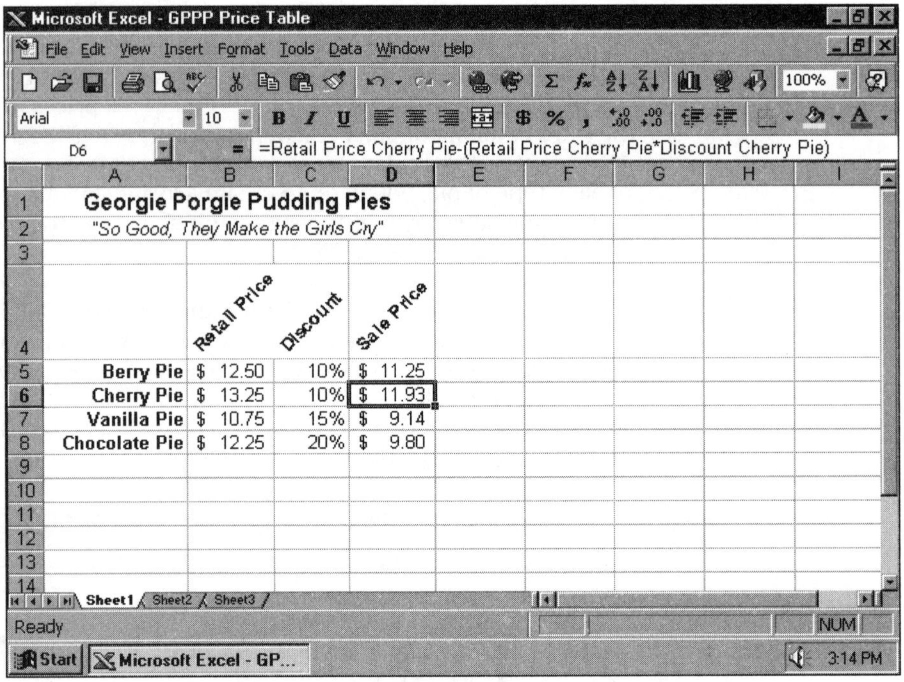

Figure 6-12:
Copying the
formula that
uses the
row and
column
headings in
the data
table.

Note that in using the row and column names in place of the cell address, I could have just as well preceded the column heading for each cell with the row, as in:

```
=Berry Pie Retail Price-(Berry Pie Retail Price*Berry Pie
Discount)
```

Figure 6-12 shows the data table after copying this original formula for calculating the sales price in cell D5 down to the cell range D6:D8 and then selecting cell D6. Note the contents of the formula copied to cell D6:

```
=Retail Price Cherry Pie-(Retail Price Cherry Pie*Discount
Cherry Pie)
```

When you create a formula using the row and column headings in a data table, these row and column headings are copied and automatically adjusted to suit the cells actually used in the new formula. So there you have it: an easy method for creating descriptive formulas (both in the original and its copies) without having to go to the trouble of "formally" naming the cells!

"Seek and Ye Shall Find . . ."

When all else fails, you can use Excel's Find feature to locate specific information in the worksheet. When you choose Edit⇨Find on the menu bar, or press Ctrl+F or Shift+F5, Excel opens the Find dialog box (see Figure 6-13). In the Find what edit box, enter the text or values you want to locate and then click the Find Next button or press Enter to start the search.

When you search for a text entry with the Find feature, be mindful of whether the text or number you enter in the Find what edit box is separate in its cell or occurs as part of another word or value. For example, if the characters "ca" are in the Find what edit box and the Find entire cells only check box is not selected, Excel finds

 ✔ the field name *Ca* in *Case No* cell A2

 ✔ the state code *CA* (for California) in cells F8, F9, and F11

 ✔ the *ca* that occurs in *Rebecca* in cell C31

If you checked the Find entire cells only check box in the Find dialog box before starting the search, Excel would not consider the *Ca* in *Case No* or the *ca* in *Rebecca* to be a match because both of these cases have other text surrounding the text you are searching for.

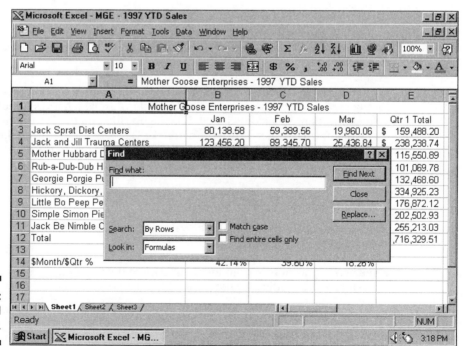

Figure 6-13:
The Find
dialog box.

When you search for text, you can also specify whether or not you want Excel to match the case you use (upper- or lowercase) when entering the search text in the Find what edit box. By default, Excel ignores case differences between text in cells of your worksheet and the search text you enter in the Find what edit box. To conduct a case-sensitive search, you need to select the Match case check box.

When you search for values in the worksheet, be mindful of the difference between formulas and values. For example, cell K24 of the Bo Peep clients list (refer to Figure 6-7) contains the value $15,000. (You can't see it on-screen, but trust me, it's there.) However, if you enter **15000** in the Find what edit box and press Enter to search for this value, Excel displays an alert box with the following message:

```
Cannot find matching data
```

instead of finding the value 15000 in cell K24. This is because the value in this cell is calculated by the following formula:

```
=I24*J24
```

and nowhere in that formula does the value 15000 show up. To get Excel to find the 15000s displayed in the cells of the worksheet, you need to choose Values in the Look in pop-up menu of the Find dialog box in place of the normally used Formulas option.

If you want to restrict the search to just the text or values in the text of the comments in the worksheet, you need to choose the Comments option in this pop-up menu.

If you don't know the exact spelling of the word or name, or the precise value or formula you're searching for, you can use *wildcards,* which are symbols that stand for missing or unknown text. Use the question mark (?) to stand for a single unknown character; use the asterisk (*) to stand for any number of missing characters. Suppose that you enter the following in the Find what edit box and choose the Values option in the Look in pop-up menu:

```
7*4
```

Excel stops at cells that contain the values *74, 704,* and *7,5234,* and even finds the text entry *782 4th Street.*

If you actually want to search for an asterisk in the worksheet rather than use the asterisk as a wildcard, precede it with a tilde (~), as follows:

```
~*4
```

This arrangement enables you to search the formulas in the worksheet for one that multiplies by the number 4 (remember that Excel uses the asterisk as the multiplication sign).

The following entry in the Fi_n_d what edit box finds cells that contain *Jan, January, June, Janet,* and so on.

```
J?n*
```

Normally, Excel searches only the current worksheet for the search text you enter. If you want the program to search all of the worksheets in the workbook, you must select all the worksheets prior to entering the search text in the Find dialog box and starting the search. To select all the worksheets in a workbook, you click one of the tabs at the bottom of the document window with the secondary mouse button and choose the _S_elect All Sheets command on the shortcut menu that appears. (See Chapter 7 for more on working with more than one worksheet in a workbook.)

When Excel locates a cell in the worksheet that contains the text or values you're searching for, it selects that cell while at the same time leaving the Find dialog box open (remember that you can move the Find dialog box if it obscures your view of the cell). To search for the next occurrence of the text or value, click the _F_ind Next button (the simplest way to do this is by pressing Enter).

Excel normally searches down the worksheet by rows. To search across the columns first, choose the By Columns option in the _S_earch pop-up menu. To reverse the search direction and revisit previous occurrences of matching cell entries, press the Shift key as you click the _F_ind Next button in the Find dialog box.

You Can Be Replaced!

If your purpose for finding a cell with a particular entry is so that you can change it, you can automate this process by choosing _E_dit➪_R_eplace instead of _E_dit➪_F_ind on the menu bar (Ctrl+H). After entering the text or value you want to replace in the Fi_n_d what edit box, enter the text or value you want entered as the replacement in the _R_eplace with edit box.

When you enter replacement text, enter it exactly as you want it to appear in the cell. In other words, if you replace all occurrences of *Jan* in the worksheet with *January,* enter the following in the _R_eplace with edit box:

```
January
```

Make sure that you use the capital J in the Replace with edit box, even though you can enter the following in the Find what edit box (providing you don't check the Match Case check box):

```
jan
```

After specifying what to replace and what to replace it with, you can have Excel replace occurrences in the worksheet on a case-by-case basis or globally. To replace all occurrences in a single operation, click the Replace All button.

Be careful with global search-and-replace operations; they can really mess up a worksheet in a hurry if you inadvertently replace values, parts of formulas, or characters in titles and headings that you hadn't intended to change. With this in mind, always follow one rule:

> Never undertake a global search-and-replace operation on an unsaved worksheet.

Also, verify whether or not the Find entire cells only check box is selected before you begin. You can end up with a lot of unwanted replacements if you leave this check box unselected when you really only want to replace entire cell entries (rather than matching parts in cell entries).

If you do make a mess, choose the Edit⇨Undo Replace command (Ctrl+Z) to restore the worksheet.

To see each occurrence before you replace it, click the Find Next button or press Enter. Excel selects the next cell with the text or value you entered in the Find what edit box. To have the program replace the selected text, click the Replace button. To skip this occurrence, click the Find Next button to continue the search. When you finish replacing occurrences, click the Close button to close the Replace dialog box.

You Can Be So Calculating

Locating information in a worksheet — although admittedly extremely important — is only a part of the story of keeping on top of the information in a worksheet. In really large workbooks that contain many completed worksheets, you may want to switch to manual recalculation so that you can control when the formulas in the worksheet are calculated. You need this kind of control when you find that Excel's recalculation of formulas each time you enter or change information in cells has slowed the program's response to a crawl. By holding off recalculations until you are ready to save or print the workbook, you find that you can work with Excel's worksheets without interminable delays.

To put the workbook on manual recalculation, choose Tools⇨Options on the menu bar and click the Calculation tab. Then select the Manual radio button in the Calculation area. When doing this, you probably won't want to remove the check mark from the Recalculate before save check box (not generally a very smart idea) so that Excel will still automatically recalculate all formulas before saving the workbook. By keeping this setting active, you are assured of saving only the most up-to-date values.

After switching to manual recalculation, Excel displays the message

```
Calculate
```

on the status bar whenever you make a change to the worksheet that somehow affects the current values of its formulas. Whenever you see Calculate on the status bar, this is the signal you need to bring the formulas up to date before saving the workbook (as you would before printing its worksheets).

To recalculate the formulas in a workbook when calculation is on manual, you press F9 or Ctrl+= (equal sign) or click the Calc Now (F9) button in the Calculation tab of the Options dialog box.

Excel then recalculates the formulas in all the worksheets in your workbook. If you've only made changes to the current worksheet and don't want to wait around for Excel to recalculate every other worksheet in the workbook, you can restrict the recalculation to the current worksheet by clicking the Calc Sheet button on the Calculation tab of the Options dialog box or pressing Shift+F9.

Putting On the Protection

After you've more or less finalized a worksheet by checking out its formulas and proofing its text, you often want to guard against any unplanned changes by protecting the document.

Each cell in the worksheet can be *locked* or *unlocked*. By default, Excel locks all the cells in a worksheet so that, when you follow these steps, Excel locks the whole thing up tighter than a drum.

1. **Choose Tools⇨Protection⇨Protect Sheet on the menu bar.**

   Excel opens the Protect Sheet dialog box where the Contents, Objects, and Scenarios check boxes are all selected.

2. **If you want to assign a password that must be supplied before you can remove the protection from the worksheet, type the password in the Password (optional) edit box.**

3. Click OK or press Enter.

If you typed a password in the Password (optional) edit box, Excel opens the Confirm Password dialog box. Reenter the password in the Reenter password to proceed edit box exactly as you typed it into the Password (optional) edit box in the Protect Sheet dialog box and click OK or press Enter.

If you want to go a step further and protect the layout of the worksheets in the workbook, you protect the entire workbook as follows:

1. Choose Tools⇨Protection⇨Protect Workbook on the menu bar.

Excel opens the Protect Workbook dialog box where the Structure check box is selected and the Windows check box is not selected. With the Structure check box selected, Excel won't let you mess around with the sheets in the workbook (by deleting them or rearranging them). If you want to protect any windows that you've set up (as described at the beginning of this chapter), you need to select the Windows check box as well.

2. If you want to assign a password that must be supplied before you can remove the protection from the worksheet, type the password in the Password (optional) edit box.

3. Click OK or press Enter.

If you typed a password in the Password (optional) edit box, Excel opens the Confirm Password dialog box. Reenter the password in the Reenter password to proceed edit box exactly as you typed it into the Password (optional) edit box in the Protect Sheet dialog box and click OK or press Enter.

Selecting the Protect Sheet command makes it impossible to make further changes to the contents of any of the locked cells in that worksheet. Selecting the Protect Workbook command makes it impossible to make further changes to the layout of the worksheets in that workbook.

Excel displays an alert dialog box with the following message when you try to edit or replace an entry in a locked cell:

```
Locked cells cannot be changed
```

Usually, your intention in protecting a worksheet or an entire workbook is not to prevent *all* changes but to prevent changes in certain areas of the worksheet. For example, in a budget worksheet, you may want to protect all the cells that contain headings and formulas but allow changes in all the cells where you enter the budgeted amounts. That way, you can't inadvertently wipe out a title or formula in the worksheet simply by entering a value in the wrong column or row (not an uncommon occurrence).

To leave certain cells unlocked so that you can still change them after protecting the worksheet or workbook, follow these steps:

1. **Select the cells you want to still be able to change after turning on the worksheet or workbook protection.**

2. **Open the Format Cells dialog box by choosing Format⇨Cells on the menu bar (Ctrl+1); then select the Protection tab.**

3. **Remove the check mark from the Locked check box in the Protection tab of the Format Cells dialog box; then click OK or press Enter.**

4. **Turn on protection in the worksheet by choosing Tools⇨Protection⇨ Protect Sheet on the menu bar and then click OK or press Enter in the Protect Sheet dialog box.**

To remove protection from the current worksheet or workbook document so that you can once again make changes to its cells (be they locked or unlocked), choose Tools⇨Protection and then choose either the Unprotect Sheet or the Unprotect Workbook command on the cascading menu. If you assigned a password when protecting the worksheet or workbook, you must then reproduce the password exactly as you assigned it (including any case differences) in the Password edit box of the Unprotect Sheet or Unprotect Workbook dialog box.

Be very careful with passwords. If you forget the password for a worksheet, you cannot ever again change any locked cells and you cannot unlock any more cells in the worksheet. If you forget the password for a workbook, you can make no further changes to the layout of its worksheets.

Chapter 7
Maintaining Multiple Worksheets

• •

In This Chapter

▶ Moving from sheet to sheet in your workbook

▶ Adding more sheets to a workbook

▶ Deleting sheets from a workbook

▶ Selecting a bunch of sheets for editing as a group

▶ Naming sheet tabs something else besides Sheet1, Sheet2, and so on

▶ Putting the sheets in a different order in a workbook

▶ Displaying parts of different sheets on the same screen

▶ Copying or moving sheets from one workbook to another

▶ Creating formulas that refer to values on different worksheets in a workbook

• •

*W*hen you're brand-new to spreadsheets, you have enough trouble keeping track of a single worksheet — let alone three worksheets — and the very thought of working with more than one is a little more than you can take. However, as soon as you get a little experience under your belt, you find that working with more than one worksheet in a workbook is no more taxing than working with just a single worksheet.

Don't confuse the term *workbook* with *worksheet*. The workbook forms the document (file) that you open and save as you work. Each workbook (file) normally contains three blank worksheets. These worksheets are like the loose-leaf pages in a notebook binder from which you can delete or to which you can add as you need. To help you keep track of the worksheets in your workbook and navigate between them, Excel provides sheet tabs (Sheet1 through Sheet3) that are kinda like tab dividers in a loose-leaf notebook.

Juggling Worksheets

You need to see *how* to work with more than one worksheet in a workbook, but it's also important to know *why* you'd want to do such a crazy thing in the first place. The most common situation is, of course, when you have a bunch of worksheets that are somehow related to each other and, therefore, naturally belong together in the same workbook. For example, take the case of Mother Goose Enterprises with its different companies: Jack Sprat Diet Centers, Jack and Jill Trauma Centers, Mother Hubbard Dog Goodies; Rub-a-Dub-Dub Hot Tubs and Spas; Georgie Porgie Pudding Pies; Hickory, Dickory, Dock Clock Repair; Little Bo Peep Pet Detectives; Simple Simon Pie Shoppes; and Jack Be Nimble Candlesticks. To keep track of the annual sales for all these companies, you could create a workbook containing a worksheet for each of the nine different companies.

By keeping the sales figures for each company in a different sheet of the same workbook, you gain all of the following benefits:

- ✓ You can enter the stuff that's needed in all the sales worksheets (if their sheet tabs are selected) just by typing it once into the first worksheet (see "Editing en masse," later in this chapter).

- ✓ In order to help you build the worksheet for the first company's sales, you can attach *macros* to the current workbook so that they are readily available when you create the worksheets for the other companies (see Chapter 12 for details on recording macros in the current workbook).

- ✓ You can quickly compare the sales of one company to the sales of another (see "Opening Windows on Your Worksheets," later in this chapter).

- ✓ You can print all of the sales information for each store as a single report in one printing operation. (Refer to Chapter 5 for specifics on printing an entire workbook or particular worksheets in a workbook.)

- ✓ You can easily create charts that compare certain sales data from different worksheets (see Chapter 8 for details).

- ✓ You can easily set up a summary worksheet with formulas that total the quarterly and annual sales for all nine companies (see "To Sum Up . . ." later in this chapter).

Sliding between the sheets

Each workbook that you create contains three worksheets, rather predictably named Sheet1 through Sheet3. In typical Excel fashion, these names appear on tabs at the bottom of the workbook window. To go from one worksheet to another, you simply click the tab that contains the name of the sheet you want to see. Excel then brings that worksheet to the top of the stack, displaying its information in the current workbook window. You can always tell which worksheet is current because its name is displayed in bold type on the tab and its tab appears without any dividing line as an extension of the current worksheet.

The only problem with moving to a new sheet by clicking its sheet tab occurs when you add so many worksheets to a workbook (as described later in this chapter in the section called "Don't Short-Sheet Me!") that not all the sheet tabs are visible at any one time and the sheet tab you want to click is not visible in the workbook. To deal with this problem, Excel provides tab scrolling buttons (see Figure 7-1) that you can use to bring new sheet tabs into view.

 ✔ Click the tab scroll button with the triangle pointing right to bring the next unseen tab of the sheet on the right into view.

 ✔ Click the tab scroll button with the triangle pointing left to bring the next unseen tab of the sheet on the left into view.

 ✔ Click the tab scroll button with the triangle pointing right to the vertical bar to bring the last group of sheet tabs, including the very last tab, into view.

 ✔ Click the tab scroll button with the triangle pointing left to the vertical bar to bring the first group of sheet tabs, including the very first tab, into view.

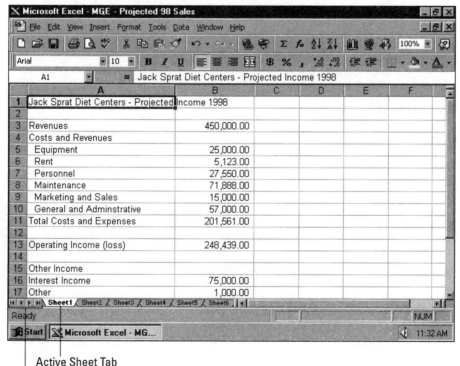

Figure 7-1:
Using the
sheet tab
scrolling
buttons to
bring new
sheet tabs
into view.

Active Sheet Tab

Tab Scrolling Buttons

Just don't forget that scrolling the sheet tab you want into view is not the same thing as *selecting* it: You still need to click the tab for the desired sheet to bring it to the front of the stack.

To make it easier to find the sheet tab you want to select without having to do an inordinate amount of tab scrolling, you can drag the tab split bar (see Figure 7-2) to the right to reveal more sheet tabs (consequently making the horizontal scroll bar shorter). If you don't care at all about using the horizontal scroll bar, you can maximize the number of sheet tabs in view by actually getting rid of this scroll bar. To do this, you drag the tab split bar to the right until it's right up against the vertical split bar, which gives you a view of about 12 sheet tabs at a time (on a standard 14-inch monitor in a resolution of 640 by 480 pixels).

When you decide that you then want to restore the horizontal scroll bar to its normal length, you can either manually drag the tab split bar to the left or simply double-click it.

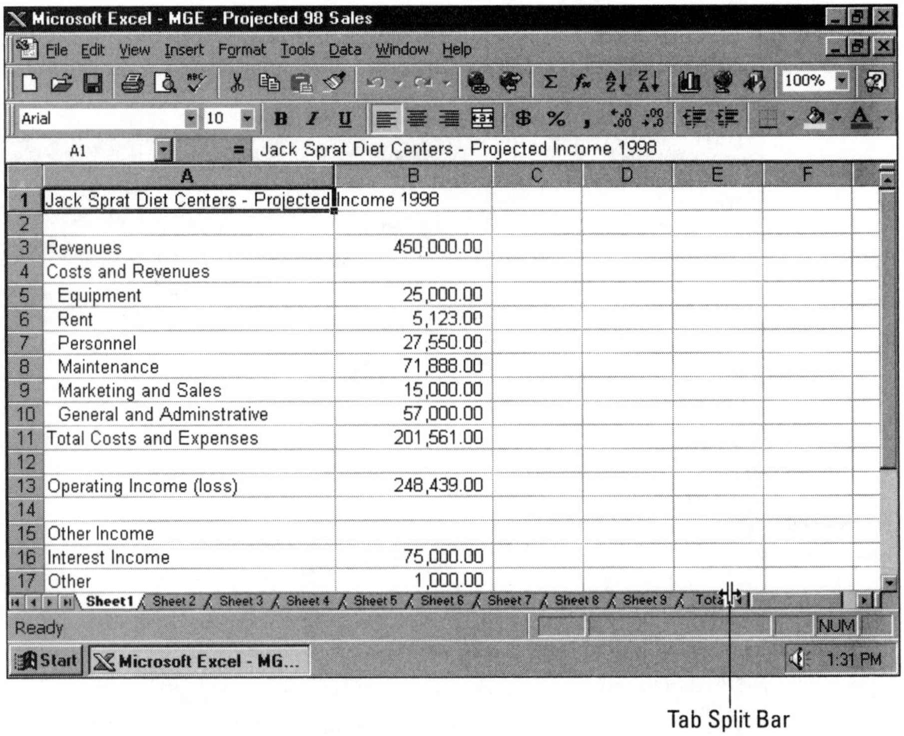

Figure 7-2:
Using the tab split bar to display more sheet tabs by making the horizontal scroll bar shorter.

Tab Split Bar

Going sheet to sheet via the keyboard

You can forget all about the darned tab scrolling buttons and sheet tabs and just go back and forth through the sheets in a workbook with the keyboard. To move to the next worksheet in a workbook, press Ctrl+PgDn. To move to the previous worksheet in a workbook, press Ctrl+PgUp. The nice thing about Ctrl+PgDn and Ctrl+PgUp is that these keystroke shortcuts work whether or not the next or previous sheet tab is currently displayed in the workbook window!

Editing en masse

Each time you click a sheet tab, you select that worksheet and make it active, enabling you to make whatever changes are necessary to its cells. There are times, however, when you want to select bunches of worksheets so that you can make the same editing changes to all of them simultaneously. When multiple worksheets are selected, any editing change you make to the current worksheet, such as entering information in cells or deleting stuff from them, affects the same cells in all of the selected sheets in exactly the same way.

In other words, say you needed to set up three worksheets in a new workbook, all of which contain the names of the 12 months in row 3 starting in column B. Prior to entering January in cell B3 and then using the AutoFill handle to fill in the rest of the 11 months across row 3, you would select all three worksheets (say Sheet1, Sheet2, and Sheet3 for argument's sake). That way, Excel would insert the names of the 12 months in row 3 of all three selected worksheets just by your entering them once in the third row of the first sheet (pretty slick, huh?).

Likewise, say you have another workbook where you need to get rid of Sheet2 and Sheet3. Instead of clicking Sheet2, choosing Edit⇨Delete Sheet, and then clicking Sheet3 and repeating the Edit⇨Delete Sheet command, you can select both worksheets and then zap them out of existence in one fell swoop by choosing the Edit⇨Delete Sheet command.

To select a bunch of worksheets in a workbook, you have the following choices:

- ✔ To select a group of neighboring worksheets, click the first sheet tab and then scroll the sheet tabs until you see the tab of the last worksheet you want to select. Hold the Shift key as you click the last sheet tab to select all of the tabs in between — the old shift-click method applied to worksheet tabs.

- ✔ To select a group of non-neighboring worksheets, click the first sheet tab and then hold down the Ctrl key as you click the tabs of the other sheets to be selected.

Excel shows you which worksheets are selected by turning their sheet tabs white (although only the active sheet's tab name appears in bold) and displaying [Group] after the filename of the workbook on the Excel window's title bar.

To deselect the group of worksheets when you've finished your "group editing," you simply click a nonselected (that is, gray) worksheet tab. You can also deselect all the selected worksheets by Shift+clicking the active sheet or by choosing the Ungroup Sheets command on any tab's shortcut menu.

Don't Short-Sheet Me!

For some of you, the three worksheets automatically put into each new workbook that you start are as many as you would ever, ever need (or want) to use. For others of you, a measly three worksheets might seldom, if ever, be sufficient for the workbooks you create (for instance, say your company operates in ten locations, or you routinely create budgets for 20 different departments or track expenses for 40 account representatives).

Excel makes it easy to insert additional worksheets in a workbook or remove those that you don't need. To insert a new worksheet in the workbook, follow these steps:

1. **Select the tab of the sheet where you want Excel to insert the new worksheet.**

2. **Choose Insert⇨Worksheet on the menu bar or choose Insert on the sheet tab's shortcut menu.**

   If you choose the Insert⇨Worksheet command, Excel inserts a new worksheet and gives its tab the next available number (like Sheet4). If you choose the Insert command on the sheet tab's shortcut menu, Excel opens the Insert dialog box where you can specify the type of sheet to insert (such as Worksheet, Chart, MS Excel 4.0 Macro, or MS Excel 5.0 dialog), and you need to proceed to step 3.

3. **Make sure that the Worksheet icon on the General tab of the Insert dialog box is selected and then click OK or press Enter.**

To insert a bunch of new worksheets in a row in the workbook, select a group with the same number of tabs as the number of new worksheets you want to add, starting with the tab where the new worksheets are to be inserted. Next, choose Insert⇨Worksheet on the menu bar or choose Insert on the tab's shortcut menu. Finally, click OK in the Insert dialog box or press Enter.

To delete a worksheet from the workbook, follow these steps:

1. **Click the tab of the worksheet you want to delete.**

2. **Choose Edit⇨Delete Sheet on the Edit menu or choose Delete on the tab's shortcut menu.**

   Excel then displays a scary message in an alert box about how you're going to permanently delete the selected sheets.

3. **Go ahead and click the OK button or press Enter if you're really sure that you want to zap the entire sheet.**

   Just keep in mind that this is one of those situations where Undo is powerless to put things right by restoring the deleted sheet to the workbook.

To delete a bunch of worksheets from the workbook, select all the worksheets you want to delete and choose Edit⇨Delete Sheet on the menu bar or choose Delete on the tab's shortcut menu. Then, if you're sure that none of the worksheets will be missed, click OK or press Enter when the alert dialog box appears.

If you find that you're constantly having to monkey around with the number of worksheets in a workbook, either by adding new worksheets or deleting a bunch, you might want to think about changing the default number of worksheets in a workbook. To change the magic number of three sheets to a more realistic number for your needs, choose Tools⇨Options to open the Options dialog box, select the General tab, and enter a new number in the Sheets in new workbook edit box or select a new number with the spinner buttons before you click OK.

A sheet by any other name . . .

Let's be honest: The sheet names that Excel comes up with for the tabs in a workbook (Sheet1 through Sheet3) are, to put it mildly, not very original — and are certainly not descriptive of their function in life! Luckily, you can easily rename a worksheet tab to whatever helps you remember what you put on the worksheet (provided that this descriptive name is no longer than 31 characters).

To rename a worksheet tab, just follow these steps:

1. **Double-click the sheet tab with the primary mouse button or choose the Rename command on the sheet tab's shortcut menu (opened by clicking on the sheet tab with the secondary mouse button).**

   This selects the current name on the sheet tab.

2. **Replace the current name on the sheet tab by typing in the new sheet name.**

3. **Press Enter.**

   Excel displays the new sheet name on its tab at the bottom of the workbook window.

Getting your sheets in order

Sometimes, you may find that you need to change the order in which the sheets appear in the workbook. Excel makes this possible by letting you drag the tab of the sheet you want to arrange in the workbook to the place where it should be inserted. As you drag the tab, the pointer changes to a sheet icon with an arrowhead on it, and the program marks your progress among the sheet tabs (see Figures 7-3 and 7-4 for example). When you release the mouse button, Excel reorders the worksheets in the workbook by inserting the sheet at the place where you dropped the tab off.

If you hold down the Ctrl key as you drag the tab, Excel inserts a *copy* of the worksheet at the place where you release the mouse button. You can tell that Excel is copying the sheet, rather than just moving it in the workbook, because the pointer shows a plus on the sheet icon containing the arrowhead. When you

Figure 7-3: Reordering the sheets in the MGE-1998 Projected Income workbook by dragging the Total Income sheet tab to the front.

	X Microsoft Excel - MGE - Projected 98 Sales							
	File Edit View Insert Format Tools Data Window Help							
	A1	=	Mother Goose Enterprises - 1998 Projected Income					
	A	B	C	D	E	F	G	
1	Mother Goose Enterprises - 1998 Projected Income							
2								
3	Revenues	6,681,450.78						
4	Costs and Revenues							
5	Equipment	882,387.00						
6	Rent	1,287,923.88						
7	Personnel	346,452.79						
8	Maintenance	616,404.88						
9	Marketing and Sales	892,856.06						
10	General and Administrative	219,925.60						
11	Total Costs and Expenses	4,245,950.21						
12								
13	Operating Income (loss)	2,435,500.57						
14								
15	Other Income							
16	Interest Income	218,430.60						
17	Other	103,769.00						

Sprat Diet Ctr.   J&J Trauma Ctr.   Hubbard Dog Goodies   R-D-D Hot Tubs   Porgie Puddin

Ready   NUM

Start   Microsoft Excel - MG...   12:07 PM

Short and sweet (sheet names)

Although Excel allows up to 31 characters (including spaces) for a sheet name, you're gonna want to keep your sheet names much briefer for two reasons:

✔ First, the longer the name, the longer the sheet tab. And the longer the sheet tab, the fewer tabs that can be displayed. And the fewer the tabs, the more tab scrolling you'll have to do to select the sheets you want to work with.

✔ Second, should you start creating formulas that use cells in different worksheets (see "To Sum Up. . .," later in this chapter, for an

example of this), Excel uses the sheet name as part of the cell reference in the formula (how else could Excel keep straight the value in cell C1 on Sheet1 from the value in cell C1 on Sheet2!). Therefore, if your sheet names are long, you'll end up with unwieldy formulas in the cells and on the formula bar even when you're dealing with simple formulas that only refer to cells in a couple of different worksheets.

So remember: As a general rule, the fewer characters in a sheet name, the better.

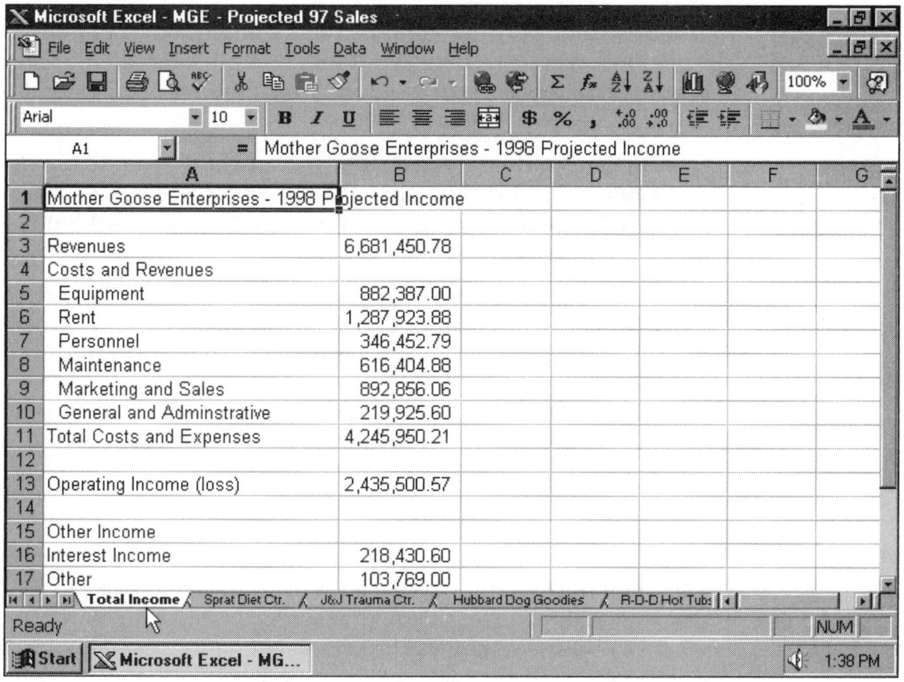

Figure 7-4:
The worksheet after moving the Total Income sheet to the front of the workbook.

release the mouse button, Excel inserts the copy in the workbook, which is designated by the addition of (2) after the tab name. For instance, if you copy Sheet5 to another place in the workbook, the sheet tab of the copy is named Sheet5 (2). You can then rename the tab to something civilized (see "A sheet by any other name . . ." earlier in this chapter, for details).

Opening Windows on Your Worksheets

Just as you can split up a single worksheet into window panes so that you can view and compare different parts of that same sheet on the screen (see Chapter 6), you can split up a single workbook into worksheet windows and then arrange the windows so that you can view different parts of each worksheet on the screen.

To open up the worksheets that you want to compare in different windows, you simply insert new workbook windows (in addition to the one that Excel automatically opens when you open the workbook file itself) and then select the worksheet that you want displayed in the new window. You can accomplish this with the following steps:

1. **Choose Window⇨New Window on the menu bar to create a second worksheet window; then click the tab of the worksheet that you want displayed in this second window (indicated by the :2 added to the end of the filename in the title bar).**

2. **Choose the Window⇨New Window command again to create a third worksheet window; then click the tab of the worksheet that you want displayed in this third window (indicated by the :3 added to the end of the filename in the title bar).**

3. **Continue in this manner, using the Window⇨New Window command to create a new window and then selecting the tab of the worksheet to be displayed in that window for each worksheet that you want to compare.**

4. **Choose the Window⇨Arrange command and select one of the Arrange options (as described next); then click OK or press Enter.**

When you open the Arrange Windows dialog box, you are presented with the following options:

✔ **The Tiled radio button:** to have Excel arrange and size the windows so that they all fit side by side on the screen in the order in which they were opened. (Figure 7-5 shows the screen after choosing the Windows of active workbook check box and choosing the Tiled radio button, when three worksheet windows are open.)

✔ **The Horizontal radio button:** to have Excel size the windows equally and then place them one above the other. (Figure 7-6 shows the screen after choosing the Windows of active workbook check box and choosing the Horizontal radio button, when three worksheet windows are open.)

✔ **The Vertical radio button:** to have Excel size the windows equally and then place them next to each other. (Figure 7-7 shows the screen after choosing the Windows of active workbook check box and choosing the Vertical radio button, when three worksheet windows are open.)

✔ **The Cascade radio button:** to have Excel arrange and size the windows so that they overlap one another with only their title bars showing. (Figure 7-8 shows the screen after choosing the Windows of active workbook check box and choosing the Cascade radio button, when three worksheet windows are open).

✔ **The Windows of active workbook check box:** to have Excel show only the windows that you've opened in the current workbook (otherwise, the program will also display all the windows in any other workbooks you have open — yes, it is possible to open more than one workbook as well as more than one window within each open workbook, provided that your computer has enough memory and you have enough stamina to keep track of all that information).

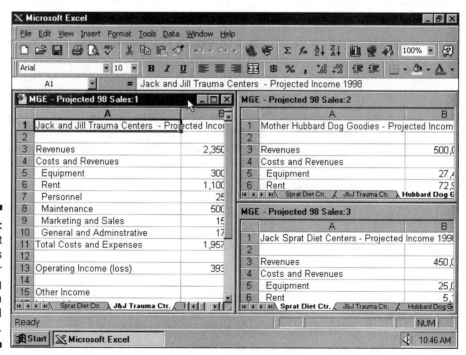

Figure 7-5: Worksheet windows after arranging them with the Tiled radio button.

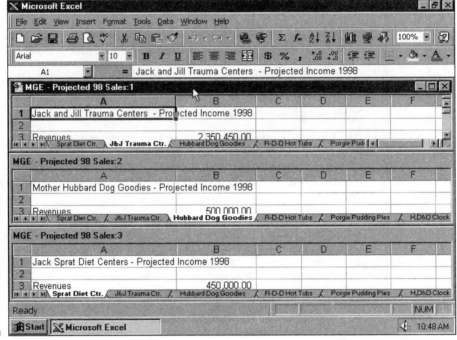

Figure 7-6:
Worksheet windows after arranging them with the Horizontal radio button.

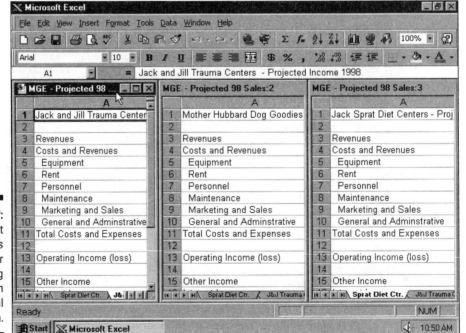

Figure 7-7:
Worksheet windows after arranging them with the Vertical radio button.

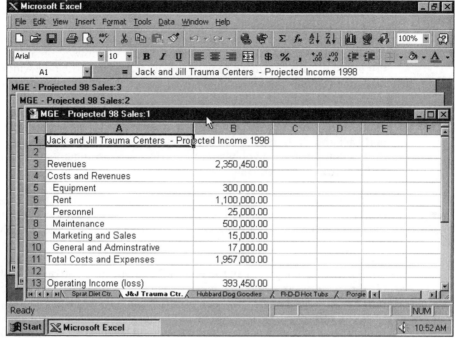

After the windows are placed in one arrangement or another, you can activate the one you want to use (if it's not already selected) by clicking it (in the case of the cascade arrangement, you need to click the window's title bar).

When you click a worksheet window that has been tiled or placed in the horizontal or vertical arrangement, Excel indicates that the window is selected by highlighting its title bar and adding scroll bars to the window. When you click the title bar of a worksheet window that has been placed in the cascade arrangement, the program displays the window on the top of the stack as well as highlighting its title bar and adding scroll bars.

You can temporarily zoom the window up to full size by clicking the Maximize button on the window's title bar. When you finish the work you need to do in the full-size worksheet window, return it to its previous arrangement by clicking the window's Restore button.

To select the next tiled, horizontal, or vertical window on the screen or display the next window in a cascade arrangement with the keyboard, press Ctrl+F6. To select the previous tiled, horizontal, or vertical window or display the previous window in a cascade arrangement, press Ctrl+Shift+F6. Note that these keystrokes work to select the next and previous worksheet window even when the windows are maximized in the Excel program window.

If you close one of the windows you've arranged by its Close button (the one with the X in the upper-right corner) or by pressing Ctrl+W, Excel does not automatically resize the other open windows to fill in the gap. Likewise, if you create another window with the Window⇨New Window command, Excel does not automatically arrange it in with the others (in fact, the new window just sits on top of the other open windows).

To fill in the gap created by closing a window or to integrate a newly opened window into the current arrangement, open the Arrange Windows dialog box and click the OK button or press Enter. (The same radio button you clicked last time is still selected; if you want to choose a new arrangement, click the new radio button before you click OK.)

Don't try to close a particular worksheet window with the File⇨Close command on the menu bar because you'll only succeed in closing the entire workbook file, while at the same time getting rid of all the worksheet windows you've created.

When you save your workbook, Excel saves the current window-arrangement as part of the file along with all the rest of the changes. If you don't want the current window arrangement saved, close all but one of the windows (by double-clicking their Control-menu buttons or selecting their windows and then pressing Ctrl+W); then click that last window's Maximize button and select the tab of the worksheet that you want displayed the next time you open the workbook before saving the file.

Passing Sheets in the Night

In some situations, you need to move a particular worksheet or copy it from one workbook to another. To move or copy worksheets between workbooks, you follow these steps:

1. **Open both workbooks with the worksheet(s) you want to move or copy and the workbook that is to contain the moved or copied worksheet(s).**

   Use the Open tool on the Standard toolbar or choose the File⇨Open command (Ctrl+O) to open the workbooks.

2. **Select the workbook that contains the worksheet(s) that you want to move or copy.**

   To select the workbook with the sheet(s) to be moved or copied, choose its name on the Window pull-down menu.

3. Select the worksheet(s) you want to move or copy.

To select a single worksheet, click its sheet tab. To select a group of neighboring sheets, click the first tab and then hold down Shift as you click the last tab. To select various nonadjacent sheets, click the first tab and then hold down Ctrl as you click each of the other sheet tabs.

4. Choose the Edit⇨Move or Copy Sheet command on the menu bar or choose the Move or Copy command on a tab's shortcut menu.

Excel opens up the Move or Copy dialog box (similar to the one shown in Figure 7-9) in which you indicate whether you want to move or copy the selected sheet(s) and where to move or copy them to.

5. In the To book drop-down list box, select the name of the workbook you want to copy or move the worksheets to.

If you want to move or copy the selected worksheet(s) to a new workbook rather than to an existing one that you have open, select the (new book) option that appears at the very top of the To book drop-down list box.

6. In the Before sheet list box, select the name of the sheet that the worksheet(s) you're about to move or copy should precede.

7. Select the Create a copy check box to copy the selected worksheet(s) to the designated workbook (rather than move them).

8. Click the OK button or press Enter to complete the move or copy operation.

Figure 7-9:
The Move or Copy dialog box where you select the workbook to move or copy the selected sheets to.

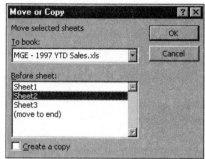

If you prefer a more direct approach, you can move or copy sheets between open workbooks by dragging their sheet tabs from one workbook window to another. Note that this method works with a bunch of sheets as well as with a single sheet; just be sure that you've selected all their sheet tabs before you begin the drag-and-drop procedure.

To drag a worksheet from one workbook to another, you must open both workbooks and then use the Window⇨Arrange command on the menu bar and select an arrangement (such as Horizontal or Vertical to put the workbook windows either on top of each other or side by side). Before you close the Arrange Windows dialog box, be sure that the Windows of active workbook check box does *not* contain a check mark.

After arranging the workbook windows, drag the worksheet tab from one workbook to another. If you want to copy rather than move the worksheet, hold down the Ctrl key as you drag the sheet icon(s). To locate the worksheet in the new workbook, position the downward pointing triangle that moves with the sheet icon in front of the worksheet tab where it's to be inserted and then release the mouse button.

Figures 7-10 and 7-11 illustrate how easy it is to move or copy a worksheet from one workbook to another using this drag-and-drop method.

In Figure 7-10, you see two workbook windows: the workbook named MGE - 1997 YTD Sales in the left pane and the workbook named MGE - Projected 1998 Sales in the right pane (arranged with the Tiled option in the Arrange Windows

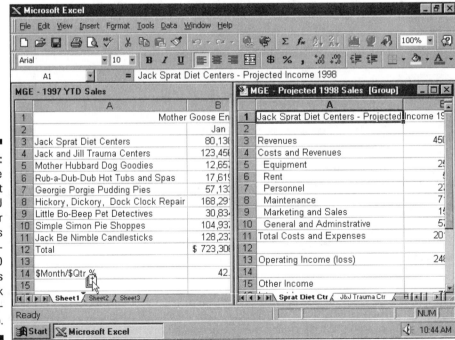

Figure 7-10: Copying the Sprat Diet Ctr and J&J Trauma Ctr worksheets to the MGE - 1997 YTD Sales workbook via drag-and-drop.

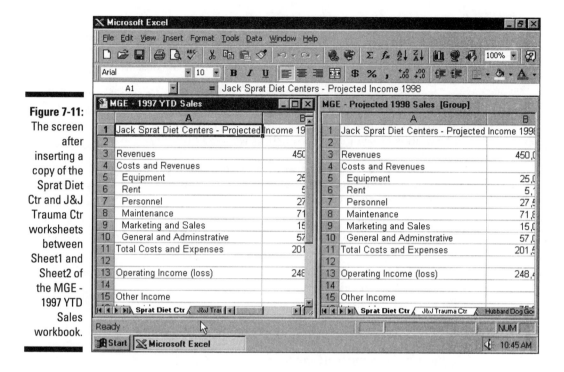

Figure 7-11:
The screen
after
inserting a
copy of the
Sprat Diet
Ctr and J&J
Trauma Ctr
worksheets
between
Sheet1 and
Sheet2 of
the MGE -
1997 YTD
Sales
workbook.

dialog box). To copy the Sprat Diet Ctr and the J&J Trauma Ctr sheets from the MGE - Projected 1998 Sales workbook to the MGE - 1997 YTD Sales workbook, you simply select both the Sprat Diet Ctr and J&J Trauma Ctr tabs and then hold down the Ctrl key as you click the Sprat Diet Ctr tab and drag the sheet icons to their new position right before Sheet2 of the MGE – 1997 YTD Sales workbook.

Figure 7-11 shows the workbooks after releasing the mouse button. As you can see, Excel inserts the copy of the Sprat Diet Ctr and the J&J Trauma Ctr worksheets into the MGE - 1997 YTD Sales workbook at the place indicated by the triangle that accompanies the sheet icon (in between Sheet1 and Sheet2 in this example).

To Sum Up . . .

I now want to introduce you to the fascinating subject of creating a *summary worksheet* that recaps or totals the values stored in a bunch of other worksheets in the workbook.

The best way that I can show you how to create a summary worksheet is to walk you through the procedure of making one (entitled Total Income) for the MGE - Projected 1998 Sales workbook, which totals the projected revenue and expenses for all of the companies owned by Mother Goose Enterprises.

Because the MGE - Projected 1998 Sales workbook already contains nine worksheets, each with the 1998 projected revenue and expenses for one of these companies, and these worksheets are all laid out in the same arrangement, creating this summary worksheet will be a breeze:

1. **I start by inserting a new worksheet in front of the other worksheets in the MGE - Projected 1998 Sales workbook and renaming its sheet tab from Sheet1 to Total Income.**

   To find out how to insert a new worksheet, refer back to "Don't Short-Sheet Me." To find out how to rename a sheet tab, refer back to "A sheet by any other name . . ." earlier in this chapter.

2. **Next, I enter the worksheet title** Mother Goose Enterprises - Projected 1998 Income **in cell A1.**

   Do this by selecting cell A1 and then typing the text.

3. **Finally, I copy the rest of the row headings for column A (containing the revenue and expense descriptions) from the Sprat Diet Ctr worksheet to the Total Income worksheet.**

   To do this, select cell A3 in the Total Income sheet; then click the Sprat Diet Ctr tab and select the cell range A3:A22 in this sheet before pressing Ctrl+C, clicking the Total Income tab again, and pressing Enter.

Now, after widening column A to accommodate the copied row headings, I am ready to create the "master" SUM formula that totals the revenues of all nine companies in cell B3 of the Total Income sheet:

1. **I start by clicking cell B3 and then clicking the AutoSum tool on the Standard toolbar.**

   Excel then puts =SUM( ) in the cell with the insertion point placed between the two parentheses.

2. **Then I click the Sprat Diet Ctr sheet tab and then its cell B3 to select the projected revenues for the Jack Sprat Diet Centers.**

   The formula bar now reads =SUM('Sprat Diet Ctr'!B3) after selecting this cell.

3. **Next I type , (the comma starts a new argument) and then click the J&J Trauma Ctr sheet tab followed by clicking its cell (B3) to select projected revenues for the Jack and Jill Trauma Centers.**

   The formula bar now reads =SUM('Sprat Diet Ctr'!B3,'J&J Trauma Ctr'!B3) after selecting this cell.

4. **I then continue in this manner, typing a comma and then selecting cell B3 with the projected revenues for all of the other companies in the following seven sheets.**

   At the end of this procedure, the formula bar now appears with the whopping SUM formula shown on the formula bar in Figure 7-12.

5. **To complete the SUM formula in cell B3 of the Total Income worksheet, I then click the Enter box in the formula bar (I could press the Enter key as well).**

   Figure 7-12 shows you the result after using AutoFit to widen column B. As you can see in the formula bar, the master SUM formula that returns 6,681,450.78 to cell B3 of the Total Income worksheet gets its result by summing the values in B3 in all nine of the supporting worksheets.

All that's left to do now is to use AutoFill to copy the master formula in cell B3 down to row 22 as follows:

1. **With cell B3 still selected, I drag the AutoFill handle in the lower-right corner of cell B3 down to cell B22 to copy the formula for summing the values for the nine companies down this column.**

2. **Then I delete the SUM formulas from cells B4, B12, B14, B15, and B19 (all of which contain zeros because these cells have no income or expenses to be totaled).**

In Figure 7-13, you see the first section of the final summary projected income worksheet after copying the formula created in cell B3 and deleting the formulas from the cells that should be blank (all those that came up 0 in column B).

Although this Total Income summary worksheet looks like it was a lot of work to create at first glance, it really was quite simple to put together. And the best part is that, because the values in the summary worksheet are tied by formula to the values entered in the income statement worksheet for each company, any update or correction made to these figures will be automatically reflected in the summary values in the Total Income sheet, giving you 100 percent accuracy in your totals without requiring any extra work on your part!

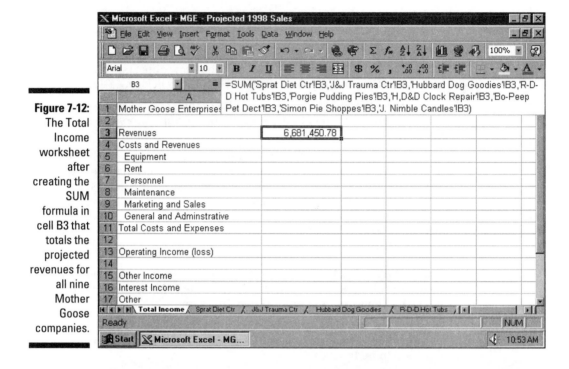

Figure 7-12: The Total Income worksheet after creating the SUM formula in cell B3 that totals the projected revenues for all nine Mother Goose companies.

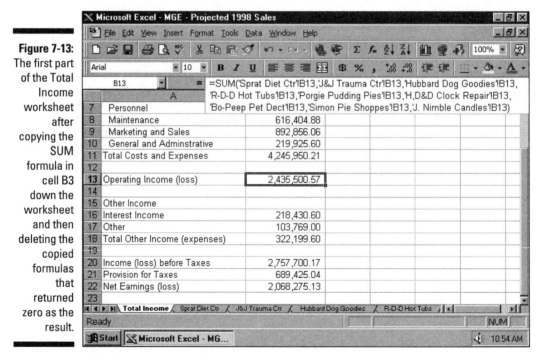

Figure 7-13: The first part of the Total Income worksheet after copying the SUM formula in cell B3 down the worksheet and then deleting the copied formulas that returned zero as the result.

Part IV
Life beyond the Spreadsheet

The 5th Wave
By Rich Tennant

*Bill Gates dreams...

* Yes, he sleeps with his glasses on.

RICHTENNANT.

JUSTICE DEPT.

"THAT'S RIGHT, MS. BINGAMAN, HE'S COLLECTING A ROYALTY FROM EVERYONE ON EARTH, AND THERE'S NOTHING WE CAN DO ABOUT IT."

In this part . . .

Don't let anybody kid you: Spreadsheets are the bread and butter of Excel 97. And for many of you, creating, editing, and printing spreadsheets is the be-all and end-all of Excel and "who could ask for anything more?" But don't get the wrong impression. Just because Excel is a whiz at spreadsheets doesn't mean that it's a one-trick pony, and just because spreadsheets may be the only thing that you churn out in your present job doesn't mean that someday you won't be moving into a job where you need to chart spreadsheet data, create and maintain Excel databases, and, who knows, even publish your worksheet data on the World Wide Web.

Part IV is here just in case you need to stray beyond the confines of the spreadsheet into such exotic areas as creating charts and adding graphic images, creating, sorting, and filtering databases, and publishing worksheets on the Internet or company intranet. Between the entertaining information in Chapter 8 about making charts, the fact-filled information in Chapter 9 on working with Excel databases, and the tips and tricks on creating hyperlinks and converting worksheet data into HTML documents, you'll be more than ready should the day arise (or already be here) when you are forced to go beyond the pale of the good old Excel spreadsheet.

Chapter 8
The Simple Art of Making Charts

*A*s Confucius said, "A picture's worth a thousand words" (or, in our case, numbers). By adding charts to worksheets, you not only heighten interest in the otherwise boring numbers but also illustrate trends and anomalies that might not be apparent from just looking at the values alone. Because Excel 97 makes it so easy to chart the numbers in a worksheet, you can also experiment with different types of charts until you find the one that best represents the data — in other words, the picture that best tells the particular story.

Just a word about charts before you find out how to make them in Excel. Remember your high-school algebra teacher valiantly trying to teach you how to graph equations by plotting different values on an x-axis and a y-axis on graph paper? Of course, you were probably too busy with more important things like cool cars and rock 'n' roll to pay too much attention to an old algebra teacher. Besides, you probably told yourself, "I'll never need this junk when I'm out on my own and get a job!"

Well, see, you just never know. It turns out that even though Excel automates almost the entire process of charting worksheet data, you may need to be able to tell the x-axis from the y-axis, just in case Excel doesn't draw the chart the way you had in mind. To refresh your memory, the x-axis is the horizontal axis, usually located along the bottom of the chart; the y-axis is the vertical one, usually located on the left side of the chart.

In most charts that use these two axes, Excel plots the categories along the x-axis at the bottom and their relative values along the y-axis on the left. The x-axis is sometimes referred to as the *time axis* because the chart often depicts values along this axis at different time periods such as months, quarters, years, and so on.

Conjuring Up Charts with the Chart Wizard

Well, that's enough background on charts. Now let's get on with the charting itself. Excel makes the process of creating a new chart in a worksheet as painless as possible with the Chart Wizard. The Chart Wizard walks you through a four-step procedure, at the end of which you have a complete and beautiful new chart.

Before you start the Chart Wizard, it's a good idea to first select the cell range that contains the information that you want charted. Keep in mind that to end up with the chart you want, the information should be entered in standard table format. With the information in this format, you can select it all as a single range (see Figure 8-1).

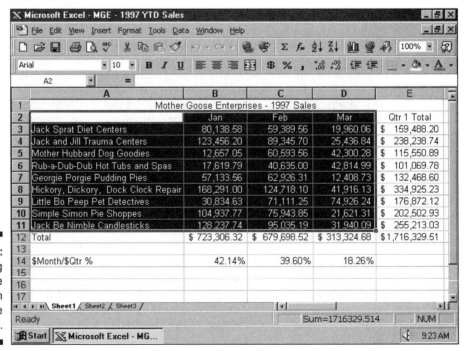

Figure 8-1: Selecting the information to be charted.

	A	B	C	D	E
1	Mother Goose Enterprises - 1997 Sales				
2		Jan	Feb	Mar	Qtr 1 Total
3	Jack Sprat Diet Centers	80,138.58	59,389.56	19,960.06	$ 159,488.20
4	Jack and Jill Trauma Centers	123,456.20	89,345.70	25,436.84	$ 238,238.74
5	Mother Hubbard Dog Goodies	12,657.05	60,593.56	42,300.28	$ 115,550.89
6	Rub-a-Dub-Dub Hot Tubs and Spas	17,619.79	40,635.00	42,814.99	$ 101,069.78
7	Georgie Porgie Pudding Pies	57,133.56	62,926.31	12,408.73	$ 132,468.60
8	Hickory, Dickory, Dock Clock Repair	168,291.00	124,718.10	41,916.13	$ 334,925.23
9	Little Bo Peep Pet Detectives	30,834.63	71,111.25	74,926.24	$ 176,872.12
10	Simple Simon Pie Shoppes	104,937.77	75,943.85	21,621.31	$ 202,502.93
11	Jack Be Nimble Candlesticks	128,237.74	95,035.19	31,940.09	$ 255,213.03
12	Total	$ 723,306.32	$ 679,698.52	$ 313,324.68	$1,716,329.51
13					
14	$Month/$Qtr %	42.14%	39.60%	18.26%	

If you create a chart that uses an x-axis and y-axis (as most do), the Chart Wizard naturally uses the row of column headings in the selected table for the category labels along the x-axis. If the table has row headings, the Chart Wizard uses these as the headings in the legend of the chart (if you choose to include one). The *legend* identifies each point, column, or bar in the chart that represents the values in the table.

After you select the information to chart, follow these steps to create the chart:

1. **Click the Chart Wizard button on the Standard toolbar to open the Chart Wizard - Step 1 of 4 - Chart Type dialog box.**

   The Chart Wizard button is the fifth tool from the right and has a picture of a column chart. When you click the Chart Wizard button as described in step 1, Excel opens the Chart Wizard - Step 1 of 4 - Chart Type dialog box shown in Figure 8-2.

2. **If you want to use a chart other than the default Clustered Column, select the new chart type and/or chart sub-type on the Standard Types or Custom Types tabs in the Chart Wizard - Step 1 of 4 - Chart Type dialog box.**

   To select another chart type, click its sample chart in the Chart type list box. To select a chart sub-type, click its representation in the Chart sub-type portion of the dialog box. To see how your data will look using the chart type and chart sub-type you've selected on the Standard Types tab, click and hold down the Press and hold to view sample button that's right below the area showing the name of the chart type and chart sub-type.

3. **Click the Next> button or press Enter to open the Chart Wizard - Step 2 of 4 - Chart Source Data dialog box.**

   The Chart Wizard - Step 2 of 4 - Chart Source Data dialog box (similar to the one shown in Figure 8-3) lets you change the data range that is to be charted (or select it from scratch, if you haven't already done so), as well as define how the series within that data range are defined.

   When this dialog box is displayed, any cell range selected prior to selecting the Chart Wizard is surrounded by the marquee in your worksheet and specified in formula form (with absolute cell references) in the Data range edit box. To modify this range (perhaps to include the row of column headings or the column of row headings), either reselect the range with the mouse or edit the cell references in the Data range edit box. Remember that if the Chart Wizard - Step 2 of 4 - Chart Source Data dialog box is in the way of the cells you need to select, you can reduce this dialog box to just this edit box by clicking the edit box's minimize button.

4. **Check the cell range shown in the Data range edit box and, if necessary, adjust the range address (either by typing or selecting the cell range in the worksheet itself).**

Normally, the Chart Wizard makes each column of values in the selected table into a separate *data series* on the chart. The *legend* (the boxed area with samples of the colors or patterns used in the chart) identifies each data series in the chart.

In terms of worksheet data selected in Mother Goose Enterprises 1997 first quarter sales worksheet (shown in Figure 8-1), this means that Excel will use each bar in the column chart to represent a different month's sales and will cluster these sales together by the nine different companies. If you want, you can switch the data series from columns to rows by clicking the Rows radio button. Choosing the Rows radio button in this example would make each bar represent the sales of one of the nine different companies and cause them to be clustered together by month.

When the chart forms the data series by columns, the Chart Wizard uses the entries in the first column (the row headings in cell range A3:A11) to label the x-axis (the so-called *category labels*). The Chart Wizard uses the entries in the first row (the column labels in cell range B2:D2) as the headings in the legend.

5. **If you want the Chart Wizard to use the rows of the selected data range as the data series of the chart (rather than the columns), click the Rows radio button next to the Series in heading.**

If you need to make individual changes to either the names or cells used in the data series, you can do so by clicking the Series tab in the Chart Wizard - Step 2 of 4 - Chart Source Data dialog box.

6. **Click the Next> button or press Enter to open the Chart Wizard - Step 3 of 4 - Chart Options dialog box.**

The Chart Wizard - Step 3 of 4 - Chart Options dialog box (shown in Figure 8-4) lets you assign a whole bunch of options, including the titles to appear in the chart, whether or not gridlines are used, where the legend is displayed, whether or not data labels appear next to their data series, and whether or not the Chart Wizard draws a data table showing the values that are being charted right below the data series in the chart.

7. **Select the tab for the options you want to change (Titles, Axes, Gridlines, Legend, Data Labels, or Data Table) and then change the option settings as necessary (see "Changing the Chart Options" later in this chapter for more information).**

8. **Click the Next> button in the dialog box or press Enter to open the Chart Wizard - Step 4 of 4 - Chart Location dialog box.**

The Chart Wizard - Step 4 of 4 - Chart Location dialog box (shown in Figure 8-5) lets you place your new chart either on its own chart sheet in the workbook or as a new graphic object on one of the worksheets in your workbook.

9a. **To place the chart on its own sheet, click the As new sheet radio button; then, if you wish, enter a new name for the sheet (besides Chart1, Chart2, and so on) in the edit box to its right.**

9b. **To place the chart somewhere on one of the worksheets in your workbook, make sure that the As object in radio button is selected and then select the name of the worksheet in the pop-up menu to its right (if you want to rename the worksheet at the same time, you can do so by typing in a new sheet name — which replaces the original sheet name because its already highlighted).**

10. **Click the Finish button or press Enter to close the last Chart Wizard dialog box.**

    If you selected the As new sheet option, your new chart will appear on its own chart sheet and the Chart toolbar magically appears floating in the workbook document window. If you selected the As object in radio button, your chart appears as a selected graphic — along with the floating Chart toolbar — on the designated worksheet (similar to the one shown in Figure 8-6, which shows the column chart created for the Mother Goose Enterprises 1997 first quarter sales).

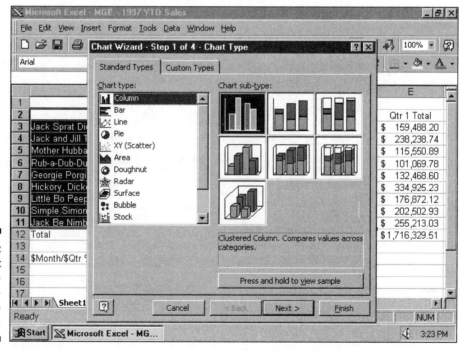

Figure 8-2:
The Chart
Wizard -
Step 1 of 4 -
Chart Type
dialog box.

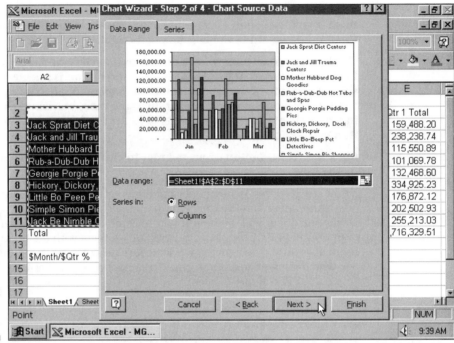

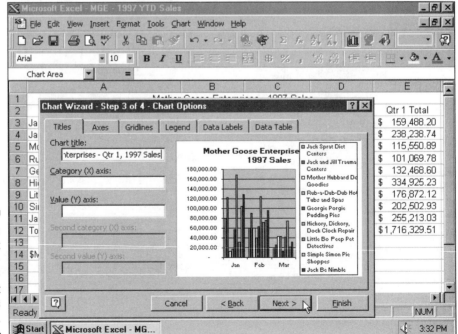

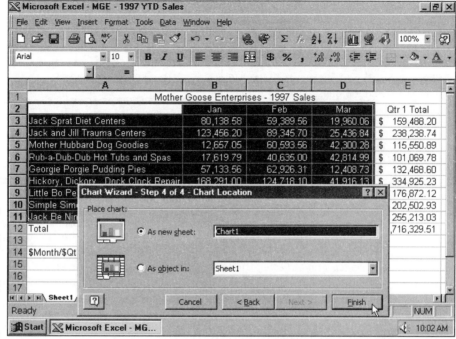

Figure 8-5:
The Chart
Wizard -
Step 4 of 4 -
Chart
Location
dialog box.

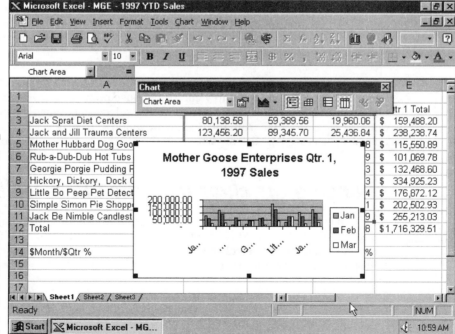

Figure 8-6:
The
completed
Cluster
Column
chart
representing
Qtr. 1 sales
as it
appears in
the
worksheet.

Instant Charts with F11!

If you just don't have time for the Chart Wizard and its four-step process outlined earlier, you can create a finished chart in an instant by doing these two steps:

1. Select the cells with the labels and values to be charted.

2. Press the function key F11.

Excel then creates a new Clustered Column chart using the selected data on its own chart sheet.

After creating a new chart as a graphic object in a worksheet, you can easily move or resize the chart right after creating it because the chart is still selected. (You can always tell when a graphic object like a chart is selected because you see *selection handles* — those tiny squares — around the edges of the object.) Immediately after creating the chart, the Chart toolbar appears floating above in the workbook document window.

- ✔ To move the chart, position the mouse pointer somewhere inside the chart and drag the chart to a new location.

- ✔ To resize the chart (you may want to make it bigger if it seems distorted in any way), position the mouse pointer on one of the selection handles. When the pointer changes from the arrowhead to a double-headed arrow, drag the side or corner (depending on which handle you select) to enlarge or reduce the chart.

When the chart is properly sized and positioned in the worksheet, set the chart in place by deselecting it (simply click the mouse pointer in any cell outside the chart). As soon as you deselect the chart, the selection handles disappear, as does the Chart toolbar, from the document window. To reselect the chart (to edit, size, or move it), click anywhere on the chart with the mouse pointer.

Changing the chart with the Chart toolbar

After you create a chart, you can use the buttons on the Chart toolbar (shown in Figure 8-7) to make all kinds of changes to it. Remember that this toolbar appears whenever you select the chart in the worksheet. You can use the buttons on the Chart toolbar to make the following changes to a chart that's selected in a worksheet:

✓ **Chart Objects:** To select the part of the chart to be changed, click the Chart Objects drop-down button and click the object's name on the pop-up menu or click the object directly in the chart itself with the mouse pointer. When you click a new object in a chart, its name automatically appears in the Chart Objects edit box.

✓ **Format:** To change the formatting of the selected chart object (whose name is shown in the edit box of the Chart Objects button), click the Format button to open a dialog box with the formatting options you can modify. Note that the name of this button as shown with screen tips changes to match the chart object that you've selected so that if Chart Area appears in the Chart Objects' edit box, the button is called Format Chart Area. So too, if Legend appears as the selected chart object in this edit box, the button's name changes to Format Legend.

✓ **Chart Type:** To change the type of chart, click the Chart Type drop-down button and then click the new chart type in the pop-up palette.

✓ **Legend:** Click the Legend button to hide or display the chart's legend.

✓ **Data Table:** Click the Data Table button to add or remove a data table that encapsulates the values that are represented by the chart's graphics (Figure 8-8 shows an example of a data table added to the Clustered Column chart added to the 1997 Sales worksheet).

✓ **By Row:** Click the By Row button to have the data series in the chart represent the rows of values in the selected data range.

✓ **By Column:** Click the By Column button to have the data series in the chart represent the columns of values in the selected data range.

✓ **Angle Text Downward:** Click the Angle Text Downward button when the Category Axis or Value Axis objects are selected to have the text of their labels slanted down 45 degrees as shown with the *ab* that appears on this button.

✓ **Angle Text Upward:** Click the Angle Text Upward button when the Category Axis or Value Axis objects are selected to have the text of their labels appear slanted up 45 degrees as shown with the *ab* that appears on this button.

Editing the chart directly in the worksheet

At times, you may want to make changes to specific parts of the chart (for example, selecting a new font for titles or repositioning the legend). To make these kinds of changes, you must double-click the particular object (such as the title, legend, plot area, and so on). When you double-click a chart object, Excel selects it and displays a format dialog box specific to the part of the chart you double-clicked. For example, if you double-click somewhere on the legend of a chart, the Format Legend dialog box with its three tabs (Patterns, Font, and Placement) as shown in Figure 8-9 appears. You can then use the options on any of these tabs to spruce up its appearance.

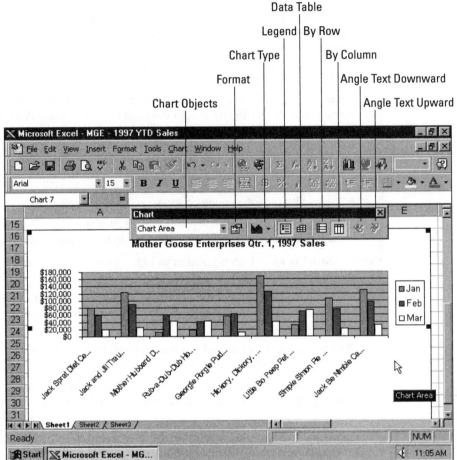

Figure 8-7:
The Chart
toolbar.

Note that you can also edit a chart by selecting the part you want to change as follows:

- ✔ To select one of these chart objects, simply click it.

- ✔ You can tell when an object is selected because selection handles appear around it. (Figure 8-9 shows the selection handles around the chart legend.) With some objects, you can use the selection handles to resize or reorient the object.

- ✔ After selecting some chart objects, you can move them within the chart by positioning the arrowhead pointer in their midst and then dragging their boundary.

- ✔ To display a chart object's shortcut menu, you click the object with the secondary mouse button and then drag to the desired command on the menu or click it with the primary mouse button.

- ✔ To remove the selected part from the chart, press the Delete key.

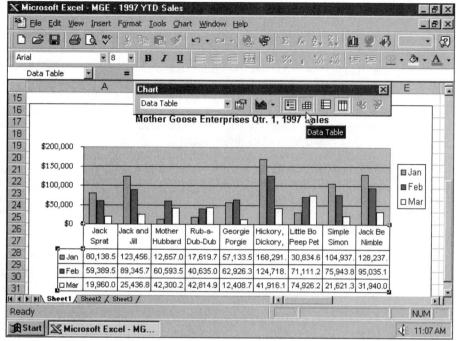

Figure 8-8:
A Clustered
Column
chart with
a data table
containing
the Qtr. 1
sales
figures.

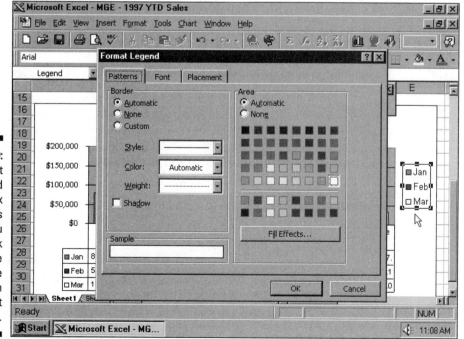

Figure 8-9:
The Format
Legend
dialog box
appears
when you
double-click
somewhere
on the
legend in
the chart
itself.

After you select one object in the chart by clicking on it, you can cycle through and select the other objects in the chart by pressing the ↑ and ↓ keys. Pressing → selects the next object; pressing ← selects the previous object.

All the parts of the chart that you can select in a chart window have shortcut menus attached to them. If you know that you want to choose a command from the shortcut menu as soon as you select a part of the chart, you can both select the object and open the shortcut menu by clicking the chart object with the *secondary* mouse button. (You don't have to click the object with the left button to select it and then click again with the right to open the menu.)

Note that you can move the chart title by dragging it to a new position within the chart. In addition to moving the title, you can also break up the title on several different lines. Then, if you want, you can use options in the Alignment tab of the Format Chart Title dialog box to change the alignment of the broken-up text.

To force part of the title onto a new line, click the insertion point at the place in the text where the line break is to occur. After the insertion point is positioned in the title, press Enter to start a new line.

In addition to changing the way the titles appear in the chart, you can modify the way the data series, legend, and x- and y-axes appear in the chart by opening their shortcut menus and selecting the appropriate commands from them.

Changing the Chart Options

If you find that you need to make some substantial alterations to your chart, you can open the Chart Options dialog box (which contains the same tabs and options as you saw in the Chart Wizard - Step 3 of 4 - Chart Options dialog box when creating the chart — refer to Figure 8-4). You can open this dialog box by choosing Chart⇨Chart Options on the menu bar or by clicking somewhere in the chart area (while at the same time avoiding a particular object like a title, axis, data table, legend, and the like) with the secondary mouse button and then choosing Chart Options on the Chart Area's shortcut menu.

The Chart Options dialog box can contain up to six tabs (depending upon the type of chart you've selected — pie charts for instance have only the first three tabs) with options for doing the following stuff:

✔ **Titles:** You can use the options on the Titles tab to add or modify the Chart title (that appears at the top of the chart), the Category title (that appears below the x-axis), or the Value title (that appears to the left of the y-axis).

✔ **Axes:** You can use the options on the Axes tab to hide or display the tick marks and labels along the Category (x) axis or the Value (y) axis.

✔ **Gridlines:** You can use the options on the Gridlines tab to hide or display the major and minor gridlines that appear from the tick marks along the Category (x) axis or the Value (y) axis.

✔ **Legend:** You can use the options on the Legend tab to hide or display the legend or to change its placement in relation to the chart area (by choosing the Bottom, Corner, Top, Right, or Left radio button).

✔ **Data Labels:** You can use the options on the Data Labels tab to hide or display labels that identify each data series in the chart. You can also specify the appearance of the data label (by choosing the Show value, Show percent, Show label, Show label and percent, or Show bubble sizes radio button).

✔ **Data Table:** You can use the options in the Data Table tab to add or remove a data table that shows the worksheet values being charted (refer to Figure 8-8 for an example of a chart with a data table).

Telling all with a text box

Figure 8-10 shows a couple of other changes you can easily make to a chart. In this figure, you see the chart for the Mother Goose Enterprises 1997 first quarter sales (as an Area chart) after adding a text box with an arrow that points out how extraordinary the sales were for the Hickory, Dickory, Dock Clock Repair shops in this quarter and after formatting the values on the y-axis with the Currency number format.

To add a text box to the chart, open the Drawing toolbar by clicking the Drawing button on the Standard toolbar. As you can see in Figure 8-11, the Drawing toolbar automatically docks itself at the bottom of the workbook window. Then click its Text Box button. When you click the Text Box button, Excel changes the mouse pointer to a narrow vertical line with a short cross near the bottom, which you can click at the place where you want the text box drawn or use to draw the text box either in the chart or the worksheet by dragging its outline. When you click this mouse pointer, Excel draws a square text box. When you release the mouse button after dragging this mouse pointer, Excel draws a text box in the shape and size of the outline.

After creating the text box, the program positions the insertion point at the top, and you can then type the text you want to appear within it. The text you type appears in the text box and wraps to a new line when you reach the right edge of the text box. (Remember: You can press Enter when you want to force text to appear on a new line.) When you've finished entering the message for your text box, click anywhere outside the box to deselect it.

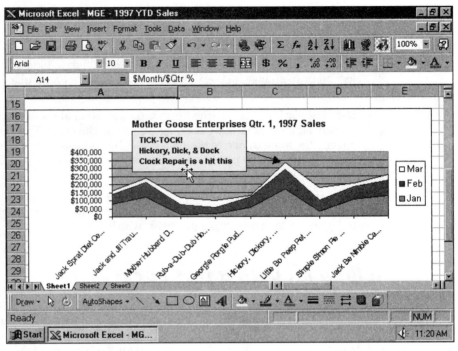

Figure 8-10:
An Area chart after adding a text box with arrow and formatting the values on the y-axis with the Currency style.

After adding a text box to a chart (or worksheet), you can edit as follows:

✔ You can move the text box to a new location in the chart by dragging it.

✔ You can resize the text box by dragging the appropriate selection handle.

✔ Change or remove the border around the text box by opening the Format Text Box dialog box either by choosing Format⇨Text Box (Ctrl+1) or by choosing the Format Text Box command on the text box shortcut menu and then choosing the Colors and Lines tab in the dialog box. To remove all borders from the text box, select No Line on the Color pop-up menu under Line.

✔ To add the drop-shadow effect, select the text box, then click the Shadow button on the Drawing toolbar (the one with the picture of a drop shadow behind a rectangle), and select the type of drop shadow to apply in the pop-up palette.

✔ To make the text box three-dimensional, select the text box, then click the 3D button on the Drawing toolbar (the last one with the 3-D rectangle), and select the 3-D box shape you want to apply in the pop-up palette.

When creating a text box, you may want to add an arrow to point directly to the object or part of the chart you're talking about. To add an arrow, click the

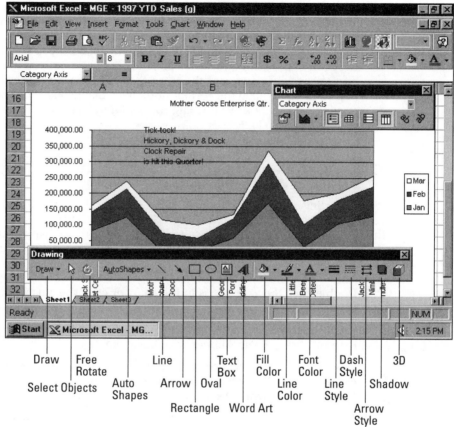

Figure 8-11:
The
Drawing
toolbar.

Draw — Free Rotate — Line — Text Box — Fill Color — Font Color — Dash Style — 3D

Select Objects — Auto Shapes — Arrow — Oval — Line Color — Line Style — Shadow

Rectangle — Word Art — Arrow Style

Arrow button on the Drawing toolbar and then drag the crosshair from the place where the end of the arrow (the one *without* the arrowhead) is to appear to the place where the arrow starts (and the arrowhead appears) and release the mouse button.

Excel then draws a new arrow, which remains selected (with selection handles at the beginning and end of the arrow). You can then modify the arrow as follows:

✔ To move the arrow, drag it into position.

✔ To change the length of the arrow, drag one of the selection handles.

✔ As you change the length, you can also change the direction of the arrow by pivoting the mouse pointer around a stationary selection handle.

✔ If you want to change the shape of the arrowhead or the thickness of the arrow's shaft, select the arrow in the worksheet, then click the Arrow Style button on the Drawing toolbar (the one with the three arrows), and choose the type of arrowhead to apply in the pop-up menu. If you need to change the color of the arrow, thickness or style of the line, or want to create a custom arrowhead, choose the More Arrows command at the bottom of pop-up menu to open the Format AutoShape dialog box (you can also open this dialog box by choosing Format⇨AutoShape on the menu bar or by pressing Ctrl+1).

Formatting the x- or y-axis

When charting a bunch of values, Excel isn't too careful how it formats the values that appear on the y-axis (or the x-axis when using some chart types like the 3-D Column chart or the XY Scatter chart). If you're not happy with the way the values appear on either the x- or y-axis, you can change the formatting as follows:

1. **Double-click the x- or y-axis in the chart or click the axis and then choose Format⇨Selected Axis on the menu bar (or press Ctrl+1).**

   Excel opens the Format Axis dialog box containing the following tabs: Patterns, Scale, Font, Number, and Alignment.

2. **To change the appearance of the tick marks along the axis, change the options on the Patterns tab (which is automatically selected when you first open the Format Axis dialog box) as required.**

3. **To change the scale of the selected axis, click the Scale tab and change the Scale options as required.**

4. **To change the font of the labels that appear at the tick marks on the selected axis, click the Font tab and change the Font options as required.**

5. **To change the formatting of the values that appear at the tick marks on the selected axis, select the Number tab; then choose the appropriate options in the Category list box, Decimal places edit box, and Symbol pop-up menu.**

   For example, to select the Currency format with no decimal places, you select Currency in the Category list box; then enter 0 in the Decimal places edit box or select 0 with the spinner buttons.

6. **To change the formatting of the orientation of the labels that appear at the tick marks on the selected axis, select the Alignment tab; then indicate the new orientation by clicking it in the sample Text box or by entering the number of degrees (between 180 and -180) in the Degrees edit box (or selecting this number with the spinner buttons).**

7. **Click the OK button or press Enter to close the Format Axis dialog box.**

As soon as you close the Format Axis box, Excel redraws the axis of the chart according to the new settings. For instance, if you choose a new number format for a chart, Excel immediately formats all the numbers that appear along the selected axis using that format.

Vacillating values mean changing charts

As soon as you finish modifying the objects in a chart, you can deselect the chart and return to the normal worksheet and its cells by clicking the pointer anywhere outside the chart. After a chart is deselected, you can once again move the cell pointer all over the worksheet. Just keep in mind that if you use the arrow keys to move the cell pointer, the cell pointer disappears when you move to a cell in the worksheet that's hidden behind the chart (of course, if you try to select a cell covered by a chart by clicking it with the mouse pointer, you'll only succeed in selecting the chart itself).

Keep in mind that worksheet values represented graphically in the chart remain dynamically linked to the chart so that, should you make a change to one or more of the charted values in the worksheet, Excel will automatically update the chart to suit.

Changing perspectives

Figure 8-12 shows the chart in a chart window in yet another guise: this time, as a 3-D Area chart. When you select this kind of chart (as well as the 3-D Column, 3-D Line, and 3-D Surface charts), Excel draws the chart in perspective view by adding a third axis to the chart. Now you have the category (x) axis with the companies running along the bottom of the closest side, the data series (y) axis with the months running along the bottom of the other side, and the value (z) axis with the dollar amounts running up the left wall.

These three axes form a kind of open box with the category and series axes on the two sides of the floor and the values axis on the left side of the wall of the box. You can modify the view of this type of 3-D-perspective chart by rotating the box, thereby changing the viewing angles of its walls and floor.

To do this, click the chart (double-click if the chart is on a worksheet rather than a chart sheet); then select the frame of the 3-D chart by clicking one of its corners and hold down the mouse button. (If the 3-D chart is on a chart sheet, you can tell when you've clicked a corner because the word *Corners* appears on the formula bar where the current cell address usually appears.) In a second, assuming that you don't let up on the mouse button prematurely and that you have really clicked a corner of the frame and not one of the data series inside the frame, everything disappears from the 3-D chart except for the wire frame representing its orientation (see Figure 8-13).

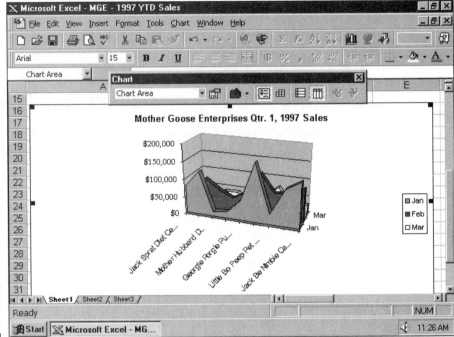

Figure 8-12:
Sales
information
as a 3-D
Area chart
in its own
chart sheet.

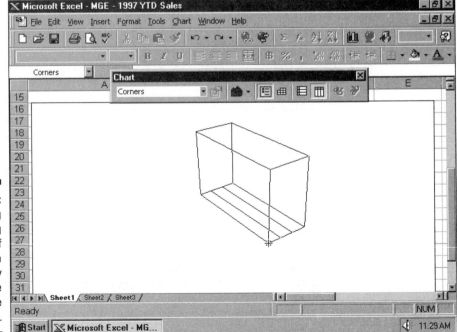

Figure 8-13:
Modifying
the viewing
angles of
the 3-D Area
chart by
rotating the
wire-frame
box.

You can then drag the corner of the wire-frame box around to reorient the entire 3-D chart. When the wire-frame box is positioned the way you want the 3-D chart, release the mouse button. Excel draws the 3-D chart using the new viewing angles. Figure 8-13 shows the wire-frame of the 3-D Area chart after rotating its lower-right corner down and around to the left before releasing the mouse button and redrawing the chart. Figure 8-14 shows you how the rotated 3-D Area chart appears after releasing the mouse button.

Notice how this change to the orientation of the 3-D Area chart causes Excel to flip the category labels with the names of the companies all the way from the lower side of the chart to its right side.

Picture This!

Charts are not the only kind of graphics you can add to a worksheet. Indeed, Excel lets you spruce up a worksheet with drawings, text boxes, and even graphic images imported from other sources, like scanned images or drawings created in other graphics programs.

To bring in a piece of clip art included with Office 97, you choose the Insert⊅ Picture⊅Clip Art command on the menu bar and select the image from the Clip Art tab in the Microsoft Clip Gallery dialog box (similar to the one shown in

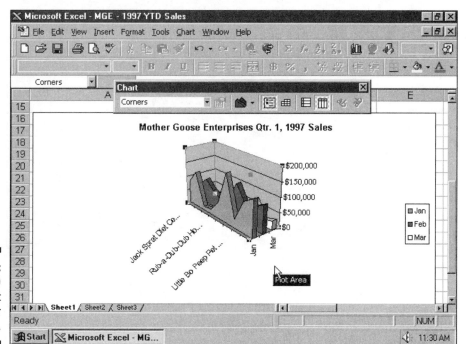

Figure 8-14:
The 3-D Area chart after rotating it.

Figure 8-15). To select a clip art image, first click the category of the art image in the left pane of the dialog box, then click the clip art image itself in the right pane before you click the Insert button or press Enter.

If you want to bring in a graphic image created in another program and saved in its own graphics file, you choose the Insert⇨Picture⇨From File command and then select the graphic file in the Insert Picture dialog box (which works just like opening an Excel 97 workbook file in the Open dialog box).

If you want to bring in a graphic image created in another graphics program that's not saved in its own file, you select the graphic in that program and then copy it to the Clipboard (using Ctrl+C or the Edit⇨Copy command on the menu bar) before returning to the Excel worksheet. When you get back to your worksheet, place the cursor where you want the picture to go and then paste the image in place (using Ctrl+V or the Edit⇨Paste command).

In addition to ready-made graphics or images drawn in other graphics programs, you can use the tools on the Drawing toolbar to create your own graphics within Excel. The Drawing toolbar contains all sorts of drawing tools that you can use to draw outlined or filled shapes like lines, rectangles, squares, and ovals.

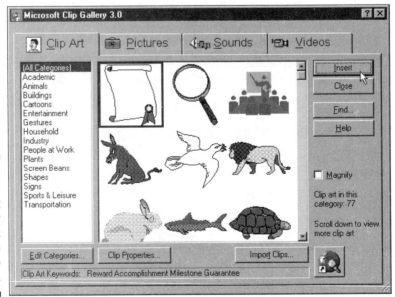

Figure 8-15:
The
Microsoft
Clip Gallery
dialog box
with the Clip
Art tab
selected.

Along with these tools for drawing traditional lines and shapes, the Drawing toolbar contains a new AutoShapes button that gives you access to a whole bunch of ready-made, specialized lines and shapes. To select one of these lines or shapes, you click it on the particular cascading palette that opens when you choose the Lines, Connectors, Basics Shapes, Block Arrows, Flowchart, Stars and Banners, or Callouts pop-up menu that appears when you click the AutoShapes button.

Working with WordArt

If having the specialized lines and shapes available with the AutoShapes button doesn't provide enough variety for jazzing up your worksheet, you may want to try adding some fancy text to the worksheet with the new WordArt button on the Drawing toolbar. You can add this kind of text to your worksheet by following these steps:

1. **Select the cell in the area of the worksheet where the WordArt text is to appear.**

   Because WordArt is created as a graphics object on the worksheet, you can size and move the text after it's been created as you would any other worksheet graphic.

2. **Click the WordArt button (the one with the picture of the letter "A" angled downward) on the Drawing toolbar.**

   When you click the WordArt button, Excel displays the WordArt Gallery dialog box, as shown in Figure 8-16.

3. **Click the picture of the WordArt style you want to use in the WordArt Gallery dialog box and then click OK or press Enter.**

   Excel opens the Edit WordArt Text dialog box (similar to the one shown in Figure 8-17) where you enter the text you want to appear in the worksheet and select its font and font size.

4. **Type the text you want displayed in the worksheet in the Text edit box.**

   As soon as you start typing, Excel replaces the highlighted "Your Text Here" with the text you want to appear in the worksheet.

5. **Select the font you want to use in the Font pop-up list box and the font size in the Size pop-up list box.**

6. **Click the OK button or press Enter.**

   Excel draws your WordArt text in the worksheet at the cell pointer's position, while at the same time displaying the floating WordArt toolbar (as shown in Figure 8-18). You can use the buttons on this toolbar to further format the basic WordArt style or to edit the text.

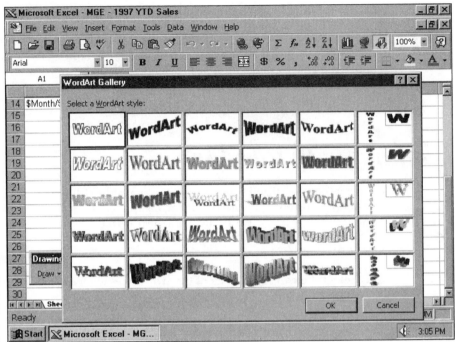

Figure 8-16:
The
WordArt
Gallery.

Figure 8-17:
The Edit
WordArt
Text dialog
box.

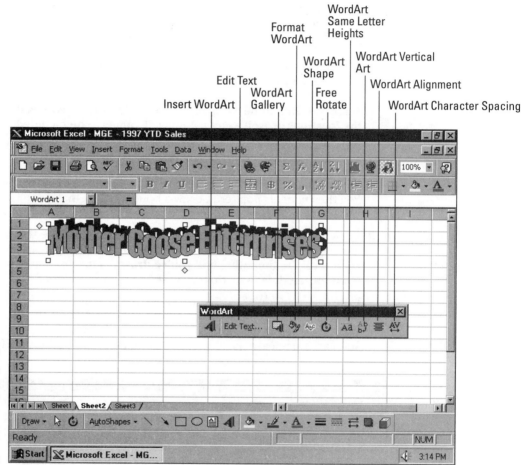

Figure 8-18:
Worksheet
immediately
after adding
WordArt
text.

7. **After making any final adjustments to the size, shape, or format of the WordArt text, click a cell somewhere outside of the text to deselect the graphic.**

When you click outside of the WordArt text, Excel deselects the graphic and the WordArt toolbar is hidden. (If you ever want the toolbar to reappear, all you have to do is click somewhere on the WordArt text to select the graphic.)

Map Madness

The Data Map feature in Excel 97 lets you represent geographical data such as sales in a particular state or foreign country or locations of different out-of-state or foreign offices in graphical form. All you have to do is enter the numbers in one column accompanied by the names of the states or countries they pertain to as row headings in the previous column (similar to the data shown selected in Figure 8-19).

After entering the geographical data in a particular worksheet, you create its data map by following these steps:

1. **Select the data to be mapped, including the row headings that identify the locations as well as all columns of values to be included.**

2. **Click the Map button on the Standard toolbar (the one with the globe, between the Chart Wizard and Drawing buttons).**

   When you click the Map button, the mouse pointer changes to a crosshair. You then use this pointer to draw a bounding box that establishes the size and location of the data map.

3. **Click the crosshair at the place in the worksheet where the upper-left corner of the data map should appear and then drag down and to the right until the bounding box you've drawn is the size and shape you want for the data map; then release the mouse button.**

   Note that you don't have to be too precise with drawing the data map bounding box because you can always move and resize the data map after you've created it, just as you would any other graphic object in Excel. As soon as you release the mouse button, Excel 97 draws the map in the

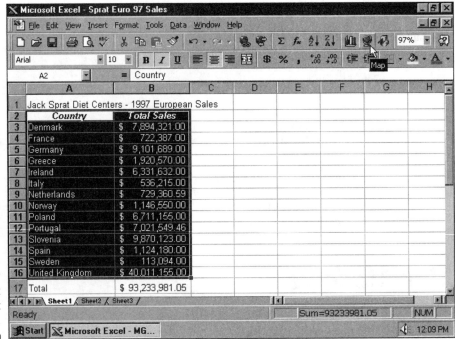

Figure 8-19: Use the Map button to create a data map representing the European sales for Jack Sprat Diet Centers.

worksheet and displays the Data Map toolbar (with all its buttons grayed out) at the top of the workbook window (temporarily hiding both the Standard and the Formatting toolbars).

4. **Select the map that you want to use in the list box of the Multiple Maps Available dialog box and then click OK or press Enter.**

In some cases, Excel may not be able to identify a particular heading as representing geographical data in the map that you've selected. When this is the case, you have to deal with a Resolve Unknown Geographic Data dialog box, where you either change the name of the heading to something Excel recognizes or you eliminate it with the Discard button.

After you select the map to use, Excel draws the map in the worksheet and displays the Microsoft Map Control dialog box (similar to the one shown in Figure 8-20), which determines which data is represented and how it's represented.

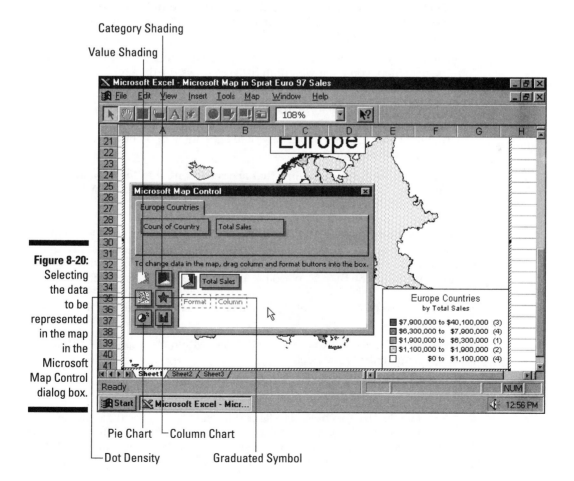

Figure 8-20: Selecting the data to be represented in the map in the Microsoft Map Control dialog box.

Category Shading

Value Shading

Pie Chart — Column Chart

Dot Density — Graduated Symbol

Left to its own devices, Excel chooses whatever column in the cell selection it can identify as representing values like total sales or number of employees and chooses Value Shading as the way to format these values (by representing their density with different types of gray shading and patterns).

5. **To change which columns are represented in the data map, drag the appropriate column button from the top area to the list box area in the Microsoft Map Control dialog box.**

   To remove a column from the data map, drag its button out of the list box area until the pointer changes to the recycle bin icon and then release the mouse button.

   Each time you change which columns are included in the data map, you must wait until Excel redraws the map in the worksheet before you can make any more changes to it.

6. **To change the way a column of data is formatted in the data map, drag the desired format icon from the left area and drop it on top of the current formatting icon.**

   Each time you choose a new formatting icon for a column represented in the data map, you must wait until Excel redraws the data map using that formatting.

   When deciding on the formatting, you might want to play around with the formatting icons until you get the data map looking the way you want (different formats look better or worse depending upon how much territory the map includes).

7. **When you've got the columns that are represented in the data map formatted the way you want them, click the Close box in the Microsoft Map Control dialog box to get rid of it.**

Even after you get rid of the Microsoft Map Control dialog box, the data map remains selected in the worksheet and the Data Map toolbar remains displayed right below the Excel pull-down menus (as shown in Figure 8-21). You can then use the buttons on the Data Map toolbar to continue to enhance your data map:

- ✔ **Select Objects:** Use this button to select things in the data map like titles or map pins.

- ✔ **Grabber:** Use this button to move the map within the boundaries of the data map on the worksheet.

- ✔ **Center Map:** Use this button to specify the center of the map within the boundaries of the data map on the worksheet.

- ✔ **Map Labels:** Use this button to label different parts of the data map, either with the geographical names (like those for the states or countries shown) or with the worksheet values entered for each place in the data map. When you click this button, Excel opens the Map Labels dialog box where you

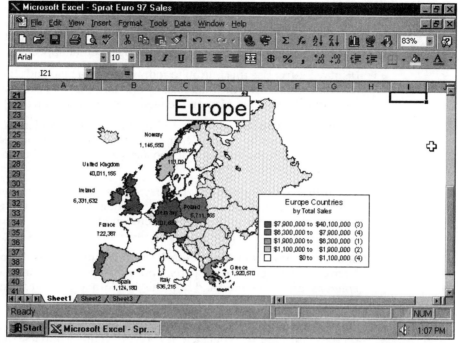

Figure 8-21:
The final
data map
showing the
location and
relative
values of the
European
sales of
Jack Sprat
Diet
Centers.

can choose between creating labels for the places on the map (Map feature names) or the labels for the values in a particular column. After you click OK and close this dialog box, the mouse pointer changes to a crosshair pointer. Each time you pass this pointer over a part of the map, Excel displays the appropriate label (name or value) for that place. To enter that label in the data map, you need to click the place with the mouse pointer. To move the label, you need to drag the label by one of its sides. You can also do this by choosing Tools➪Labeler on the menu bar.

✔ **Add Text:** Use this button to add text anywhere on the data map. Note that you can edit text by choosing the Select Objects tool (see the first item in this list) and then double-clicking the text to open its Edit Text Object dialog box.

✔ **Custom Pin Map:** Use this button to mark the data map with pins. When you first click this button, Excel opens the Custom Pin Map dialog box where you designate a name for a new custom map pin or select one of the existing map pins. When you click OK or press Enter to close this dialog box, Excel changes the mouse pointer to a thumbtack. To add a map pin to the map (which appears as a tiny, red pushpin), simply click the place with the thumbtack mouse pointer; then enter the label that is to appear next to the pushpin on the data map in the Edit Text Object dialog box that automatically opens before you click OK or press Enter.

To use another symbol besides the pushpin for your map pins, choose the Select Objects tool (see the first item in this list) and click a map pin with the secondary mouse button. Then choose Format on the shortcut menu and select a character in the Symbol dialog box that appears.

✔ **Display Entire:** Use this button to redraw the data map and all its labels so that they all fit within the data map's bounding box. You can also do this by choosing View⇨Entire Map on the menu bar or by pressing Ctrl+Space bar.

✔ **Redraw Map:** Use this button to redraw the data map and minimize any stretching caused by moving the map with the Grabber tool (see Grabber above). You can also do this by choosing View⇨Redraw Map on the menu bar.

✔ **Map Refresh:** Unlike with Excel charts, data maps are not automatically redrawn when you change one or more of their underlying values in the worksheet. To see your changes reflected in the data map, you need to click the Map Refresh button to have the entire data map redrawn.

✔ **Show/Hide Microsoft Map Control:** Use this button to display or hide the Microsoft Map Control dialog box, from which you can change what columns are represented and how they are formatted. You can also do this by choosing View⇨Microsoft Map Control on the menu bar.

✔ **Zoom Percentage of Map:** Use this drop-down list box to zoom in and out on the map either by typing a new zoom percentage into its edit box or by selecting a new percentage from its pop-up list. After zooming in, use the Grabber tool (see above) to drag a new part of the map into view within the data map's boundaries.

✔ **Help:** Use this button to get context sensitive help on one of the commands on the data map menu bar or toolbar or on a part of the data map simply by clicking it with the mouse pointer.

When you finish enhancing your data map with the buttons on the Data Map toolbar or the commands on the menu bar, you still need to remember to deselect the map (by clicking outside the data map, preferably on one of the worksheet cells). When you deselect the data map, Excel automatically removes the heavy border from around the data map and hides the Data Map toolbar, thus restoring your normal screen display and making the data map appear as though it were any other chart that you had added to the worksheet.

One on top of the other . . .

In case you haven't noticed, graphic objects float on top of the cells of the worksheet. Most of the objects (including charts) are opaque, meaning that they hide (*without* replacing) information in the cells beneath. If you move one opaque graphic on top of another, the one on top hides the one below, just as putting one sheet of paper over another hides the information on the one below. This means that, most of the time, you should make sure that graphic objects don't overlap one another or overlap cells with worksheet information that you want to display.

Sometimes, however, you can create some interesting special effects by placing a transparent graphic object (such as a circle) in front of an opaque one. The only problem you might encounter is if the opaque object gets on top of the transparent one. If this happens, switch their positions by selecting the opaque object and then choosing the Order⇨Send to Back command on the object's shortcut menu. If you ever find a situation where you need to bring up a graphic that's underneath another, click this underlying graphic and then choose the Order⇨Send to Front command on the object's shortcut menu.

Sometimes you may find that you need to group several objects together so that they act as one unit (like a text box with its arrow). That way, you can move these objects or size them together in one operation. To group objects together, you need to select each object to be grouped (by clicking each one as you hold down the Shift key) and then choose the Grouping⇨Group command on the object's shortcut menu. After grouping several objects, whenever you click any part of the mega-object, every part is selected (and selection handles appear only around the perimeter of the combined object).

Should you later decide that you need to independently move or size objects that have been grouped together, you can ungroup them by selecting the grouped object and then choosing Grouping⇨Ungroup on the object's shortcut menu.

When you need to ditch the graphics

Here's something you'll want to know about the graphics you add to a worksheet: how to hide them. You see, adding graphics to a worksheet can appreciably slow down the screen response because Excel has to take the time to redraw each and every little picture in the document window whenever you scroll the view even slightly. To keep this sluggishness from driving you crazy, either hide the display of all the graphics (including charts) while you edit other things in the worksheet, or temporarily replace them with gray rectangles that continue to mark their places in the worksheet but don't take nearly as long to redraw.

To hide all the graphics or replace them with gray placeholders, choose the Tools⇨Options command on the menu bar and then select the View tab. Click the Hide all radio button under Objects to get rid of the display of all graphics entirely. Click the Show placeholders radio button to temporarily replace the graphics with shaded rectangles. (This is the safest bet, because the placeholders give you a general idea of how changes to the cells of the worksheet impact the graphics.)

Before you print the worksheet, be sure that you redisplay the graphic objects: Open the Options dialog box, select the View tab, and then click the Show all radio button.

Printing Charts Only

Sometimes, you may want to print only a particular chart in the worksheet (independent of the worksheet data it represents or any of the other stuff you've added). To do this, first make sure that the graphic objects are displayed in the worksheet. (For details, refer to "When you need to ditch the graphics" earlier in this chapter.) Then double-click the chart (to display the heavy border drawn with diagonal lines). Next, choose the File⇨Print command on the menu bar (Ctrl+P) or click the Print tool on the Standard toolbar.

If you choose the File⇨Print command on the menu bar rather than click the Print tool, you see that the Selected Chart radio button under Print What is selected. By default, Excel prints the chart at full size on the page. This may mean that all of the chart cannot be printed on a single page — be sure to click the Preview button to make sure that your entire map fits on one page.

If you find in Print Preview that you need to change the printed chart size or the orientation of the printing (or both), click the Setup button in the Print Preview window. To change the orientation of the printing (or the paper size), select the Page tab in the Page Setup dialog box and change these options. When everything looks good in the Print Preview window, start printing the chart by choosing the Print button.

Chapter 9
How to Face a Database

In This Chapter

▶ Setting up a database in Excel

▶ Creating a data form for entering and editing records in the database

▶ Adding records via the data form

▶ Finding, editing, and deleting records through the data form

▶ Sorting records in the database

▶ Filtering records in the database so that you end up with just those you want to see

▶ Setting up custom criteria when filtering records

*T*he purpose of all the worksheet tables I've discussed up to this point in the book has been to perform essential calculations (such as to sum monthly or quarterly sales figures) and then present the information in an understandable form. But you can create another kind of worksheet table in Excel: a *database*. The purpose of a database is not so much to calculate new values but rather to store lots and lots of information in a consistent manner. For example, you can create a database that contains the names and addresses of all your clients, or you can create a database that contains all the essential facts about your employees.

Creating a database is much like creating a worksheet table. When setting up a database, you start by entering a row of column headings (technically known as *field names* in database parlance) to identify the different kinds of items you need to keep track of (such as First Name, Last Name, Street, City, State, and so on). After you enter the row of field names, you start entering the information for the database in the appropriate columns of the rows immediately below the field names.

As you proceed, notice that each column of the database contains information for a particular item you want to track in the database, such as the client's company name or an employee's telephone extension. Each column is also known as a *field* in the database. In looking back over your work, you see that each row of the database contains complete information about a particular person or thing you're keeping track of in the database, whether it's a company such as Valuerite Reality or a particular employee such as Johnny Hayseed. The individuals or entities described in the rows of the database are also known as the *records* of the database. Each record (row) contains many fields (columns).

Maintaining vast quantities of data in a tabular format is but one small part of the database story in Excel. Excel provides you with very powerful features for organizing the data as well as for displaying just the information you need. For instance, suppose that you entered the clients in a database alphabetically by company name but now want to see them listed alphabetically by company name *and* grouped by states and cities. No problem: Sort the records of the database by their State, City, and then Company fields.

Or suppose that you only want to work with clients who live in New York City and who have already established credit accounts with you. It's simple: You choose Data⇨Filter⇨AutoFilter on the menu bar to add drop-down buttons to each field name in the database complete with its own little pop-up list. Then, to display only the records you want to see, you click the drop-down list button for the appropriate field(s) and select the entry in the pop-up list by which you want the database to be filtered (for this example, you would select New York in the City drop-down list and Yes in the Credit drop-down list). And, just like that, Excel hides all the records in your database except those containing the entries you selected (referred to as *filter criteria*). In this example, Excel displays only the records in the database where the City field contains New York and the Credit field contains Yes.

Designing the Data Form

Setting up and maintaining a database is easy with Excel's handy, built-in *data form*. You use the data form to add, delete, or edit records in the database. To create a data form for a new database, you first enter the row of column headings used as field names and one sample record in the following row (check out the client database in Figure 9-1). Then you format each field entry just as you want all subsequent entries in that column of the database to appear. Then position the cell pointer in any one of the cells in these two rows and choose the Data⇨Form command on the menu bar.

As soon as you choose the Data⇨Form command on the menu bar, Excel analyzes the row of field names and entries for the first record and creates a data form that lists the field names down the left side of the form with the entries for the first record in the appropriate edit boxes next to them. Figure 9-1 shows the data form for the new Little Bo Peep Pet Detective client database; it looks kind of like a customized dialog box. The data form Excel creates includes the entries you made in the first record. The data form also contains a series of buttons on the right side that you use to add, delete, or find specific records in the database. Right above the first button (New), the data form lists the number of the record you're looking at followed by the total number of records (1 of 1 when you first create the data form).

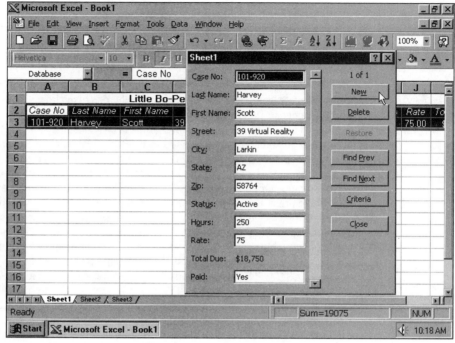

Figure 9-1:
The data
form for
a new
database
with a row
of field
names
followed by
a single
data record
(row).

If you don't format any of the cells in the row of field names or the row with the entries for the first record in some manner beyond the default formatting automatically applied by Excel, the program won't be able to automatically distinguish the row of field names from the row of entries for the first database record when you choose the Data⇨Form command. In such a case, Excel will then display a nasty-looking alert dialog box indicating that it can't determine which row in your list contains the column labels (that is, the field names). To have Excel use the first row as the field names, click the OK button or choose Enter.

To avoid having to deal with this alert dialog box entirely, be sure to add some sort of non-default formatting to one or more of the entries in either the row with the field names or the row with the entries for the first record. To avoid this dialog box, I usually format the cells in the top row with the field names by centering and boldfacing their entries. You could also avoid the alert dialog box by applying a new font or font size to the cells with the field names.

Adding records to the database

After you create the data form with the first record, you can use the form to add the rest of the records to the database. The process is simple. When you click the New button, Excel displays a blank data form (marked New Record at the right side of the data form), which you get to fill in.

Creating a data form from field names alone

You can create a data form for a new database simply by entering a row of field names and selecting them before you choose Data⬧Form on the menu bar. When you do this, Excel displays the alert dialog box indicating that the program can't determine which row in your list contains the column labels (that is, the field names). To have Excel use the selected row as the field names, click OK or press Enter. Excel will then create a blank data form listing all of the fields down the form in the same order as they appear across the selected row.

Creating a blank data form from field names alone is just fine, provided that your database doesn't contain any calculated fields (that is, fields whose entries result from a formula's computation rather than from manual entry). If your new database will contain calculated fields, you need to build their formulas in the appropriate fields of the first record. Then select both the row of field names and the first database record with the formulas indicating how the entries are calculated before you choose Form on the Data menu. Excel knows which fields are calculated and which are not (you can tell that a field is a calculated field in the data form because Excel lists its field name but does not provide an edit box for you to enter any information for it).

After you enter the information for the first field, press the Tab key to advance to the next field in the record.

Whoa! Don't press the Enter key to advance to the next field in a record. If you do, you'll insert the new, incomplete record into the database.

Continue entering information for each field and pressing Tab to go to the next field in the database.

- ✔ If you notice that you've made an error and want to edit an entry in a field you already passed, press Shift+Tab to return to that field.

- ✔ To replace the entry, just start typing.

- ✔ To edit some of the characters in the field, press ← or click the I-beam pointer in the entry to locate the insertion point; then edit the entry from there.

When entering information in a particular field, you can copy the entry made in that field for the previous record by pressing Ctrl+" (quotation mark). Press Ctrl+", for example, to carry forward the same entry in the State field of each new record when entering a series of records for people who all live in the same state.

When entering dates in a date field, use a consistent date format that Excel knows (for example, enter something like **2/19/93**). When entering zip codes that sometimes use leading zeros that you don't want to disappear from the entry (such as zip code **00102**), format the first field entry with the Special Zip Code number format (refer to "Sorting through the Special number formats" in Chapter 3 for details). In the case of other numbers that use leading zeros (like part numbers), you can put an ' (apostrophe) before the first 0. The apostrophe tells Excel to treat the number like a text label but doesn't show up in the database itself (the only place you can see the apostrophe is on the formula bar when the cell pointer's in the cell with the numeric entry).

Press the ↓ key when you've entered all the information for the new record. Instead of the ↓ key, you can press Enter or click the New button (see Figure 9-2). Excel inserts the new record as the last record in the database in the worksheet and displays a new blank data form in which you can enter the next record (see Figure 9-3).

When you finish adding records to the database, press the Esc key or click the Close button at the bottom of the dialog box to close the data form. Then save the worksheet with the File⇨Save command on the menu bar or click the Save tool on the Standard toolbar.

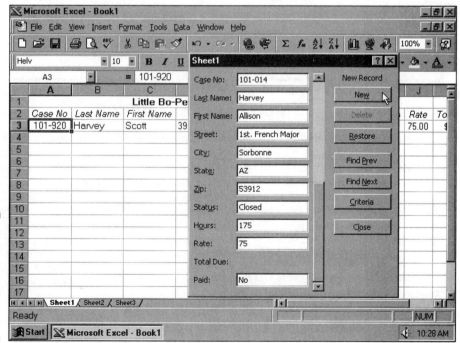

Figure 9-2: Entering information in the data form for the second record.

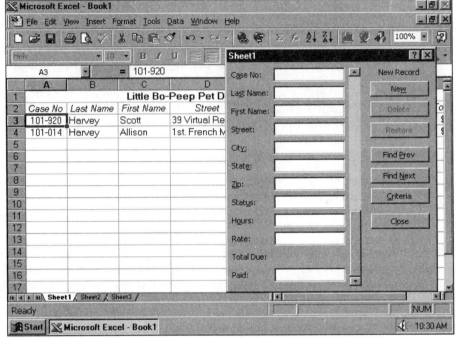

Figure 9-3:
The
database
after
entering the
second
record.

Calculated field entries

When you want Excel to calculate the entries for a particular field by formula, you need to enter that formula in the correct field in the first record of the database. Then select both the row of field names and the first record when creating the data form, and Excel copies the formula for this calculated field to each new record you add with the data form.

In the Bo Peep clients database, for example, the Total Due field in cell K3 of the first record is calculated by the formula =I3*J3Rate (cell I3 with the number of case hours having been named Hours and cell J3 with the hourly rate having

been named Rate). This formula then computes what the client owes by multiplying the number of case hours by the hourly rate. As you can see, Excel adds the calculated field, Total Due, to the data form but doesn't provide an edit box for this field (calculated fields can't be edited). When you enter additional records to the database, Excel calculates the formula for the Total Due field. If you then redisplay the data for these records, you see the calculated value following Total Due (although you won't be able to change it).

Locating, changing, and deleting records

After the database is underway and you're caught up with entering new records, you can start using the data form to perform routine maintenance on the database. For example, you can use the data form to locate a record you want to change and then make the edits to the particular fields. You can also use the data form to find a specific record you want to remove and then delete it from the database.

- ✔ Begin editing by positioning the cell pointer somewhere in the database (either in a cell with one of the database's field names or a in cell that forms a record with a field entry).

- ✔ Locate the record you want to edit in the database by bringing up its data form (see Table 9-1 and the following two sections "Scrolling the night away!" and "Finders keepers" for hints on locating records).

- ✔ To edit the fields of the current record, move to that field by pressing Tab or Shift+Tab and replace the entry by typing a new one.

- ✔ Alternatively, press ← or → or click the I-beam cursor to reposition the insertion point and then make your edits.

- ✔ To clear a field entirely, select it and then press the Delete key.

To delete the entire record from the database, click the Delete button. Excel displays an alert box with the following dire warning:

```
Displayed record will be deleted permanently
```

To go ahead and get rid of the record displayed in the data form, click OK. To play it safe and keep the record intact, click Cancel.

Please keep in mind that you *cannot* use the Undo feature to bring back a record you removed with the Delete button! Excel is definitely *not* kidding when it uses words like "deleted permanently." As a precaution, always save a backup version of the worksheet with the database before you start removing old records.

Scrolling the night away!

After you display the data form in the worksheet by positioning the cell pointer somewhere in the database and then choosing the Form command from the Data pull-down menu, you can use the scroll bar to the right of the list of field names or various keystrokes (both summarized in Table 9-1) to move through the records in the database until you find the one you want to edit or delete.

✔ To move to the data form for the next record in the database: Press ↓, press Enter, or click the down scroll arrow at the bottom of the scroll bar.

✔ To move to the data form for the previous record in the database: Press ↑, press Shift+Enter, or click the up scroll arrow at the top of the scroll bar.

✔ To move to the data form for the first record in the database: Press Ctrl+↑, press Ctrl+PgUp, or drag the scroll box to the very top of the scroll bar.

✔ To move to the data form for the last record in the database: Press Ctrl+↓, press Ctrl+PgDn, or drag the scroll box to the very bottom of the scroll bar.

Table 9-1	Ways to Get to a Particular Record
Keystrokes or Scroll Bar Technique	*Result*
Press ↓ or Enter or click the down scroll arrow or the Find Next button	Moves to the next record in the database and leaves the same field selected
Press ↑ or Shift+Enter or click the up scroll arrow or the Find Prev button	Moves to the previous record in the database and leaves the same field selected
Press PgDn	Moves forward ten records in the database
Press PgUp	Moves backward ten records in the database
Press Ctrl+↑ or Ctrl+PgUp or drag the scroll box to the top of the scroll bar	Moves to the first record in the database
Press Ctrl+↓ or Ctrl+PgDn or drag the scroll box to the bottom of the scroll bar	Moves to the last record in the database

Finders keepers

In a really large database, trying to find a particular record by moving from record to record — or even moving 10 records at a time with the scroll bar — can take all day. Rather than waste time trying to manually search for a record, you can use the Criteria button in the data form to look it up.

When you click the Criteria button, Excel clears all the field entries in the data form (and replaces the record number with the word *Criteria*) so that you can enter the criteria to search for in the blank edit boxes.

For example, suppose that you need to edit Old King Cole's file status (you've finally located his missing animals!). Unfortunately, his paperwork doesn't include his case number. All you know is that currently his case is open (meaning the Status field for his record contains "Active" rather than "Closed"), and you're pretty sure that he spells his last name with a *C* instead of a *K*.

To find his record, you can at least use the information you have to narrow the search down to all the records where the last name begins with the letter *C* and the Status field contains *Active*. To limit your search in this way, open the data form for the client database, click the Criteria button, and then enter the following in the edit box for the Last Name field:

```
C*
```

Also enter the following in the edit box for the Status field (see Figure 9-4):

```
Active
```

When you enter search criteria for records in the blank edit boxes of the data form, you can use the ? (question mark) and * (asterisk) *wildcard* characters. In Chapter 6, I show you how to use these wildcard characters with the Edit⇨Find command on the menu bar to locate cells with particular entries.

Now click the Find Next button. Excel displays in the data form the first record in the database where the last name begins with the letter C and the Status field contains *Active*. As shown in Figure 9-5, the first record in this database that

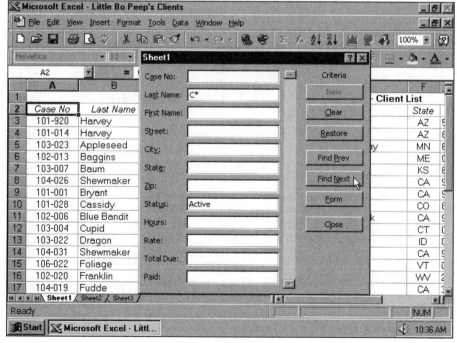

Figure 9-4: The data form after selecting the Criteria button and entering the search criteria in the blank field edit boxes.

meets these criteria is for Eros Cupid. To press on and find our Old King Cole's record, click the Find Next button again. Figure 9-6 shows Old King Cole's record. Having located Cole's record, you can then edit his case status in the edit box for the Status field. When you click the Close button, Excel records his new Closed case status in the database.

When you use the Criteria button in the data form to find records, you can include the following operators in the search criteria you enter to locate a specific record in the database:

Operator	*Meaning*
=	Equal to
>	Greater than
>=	Greater than or equal to
<	Less than
<=	Less than or equal to
<>	Not equal to

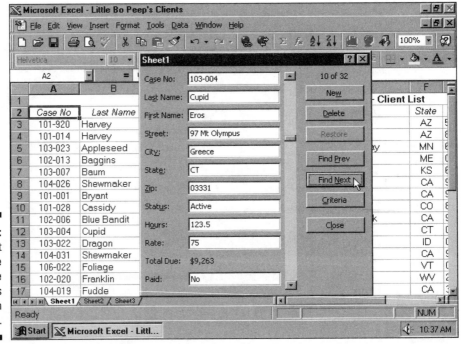

Figure 9-5: The first record in the database that meets the search criteria.

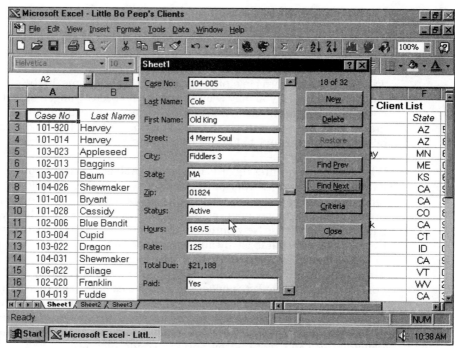

Figure 9-6:
Eureka! The
king's long
lost record
is found.

For example, to display only those records where a client's total due is greater than or equal to $50,000, enter **>=50000** in the edit box for the Total Due field before choosing the Find Next button.

When specifying search criteria that fit a number of records, you may have to click the Find Next or Find Prev button several times to locate the record you want. If no record fits the search criteria you enter, the computer beeps at you when you click these buttons.

To change the search criteria, first clear the data form by choosing the Criteria button again and then choosing the Clear button. Then select the appropriate edit boxes and clear out the old criteria before you enter the new. (You can just replace the criteria if you're using the same fields.)

To switch back to the current record without using the search criteria you enter, click the Form button (this button replaces the Criteria button as soon as you click the Criteria button).

Sorting It All Out

Every database you put together in Excel will have some kind of preferred order for maintaining and viewing the records. Depending on the database, you may want to see the records in alphabetical order by last name. In the case of a database of clients, you may want to see the records arranged alphabetically by company name. In the case of the Little Bo Peep clients database, the preferred order is in numerical order by the case number assigned to each client when he or she hires the agency to find his or her pets.

When you initially enter records for a new database, you no doubt enter them either in the preferred order or the order in which you get a hold of their records. However you start out, as you will soon discover, you don't have the option of adding subsequent records in that preferred order. Whenever you add a new record with the New button in the data form, Excel tacks that record onto the bottom of the database by adding a new row.

This means that if you originally enter all the records in alphabetical order by company (from *Acme Pet Supplies* to *Zastrow and Sons*) and then you add the record for a new client named *Bambi's Pasta Palace,* Excel puts the new record at the bottom of the barrel, in the last row right after *Zastrow and Sons* instead of inserting it in its proper position somewhere after *Acme Pet Supplies* but definitely well ahead of Zastrow and his wonderful boys!

And this is not the only problem you can have with the order used in originally entering records. Even if the records in the database remain fairly stable, the preferred order merely represents the order you use *most* of the time. But what about those times when you need to see the records in another, special order?

For example, although you usually like to work with the clients database in numerical order by case number, you may need to see the records in alphabetical order by the client's last name to quickly locate a client and look up his or her total due in a printout. When using the records to generate mailing labels for a mass-mailing, you want the records in zip-code order. When generating a report for your account representatives that shows which clients are in whose territory, you need the records in alphabetical order by state and maybe even by city.

It seems that flexibility in the record order is exactly what's required to keep up with the different needs you have for the data. This is precisely what the Data⇨Sort command offers you, once you understand how to use it.

To have Excel correctly sort the records in a database, you must specify the fields whose values determine the new order of the records (such fields being technically known as the *sorting keys* in the parlance of the database enthusiast). Further, you must specify what type of order should be created using the information in these fields. There are two possible orders: *ascending order,* in which text entries are placed in alphabetical order (A to Z) and values are placed in numerical order (from smallest to largest); and *descending order,* which is the exact reverse of alphabetical order (Z to A) and numerical order (largest to smallest).

When you sort records in a database, you can specify up to three fields on which to sort (you can also choose between ascending and descending order for each field you specify). You need to use more than one field only when the first field you use in sorting contains duplicate values and you want a say in how the records with duplicates are arranged. (If you don't specify another field to sort on, Excel just puts the records in the order in which you entered them.)

The best and most common example of when you need more than one field is when sorting a large database alphabetically in last-name order. Say that you have a database that contains several people with the last name Smith, Jones, or Zastrow (as is the case when you work at Zastrow and Sons). If you specify the Last Name field as the only field to sort on (using the default ascending order), all the duplicate Smiths, Joneses, and Zastrows are placed in the order in which their records were originally entered. To better sort these duplicates, you can specify the First Name field as the second field to sort on (again using the default ascending order), making the second field the tie-breaker, so that Ian Smith's record precedes that of Sandra Smith, and Vladimir Zastrow's record comes after that of Mikhail Zastrow.

To sort records in an Excel database, follow these steps:

1. **Position the cell pointer in the first field name of the database.**

2. **Choose <u>D</u>ata⇨<u>S</u>ort on the menu bar.**

   Excel selects all the records of the database (without including the first row of field names) and opens the Sort dialog box shown in Figure 9-7. By default, the first field name appears in the Sort by drop-down list box and the <u>A</u>scending radio button is selected at the top of the Sort dialog box.

Up and down the ascending and descending sort orders

When you use the ascending sort order with a key field that contains many different kinds of entries, Excel places numbers (from smallest to largest) before text entries (in alphabetical order), followed by any logical values (TRUE and FALSE), error values, and finally, blank cells.

When you use the descending sort order, Excel arranges the different entries in reverse: numbers are still first, arranged from largest to smallest; text entries go from Z to A; and the FALSE logical value precedes the TRUE logical value.

3. **Select the name of the field you first want the database records sorted by in the Sort by drop-down list box.**

   If you want the records arranged in descending order, remember also to choose the <u>D</u>escending radio button to the right.

4. **If the first field contains duplicates and you want to specify how these records are sorted, select a second field to sort on in the Then by drop-down list box and select between the As<u>c</u>ending and Desce<u>n</u>ding radio buttons to its right.**

5. **If necessary, specify a third field to sort the records by, using the second Then by drop-down list box and decide on the sort order to use.**

6. **Click OK or press Enter.**

   Excel sorts the selected records. If you see that you sorted the database on the wrong fields or in the wrong order, choose the <u>E</u>dit⇨<u>U</u>ndo Sort command on the menu bar or press Ctrl+Z to immediately restore the database records to their previous order.

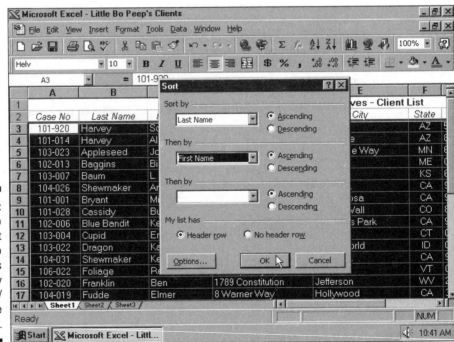

Figure 9-7:
Setting up the Sort dialog box to sort records alphabetically in last-name/first-name order.

Figure 9-7 shows the Sort dialog box after the Last Name field in the Bo Peep clients database is selected as the first field to sort on and the First Name field is selected as the second field on which to sort (these being the records with duplicate entries in the Last Name field). The settings in this dialog box specify that records in the Bo Peep clients database be sorted in alphabetical (ascending) order by last name and then first name. Figure 9-8 shows the clients database right after sorting (note how the Harveys — Allison, Chauncey, and Scott — are now arranged in the proper first name/last name alphabetical order).

You can use the Sort Ascending tool (the button with the A above the Z) or the Sort Descending tool (the button with the Z above the A) on the Standard toolbar to sort records in the database on a single field.

  ✔ To sort the database in ascending order by a particular field, position the cell pointer in that field's name at the very top of the database and then click the Sort Ascending button on the Standard toolbar.

  ✔ To sort the database in descending order by a particular field, position the cell pointer in that field's name at the very top of the database and then click the Sort Descending button on the Standard toolbar.

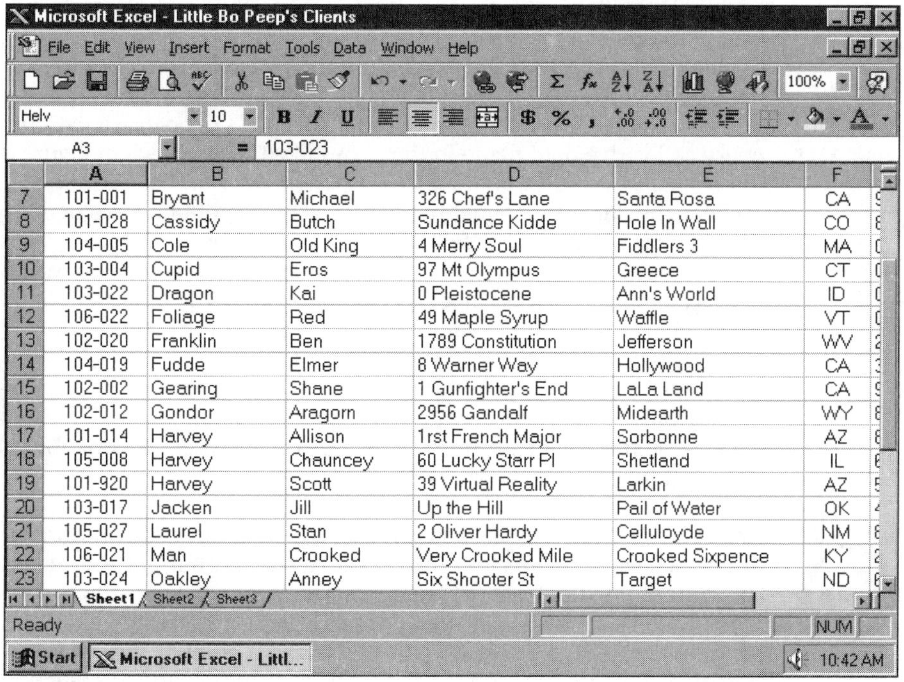

Figure 9-8:
The clients database sorted in alphabetical order by last name and then by first name.

	A	B	C	D	E	F
7	101-001	Bryant	Michael	326 Chef's Lane	Santa Rosa	CA
8	101-028	Cassidy	Butch	Sundance Kidde	Hole In Wall	CO
9	104-005	Cole	Old King	4 Merry Soul	Fiddlers 3	MA
10	103-004	Cupid	Eros	97 Mt Olympus	Greece	CT
11	103-022	Dragon	Kai	0 Pleistocene	Ann's World	ID
12	106-022	Foliage	Red	49 Maple Syrup	Waffle	VT
13	102-020	Franklin	Ben	1789 Constitution	Jefferson	WV
14	104-019	Fudde	Elmer	8 Warner Way	Hollywood	CA
15	102-002	Gearing	Shane	1 Gunfighter's End	LaLa Land	CA
16	102-012	Gondor	Aragorn	2956 Gandalf	Midearth	WY
17	101-014	Harvey	Allison	1rst French Major	Sorbonne	AZ
18	105-008	Harvey	Chauncey	60 Lucky Starr Pl	Shetland	IL
19	101-920	Harvey	Scott	39 Virtual Reality	Larkin	AZ
20	103-017	Jacken	Jill	Up the Hill	Pail of Water	OK
21	105-027	Laurel	Stan	2 Oliver Hardy	Celluloyde	NM
22	106-021	Man	Crooked	Very Crooked Mile	Crooked Sixpence	KY
23	103-024	Oakley	Anney	Six Shooter St	Target	ND

Sorting something besides a database

The Sort command is not just for sorting records in the database. You can use it to sort financial data or text headings in the spreadsheets you build as well. When sorting regular worksheet tables, just be sure to select all the cells with data to be sorted (and only those with the data to be sorted) before you choose Sort from the Data pull-down menu.

Also note that Excel automatically excludes the first row of the cell selection from the sort (on the assumption that this row is a header row containing field names that shouldn't be included). To include the first row of the cell selection in the sort, be sure to select the No Header Row radio button in the My List Has section before you click the OK button to begin sorting.

You AutoFilter the Database to See the Records You Want

Excel's AutoFilter feature makes it a breeze to hide everything in a database except the records you want to see. All you have to do to filter a database with this incredibly nifty feature is position the cell pointer somewhere in the database before you choose Data➪Filter➪AutoFilter on the menu bar. When you choose the AutoFilter command, Excel adds drop-down list buttons to every cell with a field name in that row (like those shown in Figure 9-9).

To filter the database to just those records that contain a particular value, you then click the appropriate field's drop-down list button to open a list box containing all of the entries made in that field and select the one you want to use as a filter. Excel then displays only those records that contain the value you selected in that field (all other records are temporarily hidden).

For example, in Figure 9-9, I filtered the Little Bo Peep clients database to display only those records where the State field contains AZ (for Arizona) by clicking on the State's drop-down list button and then clicking AZ in the drop-down list box. (It was as simple as that.)

After you've filtered a database so that only the records you want to work with are displayed, you can copy those records to another part of the worksheet to the right of the database (or better yet, another worksheet in the workbook). Simply select the cells and then choose Edit➪Copy on the menu bar (Ctrl+C), move the cell pointer to the first cell where the copied records are to appear, and press Enter. After copying the filtered records, you can then redisplay all the records in the database or apply a slightly different filter.

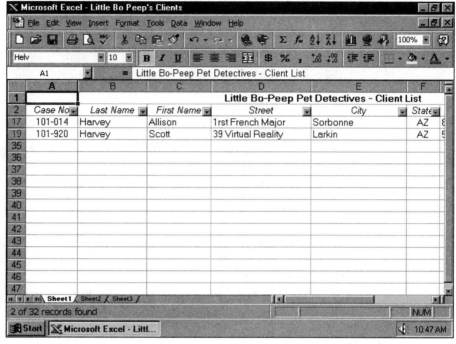

Figure 9-9:
The clients
database
after
filtering out
all records
except
those where
the State
is AZ.

If you find that filtering the database by selecting a single value in a field drop-down list box gives you more records than you really want to contend with, you can further filter the database by selecting another value in a second field's drop-down list box. For example, say that you select CA as the filter value in the State field's drop-down list box and end up with hundreds of California records still displayed in the worksheet. To reduce the number of California records to a more manageable number, you could then select a value like San Francisco in the City field's drop-down list box to further filter the database and reduce the records you have to work with on-screen. When you finish working with the San Francisco, California, records, you can display another set by choosing the City field's drop-down list box again and changing the filter value from San Francisco to some other city (such as Los Angeles).

When you're ready to once again display all the records in the database, choose Data⇨Filter⇨Show All on the menu bar. You can also remove a filter from a particular field by selecting its drop-down list button and then selecting the (All) option at the top of the drop-down list.

Note that if you've only applied a single field filter to the database, choosing the (All) option is tantamount to selecting the Data⇨Filter⇨Show All command on the menu bar.

Viewing the top ten records

Excel 97 contains an AutoFilter option called Top 10. You can use this option on a numerical field to show only a certain number of records (like the ones with the ten highest or lowest values in that field or those in the ten highest or lowest percent in that field). To use the Top 10 option to filter a database, follow these steps:

1. **Choose Data⇨Filter⇨AutoFilter on the menu bar.**

2. **Click the drop-down list button in the field that you want to use in filtering the database records.**

3. **Select the (Top 10) option in the drop-down list box.**

   Excel opens the Top 10 AutoFilter dialog box, similar to the one shown in Figure 9-10.

   By default, the Top 10 AutoFilter chooses to show the top ten items in the selected field. You can, however, change these default settings before filtering the database.

4. **To show only the bottom ten records, change Top to Bottom in the pop-up list box.**

5. **To show more than the top or bottom ten records, enter the new value in the edit box that currently holds 10 or select a new value using the spinner buttons.**

6. **To show those records that fall into the top or bottom 10 (or whatever)** *percent,* **change Items to Percent in its pop-up list box.**

7. **Click OK or press Enter to filter the database using your Top Ten settings.**

Figure 9-11 shows the Little Bo Peep clients database after using the Top Ten option (with all its default settings) to show only those records whose Total Due values are in the top ten. David Letterman would be proud!

Getting creative with custom AutoFilters

In addition to filtering a database to records that contain a particular field entry (such as *Newark* as the City or *CA* as the State), you can create custom AutoFilters that enable you to filter the database to records that meet less-exacting criteria (such as last names starting with the letter M) or ranges of values (such as salaries between $25,000 and $35,000 a year).

To create a custom filter for a field, you click the field's drop-down list button and then select the (Custom) option at the top of the pop-up list box — between (Top Ten) and the first field entry in the list box. When you select the (Custom) option, Excel displays the Custom AutoFilter dialog box, similar to the one shown in Figure 9-12.

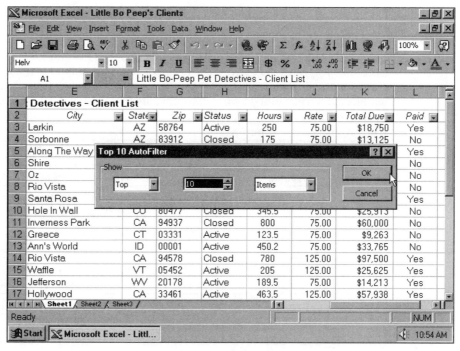

Figure 9-10:
The Top 10
AutoFilter
dialog box.

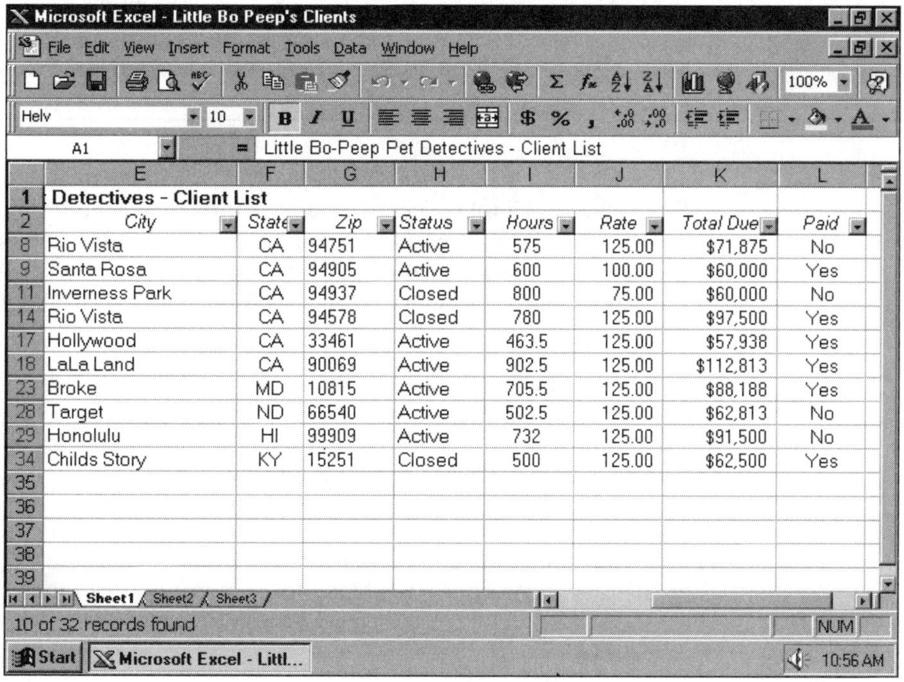

Figure 9-11:
The
database
after using
the Top 10
AutoFilter to
filter out all
records
except
those with
the ten
highest
Total Due
amounts.

In this dialog box, you first select the operator that you want to use in the first drop-down list box (=, >, <, >=, <=, or <> — see Table 9-2 for details) and then enter the value (be it text or numbers) that should be met, exceeded, fallen below, or not found in the records of the database in the edit box to the right. Note that you can select any of the entries made in that field of the database by choosing the drop-down list button and selecting the entry in the drop-down list box (much like you do when selecting an AutoFilter value in the database itself).

Table 9-2	Operators Used in Creating Custom AutoFilters		
Operator	*Meaning*	*Example*	*What It Locates in the Database*
=	Equal to	Last Name=D*	Records where the last name starts with the letter D
>	Greater than	ZIP >42500	Records where the number in the ZIP field comes after 42,500
<	Less than	Salary<25000	Records where the value in the Salary field is less than 25,000 a year
>=	Greater than	Hired>=1/11/92	Records where the date in or equal to the Hired field is on or after January 11, 1992
<=	Less than	Joined<=2/15/91	Records where the date in the or equal to Joined field is on or before February 15, 1991
<>	Not equal to	State<>NY	Records where the entry in the State field is not NY (New York)

If you only want to filter records where a particular field entry matches, exceeds, falls below, or simply is not the same as the one you enter in the edit box, you then click OK or press Enter to apply this filter to the database. However, you can use the Custom AutoFilter dialog box to filter the database to records with field entries that fall within a range of values or meet either one of two criteria.

To set up a range of values, you select the > or >= operator for the top operator and then enter or select the lowest (or first) value in the range. Then make sure that the And radio button is selected and select < or <= as the bottom operator and enter the highest (or last) value in the range.

Figures 9-12 and 9-13 illustrate how to filter the records in the clients database so that only those records where Total Due amounts are between 25,000 and 50,000 are displayed. As shown in Figure 9-12, you set up this range of values as

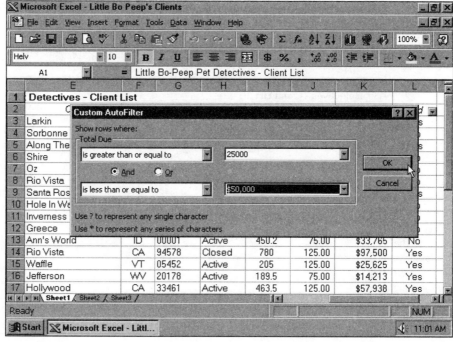

Figure 9-12:
Custom
AutoFilter
where the
Total Due is
greater than
or equal to
$25,000 or
less than or
equal to
$50,000.

the filter by first selecting >= as the operator and 25000 as the lower value of the range. Then, with the And radio button selected, you select <= as the operator and 50000 as the upper value of the range. Figure 9-13 shows the result of applying this filter to the clients database.

To set up an either/or condition in the Custom AutoFilter dialog box, you normally choose between the = (equal) and <> (unequal) operators (whichever is appropriate) and then enter or select the first value that must be met or must not be equaled. Then you select the Or radio button and select whichever operator is appropriate and enter or select the second value that must be met or must not be equaled.

For example, if you want to filter the database so that only records where the state is WA (Washington) or OR (Oregon) are displayed, you select = as the first operator and then select or enter WA as the first entry. Next, you select the Or radio button, select = as the second operator, and then select or enter OR as the second entry. When you then filter the database by choosing OK or pressing Enter, Excel displays only those records where either WA or OR is entered as the code in the State field.

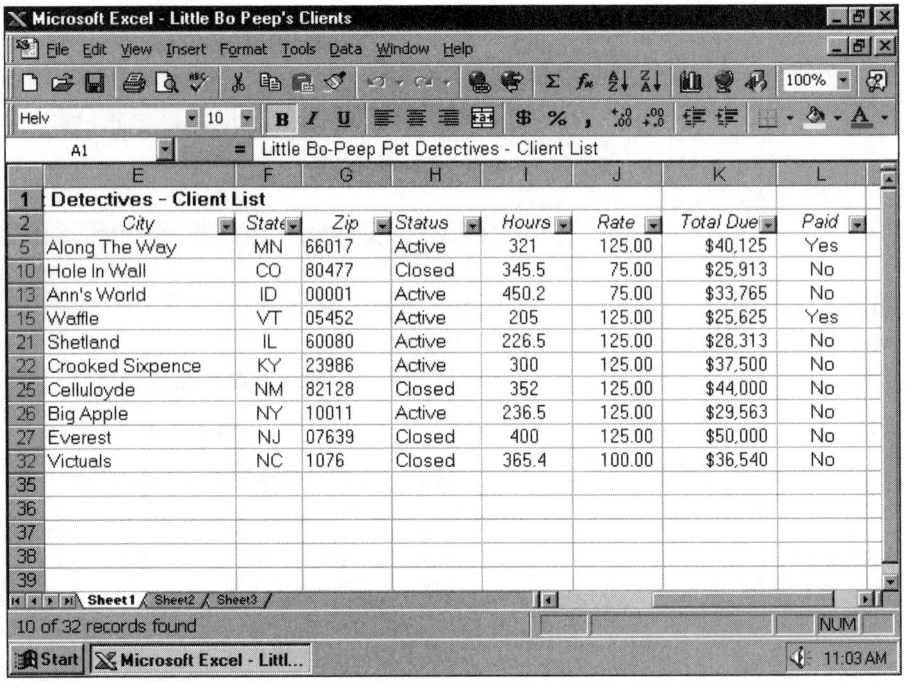
Microsoft Excel - Little Bo Peep's Clients
File Edit View Insert Format Tools Data Window Help
Helv 10
A1 = Little Bo-Peep Pet Detectives - Client List
Sheet1 Sheet2 Sheet3
10 of 32 records found
NUM
Start Microsoft Excel - Littl...
11:03 AM

	E	F	G	H	I	J	K	L
1	Detectives - Client List							
2	City	State	Zip	Status	Hours	Rate	Total Due	Paid
5	Along The Way	MN	66017	Active	321	125.00	$40,125	Yes
10	Hole In Wall	CO	80477	Closed	345.5	75.00	$25,913	No
13	Ann's World	ID	00001	Active	450.2	75.00	$33,765	No
15	Waffle	VT	05452	Active	205	125.00	$25,625	Yes
21	Shetland	IL	60080	Active	226.5	125.00	$28,313	No
22	Crooked Sixpence	KY	23986	Active	300	125.00	$37,500	No
25	Celluloyde	NM	82128	Closed	352	125.00	$44,000	No
26	Big Apple	NY	10011	Active	236.5	125.00	$29,563	No
27	Everest	NJ	07639	Closed	400	125.00	$50,000	No
32	Victuals	NC	1076	Closed	365.4	100.00	$36,540	No
35								
36								
37								
38								
39								

Figure 9-13: The database after applying the custom AutoFilter.

Chapter 10
Of Hyperlinks and HTML

● ●

In This Chapter

▶ Creating a hyperlink to another Office document, Excel workbook, worksheet, or cell range

▶ Creating a hyperlink to a Web page

▶ Changing the Hyperlink and Followed Hyperlink styles

▶ Converting an Excel data table into an HTML table

▶ Viewing your HTML table with your Web browser

▶ Publishing your worksheet data on the World Wide Web

● ●

 N ow that everyone and his brother seems to have a heavy dose of Internet fever and the World Wide Web has become the greatest thing since sliced bread, it should come as no surprise to learn that Excel 97 has added a whole bunch of exciting, new Web-related features. Chief among these features are the ability to add *hyperlinks* to the cells of your worksheet and the ability to convert your worksheet data to *HTML* (*H*yper*t*ext *M*arkup *L*anguage) tables.

Hyperlinks in a worksheet make the opening of other Office documents, Excel workbooks and worksheets (whether these documents are located on your hard disk, a server on your LAN [Local Area Network], or Web pages on the Internet or the company's intranet) just a mouse click away. HTML tables let you publish your worksheet on your Web pages (whether these pages are located on your company's intranet or the company's Web site on the Internet) more or less as you formatted them with Excel 97.

Adding Hyperlinks to a Worksheet

The hyperlinks that you add to your Excel worksheets can be of these types: *hypertext* that normally appears in the cell as underlined blue text, graphics from files that you've inserted into the worksheet, or graphics that you've drawn with the tools on the Drawing toolbar — in effect turning the graphic images into buttons.

When adding a hyperlink of either text or graphics, you can link it to an external file or Internet *URL* (*U*niform *R*esource *L*ocator) or to a named location in the worksheet. The named location can be a cell reference or named cell range (see Chapter 6 for details on naming cell ranges) in a particular worksheet.

To create the text in a cell to which the hyperlink is to be attached, follow these steps:

1. **Select the cell in the worksheet of the workbook that is to contain the hyperlink.**

2. **Enter the text for the hyperlink in the cell; then click the Enter button on the formula bar.**

To insert a graphics file into the worksheet to whose image the hyperlink is to be attached, follow these steps:

1. **Choose Insert⇨Picture⇨From File; then select the file with the image you want to use in the Insert Picture dialog box and click the Insert button or press Enter.**

   Excel inserts the graphic image into your worksheet. This graphic is selected (as evidenced by the sizing handles around the boundary box that surrounds it).

2. **Use the sizing handles to size the graphic image; then drag it to the place in the worksheet where you want the hyperlinked image to appear.**

To link the text or graphic image to another file, Web site, or named location in the workbook, follow these steps:

1. **Select the cell with the text or click the graphic to be linked.**

2. **Choose Insert⇨Hyperlink on the menu bar or click the Insert Hyperlink button (the one with the picture of a piece of chain link in front of the globe) on the Standard toolbar.**

   Excel opens the Insert Hyperlink dialog box (similar to the one shown in Figure 10-1) where you indicate the file, the Web address (URL), or the named location in the workbook.

3a. **To open another document, a Web page on the company's intranet, or a Web site on the Internet, enter the directory path to the document in the Link to file or URL edit box.**

   If the document you want to link to is located on your hard disk or a hard disk that is mapped on your computer, click the Browse button and select its file in the Link to File dialog box (which works just like the Open dialog box that I describe in Chapter 2) before you click OK.

   If the document you want to link to is located on a Web site and you know its Web address (the `http://www.dummies.com/excel97.htm`-like thing), you can type it into the Link to file or URL edit box.

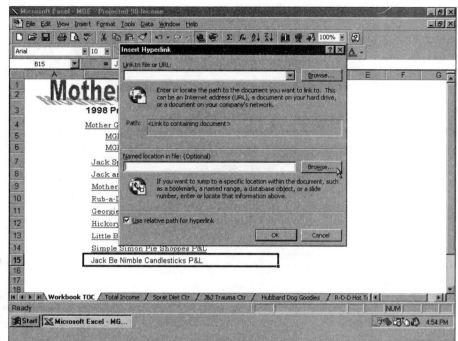

Figure 10-1:
The Insert
Hyperlink
dialog box.

If you're not sure what the exact address is for the Web page you want to link to (and you must enter it exactly as it is in the Link to file or URL edit box) but the Web page is one of those listed on Internet Explorer's Favorites pull-down menu, visit the Web page with your Web browser by selecting the page on the Favorites menu if you're using Internet Explorer or the Bookmarks menu if you're using Netscape Navigator; then switch to Excel 97 and open the Insert Hyperlink dialog box. Then click the Link to file or URL drop-down button: The URL address of the Web page you just visited will be listed at the bottom of the drop-down menu, and you can enter it into the edit box by selecting it on this menu.

3b. To move the cell pointer to another cell or cell range in the same workbook, select the Named location in file (Optional) edit box and enter the sheet name followed by the cell address or the defined range name.

The easiest way to enter the worksheet name and cell address or range name is to click the Browse button and then select the sheet name and cell reference or the defined range name in the Browse Excel Workbook dialog box (similar to the one shown in Figure 10-2). To select a cell reference in a worksheet, choose the Sheet Name radio button, click the worksheet name in the list box, and then enter the cell reference in the Reference edit box before you click OK. To select a range name, select the Defined Name radio button; then click the range name in the list box before you click OK.

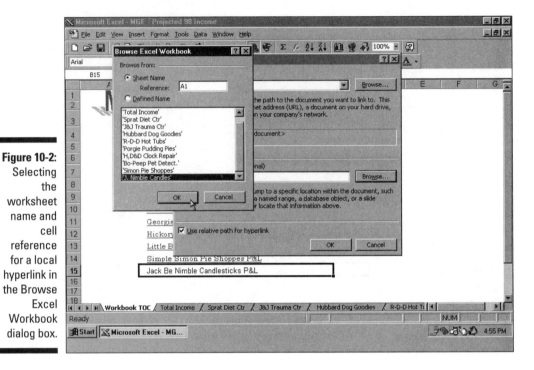

Figure 10-2:
Selecting
the
worksheet
name and
cell
reference
for a local
hyperlink in
the Browse
Excel
Workbook
dialog box.

4. **Click the OK button or press Enter to close the Insert Hyperlink dialog box.**

Follow those hyperlinks!

After you create a hyperlink in a worksheet, you can follow it to whatever external document, Web page, or cell range within the same workbook that is associated with the hyperlink. To follow a hyperlink, position the mouse pointer over the underlined blue text (if you assigned the hyperlink to text in a cell) or the graphic image (if you assigned the hyperlink to a graphic inserted in the worksheet). When the mouse pointer changes to a hand with the index finger pointing upward, click the hypertext or graphic image and Excel 97 makes the jump to the designated external document, Web page, or cell within the work-book. What happens when you make the jump depends on the destination of the hyperlink as follows:

✔ **Hyperlinks to external documents:** Excel opens the document in its own window. If the program that created the document (like Word 97 or PowerPoint 97) is not already running, Windows 95 will launch the pro-gram at the same time it opens the target document.

✔ **Hyperlinks to Web pages:** Excel opens the Web page in its own Web browser window. If you are not online at the time you click this hyperlink, Windows 95 opens the Connect To dialog box and you need to select the Connect button. If Internet Explorer is not open at the time you click this hyperlink, Windows 95 opens this Web browser prior to opening the Web page whose URL address is listed in the hyperlink.

✔ **Hyperlinks to cell ranges within the same workbook:** Excel activates the worksheet and selects the cell or cells whose sheet and cell range address is listed in the hyperlink.

After you follow a hypertext link to its destination, the color of its text changes from the traditional blue to a dark shade of purple (without affecting its underlining). This color change indicates that the hyperlink has been used (note, however, that graphic hyperlinks do not show any change in color after you follow them). To restore the hypertext links that you've followed to their original blue text color, you simply click the Refresh Current Page button on the Web toolbar (shown in Figure 10-3). You can display the Web toolbar by clicking the Web Toolbar button on the Standard toolbar or by choosing View➪ Toolbars➪ Web on the menu bar.

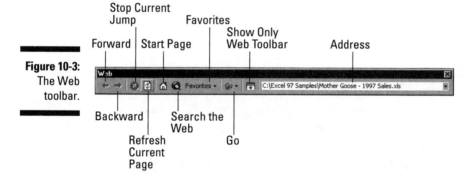

Figure 10-3: The Web toolbar.

Figures 10-4 through 10-6 illustrate how you might use hyperlinks to jump to different parts of the same workbook. Figure 10-4 shows a worksheet that contains an interactive table of contents to all of the Profit and Loss data tables and charts in this workbook. This interactive table of contents consists of a list of the data tables and charts contained in the workbook. A hypertext link to the appropriate worksheet and cell range has been added to each entry of this list in the cell range B4:B15 (I removed the gridlines from this worksheet to make it easier to see and use the hyperlinks).

Figure 10-5 shows what happens when I click the <u>Mother Goose Enterprises P&L</u> hyperlink. Excel immediately takes me to cell A1 of the Total Income worksheet. In this worksheet, the graphic image of a house (downloaded, by the way, from the Clip Art Gallery on Microsoft's Web site) appears to the right of the worksheet title in cell A1. This graphic contains a hyperlink that, when clicked, takes me to cell A1 of the Workbook TOC worksheet (the one shown in Figure 10-4).

Figure 10-6 shows what happens when I click the <u>MGE Projected Expenses Pie Chart</u> hypertext link. This hyperlink is attached to the named cell range, Exp_Pie. This cell range encompasses the cells A28:D45 in the Total Income worksheet. Note that clicking this hypertext link selects all cells in this named cell range, which just happen to be the ones that lie under the 3-D pie chart that shows the breakdown of the projected expenses anticipated in 1998. Because there is no way to attach a hyperlink directly to a chart that you add to a worksheet, you have to resort to selecting the underlying cells when you want a hyperlink to display a particular chart that's been added to a worksheet.

To the right of the MGE Projected 1998 Expenses pie chart, you see a star burst graphic (that I created with the Drawing toolbar, using the <u>S</u>tars and Banners option on the A<u>u</u>toShapes pop-up menu). This handmade graphic image contains the same hyperlink as the house Clip Art graphic (shown in Figure 10-5) so that, when clicked, it too takes me back to cell A1 of the Workbook TOC worksheet.

Figure 10-4:
Interactive
table of
contents
with
hypertext
links to
sheets with
P&L data
and pie
charts.

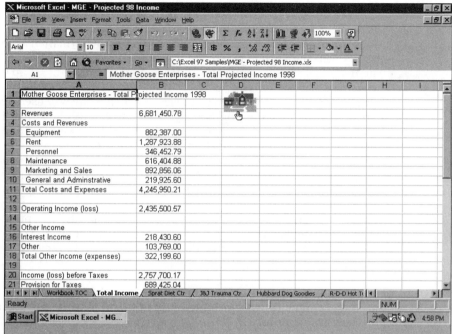

Figure 10-5:
Following the Mother Goose Enterprise P&L hypertext link.

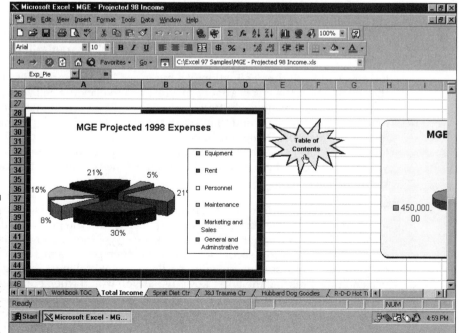

Figure 10-6:
Following the MGE Projected Expenses Pie Chart hypertext link.

Editing and formatting hypertext links

The contents of cells that contain hypertext links are formatted according to the settings contained in two built-in workbook styles: Hyperlink and Followed. The Hyperlink style is applied to all new hypertext links you set up in a worksheet that you haven't yet used. The Followed Hyperlink is applied to all hypertext links that you used. If you want to change the way used and unused hypertext appears in the workbook, you need to change the formatting used in Followed Hyperlink and Hyperlink styles respectively. (Refer to "Showing Off in Styles" in Chapter 3 for information on modifying styles.)

If you need to edit the contents of a cell containing a hypertext link, you must be careful that, while getting Excel 97 into Edit mode so that you can change the text, you don't inadvertently follow the link. This means that under *no* circumstances can you click the cell with the hypertext link with the (primary) mouse button because that's the way you follow the hypertext link to your destination! The best way to get around this problem, if you're used to selecting cells by clicking them, is by doing the following:

1. **Click a cell right next door to the one with the hypertext link (above, below, right, or left), provided that this neighboring cell doesn't contain its own hyperlink.**

2. **Press the appropriate arrow key to then select the cell with the hypertext link to be edited (↓, ↑, →, or ←).**

3. **Press F2 to put Excel 97 into Edit mode.**

4. **Make your changes to the contents of the hypertext in the cell; then click the Enter button or press Enter to complete your edits.**

If you need to edit the destination of a hypertext link (as opposed to contents of the cell to which the link is attached), you need to click the cell with the link with the secondary mouse button to open the cell's shortcut menu (and avoid following the hyperlink) and then select the Hyperlink⇨Edit Hyperlink command on this menu. Doing this opens the Edit Hyperlink dialog box (which looks suspiciously like the Insert Hyperlink dialog shown in Figure 10-1 after you've filled it in) where you can change either the type and/or the location of the hyperlink.

To copy a hyperlink from one cell to another, you click the cell with the secondary mouse button (be sure that you don't click it with the primary button or Excel will follow the hyperlink) and then select Hyperlink⇨Copy Hyperlink commands on the cell's shortcut menu. Excel then places a marquee around the cell and you can paste the copied hyperlink in a new cell by selecting the new cell and then pressing the Enter key (just as you would when copying the contents of the cell). Note that if you copy a hyperlink to an empty cell in the workbook, the directory path or URL address of the destination appears in the cell. Then, when you enter data in that cell, the hyperlink destination disappears and the data entry appears in the Hyperlink cell style.

If you want to remove the cell entry along with the hypertext link from a cell, you choose Edit⇨Clear⇨All on the menu bar. If you want to delete the hypertext link but leave the entry in the cell, you choose Edit⇨Clear⇨Hyperlinks instead. Just don't trying deleting a hypertext link by selecting the cell and pressing the Delete key: Doing this succeeds only in removing the entry from the cell without getting rid of the underlying hypertext link. Because pressing the Delete key merely removes the cell entry while leaving the hyperlink behind, if you click this seemingly empty cell, Excel 97 will jump you to the hyperlink's destination.

Editing and formatting graphics with hyperlinks

When it comes to editing the graphics images to which you assign hyperlinks, you can edit the graphic image either by holding the Ctrl key as you click the image and then choosing Format⇨Object on the menu bar (Ctrl+1) or by clicking the image with the secondary mouse button and then choosing Format Object on the graphic's shortcut menu. Doing this opens the Format Object dialog box where you can modify various and sundry attributes of the image such as its color, fill, brightness and contrast, how it's cropped, and whether or not the image moves and is resized when you edit the underlying cells.

If you want to manually resize the graphic image or move it to a new place in the worksheet, you need to Ctrl+click the graphic and then manipulate it with the mouse. To resize the graphic image, you drag the appropriate sizing handles. To relocate the graphic image, you drag the graphic (when the mouse pointer changes to an arrowhead pointing to two double-headed arrows in the form of a cross) to its new position in the worksheet.

To copy a graphic image along with its hyperlink, you can click the image as you hold down the Ctrl key and then (without releasing the Ctrl key) drag a copy of the image to its new location. Alternately, you can click the graphic image with the secondary mouse button and then put it into the Clipboard by choosing the Copy command on the graphics' shortcut menu. After you've copied the graphic with its hyperlink to the Clipboard, you can paste it into a worksheet by choosing Edit⇨Paste on the regular Excel menu bar (Ctrl+V) or by choosing the Paste button on the Standard toolbar.

To delete a graphic image and at the same time remove its hyperlink, you Ctrl+click the graphic to select it and then press the Delete key. To remove a hyperlink without deleting the graphic image, Ctrl+click the graphic and then choose Edit⇨Clear⇨Hyperlinks on the menu bar. To edit the hyperlink's destination, click the graphic image with the secondary mouse button; then select the Hyperlink⇨Edit Hyperlink command on the image's shortcut menu to open the Edit Hyperlink dialog box where you can modify the location to be followed.

Spreadsheets on the Web?

Actually, the concept of publishing Excel spreadsheet data on the World Wide Web makes a heck of a lot of sense, both from the standpoint of the worksheet's tabular layout and the worksheet's calculated contents. As anyone who's tried to code an HTML table will tell you, this is one of the nastiest jobs a person can perform. Even creating the simplest HTML table is a pain because you have to use <TH> and </TH> tags to set up the column headings in the table along with <TR> and </TR> tags to set up the rows of the table and <TD> and </TD> tags to define the number and width of the columns as well as what data goes in each cell of the table.

Even when using an HTML authoring tool that doesn't make you go through this kind of brute-force table making with the objectionable HTML table tags (like the Internet Assistant for Word, which lets you set up and fill in a table from the menu bar just like you would in a regular Word document), you don't end up with a fancy table with sculpted borders between the cells and you still don't have the luxury of performing calculations between data in the table cells like you do when using the Internet Assistant for Excel to convert your worksheet data tables.

By using the Internet Assistant Wizard in Excel 97, you get the best of both worlds: You can use all of Excel's calculation power, while at the same time automatically generating very fancy-looking HTML tables for your Web pages.

Converting worksheet data into an HTML table

The Internet Assistant Wizard walks you through the steps (which are really quite straightforward) for converting your data table in the current worksheet into an HTML table. During this procedure, you can either choose to have the HTML table placed in a brand new HTML document or into an existing HTML document.

Creating a table in a new HTML document

To convert Excel worksheet data to an HTML table in a new HTML document, follow these steps:

1. **Open the workbook with the data to be converted; then activate its worksheet and select the cells as a range.**

2. **Choose File➪Save as HTML on the menu bar.**

   Doing this opens the Internet Assistant Wizard - Step 1 of 4 dialog box (similar to the one shown in Figure 10-7).

3a. (Optional) To add other data ranges to be included in the HTML document, click the <u>A</u>dd button; then type in the address of the new cell range or select its cells in the worksheet and click OK or press Enter.

3b. (Optional) To change the order in which the data ranges and charts appear in the HTML document, click the name of the range or chart in the Ranges or charts to convert list box; then click the appropriate Move arrow button (clicking the one pointing up moves the selected range or chart up one position in the list, and clicking the one pointing down moves the selected range or chart down one position in the list).

3c. (Optional) To remove a data range or chart listed in the Ranges or charts to convert list box from the HTML document, click its name in this list box and then click the <u>R</u>emove button.

4. When the Ranges and charts to convert list box contains the data ranges and charts you want included in the correct order, click the Next> button or press Enter.

When you choose Next>, Excel displays the Internet Assistant Wizard - Step 2 of 4 dialog box (similar to the one shown in Figure 10-8).

5. By default, the Internet Assistant Wizard creates a new HTML document that contains the converted worksheet and chart data along with a header and footer so that you just need to click the Next> button or press Enter to move on to the Step 3 dialog box.

When you choose Next>, the Internet Assistant Wizard displays the Internet Assistant Wizard - Step 3 of 4 dialog box (similar to the one shown in Figure 10-9).

6. When creating a new HTML document, you can enter the text to be displayed as the document's title; header; description below the header; and a footer with the date last updated, name, and e-mail address. You can also have the Internet Assistant insert a horizontal rule above and below the HTML table. When you have finished making your choices in this dialog box, click Next> or press Enter to move to the next dialog box.

The Internet Assistant Wizard - Step 4 of 4 dialog box (shown in Figure 10-10) then appears, where you can indicate the language and operating system used for your Web page, whether or not you want the Internet Assistant Wizard to save the result as plain old HTML file or an HTML file that can be edited with the Microsoft FrontPage Editor (part of the FrontPage program that lets you create and maintain your Web site) as well as indicate the path and filename for the new HTML document.

7. By default, the Internet Assistant Wizard saves the result as an HTML file associated with whatever you've designated as your default Web browser (probably either Internet Explorer or a version of Netscape Navigator). If you use the Microsoft FrontPage program to create and edit Web pages for your company's intranet or the Internet, you can choose the <u>A</u>dd the result to my FrontPage Web radio button to have the new HTML file associated with its FrontPage Editor.

8. **Edit the path and filename in the File path edit box in the Step 4 dialog box or use the Browse button to open the destination folder and to enter the new filename before you click the Finish button or press Enter.**

   When you choose the Finish button, the Internet Assistant Wizard creates a new HTML document with a table containing the selected worksheet and chart data.

9. **Deselect the data in the Excel worksheet.**

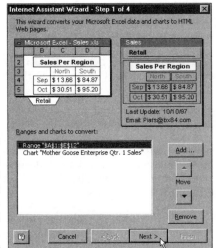

Figure 10-7:
The Internet
Assistant
Wizard -
Step 1 of 4
dialog box.

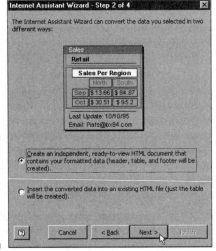

Figure 10-8:
The Internet
Assistant
Wizard -
Step 2 of 4
dialog box.

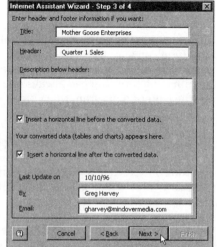

Creating a table in an existing HTML document

Many times you will want to add a table of worksheet data or a chart to an existing HTML document. To insert the data and charts into an existing HTML document, you must have already indicated the place in this HTML document where the converted data are to appear. To do this, you enter this weird-looking comment tag:

```
<!--##Table##-->
```

on its own line in the HTML document where the converted HTML tables and charts are to be inserted. To do this, you can simply open the HTML document with your favorite HTML authoring tool (like the Microsoft FrontPage Editor). If you don't have a favorite HTML authoring tool, you can always open up and edit the HTML document with the Notepad program that comes with Windows 95.

After you have inserted this comment tag into the existing HTML document, you follow the same first four steps for saving the data in an HTML document as outlined in the earlier section, "Creating a table in a new HTML document." Then, with the Internet Assistant Wizard - Step 2 dialog box (shown in Figure 10-8) open, take these new steps:

1. **Select the Insert the converted data into an existing HTML file (just the table will be created) radio button in the Internet Assistant Wizard - Step 2 dialog box.**

2. **Click the Next> button or press Enter.**

   When you choose Next>, Excel displays the Internet Assistant Wizard - Step 3 of 4 dialog box (similar to the one shown in Figure 10-11).

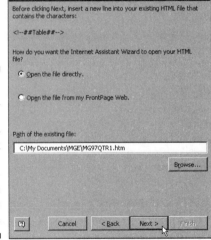

Figure 10-11: The HTML Wizard - Step 3 of 4 dialog box when inserting the table into an existing HTML file.

3. **By default, the Internet Assistant Wizard opens your HTML file directly. If, however, you use the Microsoft FrontPage program to create and edit Web pages for your company's intranet, select the Open the file from my FrontPage Web radio button.**

4. **Enter the path and name of the HTML document into which the new table is to be inserted in the Path of the existing file edit box or use the Browse button to open its folder and select the file before you click Next or press Enter.**

The Internet Assistant Wizard then checks the specified HTML file for the <--##Table##--> comment tag indicating where the new table is to be inserted. If this tag is not found in the specified HTML file, Excel 97 displays an alert box (as shown in Figure 10-12) indicating that you need to use your Web browser or a text editor to add this string to the HTML document. At that point, you must click OK or press Enter to close the alert box; then open the designated HTML file, add this tag, and save the document before you return to Internet Assistant Wizard in Excel 97, where you can try clicking the Next> button again.

Assuming that this code is found when you choose Next>, the Internet Assistant Wizard - Step 4 of 4 dialog box then appears where you can indicate whether or not to save the revised document as a standard HTML file or as an HTML page for your Web site created and maintained with the Microsoft FrontPage program.

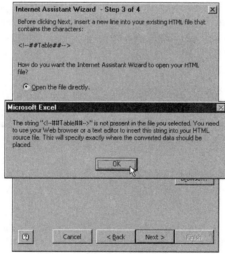

Figure 10-12: An alert box indicating that the Internet Assistant Wizard has not found the <!- -##Table ## - -> tag in your HTML file.

5. **By default, the Internet Assistant Wizard saves result as an HTML file associated with whatever you've designated as your default Web browser (probably either Internet Explorer or a version of Netscape Navigator). If you use the Microsoft FrontPage program to create and edit Web pages for your company's intranet or the Internet, you can choose the Add the result to my FrontPage Web radio button to have the new HTML file associated with its FrontPage Editor.**

6. **Edit the path and filename in the File path edit box in the Step 4 dialog box or use the Browse button to open the destination folder. Save the revised HTML document under a new filename before you click the Finish button or press Enter.**

When you click the Finish button, the Internet Assistant Wizard creates a new a table containing the selected worksheet data in the existing HTML document you specified.

Checking your HTML table with your Web browser

After the HTML table has been created from your Excel worksheet data, you will want to check out the results with your favorite Web browser. You can do this locally on your computer's hard disk before you (or your company's Web master) download or copy the HTML document to your Web server. Just follow these steps:

1. **If you use Internet Explorer as your Web browser, double-click The Internet shortcut on your desktop. If you use Netscape Navigator (and you don't have a comparable Navigator shortcut on your desktop that you can double-click), click the Start button, highlight Programs on the Start menu, and click Netscape Navigator on the Programs continuation menu.**

Doing this opens the Connect To dialog box, which connects you to your Internet Service Provider (you know, that ISP thing).

2. **If you use a dial-up account to access the Internet, click the Cancel button in the Connect To dialog box that appears.**

Selecting the Cancel button generates an Internet Explorer or Netscape Navigator alert dialog box with an error message telling you that the Home site or server at the address shown in the Address or Location edit box could not be located.

3. **If an alert box telling you that the address indicated in the Address or Location edit box could not be located, click OK or press Enter to get rid of the alert dialog box.**

4. **Choose File⇨Open on the Web browser's pull-down menu or press Ctrl+O.**

Doing this opens an Open dialog box where you can specify the folder and name of the HTML file that contains the HTML table that you want to check.

5a. If you're using Internet Explorer, you can type in the path and filename of the HTML document containing your worksheet data and charts in the Open edit box or click the Browse button to display the regular Open dialog box where you can select the folder in the Look in drop-down menu and then select the file in the list box or specify its filename in the File name edit box. After designating the folder and file in this dialog box, click the Open button or press Enter to return to the original Open dialog box and then click the OK button or press Enter again to open the HTML file in the Internet Explorer window.

5b. If you're using Netscape, select the folder in the Look in drop-down menu and then select the file in the list box or specify its filename in the File name edit box. After designating the folder and file in this dialog box, click the Open button or press Enter to open the HTML file in the Navigator window.

After you complete these steps, your Web browser loads the HTML document, displaying its data tables and charts exactly as it will appear to other users who visit your Web site when you (or your Web master) put the document up with the other Web pages.

Figure 10-13 shows you the top part of the HTML table created from sample worksheet data when viewed in Microsoft's Internet Explorer 3.0. (The process of creating this table in a new HTML document is outlined in Figures 10-7 through 10-10 in the section "Creating a table in a new HTML document.") Figure 10-14 shows the very bottom part of this same HTML table when viewed with Netscape Navigator 3.0.

Note how the information entered into the Internet Assistant Wizard - Step 3 dialog box (shown back in Figure 10-9) appears in the final HTML document shown in these two figures. The Title information appears at the beginning of the title bar of Internet Explorer (Figure 10-13) and in brackets after Navigator in the title bar of Netscape Navigator (Figure 10-14). The Header and Description below header information appear in Figure 10-13 above the first rows of the HTML table separated by a rule (the horizontal line). The Last Update, By (my name), and Email information appear in Figure 10-14 below the last rows of the HTML table separated by a second rule. Note that the Email information near the bottom of Figure 10-14 is a live hypertext link. If you wanted to send me a message, all you would have to is click the hypertext gharvey@mindovermedia.com and Netscape Navigator would open a brand new e-mail message form that you could fill-in and then send to me by clicking its Send Now button.

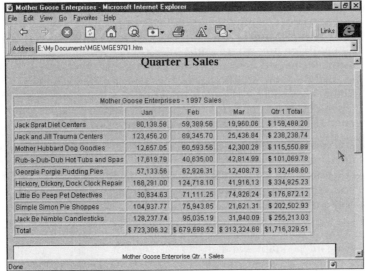

Figure 10-13:
The top part of the HTML table created from the worksheet data shown in Microsoft's Internet Explorer 3.0 browser.

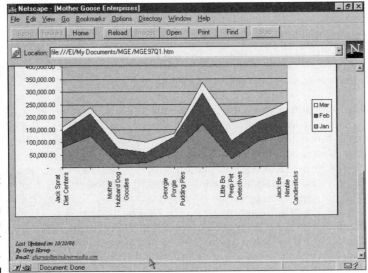

Figure 10-14:
The bottom part of the HTML table created from the worksheet data shown in the Netscape Navigator 3.0 browser.

Part V
Doing a Custom Job

The 5th Wave   By Rich Tennant

MEN

PRINTER PAPER

In this part . . .

In case you haven't noticed, one of the biggest problems with computers is how rigid they are, working for you only when you do exactly what they want you to do, right when they want you to do it. And, like it or not, software programs like Excel 97 are no different with their demanding command sequences and inflexible procedures.

Having seen how Excel 97 wants things done, I say it's high time to turn the tables and find out how to make the program work the way you want it to. To that end, Part V concentrates on all the areas that you can customize. This includes changing the default settings in Chapter 11, streamlining routine procedures with macros in Chapter 12, and creating tailor-made toolbars in Chapter 13.

Chapter 11

Stating Your Preferences

. . . .

In This Chapter

▶ Changing the way stuff is displayed on-screen

▶ Customizing general settings

▶ Customizing the colors displayed on a color monitor

▶ Changing the way Excel works when editing your worksheets

. . . .

*E*ach time you open a new workbook, Excel 97 makes a whole bunch of assumptions about how you want the spreadsheet and chart information you enter into it to appear on-screen and in print. These assumptions may or may not fit the way you work and the kinds of spreadsheets and charts you need to create.

In this chapter, you get a quick rundown on how to change the default or *preference* settings in the Options dialog box. This is the biggest dialog box in Excel, with a billion tabs (eight actually), which explains why it takes so long to open. From the Options dialog box, you can see what things appear on-screen and how they appear, as well as when and how Excel calculates worksheets.

Nothing in this chapter is critical to your being able to operate Excel. Just know that if you find yourself futzing with the same setting over and over again in most of the workbooks you create, then it's high time to get into the Options dialog box and modify that setting so that you won't end up wasting anymore time tinkering with the same setting in future workbooks.

Varying the View Options

Excel 97 gives you a lot of control over what appears on-screen and how it looks. The options for controlling the appearance of the Excel program and workbook windows mostly show up on the View tab of the Options dialog box. In addition, you can customize the cell-reference style, the menus used, the number of worksheets in a new workbook, and the font that each new work-book uses — all in the General tab of the Options dialog box (discussed in the next section, "Fooling Around with the General Options").

Figure 11-1 shows the options on the View tab of the Options dialog box. To open this dialog box, choose Tools⇨Options on the menu bar and then select the View tab. The View tab contains a mess of check boxes that turn on and off the display of various elements in both the Excel program window and a particular workbook document window. As you would expect, all the options that have check marks in their check boxes are turned on, whereas all the options with empty check boxes are turned off.

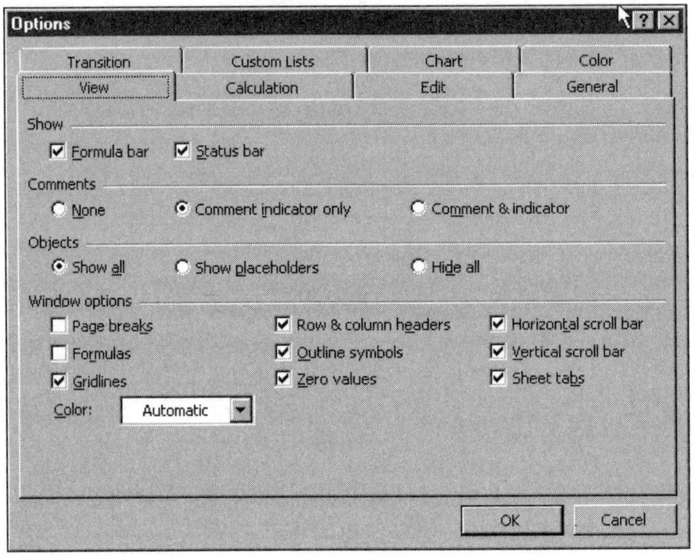

Figure 11-1:
The View tab in the Options dialog box.

The check boxes and radio buttons in the Show, Comments, and Objects areas of this dialog box control which elements are displayed in the Excel program window. In the Show area, you find these two check boxes:

- **Formula bar:** to hide or show the formula bar right below the Formatting toolbar at the top of the program window (see Chapter 2).

- **Status bar:** to hide or show the status bar at the bottom of the program window (see Chapter 1).

In the Comments area, you find these three radio buttons:

- **None:** to hide both the comment indicators (the little red triangle in the upper-right corner) and the display of the comment's text box.

- **Comment indicator only:** to show only the comment indicators in the cells without displaying the contents of the comment in the text box. (See Chapter 6 for information on creating comments.)

- **Comments & indicator:** to display both the comment indicators and the text boxes with the comments in the workbook.

In the Objects area, you find these three radio buttons (see Chapter 8 for more on graphics objects in Excel 97):

✔ **Show all:** to show all graphic objects (such as charts, clip art, and other types of graphics) in the workbook.

✔ **Show placeholders:** to show grayed out rectangles where the graphic objects normally appear.

✔ **Hide all:** to hide all graphic objects in the workbook.

The check box options in the Window options area of the View tab determine whether or not a number of elements in the current worksheet are displayed. Keep in mind that turning off a particular element in the current worksheet does not turn it off in any other worksheet in that workbook. All of the following option settings are saved as part of your worksheet when you save the workbook, except for the Automatic Page Breaks option (which always reverts to the default of being hidden):

✔ **Page breaks:** to hide or show the page breaks that Excel puts in the worksheet when you print it or look at it in Print Preview mode.

✔ **Formulas:** to switch between showing the formulas in the cells of your worksheet and showing the calculated values (the normal state of affairs). When you select this check box, Excel also automatically widens all the columns and left-aligns all of the information in the cells.

✔ **Row & column headers:** to hide or show the row of column letters at the top of the worksheet and the column of row numbers at the left.

✔ **Gridlines:** to hide or show the column and row separators that define the cells in your worksheet. Note that you can also change the color of the gridlines (when they're displayed, of course) by choosing a new color in the color palette that appears when you click the Color drop-down list button (I find that navy blue is rather fetching).

✔ **Outline symbols:** to hide or show all the various symbols that appear when you outline a worksheet table (something you only do with really large tables so that you can collapse the table to its essentials by hiding all but particular levels) or when you use the Subtotals feature to calculate subtotals, totals, and grand totals for certain fields in a database. (For a complete discussion on outlining worksheet data, see my *MORE Excel 97 For Windows For Dummies.*)

✔ **Zero values:** to hide or display entries of zero in the worksheet. Deselect this check box if you want to suppress the display of all zeros in a worksheet (as you might in a worksheet template if you don't want to see all those zeros in a new worksheet generated from the template).

✔ **Horizontal scroll bar:** to hide or display the horizontal scroll bar to the right of the worksheet tabs at the bottom of the workbook document window. When you hide the horizontal scroll bar and leave the sheet tabs displayed (see Sheet ta**b**s below), Excel fills the area normally reserved for the horizontal scroll bar with more sheet tabs. Note that this option affects the display of every worksheet in your workbook.

✔ **Vertical scroll bar:** to hide or display the vertical scroll bar on the right side of the workbook document window. This option also affects the display of every worksheet in your workbook.

✔ **Sheet ta**b**s:** to hide or display the tabs that enable you to activate the various worksheets in your workbook. Note that when you remove the display of the sheet tabs, you can still use Ctrl+PgDn and Ctrl+PgUp to move between worksheets. However, without the tabs, you won't know which worksheet you're looking at unless you can recognize the sheet from its data alone.

Fooling Around with the General Options

The General tab in the Options dialog box (shown in Figure 11-2) contains a number of program-setting options that you might want to change (if not right away, then after working with Excel 97 a little more). Of special interest to some might be the **S**heets in new workbook option that sets the number of blank worksheets in each new workbook (you might routinely need more than three and want to choose a more realistic number: hey, like five, or maybe, if you're feeling wild, ten); the St**a**ndard font option that sets the font used in every cell of a new workbook; and the **D**efault file location that determines which directory Excel automatically chooses when you try to open or save a workbook document.

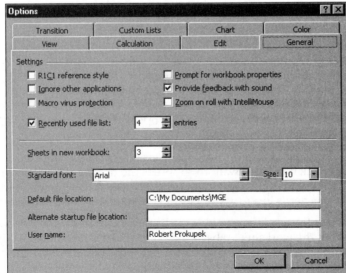

Figure 11-2:
The General
tab in the
Options
dialog box.

✔ **R1C1 reference style:** This box switches you out of the A1, B1, and so on cell reference system that Excel normally uses into the creepy R1C1 alternate style in which each column is numbered just like the rows, and the row (that's the R part) reference number precedes the column (that's the C part) reference number. In this system, the cell you know and love as B2 would be cell R2C2. (Hey, wasn't that the name of that vacuum-cleaner-like droid in *Star Wars?!*)

✔ **Ignore other applications:** When this check box contains a check mark, Excel ignores requests made from other programs using DDE (which stands for Dynamic Data Exchange, as if you care). This is of interest only if you are using data created with other programs in your Excel workbooks (in which case, you definitely want leave this check box alone).

✔ **Macro virus protection:** When this check box contains a check mark, Excel displays a warning message when you open workbooks with macros (see Chapter 12), customized toolbars, menus, or shortcuts (see Chapter 13) on the assumption that they may contain viruses. Note that this option doesn't check your macros, customized toolbars, and the like to determine whether or not they actually contain viruses, but this option just warns you that this might be the case (especially if the workbooks were developed out-of-house and were downloaded from a unsecured network or Internet site).

✔ **Prompt for workbook properties:** Normally, Excel does not display a Properties dialog box where you can enter summary information about the subject of the workbook as well as key words that you later use when searching for the file. That can all change if you put a check mark in this check box as Excel 97 will then automatically remind you to enter summary information for each new workbook that you save.

✔ **Provide feedback with sound:** When you select this check box, Excel plays available sounds associated with routine events like opening and saving workbooks and displaying alert dialog boxes. Note that if you deselect this check box, you not only turn off sound feedback in Excel 97 but in all other Office 97 application programs (like Word 97, PowerPoint 97, and so on) as well. To change a sound that is associated with a particular event, you need to open the Sounds folder in the Control Panel (opened by clicking the Start button and then choosing Settings⇨Control Panel on the pop-up menu) and make the changes in the Sounds Properties dialog box.

✔ **Zoom on roll with IntelliMouse:** If you're using Microsoft's new Intelli-Mouse (see "Scrolling with the IntelliMouse" in Chapter 1) with Excel 97 and you select this check box, you can zoom in and out on the current worksheet (as explained in Chapter 6) just by rolling its wheel. When you roll the wheel down one click, Excel zooms out on the worksheet by reducing the magnification by 15 percent (until the magnification reaches 10 percent). When you roll the wheel up one click, Excel zooms in on the worksheet by increasing the magnification by 15 percent (until the magnification reaches 100 percent).

✔ **Recently used file list:** When you select this check box, Excel lists the last four documents you opened (in the order that you opened them) at the bottom of the File menu. You can then open any of these four files simply by selecting its name (or number) after you open the File menu.

✔ **Sheets in new workbook:** Normally, Excel puts three blank worksheets in each new workbook you open. If you're never in a million years gonna use more than one or two worksheets, you can select this option and reduce the number. On the other hand, you can also use this option to increase the number of worksheets in a new workbook if you find that you're routinely using more than three sheets and you're getting tired of having to use the Insert➪Worksheet command. (See Chapter 7 for more information on manually inserting and removing worksheets from a workbook.)

✔ **Standard font** and **Size:** Use these options to change the font and/or font size that Excel automatically assigns to all the cells in a new workbook. If you have a favorite font that you like to see in most of the worksheets you create (and Arial ain't it), this is the way to select your font of choice rather than having to call upon the Font tool on the Formatting toolbar all the time (see Chapter 3).

✔ **Default file location:** If you don't specify a directory for this option when you first start Excel, the program looks for each workbook that you try to open or puts each new workbook that you save in a folder named My Documents on your hard disk. Use this option to select another folder as the repository of your precious documents by entering the path name of the folder (such as C:\Greg\Excel Stuff). Note that this folder must exist prior to using this option (it can't be one that you intend to create but just haven't gotten around to yet). Remember that you can create a new folder at the time you first save a new workbook by clicking the Create New Folder button on the Save As dialog box toolbar.

✔ **Alternate startup file location:** Normally, Excel opens any document that you put in the special Startup folder called XLStart whenever you start Excel. If you don't feel that one Startup folder is enough, you can use this option to specify another one. Again, this folder must already exist before you can designate it as your alternate startup location by entering its path in this edit box.

✔ **User name:** In my copy of Excel, this is usually Greg Harvey (unless I'm using my nom de plume, I.M. Shakes Peer), but it will differ in your copy unless you happen to go by the same name or alias. If you want to change your user name to Greg Harvey or I.M. Shakes Peer, this is where you do it.

Changing Those Crazy Color Palettes

If you're fortunate enough to have a color monitor on your computer, you can spruce up the on-screen appearance of a document by applying various colors to different parts of worksheets or charts. Excel lets you choose from a palette of 56 predefined colors; you can apply these colors to specific cells, cell borders, fonts, or graphic objects (such as an arrow or a particular data series in a chart or a text box).

- ✔ To apply a new color to a cell selection or a selected graphic object, click the Fill Color tool on the Formatting toolbar (the one with the paint bucket) and select the color you want to apply from the pop-up palette of 56 colors.

- ✔ To change the color of the font Excel uses in a cell selection or for a selected graphic object (such as a chart title or text box), choose the Font Color tool on the Formatting toolbar (the one with A underlined with the currently selected color) and select the color you want to apply in the pop-up palette of 56 colors.

- ✔ To change the color of the borders of a cell or cell selection, open the Format Cells dialog box (Ctrl+1); then select the Border tab and select the Color option or click its drop-down list button to display the palette of 56 colors from which you can select the one you want to assign to the borders of the selected cells.

If none of the 56 predefined colors exactly suits your artistic tastes, you can customize colors on the palette. Although you can't place additional colors on the palette, you can change any or all of the predefined colors, depending on how ambitious you want to get.

To customize a color on the palette, follow these steps:

1. **Choose Tools➪Options on the menu bar to open the Options dialog box.**

2. **Select the Color tab in the Options dialog box (shown in Figure 11-3).**

3. **Select the color you want to modify in any of the areas: Standard colors, Chart fills, or Chart lines.**

4. **Click the Modify button.**

When you click Modify, Excel opens the Colors dialog box, where you can select a new standard color by clicking it in the hexagonal arrangement on the Standard tab or mix a color of your own using the color mixer on the Custom tab (shown in Figure 11-4).

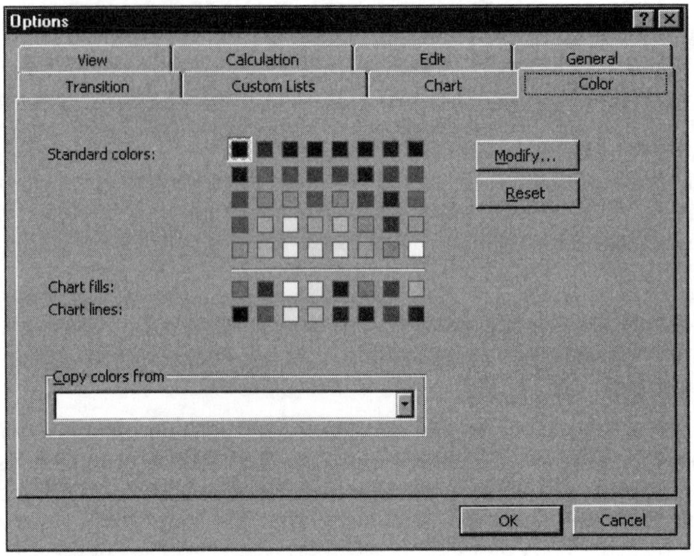

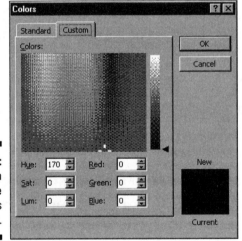

Figure 11-3:
The Color tab in the Options dialog box.

Figure 11-4:
The Custom tab of the Colors dialog box.

When mixing a custom color with the color mixer on the Custom tab, if you know something about color theory, you can modify the color by adjusting its hue (H<u>u</u>e), saturation (<u>S</u>at), and luminosity (<u>L</u>um) or its red (<u>R</u>ed), green (<u>G</u>reen), and blue (<u>B</u>lue) content. If you, like me, don't have the foggiest idea what to do with these individual settings, you can still customize the color by dragging the crosshair in the color square and/or drag the triangle up and down the color bar on the right until the desired color appears under the New sample rectangle.

✓ When you drag the crosshair, you change the color's hue and saturation.

✓ When you drag the triangle up and down the color bar, you change the color's luminosity as well as its mixture of red, green, and blue.

As you change the color settings, check how the color will appear by looking at the New/Current rectangle in the Color Picker dialog box. When you've got the color just the way you want it, click OK or press Enter to close the Colors dialog box and return to the Color tab in the Options dialog box. The custom color now appears in this dialog box.

To customize other colors in the palette, select them and repeat this modification process. To restore the predefined colors to Excel, click the Reset button in the Color tab.

After you customize the colors for a particular workbook, you can then copy your colors to another workbook (saving you all the time and effort of modifying each color individually again). To do this, follow these instructions:

1. **Open the workbook with the customized palette.**

2. **Using the Window pull-down menu, switch to the workbook to which you want to copy the palette.**

3. **Choose Tools⇨Options and click the Color tab in the Options dialog box.**

4. **Select the name of the workbook with the custom colors you want copied in Copy colors from drop-down list box.**

   Excel modifies the colors in the Color tab of the Options dialog box to match the ones in the workbook you selected.

5. **To use these colors in the new workbook, close the Options dialog box by clicking OK or pressing Enter.**

Editing the Edit Options

The Edit tab of the Options dialog box contains options that determine how editing works. As you may notice when you first select the Edit tab, most of these check-box options are already turned on for you.

✓ **Edit directly in cell:** If you deselect this option, you can't do any more editing within the cell. Instead, you have to edit the cell's contents on the formula bar after either double-clicking the cell or selecting it and then pressing F2.

✓ **Allow cell drag and drop:** If you deselect this option, you can no longer use the drag-and-drop method to copy or move cells around a worksheet, from worksheet to worksheet within a workbook, or from workbook to workbook.

✔ **Alert before overwriting cells:** If you deselect this option (which I really don't recommend), Excel no longer warns you when a drag-and-drop operation is about to obliterate stuff that you've already entered in the worksheet.

✔ **Move selection after Enter** and **Direction:** If you deselect this option, Excel no longer moves the cell pointer when you press the Enter key to complete a cell entry. If you still want Enter to complete an entry and move the cell pointer but don't want the pointer to move to the next cell down, leave the Move selection after Enter check box selected and choose a new direction (Right, Up, or Left) in the Direction drop-down list box.

✔ **Fixed decimal** and **Places:** Select this option only when you want to set all values in the worksheet to the decimal precision indicated in the associated edit box. (Refer to "The values behind the formatting" in Chapter 3 for more information.) When selecting this check box, you can modify the number of decimal places from the default of 2 by entering the new value in the edit box or by using the spinner buttons.

✔ **Cut, Copy, and Sort objects with cells:** Deselect this editing option only when you don't want graphic objects (like text boxes, arrows, and imported images) to move around when you cut, copy, or sort the cells underneath them.

✔ **Ask to update automatic links:** Deselect this option when you don't want Excel to bother you before going ahead and updating links between formulas in different workbooks.

✔ **Provide feedback with Animation:** Select this option when you want Excel to animate the process of making room for insertions or the process of pulling up and over cells to close gaps in the worksheet when making deletions.

✔ **Enable AutoComplete for cell values:** Deselect this option if you find that the AutoComplete feature gets in your way when entering columns of data in a worksheet. (See "I'm just not complete without you" in Chapter 2 for information on what the heck AutoComplete is, let alone what it does.)

Chapter 12

Macros Like Your Mom Used to Make

• •

In This Chapter

▶ Recording macros that perform common tasks

▶ Playing your macros

▶ Editing macros

▶ Adding macros to Excel toolbars

• •

*M*acros! Just hearing the word can be enough to make you want to head for the hills. But rather than think of this term as so much technobabble, keep in mind that "macro" is short for "macro instruction" and that the word "macro" refers to the BIG picture. A *macro* (at least, at the level of this book) is nothing more than a way to record the actions you take to get a particular task done (such as to enter a company name in a worksheet, save and print a worksheet, or format row headings) and have Excel 97 play those actions back for you.

Using a macro to perform a routine task instead of doing it by hand has some definite advantages. First, Excel can execute the commands involved much faster than you can (no matter how good you are at the keyboard or how familiar you are with Excel). Also, Excel performs the task flawlessly each and every time (because the macro plays back your actions exactly as recorded, you only have to worry that you record them correctly). Besides, you can even streamline the playback process by assigning keystroke shortcuts to your favorite macros, essentially reducing common tasks that otherwise require quite a few steps to just two keystrokes.

Recording Macros

The process of recording a macro is surprisingly straightforward:

1. **Open the Record New Macro dialog box to turn on the macro recorder by choosing Tools⇨Macro⇨Record New Macro.**

2. **Name the macro and (optionally) assign it a keystroke.**

3. **Perform the sequence of actions you want recorded in the macro just as you normally do in Excel.**

   You can choose commands from the pull-down or shortcut menus, click tools in the toolbars, or use shortcut keystrokes.

4. **Turn off the macro recorder when you're finished by clicking the Stop Recording button that appears in the tiny Stop Recording toolbar as soon as you start recording.**

   You can also turn off the macro recorder by choosing Tools⇨Macro⇨Stop Recording.

5. **Perform the task anytime you want simply by double-clicking the macro name in the Macro dialog box (opened by choosing Tools⇨Macro⇨ Macros or pressing Alt+F8) or by selecting the macro name and then choosing the Run button.**

   Alternately, if you bothered to assign a keystroke shortcut to the macro when you recorded it, you can run the macro by pressing the keystroke shortcut.

You'll be happy to know that, when recording your actions, Excel doesn't record mistakes (don't you wish everyone else was so forgiving?). In other words, if you're entering the heading "January" in the macro and you type **Janaury** by mistake and then correct your error, Excel does not record your pressing of the Backspace key to delete the characters "aury" and then typing **uary**. The only thing the macro records is the final, corrected result of **January**!

To record your actions, Excel 97 uses a language called *Visual Basic* (a language, by the way, that you don't need to know diddly about in order to create and use *simple* macros — the only kind you're going to get involved with in this book). Visual Basic commands are recorded in a separate module sheet (a *module sheet* is just a fancy name for a worksheet that doesn't use cells and therefore looks more like a typical page on a word processor screen).

Personally Speaking

Excel automatically assumes that you want to record your macro as part of the current workbook. Recording the macro as part of the workbook means that you can run the macro only when this workbook is open. You may want to have access to some of the macros that you create any old time you're using Excel, regardless of whether the workbook that happened to be current when you originally recorded the macro is now open or whether you're creating a new workbook or editing an existing one.

To record a macro so that it's universally available for use anytime, anywhere in Excel 97, you must record the macro in your Personal Macro Workbook rather than in the current workbook. Because your Personal Macro Workbook is automatically opened whenever you start up Excel (although it remains hidden at all times), you can run any of its macros no matter what workbook or workbooks are open at the time.

To record a macro in the Personal Macro Workbook, follow these steps:

1. **Choose Tools⇨Macro⇨Record New Macro to open the Record Macro dialog box.**

2. **Choose the Personal Macro Workbook in the Store macro in pop-up menu in the Record Macro dialog box.**

3. **Name your macro and (optionally) assign it a keystroke shortcut before you click OK and start recording the new macro.**

Excel doesn't actually create a Personal Macro Workbook for you until you take the trouble to record your first macro in that location and then save the macro in this workbook when you exit the program (no sense creating something you're never gonna use). After creating your first macro(s) in the Personal Macro Workbook and saving your changes, Excel 97 creates a workbook called PERSONAL.XLS (though you don't see the .xls in the Excel 97 displays) inside the Xlstartup folder, which itself is located within the Excel folder inside the MSOffice folder on your hard disk. After that, Excel automatically opens this PERSONAL.XLS workbook (thereby making its macros available) each and every time you launch Excel 97, while at the same time hiding the workbook.

A Macro a Day

The best way to get a feel for how easy it is to record and play back a simple macro is to follow along with the steps for creating a couple of them. The first sample macro enters and formats a company name in a cell. In these steps, you turn on the macro to record as you enter the company name, such as **Mother Goose Enterprises,** and change the font to 18-point, bold Comic Sans MS. If you're actually following along at your computer as you read these steps, be sure to adapt the basic macro so that it enters the name of *your* company in the font and type size *you* want to use.

The very first thing you need is a place in which to perform the actions you're going to have Excel record in the macro. For this example, open a new worksheet (although you can also use a blank cell in an existing worksheet). Then follow these steps:

1. **Position the pointer in the cell where you want to enter the company name.**

   For this example, position the pointer in cell A1 in a blank worksheet in the current workbook. If necessary, choose a new blank worksheet by clicking the next sheet tab or pressing Ctrl+PgDn.

2. **Choose Tools⇨Macro⇨Record New Macro on the menu bar.**

   The Record Macro dialog box, similar to the one shown in Figure 12-1, appears.

3. **Replace the temporary macro name, Macro1, in the Macro name edit box with a more descriptive macro name of your own.**

   When naming a macro, follow the same guidelines as when naming ranges (refer to Chapter 6); that is, start the name with a letter (not a number), don't use spaces (tie the parts of the name together with an underscore created by pressing Shift+hyphen), and don't use weird punctuation in the name.

   For this example, in place of Macro1, type **Company_Name**.

4. **(Optional) To assign a shortcut key to play your macro, click the Shortcut key edit box and then enter a letter from A to z (in upper- or lowercase) or a number between 0 and 9 in its edit box below.**

   The number or letter you enter is the key you use (in combination with the Ctrl key) to run the macro. Try to avoid using letters already assigned to standard Excel shortcuts (such as Ctrl+P for displaying the Print dialog box or Ctrl+S to save a workbook) because if you do, Excel will disable the standard shortcut and only play the macro when you press these keys. See the tables in Chapter 20 for a complete list of existing Excel keyboard shortcuts. If you press the Shift key when you type the letter, Ctrl will change to Ctrl+Shift+ in front of the capital letter in the Shortcut key edit box.

5. **(Optional) To store your macro in your personal macro workbook, choose Personal Macro Workbook on the Store macro in pop-up menu.**

   If you want to save the macro in a module sheet in a brand new workbook (which you can save later after recording the macro) rather than in either the current workbook (in which you will perform the actions recorded in the new macro) or in the Personal Macro Workbook, choose New Workbook on the Store macro in pop-up menu.

6. **(Optional) Edit or annotate the macro description in the Description edit box that appears beneath the Macro name edit box.**

   This is a good place to describe briefly the purpose of the macro you're creating. (You *do* know what this thing is supposed to do, don't you? Enter the name of your company, that's what.)

   Figure 12-1 shows the Record Macro dialog box just before closing the dialog box to record the macro. As you can see, the shortcut keystroke will be Ctrl+Shift+C (for Company). Also, because the company name is so often added to new workbooks, Personal Macro Workbook is selected in the Store macro in edit box so that this macro is available anytime you're using Excel 97.

7. **Click OK or press Enter to start recording your macro.**

   The Record Macro dialog box closes, and Excel shows you that the macro recorder is turned on by displaying the message, "Recording," on the status line and by displaying the Stop Recording toolbar (that consists of just two buttons, Stop Recording and Relative Reference).

8. **Perform the task you want to record.**

   For the Company_Name sample macro, you enter the company name in cell A1. Next, select the new font (Comic Sans MS in this case) from the Font drop-down list box and the font size (18 points) from the Font Size drop-down list box, and then click the Bold button.

9. **When you've finished recording all of the actions you want your macro to perform, turn off the macro recorder by clicking the Stop Recording button either in its own toolbar (shown in Figure 12-2) or by choosing Tools⇨Macro⇨Stop Recording on the menu bar.**

   As soon as you stop recording a macro, the Recording message disappears from the status bar and the Stop Recording toolbar disappears.

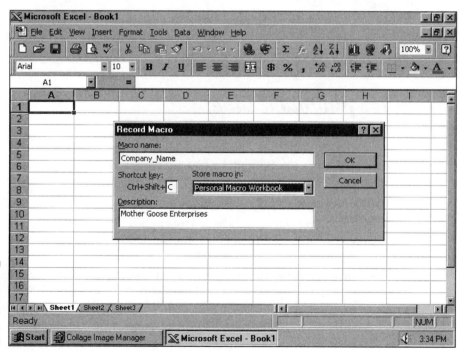

Figure 12-1:
The Record
Macro
dialog box.

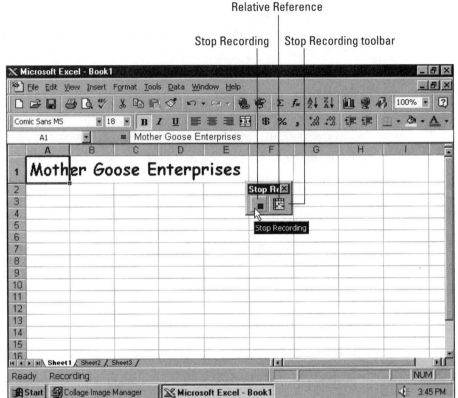

Figure 12-2:
Recording
the
Company_
Name
macro.

It's playback time!

After you turn off the macro recorder, you are ready to test the macro. If your macro enters new text or deletes some text as part of its actions, be very careful where you test it out. Be sure that the cell pointer is in a part of the worksheet where existing cell entries won't be trashed when you play back the macro. When you're ready to test the macro, you can do any of the following:

- ✔ The easiest way to play back a macro is to press the shortcut keystrokes (Ctrl+Shift+C for the sample Company_Name macro), assuming that you assigned a shortcut to your macro.

- ✔ You can choose Tools➪Macro➪Macros on the menu bar or press Alt+F8 and then double-click the macro's name in the Macro dialog box or select the name and click the Run button (this method works for any macro whether or not it has shortcut keys assigned).

If, when you play back the macro, you find it running amok in your worksheet, press Esc to stop the macro prematurely. Excel displays a macro error dialog box indicating the point at which the macro was interrupted. Click the Halt button in this dialog box to shut the macro down.

Where Excel saves your macro depends on how you created the macro in the first place:

✔ If you created the macro as part of the current workbook, Excel places the macro in a hidden module sheet (called something like Module1, Module2, and so on) that is added to the workbook. To see the contents of the macro on this hidden module sheet, you need to press Alt+F8 or choose Tools➪Macro➪Macros, select the macro in the Macro name edit box, and then click the Edit button.

✔ If you created the macro as part of the Personal Macro Workbook, Excel places the macro in a hidden module sheet (called something like Module1, Module2, and so on) in the hidden workbook called PERSONAL.XLS (although the .XLS part doesn't show in Excel 97 displays). To see the contents of the macro on this hidden module sheet, you first need to choose Window➪Unhide and then select Personal in the Unhide workbook list box before you click OK or press Enter. Then the Personal workbook is open, you need to press Alt+F8 or choose Tools➪Macro➪Macros, select the macro in the Macro name edit box, and then click the Edit button.

✔ If you saved the macro as part of a new workbook, Excel puts the macro in a hidden module sheet (called something like Module1, Module2, and so on) that is added to a new workbook (and given a temporary filename like Book1, Book2, or whatever the next available number is). To see the contents of the macro on this hidden module sheet, you need to press Alt+F8 or choose Tools➪Macro➪Macros, select the macro in the Macro name edit box, and then click the Edit button.

When you save the current workbook or the new workbook, the macros in its hidden module sheets are saved as part of the files. In the case of the hidden Personal Macro Workbook, when you exit Excel, the program asks whether you want to save changes to this macro workbook. Be sure to click the Yes button so that you can still use the macros you've placed there the next time you work in Excel 97.

A macro for all months

The second sample macro enters the 12 months of the year (from January to December) across a single row of a worksheet. This macro enters the names of the months, makes them bold and italic, and then widens their columns with the best-fit feature.

As with the first macro, first find a place in a worksheet where you can enter and format the names. For this macro, you can select a new worksheet in your workbook or use a region of an existing worksheet that has 12 unused columns so that existing cell entries don't skew how wide the best-fit feature makes the columns. (You want the length of the name of the month to determine how wide to make each column.)

Figure 12-3 shows the Record Macro dialog box for this macro. Its name, appropriately enough, is Months_of_the_Year and its shortcut keystroke is Ctrl+m.

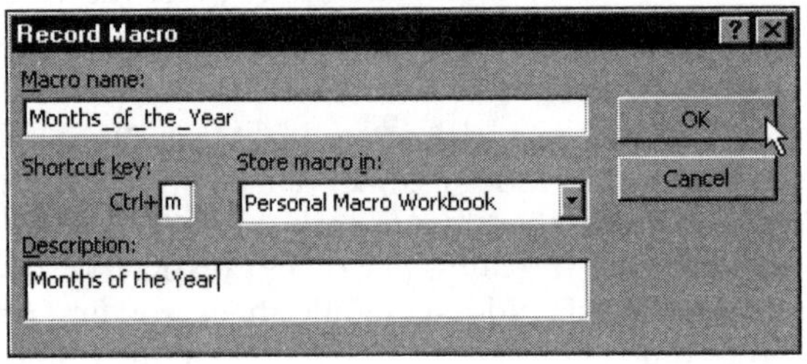

Figure 12-3:
The Record
Macro
dialog box.

To create this macro (or one like it), follow these steps:

1. **Position the cell pointer in cell A1 and choose Tools⇨Macro⇨Record New Macro.**

2. **Type** Months_of_the_Year **in the Macro name edit box in the Record Macro dialog box.**

3. **(Optional) Click the Shortcut key check box and enter a letter in its edit box.**

   In this example, I assign the macro the shortcut key, Ctrl+M.

4. **Indicate where to locate the macro in the Store macro in pop-up list box.**

   If you want to be able to use this macro in any worksheet you build (which would make the most sense), you need to choose Personal Macro Workbook in the pop-up list.

5. **(Optional) Enter a description of the macro in the Description edit box.**

6. **Click OK or press Enter to begin recording the macro.**

7. **Type** January **in cell A1, click the Enter button on the formula bar, and then use the AutoFill handle to select through cell L1 (until the screen tip says "December").**

   You didn't think that you were going to have to type out all those months, did you?

8. **Click the Bold and Italic tools on the Formatting toolbar.**

   This step adds these enhancements to the entries (the cell range A1:L1 with the month names is still selected).

9. **With the range of columns containing the months (columns A through L), still selected, choose Format⇨Column⇨AutoFit Selection on the menu bar.**

10. **Select the first cell, A1, to deselect the cell range with the names of the months.**

11. **Click the Stop Recording button on the Stop Recording toolbar or choose Tools⇨Macro⇨Stop Recording on the menu bar to stop recording.**

After turning off the macro recorder, you are ready to test your Months_ of_the_Year macro. To adequately test the macro, use some new columns to the right. For example, I tested this macro on the virgin columns N through Y in Sheet2 by placing the cell pointer in cell N1 and then pressing Ctrl+m.

If you play this macro where I did, you get a rather rude Microsoft Visual Basic error dialog box indicating that

```
Run-time error '1004,'
AutoFill method of Range of class failed
```

occurred (is that English?!). This Microsoft Visual Basic error dialog box gives you a choice between ending the macro playback right there with the End button and debugging the macro (yeah, right!) with the Debug button. All this because I didn't play this macro when the cell pointer was in cell A1, where it was recorded.

Relative macro recording

What, you may ask, causes the Months_of_the_Year macro to screw up so that it displays a Macro Error dialog box with the Run-time error '1004' when you play it back from cell N1? Chapter 4 explains the differences between copying a formula with *relative cell references* and one with *absolute cell references*. In that chapter, I explain that Excel adjusts cell references in copies of a formula unless you take steps to convert them to *absolute* (or unchanging) references.

When recording macros, just the opposite is true: When you select a cell range (or a range of columns in this case), Excel records the cell references as absolute references rather than relative ones. This is the reason that the Months_of_the_Year macro only works properly when you run it with the cell pointer in cell A1. It keeps wanting to apply AutoFill to the cell range A1:L1 when cell A1 is the active cell. When cell A1 isn't active, the Visual Basic AutoFill command can't be completed, and you end up with this lovely

```
Run-time error '1004,'
AutoFill method of Range of class failed
```

message in a Microsoft Visual Basic dialog box.

Re-recording a macro

To change the Months_of_the_Year macro so that it works correctly from any cell in the worksheet and not just in cell A1, you have to re-record it, this time using relative cell references (something that should have been done when the macro was originally recorded). To do this, follow these steps:

1. **Open up a new worksheet where you can perform the actions to be recorded.**

2. **Choose the Tools⇨Macro⇨Record New Macro on the menu bar.**

3. **Set up the Record Macro dialog box the same way you did when you first created the macro and then click OK or press Enter.**

4. **Click the Yes button when Excel prompts whether you want to replace the existing macro.**

5. **Click the Relative Reference button in the Stop Recording toolbar before you start recording the macro steps.**

6. **Perform all the actions to be re-recorded (typing** January, **using AutoFill to generate the rest of the months, applying bold and italics to the cell range, and then selecting their columns and adjusting their widths with the Format⇨Column⇨AutoFit Selection command as outlined earlier in the steps in the section called "A macro for all months").**

7. **Click the Stop Recording button in the Stop Recording toolbar or choose Tools⇨Macro⇨Stop Recording on the menu bar to stop recording.**

   This time, Excel records the command for AutoFilling the months of the year with relative column references so that the AutoFilling is always relative to the cell where the macro enters January.

After stopping the macro, test it in a new worksheet, starting in a cell other than cell A1. Now, no matter where you position the cell pointer when you run the macro, Excel is able to fill in the names of the months with AutoFill without so much as a Run-time error '1,' let alone '1004'!

Chapter 13

Button Up That Toolbar!

*A*ll of the preceding chapters have shown you how to use the tools on the various built-in toolbars (from the Worksheet Menu bar all the way to the Stop Recording macro toolbar) exactly as they are configured when they come with Excel 97. In this chapter, you find out how to customize the existing toolbars so that they contain only the tools you need, and you also discover how to create toolbars of your own.

As you will soon discover if you read this chapter, the tools found on the built-in toolbars represent just a small part of the total number of tools supplied with Excel. You can add unused tools to any of the existing toolbars or combine them to create new toolbars of your own design.

Not only can you customize Excel toolbars by creating new combinations of various built-in buttons, but you can also customize toolbars by assigning the macros that you've recorded (see Chapter 12 for details) to any of the custom buttons that come with Excel 97. Further, if none of the pictures used on the custom buttons suits the function of the macro that you're adding to a toolbar, you can use a graphic created in another program (such as a clip-art image or one that you create yourself with another graphics program).

Toolbars—Now You See 'em, Now You Don't

As you discover in previous chapters, if not in practice, Excel 97 comes with a whole truckload of built-in toolbars. Each toolbar consists of a group of buttons that the program designers thought would be most helpful in getting particular tasks done. As you know, the Menu, Standard, and Formatting toolbars that are automatically displayed at the top of the screen when you start Excel contain a wide variety of tools useful for creating, formatting, and printing documents.

Although the arrangements on most of the built-in toolbars may satisfy your needs, it's easy to modify the arrangement of any of them. For example, if there are tools you seldom or never use, you can replace them with ones more useful for the type of work you do. If you use a tool quite often but are not happy with its position in the toolbar — or even the toolbar it's on — you can move it to a more convenient position.

To display a new toolbar on screen (or hide one that's already displayed), you choose View⇨Toolbars and then select the name of the toolbar (Chart, Drawing, and so on) on the cascading menu that appears. You can also shorten this process by clicking one of the displayed toolbars with the secondary mouse button and clicking the name of the toolbar you want to display.

You can also display (or hide) a toolbar in the Excel program window from the Toolbars tab in the Customize dialog box. To open this dialog box (shown in Figure 13-1), you choose View⇨Toolbars⇨Customize on the menu bar or choose Customize on one of the toolbar's shortcut menus. After the Toolbars tab is displayed in the open Customize dialog box, you select the toolbar's check box in the Toolbars list box to display the toolbar on the screen (or hide the toolbar, if its check box is already selected).

If you click the Options tab in the Customize dialog box, you see two check boxes whose settings affect all the toolbars displayed in Excel:

✔ **Large icons:** Normally, Excel uses small icons in displaying the buttons on the toolbars. Select this check box to increase the size of the icons and, consequently, the size of the buttons. (This feature is especially helpful when you're running Excel on a computer with a really small screen, such as a laptop.)

✔ **Show ScreenTips on toolbars:** Normally, Excel shows you the name of each button on a toolbar when you position the mouse pointer on it without clicking the mouse button, the column letter or row number where you'd end up when using the scroll bars, and the address of the cell range where your cell selection will be moved or copied to when using drag-and-drop. (Microsoft refers to these descriptions as ScreenTips.) If you no longer want to see these types of indicators, you can remove the display of all ScreenTips from the program display by deselecting this check box.

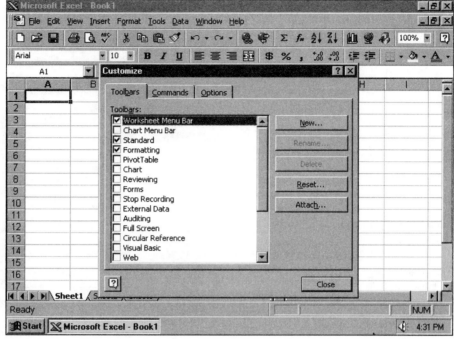

Figure 13-1:
The
Toolbars tab
in the
Customize
dialog box.

If you want more action out of your pull-down menus, you can select one of the menu animation selections (Random, Unfold, or Slide) in the Menu animations pop-up list at the bottom of the Options tab in the Customize dialog box. If you choose Random, Excel 97 randomly chooses between using the Unfold or Slide animation settings when you use the pull-down menus. If you choose Unfold, the menus and submenus cascade down from the menu bar and menu item, respectively. If you choose Slide, the menus cascade down from the menu bar, and the submenus appear to slide up to meet the menu item.

Customizing the Built-In Toolbars

To modify the contents of a particular toolbar from the Customize dialog box, you must either already have that toolbar displayed on-screen, or you must select it on the Toolbars tab of the Customize dialog box. Remember that you can select as many toolbars as you want in this list box, should you feel up to modifying more than one toolbar at a time.

After selecting the toolbar(s) that you want to modify, choose the Commands tab in the Customize dialog box (shown in Figure 13-2).

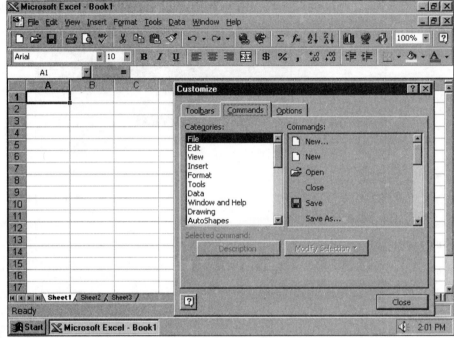

Figure 13-2:
The
Commands
tab in the
Customize
dialog box.

Adding buttons from the Customize dialog box

When you click the Commands tab in the Customize dialog box, Excel displays a Categories list box with all the groups of buttons available (File through New Menu) followed by a Commands list box that actually displays the command names alone or the command names with their icons in each group. To display a new group of commands in the Commands list box, you need only click its category name in the Categories list box. After the Commands tab of the Customize dialog box displays the commands for a particular category, you can then select individual commands just as you would any graphic object in a worksheet window.

To add one of the commands shown in the Commands list box to one of the toolbars displayed on the Excel 97 screen, you drag the command name or command name-plus-icon from the Commands list box in the Customize dialog box to its new position on the toolbar and release the mouse button.

As you drag, an icon of a generic button (representing the selected command) appears at the tip of the arrowhead mouse pointer, and a tiny box appears at the bottom of the arrowhead and slightly to the right. As long as you have the mouse pointer over a part of the screen where you can't add the button for the selected command, this tiny box at the bottom of the mouse pointer contains an **x** in it. When you finally move the mouse pointer over some place on a toolbar where you can insert the button, the **x** in this tiny box changes to the + sign. The plus sign is your signal that the toolbar will accept the button if you release the mouse button.

To let you know where the new button will be inserted in a toolbar, Excel displays an I-beam (something like one that appears when inserting cells into an existing range with drag-and-drop — see "Insertions courtesy of drag-and-drop" in Chapter 4) in the toolbar at the tip of the arrowhead mouse pointer. The I-beam shape indicates where on the toolbar the new button for the command you're adding will be inserted. When positioning the new button on the toolbar, you can insert it in front of or between any of the existing buttons.

Note that you can always find out what a particular command does by choosing its name or name-plus-icon in the Commands list box and then clicking the Description button at the bottom of the dialog box. When you click the Description button, Excel 97 displays a text box with a short description of the selected command's function. To get rid of the text box, just click anywhere on the Customize dialog box outside of the confines of the text box describing the function of the selected command.

Removing buttons from a toolbar

When the Customize dialog box is open, you can not only add new buttons to a displayed toolbar but also get rid of existing buttons by literally dragging them off the toolbar. To junk a button that you don't need, select it on the toolbar and then drag the icon of the button until it's off the toolbar before you release the mouse button. As soon as you release the mouse button, the toolbar button disappears and Excel closes up the gap on the toolbar.

Playing musical chairs with buttons

When customizing a toolbar, you may only want to reposition the buttons or move or copy them to one of the other toolbars that are displayed.

- ✔ To reposition a button on the same toolbar, drag its button icon until the I-beam indicator is positioned slightly in front of the button it is to precede and release the mouse button.

- ✔ To move a button to a different toolbar, drag its button icon to the desired position on the new toolbar and then release the mouse button.

- ✔ To copy a button to a different toolbar, hold down the Ctrl key as you drag its button icon to the new toolbar. (The plus sign will appear in the tiny little box attached to the arrowhead pointer when you position the mouse pointer over any of the toolbars displayed on the screen.)

What a bunch of spaced-out buttons!

You may have noticed how buttons on various built-in toolbars are grouped together with little gray vertical bars appearing before and after the group of buttons. You too can group various buttons when customizing a toolbar.

To insert a vertical bar on the left or right side of a button to separate it from other buttons, drag the button slightly in the opposite direction of where you want the vertical bar to appear (to the right to insert a space on its left side and to the left to insert a space on its right side) and release the mouse button. Excel inserts a vertical bar before or after the button you just dragged.

To delete a vertical bar in front of or after a button so that the button abuts — or touches — the one next to it, drag the button in the appropriate direction until it touches or slightly overlaps the neighboring button and then release the mouse button. Excel redraws the toolbar to remove the space from the button you just dragged.

It's not my default!

Sometimes, you may make changes to a built-in toolbar and then decide that you don't want to keep those changes. No matter what wild changes you make to a built-in toolbar, you can always restore the toolbar to its original form by opening the Customize dialog box (by choosing View➪Toolbars➪Customize on the menu bar or choosing the Customize command on a toolbar shortcut menu) and then selecting the toolbar's name in the Toolbars list box and choosing the Reset button.

Designing Your Own Toolbars

You are by no means limited to the built-in toolbars that come with Excel. You can create your own toolbars to combine any of the available buttons: those that are used in the built-in toolbars as well as those that are not.

To create a toolbar of your very own, follow these steps:

1. **Choose Tools➪Toolbars➪Customize on the menu bar to open the Customize dialog box.**

2. **If it's not already selected, select the Toolbars tab in the Customize dialog box and then click the New button.**

   The New Toolbar dialog box opens where you name the new toolbar.

3. **Enter a name for the new toolbar in the Toolbar name edit box and then click OK or press Enter.**

   Excel closes the New Toolbar dialog box and adds the name of your new toolbar to the bottom of the Toolbars list in the Customize dialog box. The program also opens a tiny, floating toolbar with just enough room on it for a single button and with only part of the toolbar's name showing unless you gave a one- or two-letter name (similar to the one shown in Figure 13-3).

4. **Select the Commands tab in the Customize dialog box and then choose the category containing the command for the first button you want to add to the new toolbar from the Categories list box.**

5. **Drag the button icon for the command from the Commands list box in the Customize dialog box to the tiny toolbar dialog box in the upper-left corner of the document window; then release the mouse button.**

6. **Repeat steps 4 and 5 until you have added all the buttons you want to the new toolbar.**

   After the buttons are on the new toolbar, you can rearrange and space them out as you want.

7. **Click the Close button or press Enter to close the Customize dialog box.**

As you add buttons to the new toolbar, Excel automatically widens the toolbar dialog box. When the dialog box is wide enough, the name you assigned to the toolbar appears in the title bar. If the toolbar dialog box starts running into the Customize dialog box, just drag the new toolbar down by its title bar until it's entirely clear of the Customize dialog box.

Figures 13-3 and 13-4 show the process of creating a new toolbar (called, modestly enough, Greg's Cool Tools). Figure 13-3 shows the Customize dialog box after naming the new toolbar in the New Toolbar dialog box and adding its name to the bottom of the Toolbars list box. Figure 13-4 shows Greg's Cool Tools toolbar after I added the following thirteen buttons: Clear Contents, Clear Formatting, Comments, Delete Comment, AutoFormat, Merge Cells, Unmerge Cells, Rotate Text Up, Rotate Text Down, Angle Text Downward, Angle Text Upward, Page Break Preview, and Normal.

Note how I used the vertical bars in the custom toolbar to create five groups of buttons. Each group contains buttons that perform a similar function (be it erasing, formatting, previewing, merging, or rotating text).

After creating a new toolbar, you can display, hide, move, resize, and dock it just like you do any of the built-in toolbars. If you don't want to keep a toolbar you've created, delete it by opening the Toolbars tab in the Customize dialog box and selecting the toolbar name in the Toolbars list box (so that it appears highlighted).

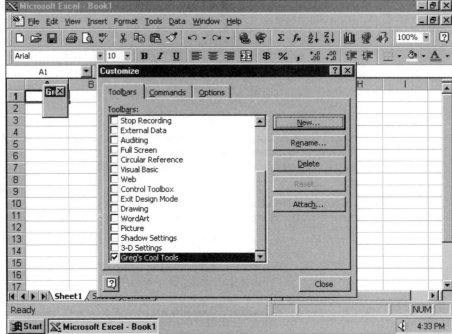

Figure 13-3:
The new
Greg's Cool
Tools
toolbar
before the
buttons
were added.

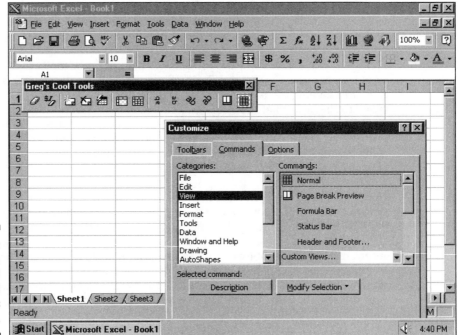

Figure 13-4:
The
completed
Greg's Cool
Tools
toolbar.

As soon as you select the name of a toolbar that you created, the Delete button becomes available. (This button remains grayed out and unavailable when you select any of the built-in toolbars.) When you click Delete, Excel displays an alert dialog box, in which you confirm the deletion by clicking OK or pressing Enter.

Adding buttons that play macros

As I hinted earlier in this chapter, you can assign macros that you've recorded (covered back in Chapter 12) to tools and then place these tools on toolbars (either on one of the built-ins or on one of your own creation). That way, you can play back a macro by clicking its button. This feature is particularly helpful when you've assigned all 26 letters (A through Z) and 10 numbers (0 through 9) as shortcut keystrokes in a particular macro sheet.

Excel 97 doesn't have much variety in the custom buttons (shown in the palette in Figure 13-5) to which you can assign macros. Come on, what's a happy-face macro supposed to do, anyway?!

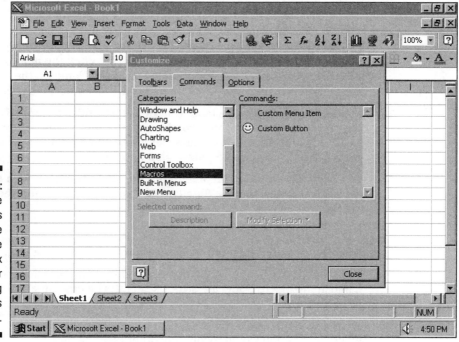

Figure 13-5: The Commands tab of the Customize dialog box after selecting the Macros category.

To assign a macro to a custom button, follow these steps:

1. **If the macro you want to assign to a toolbar button is attached to a particular workbook rather than to your Personal Macro Workbook, make sure that the workbook is open. If the workbook is not open, you need to open it with the Open tool on the Standard toolbar or the File⇨Open command on the menu bar.**

   Remember, Excel opens your Personal Macro Workbook each time you start the program, making its macros available anywhere and anytime in the program. Macros saved as part of a particular workbook, however, are only available when that workbook is open.

2. **Choose View⇨Toolbars⇨Customize on the menu bar to open the Customize dialog box.**

3. **If the toolbar to which you want to add the macro is not already displayed, click its check box in the Toolbars list box on the Toolbars tab.**

4. **Select the Commands tab and then select Macros in the Categories list box and Custom Button (the one with the Happy Face icon) in the Commands list box.**

5. **Drag the Happy Face icon from the Commands list box to the place on the toolbar where you want the macro button to appear; then release the mouse button.**

6. **(Optional) To assign your own name (that appears as the button's tooltip when you position the mouse pointer over it), click the macro button with the secondary mouse button; then choose Name on the shortcut menu, type the new button name in its edit box, and then press Enter.**

7. **(Optional) To change the icon to something besides a Happy Face, click the macro button with the secondary mouse button; then choose Change Button Image on its shortcut menu and click the new icon you want to use in the pop-up palette that appears.**

8. **To assign the macro to the macro button, click its button with the secondary mouse button; then choose Assign Macro on the shortcut menu.**

   Excel opens the Assign Macro dialog box (see Figure 13-6).

9. **Select or record the macro that you want to assign to the tool.**

   To assign an existing macro to the selected tool, double-click the macro name in the Macro Name list box or select the macro name and click OK or press Enter.

   To record a new macro for the tool, click the Record button and record a macro just as you would record any other (see Chapter 12).

10. **Repeat steps 6 through 9 for every macro you want to assign to a custom button.**

11. **Click the Close button or press Enter to close the Customize dialog box.**

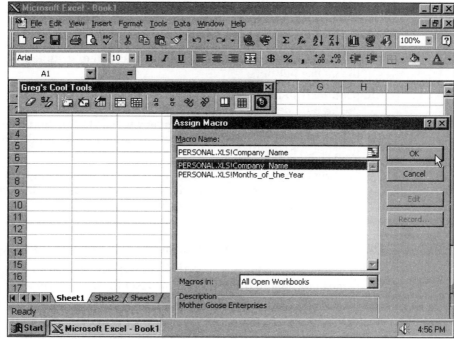

Figure 13-6:
The Assign
Macro
dialog box.

Assigning a macro to a menu item

Instead of (or in addition to) assigning a macro to a custom button on one of the toolbars, you can assign a macro as one of the items on a pull-down menu. To add a custom item to one of the pull-down menus and assign one of your macros to this item, follow these steps:

1. **If the macro you want to assign to a menu item is attached to a particular workbook rather than in your Personal Macro Workbook, make sure that the workbook is open. If the workbook is not open, you need to open it with the Open tool on the Standard toolbar or the File⇨Open command on the menu bar.**

   Normally, you will only want to assign macros that are in your Personal Macro Workbook to custom menu items. That way, the menu items will always be available when running Excel 97. If you do assign a macro from another workbook to a custom menu item, you must remember that you can only use that menu item to run the macro when the workbook it's saved in is open.

2. **Choose View⇨Toolbars⇨Customize on the menu bar to open the Customize dialog box.**

3. Select the <u>C</u>ommands tab and then select Macros in the Categories list box and Custom Menu Item in the Comman<u>d</u>s list box.

4. Drag the Custom Menu Item from the Comman<u>d</u>s list box to place on the pull-down menu where you want the macro item to appear; then release the mouse button.

5. (Optional) To assign your own name to the menu item (that appears on the menu) open the pull-down menu that contains it; then click the Custom Menu Item with the secondary mouse button and choose <u>N</u>ame on the shortcut menu, type the new button name in its edit box, and then press Enter.

6. To assign the macro to the menu item button, open its pull-down menu and then click its menu item with the secondary mouse button and choose Assign <u>M</u>acro on the shortcut menu.

   Excel opens the Assign Macro dialog box (as shown earlier in Figure 13-6).

7. Select or record the macro that you want to assign to the tool.

   To assign an existing macro to the selected tool, double-click the macro name in the <u>M</u>acro Name list box or select the macro name and click OK or press Enter.

   To record a new macro for the tool, click the Record button and record a macro just as you would record any other (see Chapter 12).

After adding a custom menu item and assigning a macro to it, you can run the macro simply by selecting its command as you would any others on the menu bar.

To remove a custom menu item, open the Customize dialog box (<u>V</u>iew⇨ <u>T</u>oolbars⇨<u>C</u>ustomize); then open the pull-down menu containing the item and drag the item off the menu before you release the mouse button.

Cute as a button

Fortunately, you aren't stuck with button images that have pictures of smiley faces, hearts, and coffee mugs. You can copy an image from another button, or, if you're an artist, you can use the Button Editor to create your own image.

To paste a picture from one button to another, follow these steps:

1. Open the Customize dialog box by choosing <u>V</u>iew⇨<u>T</u>oolbars⇨<u>C</u>ustomize on the menu bar or by choosing the <u>C</u>ustomize command on a toolbar shortcut menu.

2. If it's not already displayed, open the toolbar that contains the button image you want to copy by selecting its check box in the Tool<u>b</u>ars list box on the Tool<u>b</u>ars tab.

3. **Click the button you want to copy with the secondary mouse button; then choose Copy Button Image on its shortcut menu to copy this image to the Clipboard.**

4. **With the secondary mouse button, click the button onto which you want to copy the image that's in the Clipboard; then choose Paste Button Image on its shortcut menu.**

That's all there is to it. Excel replaces the face of the selected tool with the picture stored in the Clipboard.

If you'd prefer to create your own masterpiece rather than steal one of the existing button images (which may already be associated with a particular action if it appears on another toolbar that you use), you can edit an image with the new Button Editor. To open the Button Editor (shown in Figure 13-7), you open the Customize dialog box and, if necessary, display the toolbar; then click the button whose image you want to edit with the secondary mouse button and select Edit Button Image on the button's shortcut menu.

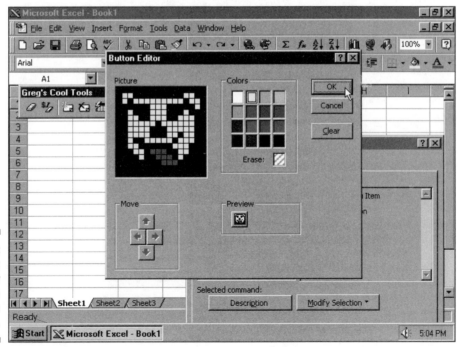

Figure 13-7:
Customizing the Happy Face icon in the Button Editor.

To edit the button's icon, click the color you want to use and then click the squares (called pixels) in the Picture area to paint with the color. If you make a mistake, you can click the pixel a second time to restore it to its original color. If you want to draw a picture from scratch rather than edit the one you selected, you need to click the Clear button before you start drawing. If you want to erase part of the image, click the Erase box in the Colors area and then click the pixels that you want to erase in the picture.

Figure 13-7 shows my artwork after editing that silly Happy Face icon in the Button Editor so that it looks more like my silly dog Spike. Figure 13-8 shows my custom toolbar after replacing the button with the image of the Happy Face with Spike's image and assigning to it the Months_of_the_Year macro created in Chapter 12. Refer to "A macro for all months" for details.

Figure 13-8:
Greg's Cool Tools custom toolbar after adding the edited Happy Face button.

Part VI
From the Home Office in Indianapolis

The 5th Wave   **By Rich Tennant**

IF BOB DYLAN HAD PURSUED A CAREER IN COMPUTERS.

"PUT HIM IN FRONT OF A TERMINAL AND HE'S A GENIUS, BUT OTHER-WISE THE GUY IS SUCH A BROODING, GLOOMY GUS HE'LL NEVER BREAK INTO MANAGEMENT."

In this part . . .

Finally, you come to the fun part of Excel for 97, the so-called Part of Tens, where the chapters all consist of lists with the top ten Excel tips on this, that, and everything in between. In homage to David Letterman (Indiana's favorite son), you'll find a chapter on the top ten new features in Excel 97, top ten things in Excel that always trip you up, top ten ways to impress your boss, as well as the top ten thousand (or so it seems) keystroke shortcuts included in this baby. And, in homage to Cecil B. deMille, Moses, and a much higher power, we've even included a chapter with the Ten Commandments of Excel 97 that, although not written in stone, when followed faithfully are guaranteed to give you heavenly results.

Chapter 14

Top Ten New Features in Excel 97

• •

*1*f you're looking for a quick rundown on what's new in Excel 97, look no further! Here it is, my official Top Ten New Features list. Just a cursory glance down the list tells you that the thrust of the new features is auto this 'n' that, such 'n' such tips, and so 'n' so Wizards.

And just in case you're interested in more than just a cursory feature description, I've included a cross-reference with chapter and verse to the place in this book where I cover the feature in more detail.

10. **Edit Formula button:** This new formula bar feature makes it easy to modify the formulas and functions you enter into a cell (See "Editing a function with the Edit Formula button" in Chapter 2.)

9. **Natural formulas:** This dandy new feature lets you use column and row headings that you've entered in a table of data instead of cell addresses in the formulas that you create to calculate totals, averages, and so on — all without having to assign a single range name. (See "Naming formulas with data table headings" in Chapter 6).

8. **Screentips:** This feature radically expands the role of tooltips — first introduced in Excel for Windows 95 — that shows you the name of a toolbar button when you position the mouse pointer over it. In Excel 97, you find that screentips are all over the place. They now appear when using the scroll bars to scroll to new cells, when using the Fill handle to fill in a series of data entries, and when moving and copying cell selections in a worksheet, keeping you informed of your current position. (See "The secrets of scrolling" in Chapter 1, "Fill 'er up with AutoFill" in Chapter 2, and "Insertions courtesy of drag-and-drop" in Chapter 4.)

7. **Save As HTML:** This command opens the Internet Assistant Wizard, which walks you through the steps for converting worksheet data to an HTML table that you can publish in Web pages for the Internet or your company's intranet. (See "Converting worksheet data into an HTML table" in Chapter 10.)

6. **Hyperlinks:** This features makes it a snap to add links to cell entries or graphic images added to a worksheet. When clicked, these links can take you to another document or workbook, another worksheet within the same workbook, or a Web page on the Internet or your company's intranet. (See "Adding Hyperlinks to a Worksheet" in Chapter 10.)

5. **Page Break preview:** This brand new preview feature not only gives you an overview of the page breaks prior to printing your report but lets you modify them. (See "When Ya Gonna Give Your Page a Break?" in Chapter 5.)

4. **IntelliMouse:** Microsoft's newest toy is a two-button mouse with a wheel in between the buttons. In Excel 97, you can use the IntelliMouse instead of the scroll bars to move very quickly to new parts of the worksheet. (See "Scrolling with the IntelliMouse" in Chapter 1.)

3. **Conditional formatting:** This new formatting feature lets you set up the conditions under which certain cell formats are to be applied to a cell selection. (See "Conditional Formatting" in Chapter 3.)

2. **Office Assistant:** In an attempt to enliven the online help, Microsoft has come up with the Office Assistant — your personal aide-de-camp who is ready to answer any of your questions about using Excel 97 as well as to suggest better ways to get things done. When you first use the Office Assistant, he takes the form of Clippit, a rather animated paper clip. If, however, you find that Clippit doesn't suit your personality, you can select any one of the eight other available characters. (See "Conferring with your Office Assistant" in Chapter 1.)

1. **New and improved cell formatting:** Excel 97 incorporates a whole bunch of really great new cell-formatting features, including automatically widening columns to accommodate the number format you apply to cells, merging cells together, indenting entries within their cells, rotating the cell entries text anywhere from -90 to $+90$ degrees, and shrinking the font in cells to suit the current column width. (See "Look Ma, no more format overflow!," "Altering the Alignment," "Intent on Indents," "Reordering the orientation," and "Shrink to Fit" in Chapter 3.)

Chapter 15
Top Ten Beginner Basics

* *

*I*f these ten items are all you ever really master in Excel 97, you'll still be way ahead of the competition. When all is said and done, this top ten list lays out all of the fundamental skills required to use Excel 97 successfully:

10. To start Excel 97 from the Windows 95 taskbar, click the Start button, choose Programs on the Start menu, and then choose Microsoft Excel on the Programs continuation menu.

9. If you're using Microsoft Office 97, you can open a workbook at the same time you start Excel 97. Click the Start button, and then choose Open Office Document at the top of the Start menu. Then open the folder with the Excel workbook in the Open dialog box and double-click the workbook's icon. (To find out more about Microsoft Office 97, check out *Microsoft Office 97 For Windows For Dummies,* written by Wallace Wang and published by IDG Books Worldwide, Inc.)

   If you don't have Microsoft Office 97, locate the Excel 97 workbook with Explorer or My Computer and then double-click its icon.

8. To locate a part of a worksheet that you cannot see on-screen, use the scroll bars at the right and bottom of the workbook window to bring new parts of the worksheet into view. When scrolling, the CellTips indicator on the scroll bar shows the letter of the column or the number of the row that will appear in the upper-left corner of the worksheet upon releasing the mouse button.

7. To start a new workbook (containing three blank worksheets), choose the New Workbook tool on the Standard toolbar (or choose File⇨New on the pull-down menus or press Ctrl+N). To insert a new worksheet in a workbook (should you need more than three), choose Insert⇨Worksheet from the menu bar or press Shift+F11.

6. To activate an open workbook and display it on-screen (in front of any others you have open), open the Window menu and select the name or number of the workbook you want. To locate a particular worksheet in the active workbook, click that worksheet's sheet tab at the bottom of the workbook document window. To display more sheet tabs, click the sheet scrolling arrows on the left side of the bottom of the workbook window.

5. To enter stuff in a worksheet, select the cell where the information should appear; then begin typing. When you're finished, click the Enter button on the formula bar or press Tab, Enter, or one of the arrow keys.

4. To edit the stuff you've already entered into a cell, double-click the cell or position the cell pointer in the cell and press F2. Excel then locates the insertion point at the end of the cell entry. When you've finished correcting the entry, click the Enter button on the formula bar or press Tab or Enter.

3. To choose one of the many commands on the pull-down menus, choose the menu name (on the menu bar) to open the menu and then choose the command name on the pull-down menu. To choose a command on a context menu, click the object (cell, sheet tab, toolbar, chart, and so on) with the secondary mouse button.

2. To save a copy of your workbook on disk the first time around, choose File⇨Save or File⇨Save As from the menu bar (or click the Save button on the Standard toolbar or press Ctrl+S); then designate the drive and folder directory where the file should be located in the Save in drop-down list box and replace the temporary BOOK1.XLS filename in the File name edit box with your own filename (up to 255 characters long, including spaces). To save changes to the workbook thereafter, click the Save tool on the Standard toolbar (or choose File⇨Save or press Ctrl+S or Shift+F12).

1. To exit Excel when you're done working with the program, choose the File⇨Exit command on the menu bar or click the program's close box or press Alt+F4. If the workbook you have open contains unsaved changes, Excel 97 asks whether you want to save the workbook before closing Excel and returning to Windows 95. Before you shut off your computer, be sure to use the Shut down command on the Start menu to shut down Windows 95.

Chapter 16

The Ten Commandments of Excel 97

● ●

*1*n working with Excel 97, you discover certain dos and don'ts that, if followed religiously, can make using this program just heavenly. Lo and behold, the following Excel ten commandments contain just such precepts for eternal Excel bliss:

10. Thou shalt commit thy work to disk by saving thy changes often (File⇨Save or Ctrl+S). If thou findest that thou tendeth to be lax in the saving of thy work, then shalt thou engage thy AutoSave add-in (Tools⇨Add-Ins⇨AutoSave) and have thy program automatically save thy work for thee at a set time interval.

9. Thou shalt nameth thy workbooks when saving them the first time with filenames of no more than twelve score and fifteen characters (255), including spaces and all manner of weird signs and symbols. So, too, shalt thou mark well into which folder thou savest thy file lest thou thinkest in error that thy workbook be lost when next thou hast need of it.

8. Thou shalt not spread wide the data in thy worksheet, but rather shalt thou gather together thy tables and avoideth skipping columns and rows unless this is necessary to make thy data intelligible. All this shalt thou do in order that thou mightest conserve the memory of thy computer.

7. Thou shalt begin all thy Excel 97 formulas with = (equal) as the sign of computation. If, however, ye be formerly of the Lotus 1-2-3 tribe, thou shalt haveth special dispensation and canst commence thy formulas with the + sign and thy functions with the @ sign.

6. Thou shalt select thy cells before thou bringeth any Excel command to bear upon them, just as surely as thou doest sow before thou reapest.

5. Thou shalt useth the Undo feature (Edit⇨Undo or Ctrl+Z) immediately upon committing any transgression in thy worksheet so that thou mayest clean up thy mess. Should thou forgeteth to useth thy Undo straightway, thou must select the action that thou wouldst undo from the pop-up menu attached to the Undo button that thou findest on the Standard toolbar. Note well that any action that thou selectest from this menu will undo not only that action but all actions that proceedeth it on this menu.

4. Thou shalt not delete, neither shalt thou insert, columns and rows in a worksheet lest thou hath first verified that no part as yet uncovered of thy worksheet will thereby be wiped out or otherwise displaced.

3. Thou shalt not print thy worksheet lest thou hath first previewed the printing (File⇨Print Preview) and art satisfied that all of thy pages are upright in the sight of the printer.

2. Thou shalt changeth the manner of recalculation of thy workbooks from automatic to manual (Tools⇨Options⇨Calculation tab⇨Manual) when thy workbook grows so great in size that Excel sloweth down to a camel crawl whenever thou doest anything in any one of its worksheets. Woe to thee, however, should thou also removest the check mark from the Recalculate before Save check box when thou setteth up manual calculation or should thou ignorest the Calculate message on the status bar and not presseth the Calculate Now key (F9) before such time as thou mayest print any of thy workbook data.

1. Thou shalt protecteth thy completed workbook and all of its worksheets from corruption and inequities at the hands of others (Tools⇨Protection⇨ Protect Sheet or Protect Workbook). And if thou be brazen enough to addeth a password to thy workbook protection, beware lest thou forgeteth thy password in any part. For verily I say unto to thee, on the day that thou knowest not thy password, that day shalt be the last upon which thou lookest upon thy workbook in any wise.

Chapter 17

Top Ten Things in Excel 97 That Can Trip You Up

● ●

*T*he following "welcome warnings" point out the most common pitfalls that get beginning Excel users. Avoid these pitfalls like the plague, and I promise that you'll be a lot happier using Excel 97:

10. Remember that Excel 97 automatically adds the file extension .XLS to whatever filename you assign to your workbook when you first save it. (This file extension indicates that the file contains Excel worksheets.) So, when you first save and name a workbook, you don't ever have to bother typing the .XLS at the end of the filename. Also, when you edit a filename in the Save As dialog box, you can leave the .XLS extension in the File name edit box if you wish, but when replacing an existing filename with a completely new filename, you never have to add this .XLS extension as part of the name you enter.

9. If you introduce a space into an otherwise completely numeric entry, Excel categorizes the entry as text (indicated by its alignment at the left edge of the cell). If you feed that entry into a formula, the text classification completely throws off the answer because text entries are treated like zeros (0) in a formula.

8. When nesting parentheses in a formula, pair them properly so that you have a right parenthesis for every left parenthesis in the formula. If you do not include a right parenthesis for every left one, Excel 97 displays an alert dialog box with the message "Parentheses do not match" when you try to enter the formula. After you close this dialog box, Excel goes right back to the formula bar, where you can insert the missing parenthesis and press Enter to correct the unbalanced condition. By the way, Excel always highlights matched parentheses.

7. You can re-enter edited cell contents by clicking the Enter box on the formula bar or by pressing Tab or Enter, but you can't use the arrow keys. When you are editing a cell entry, the arrow keys only move the insertion point through the entry.

6. Be sure that you don't press one of the arrow keys to complete a cell entry within a preselected cell range instead of clicking the Enter box on the formula bar or pressing Enter. Pressing an arrow key deselects the range of cells when Excel moves the cell pointer.

5. The Edit⇔Undo command changes in response to whatever action you just took. Because it keeps changing after each action, you'd do best to remember to strike when the iron is hot, so to speak, by using the Undo feature to restore the worksheet to its previous state *before* you choose another command. However, if you do forget, you can undo multiple actions by selecting the last action you want undone in the pop-up menu attached to the Undo button on the Standard toolbar.

4. Deleting entire columns and rows from a worksheet is risky business unless you are sure that the columns and rows in question contain nothing of value. Remember, when you delete an entire row from the worksheet, you delete *all information from column A through IV* in that row (and you can see only a very few columns in this row). Likewise, when you delete an entire column from the worksheet, you delete *all information from row 1 through 65,536* in that column.

3. Be careful with global search-and-replace operations; they can really mess up a worksheet in a hurry if you inadvertently replace values, parts of formulas, or characters in titles and headings that you hadn't intended to change. As a precaution, *never undertake a global search-and-replace operation on an unsaved worksheet.*

   Also, verify whether or not the Find Entire Cells Only check box is selected before you begin. You can end up with a lot of unwanted replacements if you leave this check box unselected when you really only want to replace entire cell entries (rather than matching parts in cell entries). If you do make a mess, choose the Edit⇔Undo Replace command (Ctrl+Z) to restore the worksheet. If you don't discover the problem in time to use Undo, close the messed-up worksheet without saving the changes and open the unreplaced version that you saved — thanks to reading this warning!

2. To make it impossible to remove protection from a particular worksheet in a workbook or an entire workbook and all its worksheets unless you know the password, enter a password in the Password (Optional) text box of the Protect Sheet or Protect Workbook dialog box (Tools⇔Protection⇔Protect Sheet or Protect Workbook). Excel masks each character you type in this text box with an asterisk. After you click OK, Excel makes you re-enter the password before protecting the worksheet or workbook. From then on, you can remove protection from the worksheet or workbook only if you can reproduce the password exactly as you assigned it (including any case differences). Be very careful with passwords. If you forget the password, you cannot change any locked cells and you cannot unlock anymore cells in the particular worksheet or, in the case of a workbook, any of its worksheets!

1. You *cannot* use the Undo feature to bring back a database record you removed with the Delete button in the data form! Excel is definitely *not* kidding when it uses words like "deleted permanently." As a precaution, always save a backup version of the worksheet with the database before you start removing old records.

Chapter 18
Top Ten Ways to Impress the Boss

*T*he ten little tips contained in this chapter are worth their weight in Intel's Pentium Pro chips (gold is out this season). Please keep them in mind as you work with Excel 97. After all, who wants computing to be any harder than it has to be?

10. Watch the Office Assistant or the Office Assistant button on the Standard toolbar if the Office Assistant isn't open. When a yellow light bulb appears in the Office Assistant button or the Office Assistant window (assuming that you have this window open), you know that Excel has some tidbits of wisdom to dispense to you based on the things you were just doing in the workbook.

    If the Office Assistant window isn't open, click the Office Assistant button on the Standard toolbar to open it. Then click the light bulb in the Office Assistant window to display a balloon with the latest tip. When you're finished reading the tip, click the Close button in the balloon to make it disappear.

9. Name any often-used cell range in a worksheet by selecting the cell or cells in the worksheet, clicking the Name box on the formula, typing the new range name in this box, and then pressing Enter. After naming a cell or cell range in this manner, you can then use its name to move to it, select its cells, or print it. Remember, you can select a range name from the pop-up menu on the Name box or by pressing the Go To key (F5) and then selecting the range name in the Go To dialog box. When you click OK, Excel not only moves you to the first cell in that range but selects all its cells as well.

8. Don't waste all day scrolling through a seemingly endless table of data. Instead, use the Ctrl+arrow key (or End and then arrow key) combination to jump from one edge of the table to another edge or to jump from the edge of one table to another.

7. If you find yourself continually entering the same list of items over and over again in new worksheets, create a custom list of items and then enter the entire list by typing just the first item in the series and then dragging out the rest of the series with the AutoFill handle. (See "Creating custom lists for AutoFill" in Chapter 2 for a refresher course on how to create a custom series.)

6. Lose the graphics in a workbook worksheet by replacing them on-screen with placeholders (Tools⊏>Options⊏>View tab⊏>Show placeholders) when you find that Excel just can't keep up with your movements in a particular worksheet. Screen response time is greatly improved by this trick — just don't forget to put the graphics back before you print the worksheet or you'll end up with shaded rectangles where the pictures ought to be!

5. When making editing and formatting changes in your Excel workbooks, don't overlook the shortcut menus attached to the things that need fixing (opened by clicking the secondary mouse button). Shortcut menus can save a lot of time that you would otherwise waste searching the menus on the menu bar to find the editing or formatting command you need. Also, don't forget how much time you can save by using the tools on the Standard and Formatting toolbars to get things done!

4. Before making changes to an unfamiliar worksheet, use the Zoom button on the Standard toolbar to zoom out to 50% or 25% so that you can get a good idea of how the information is laid out. When inserting or deleting cells in an unfamiliar worksheet, resist the temptation to insert or remove entire columns and rows, which can damage unseen tables of data. Instead, just insert or cut out the cell ranges in the region you're working in — you know, think globally, but act locally!

3. To maximize the number of worksheet cells displayed on-screen at one time without having to resort to changing the magnification with the Zoom feature, choose View⊏>Full Screen. This makes the formula bar, the Standard and Formatting toolbars, and the status bar all go away, leaving only the menu bar and scroll bars in addition to the cells in the current worksheet (giving you a view of 25 full rows rather than the normal 17). When you're ready to return to the normal (rather cramped) screen display, click the Close Full Screen button in the floating Full toolbar (which automatically appears whenever you choose View⊏>Full Screen) or, if this toolbar is hidden, choose View⊏>Full Screen a second time.

2. Give yourself a break and record a macro for doing those little tasks that you end up doing over and over and over again (choose Tools⊏>Macro⊏>Record New Macro). Using macros to get things done not only alleviates the boredom but also frees you up to do truly important things (like playing another game of Hearts or Minesweeper).

1. Name each worksheet that you use in a workbook with some intelligible English name like Invoice or Price List (by double-clicking the sheet tab, entering a new name on the tab, and then pressing Enter) rather than leave them with their normally indecipherable names like Sheet1 and Sheet2. That way, you not only know which sheets in your workbook you've already used, but you also have a fair idea of what they contain and when you should select them.

Chapter 19

Top Ten Thousand
Keystroke Shortcuts

● ●

*I*f you like using keystroke shortcuts on your computer, have I got great news
for you — Excel is loaded with them. There are keystroke shortcuts for
doing just about everything you'd probably be tempted to do with the program.
In the tables in this chapter, I've brought together the most popular of these
keystroke shortcuts and arranged them according to what kind of work they do.

For Getting Online Help

Press	To
F1	Open the Office Assistant
Shift+F1	Get context-sensitive Excel Help

For Moving through the Worksheet

Press	To
Arrow keys (↑,↓,←,→)	Move up, down, left, right one cell
Home	Move to the beginning of the row
PgUp	Move up one screenful
PgDn	Move down one screenful
Ctrl+Home	Move to the first cell in the worksheet (A1)
Ctrl+End	Move to the last active cell of the worksheet
Ctrl+Arrow key	Move to the edge of a data block

For Selecting Cells in the Worksheet

Press	To
Shift+Spacebar	Select the entire row
Ctrl+Spacebar	Select the entire column
Ctrl+Shift+Spacebar, or Ctrl+A	Select the entire worksheet
Shift+Home	Extend the selection to the beginning of the current row

For Moving around a Cell Selection

Press	To
Enter	Move the cell pointer down one cell in the selection when there's more than one row, or move one cell to the right when the selection consists of only one row
Shift+Enter	Move the cell pointer up one cell selection when there's more than one row, or move one cell to the left when the selection consists of only one row
Tab	Move the cell pointer one cell to the right in the selection when there's more than one column, or move one cell down when the selection has only one column
Shift+Tab	Move the cell pointer one cell to the left in the selection when there's more than one column, or move one cell up when the selection has only one column
Ctrl+. (period)	Move to the next corner of the current cell range
Shift+Backspace	Collapse the cell selection to just the active cell

For Sizing a Workbook or Moving through Its Sheets

Press	To
Ctrl+PgDn	Move to the next sheet in the workbook
Ctrl+PgUp	Move to the previous sheet in the workbook
Ctrl+F9	Minimize the workbook
Ctrl+F10	Maximize the workbook

For Formatting a Cell Selection

Press	To
Ctrl+Shift+~	Apply the General number format to the cell selection
Ctrl+Shift+$	Apply the Currency format with two decimal places to the cell selection
Ctrl+Shift+%	Apply the Percentage format with no decimal places to the cell selection
Ctrl+Shift+^	Apply the Scientific (exponential) number format with two decimal places to the cell selection
Ctrl+Shift+#	Apply the Date format with the day, month, and year to the cell selection (as in 27-Oct-97)
Ctrl+Shift+@	Apply the Time format with the hour, minute, and AM or PM to the cell selection (as in 12:05 PM)
Ctrl+Shift+&	Apply an outline border to the cell selection
Ctrl+Shift+_ (underscore)	Get rid of all borders in the cell selection
Ctrl+1	Display the Format Cells dialog box
Ctrl+B	Apply or get rid of bold in the cell selection
Ctrl+I	Apply or get rid of italics in the cell selection
Ctrl+U	Apply or get rid of underlining in the cell selection
Ctrl+5	Apply or get rid of strikeout in the cell selection
Ctrl+9	Hide selected rows
Ctrl+Shift+((left parenthesis)	Show all hidden rows
Ctrl+0 (zero)	Hide selected columns
Ctrl+Shift+) (right parenthesis)	Show all hidden columns

For Editing a Worksheet

Press	To
Enter	Carry out your action
Esc	Cancel a command or close the displayed dialog box
F4	Repeat your last action
Ctrl+Z	Undo your last command or action
Ctrl+Shift++ (plus sign)	Display the Insert dialog box to insert new cells, columns, or rows in the worksheet

(continued)

For Editing a Worksheet (continued)

Press	*To*
Ctrl+– (minus sign)	Display the Delete dialog box to delete cells, columns, or rows from the worksheet
Delete	Clear the contents of your cell selection
Ctrl+X	Cut the selection to the Clipboard
Ctrl+C	Copy the selection to the Clipboard
Ctrl+V	Paste the contents of the Clipboard
Shift+F2	Edit an existing comment and add a new comment to the Comment dialog box
F3	Display the Paste Name dialog box so that you can paste a range name into a formula
Shift+F3	Display the Paste Function dialog box so that you can paste a function and its arguments into a formula
Ctrl+F3	Display the Define Name dialog box so that you can assign a range name to the cell selection
Ctrl+= (equal sign) or F9	Recalculate the formulas in all open worksheets
Shift+F9	Recalculate the formulas in just the active worksheet
Alt+= (equal sign)	Create a sum formula (same as clicking the AutoSum tool on the Standard toolbar)
Ctrl+8	Toggle the outline symbols on and off or, if no outline exists, display an alert dialog box prompting you to create an outline
F7	Check spelling
Ctrl+F	Find
Ctrl+H	Replace

For Editing an Entry in the Cell

Press	*To*
F2	Activate the formula bar and position the insertion point at the end of the current entry
Ctrl+; (semicolon)	Insert the current date in the cell
Ctrl+Shift+; (semicolon)	Insert the current time in the cell (same as Ctrl+:)
Ctrl+' (apostrophe)	Copy the formula from the cell above the active cell

Press	To
Ctrl+Shift+' (apostrophe)	Copy the value from the cell above the active cell
Ctrl+Enter	Enter the contents of the formula bar in all cells in the current selection
Arrow key ($\uparrow,\downarrow,\leftarrow,\rightarrow$)	Move the insertion point one character up, down, left, or right
Home	Move the insertion point to the beginning of the formula bar
Alt+Enter	Insert a new line in the cell entry
Backspace	Delete the preceding character when editing a cell or clear the entry in the current cell and put Excel in Enter mode
Ctrl+Shift+Delete	Delete the text to the end of the line when editing a cell

For Opening, Saving, and Printing Excel Workbooks

Press	To
F11	Create a column chart from the current cell selection in a new chart sheet in the workbook
Ctrl+F12	Display the Open dialog box so that you can open an existing Excel workbook file
Ctrl+F11	Open a new macro sheet in the workbook
Alt+Shift+F2 or Shift+F12	Save the active file with the File⇨Save command
Alt+F2 or F12	Save the active file with the File⇨Save As command
Ctrl+P	Open the Print dialog box

For Running or Editing a Macro

Press	To
Alt+F8	Open the Macro dialog box
Alt+F11	Open the Visual Basic Editor

Glossary

absolute cell reference: A cell reference that Excel cannot automatically adjust. If you're about to copy a formula and you want to prevent Excel from adjusting one or more of the cell references (the program has a tendency to change the column and row reference in copies), make the cell references absolute. Absolute cell references are indicated by a dollar sign (yes, a $) in front of the column letter and the row number — $K$11, for example. You can convert a relative reference to an absolute reference by pressing the F4 key. See also *relative cell reference.*

active: The program window, workbook window, worksheet window, or dialog box currently in use. The color of the title bar of an active window or dialog box is different from the color of a nonactive window's title bars. When several document windows are displayed, you can activate an inactive window by clicking it.

arguments: Not what you have with your spouse but rather the values you give to a worksheet function to compute. Arguments are enclosed in parentheses and separated from one another by commas. See also *function* and *Function Palette.*

AutoCalculate: Refers to the area of the status bar that automatically indicates the sum of the values in any cell selection. (See "You AutoCalculate my totals" in Chapter 1 for details.)

borders: The different types of lines Excel can draw around the edges of each cell or the outside edge of a bunch of cells. Excel offers a wide variety of different line styles and colors for this purpose.

cell: The basic building block of plant and animal life and also of the Excel work-sheet. The *worksheet cell* is a block formed by the intersections of column and row gridlines displayed in the worksheet. All worksheet data is stored in cells. Each cell is identified by the letter of its column and the number of its row, the so-called *cell reference.*

cell pointer: A heavy outline that indicates which cell in the worksheet is selected. You must move the cell pointer to a particular cell before you can enter or edit information in that cell.

cell range: A bunch of cells that are all right next to each other. To select a range of cells with the mouse, you simply point at the beginning of the range, click the mouse button, and drag through the cells. See also *nonadjacent selection.*

cell reference: Identifies the location of a cell in the worksheet. Normally, the cell reference consists of the column letter followed by the row number. (For example, "B3" indicates the cell in the second column and third row of the worksheet.) When you place the cell pointer in a cell, Excel displays its cell reference at the beginning of the formula bar. See also *relative cell reference* and *absolute cell reference.*

chart: Also known as a *graph.* This is a graphic representation of a set of values stored in a worksheet. You can create a chart right on a worksheet, where it is saved and printed along with the worksheet data. You can also display a chart in its own chart window, where you can edit its contents or print it independently of the worksheet data. (Such a chart is called, appropriately enough, a *chart sheet.*)

check box: Turns an option on or off in a dialog box. If the check box is selected, the option is turned on. If the check box is blank, the option is turned off. The nice thing about check boxes is that you can select more than one of the multiple options presented as a group. See also *radio button.*

click: The simplest mouse technique. You press and immediately release the mouse button. See also *double-click.*

Clipboard: The Windows equivalent of a hand-held clipboard to which you attach papers and information you need to work with. The Windows 95 Clipboard is a special area of memory, a holding place, where text and graphics can be stored to await further action. You can paste the contents of the Clipboard into any open Excel 97 document (or any document in other Windows programs). The contents of the Clipboard are automatically replaced as soon as you cut or copy new information there (whether in Excel or some other program).

command button: A dialog-box button that initiates an action. The default command button is indicated by a dotted rectangle and a darker border. A button with an ellipsis (. . .) opens another dialog box or window. Frequently, after you choose options in the dialog box, you click the OK or Cancel command button.

comments: Notes you attach to a particular worksheet cell to remind yourself of something important (or trivial) about the cell's contents. You can display your comments in

their own text box in the worksheet by positioning the mouse pointer on the comment indicator (the red triangle that appears in the upper-right corner of the cell after adding a comment to the cell).

Control menu: A standard pull-down menu attached to all Windows programs and Excel workbook icons in the upper-left corner of their windows. This menu contains commands that open, close, maximize, minimize, or restore a window or dialog box. You can display a Control menu by clicking the program or workbook icon.

database: A tool for organizing, managing, and retrieving large amounts of information. A database is created right on a worksheet. The first row of the database contains column headings called *field names,* which identify each item of information you are tracking (such as First Name, Last Name, City, and the like). Below the field names, you enter the information you want to store for each field (column) of each record (row). See also *field* and *record.*

default: Don't be alarmed; we're not talking blame here. A *default* is a setting, value, or response that Excel automatically provides unless you choose something else. Some defaults can be changed and rearranged.

dialog box: A box containing various options that appears when you select Excel commands followed by an ellipsis (. . .). The options in a dialog box are presented in groups of buttons and boxes. (Oh, boy!) Many dialog boxes in Excel contain different tabs (see *tab*) that you click to bring up a different set of options. A dialog box can also display warnings and messages. Each dialog box contains a title bar and a Control menu but has no menu bar. You can move a dialog box around the active document window by dragging its title bar.

docking: Has nothing at all to do with the space shuttle. Docking in Excel refers to dragging one of the toolbars to a stationary position along the perimeter of the Excel window with the mouse. See also ***toolbar.***

document: See ***workbook.***

double-click: To click the mouse button twice in rapid succession. Double-clicking opens things like a program or a workbook. You can double-click to close things, too.

drag and drop: A really direct way to move stuff around on a worksheet. Select the cell or range (bunch) of cells you want to move, position the pointer on one of its edges, and then press and hold the primary mouse button. The pointer assumes the shape of an arrowhead pointing up toward the left. Hold the mouse button as you move the mouse and drag the outline of the selection to the new location. When you get to where you're going, let it all go.

drop-down list box: An edit box that displays the currently selected option, accompanied by an arrow button. When you click the associated arrow button, a pop-up list box or menu appears from the edit box with other options that you can choose. To select a new option from this list or menu and close the drop-down list box, click the option.

edit box: Also known as a *text box.* The area in a dialog box where you type a new selection or edit the current one.

error value: A value Excel displays in a cell when it cannot calculate the formula for that cell. Error values start with a number sign (#) and end with an exclamation point (!), and they have various capitalized informative words in the middle. An example is #DIV/0!, which appears when you try to divide by zero.

field: A column in an Excel database that tracks just one type of item (like a city, state, zip code, and so on). See also ***database*** and ***record.***

file: Any workbook document saved to a computer disk. See also ***workbook.***

font: Shapes for characters — typeface. Fonts have a point size, weight, and style, such as Helvetica Modern 20-point bold italic. You can pick and choose the fonts used to display information in an Excel worksheet and change their settings at any time.

footer: Information you specify to be printed in the bottom margin of each page of a printed report. See also ***header.***

formula: Ready for some math anxiety? A sequence of values, cell references, names, functions, or operators that is contained in a cell and produces a new value from existing values. In other words, a mathematical expression. Formulas in Excel always begin with an equal sign (=).

formula bar: Sound like a high-energy treat? Well, it is . . . sort of. Located at the top of the Excel window under the menu bar, the formula bar displays the contents of the current cell. (In the case of formulas, this means that you see the formula rather than the calculated result, which shows up in the cell itself.) You can also use the formula bar to enter or edit values and formulas in a cell or chart. When activated, the formula bar displays a Cancel box and Enter box between the current cell reference on the left and the Edit Formula button and the place where the cell entry appears on the right. Click the Enter box or press the Enter key to complete an entry or edit. Click the Cancel button or press Esc to leave the contents of the formula bar unchanged.

Formula Palette: This term refers to the palette in which you enter the arguments you want to specify for the function that you've chosen with the Paste Function button on the Standard toolbar. To reduce the Function Palette to just the current edit box so that you have access to any cells in the worksheet that you might want to select, you click the minimize button to the right of the edit box. After selecting cells in the worksheet, you can restore the Formula Palette by clicking the edit box's restore button (which replaces the minimize button). See also *arguments* and *function*.

function: (Let's see, I know what *dysfunction* is. . . .) A function simplifies and shortens lengthy calculations. Functions have built-in formulas that use a series of values called *arguments* to perform the specified operations and return the results. The easiest way to enter a function in a cell is with the Paste Function button, which opens the Function Palette that walks you through the entry of the function's arguments. The Paste Function tool uses the icon with the *fx* on it and appears as a button on the Standard toolbar. See also *arguments* and *Formula Palette*.

graphics object: Any of the various shapes or graphics images (including charts) that you can bring into the sheets in your workbook document. All graphics objects remain in a separate layer on top of the cells in the sheet so that they can be selected, moved, resized, and formatted independently of the other information stored in the sheet.

header: Information you specify to be printed in the top margin of each page of a printed report. See also *footer*.

HTML (HyperText Markup Language): HTML documents are text files that contain special formatting tags that can be read by Web browsers like Microsoft's Internet Explorer or Netscape's Navigator. To differentiate formatting tags from regular text in an HTML document, the tags are enclosed in a pair of angle brackets, as in <H1>, which marks the beginning of a first-level heading in the document. Many formatting tags work in pairs, with one tag to indicate where a particular format begins and another (such as </H1>) to mark where it ends. When you use the Internet Assistant Wizard in Excel 97 (as explained in Chapter 10) to convert a table of worksheet data into an HTML table, the Internet Assistant automatically adds all the necessary HTML table formatting tags to the data so that your Web browser can render its labels and values in the familiar row and column format.

Hyperlink: Hyperlink refers to a text entry or a graphic image that, when clicked, jumps you to another place in the same document or opens another document altogether. Hyperlinks assigned to text are indicated in a worksheet by underlining the text, displaying it in blue, and by the fact that the mouse pointer changes from an arrowhead to a hand when the pointer is positioned over the text. Hyperlinks assigned to graphics images are indicated only by the change of the mouse pointer to the hand shape when the pointer's positioned over the graphic. In an Excel 97 workbook, you can assign a hyperlink to a cell entry or a graphic image added to the worksheet. Such hyperlinks, when clicked, can take you to another place in the same workbook, to another Office 97 document, or to a Web page on the Internet or your company's intranet. (See Chapter 10 for details.)

I-beam cursor: The I-beam shape (looks just like the end of a girder or a capital letter I) that the mouse pointer assumes when you position it in a place on-screen where you can enter or edit text. Click the I-beam cursor in the formula bar or a text box in a dialog box, for example, to place the insertion point where you want to add or delete text. When you double-click a cell, Excel positions the insertion point exactly where you clicked. If you press F2, Excel positions the insertion point at the end of the entry in that cell. You can then click the I-beam cursor in the cell entry to reposition the insertion point for editing. See also **insertion point.**

insertion point: The blinking vertical bar that indicates your current location in the text. The insertion point shows where the next character you type will appear or the next one you delete will disappear. See also **I-beam cursor.**

list box: A boxed area in a dialog box that displays a list of choices you can choose from. When a list is too long for all the choices to be displayed, the list box has a scroll bar you can use to bring new options into view. Most list boxes are already open and have the list on display. Those that you must open by clicking an arrow button are called *drop-down list boxes.*

macro: A sequence of frequently performed, repetitive tasks and calculations that you record. At the touch of a couple keystrokes, Excel can play back the steps in the macro much faster than is humanly possible.

marquee: Those moving dotted lights around movie stars' names, right? Well, a *marquee* exists in Excel in a slightly toned-down version. It's the moving dotted line around a selection that shows what information is selected when you move or copy data with the Cut, Copy, and Paste commands on the Edit menu.

maximize button: The center button of the three on the right side of the title bar on the less-than-full-size Excel program or workbook window. When you click the Maximize button, the workbook or program window expands to full size and fills the screen. See also **minimize button** and **restore button.**

menu: A vertical list of commands that can be applied to the active window or application. Also known as a *pull-down menu* because the menu opens down from the menu bar when you select the menu name. When an option is currently unavailable on a pull-down menu, the option is dimmed. See also **shortcut menus.**

menu bar: The row at the top of a program window that contains the names of the menu items available for the active document window.

message box: Also known as an *alert box.* This is a type of dialog box that appears when Excel gives you information, a warning, or an error message, or when it asks for confirmation before carrying out a command.

minimize button: The first of the three buttons on the right side of the title bar in the Excel program or workbook window. When you click a minimize button in a workbook window, the window shrinks to an icon at the bottom of the Excel screen. When you click the minimize button in the Excel program window, the Excel window shrinks to a button on the Windows 95 taskbar. See also **maximize button** and **restore button.**

mode indicators: The information on the right side of the status bar (the row at the bottom of the screen) that tells you what keyboard modes are currently active. Some examples are ADD, NUM, and CAPS.

mouse pointer: Indicates your position on-screen as you move the mouse on the desk. The mouse pointer assumes various forms to indicate a change in the action when you use different features: the *arrowhead* when you point, select, or drag; the *I-beam* when you place the insertion point in text; the *double-headed arrow* when you drag to adjust row height or column width; and the *hourglass* when you need to wait.

nonadjacent selection: Also called a *discontiguous selection.* (Is that any better?) A nonadjacent selection is one composed of various cells and cell ranges that don't all touch each other. To accomplish this feat, click the first cell or click and drag through the first range; then hold down Ctrl as you click or drag through the remaining cells or ranges you want to select. See also *cell range.*

pane: A part of a divided worksheet window. You can display different parts of the same worksheet together on one window in different panes. Horizontal and vertical split bars are involved with creating and sizing.

paste: Yum, yum, remember kindergarten? Alas, in the computer age, paste means to transfer the cut or copied contents of the Clipboard into a document, either in the cell with the cell pointer or in a line of text at the location of the insertion point.

pointing: Babies do it, politicians do it, and so can you. *Pointing* also means selecting a cell or cell range as you enter a formula in the formula bar to automatically record cell references.

primary mouse button: Politically correct name for the mouse button that used to be known as the left mouse button (on the two-button mouse commonly used with IBM compatibles). This is the button that you use to click pull-down menus, cells, charts, or whatever. If you're right-handed and you keep the mouse on the right side of your keyboard, the primary mouse button continues to be the left button. If, however, you are left-handed, have switched the mouse button functions, and keep the mouse on the left side of the keyboard, the right mouse button becomes the primary mouse button. In both cases, we are talking about the inmost button closest to the keyboard. Calling this button the primary button (rather than the inmost button) calls attention to the fact that, in Excel, you use the secondary mouse button mainly to open shortcut menus. See also *secondary mouse button* and *shortcut menus.*

radio button: When it's selected, a radio button in a dialog box looks like an old-fashioned radio push button (because it has dot in the middle). Radio buttons are used for dialog box items that contain mutually exclusive options. This means that you can select only one of the options at a time. (Only one can have the dot in the middle.) See also *check box.*

range: Also called a *cell range.* A range is a bunch of neighboring cells that form some type of solid block when selected with the mouse or the keyboard.

record: A single row in a database that defines one entity (like an employee, a client, or a sales transaction). See also *database* and *field.*

relative cell reference: The normal cell reference (like A2) that is automatically adjusted when you copy formulas that refer to the cell. Row references are adjusted when you copy up or down; column references are adjusted when you copy to the left or right. See also *absolute cell reference* and *cell reference.*

restore button: The center of the three buttons on the right side of the title bar when the Excel program window or a workbook window is displayed full-size on the screen. Mouse users can click the restore button to shrink a window or return a window to the size and location it had before being zoomed to full size. See also *maximize button* and *minimize button.*

screentips: Screentips refers to all the little indicators that appear next to the mouse pointer as you do stuff like scroll to new part of a worksheet with scroll bars, copy or move data in a worksheet with drag-and-drop, or create a series of values with the fill handle.

scroll bar: The vertical or horizontal bar in the active document window and in some list boxes. Use a scroll bar to move rapidly through a document or list by clicking the scroll arrows or dragging the slider box.

secondary mouse button: Politically correct name for what used to be known as the right mouse button. This is the button that you use to click various screen objects in Excel to display its shortcut menu. If you're right-handed and you keep the mouse on the right side of your keyboard, the secondary mouse button continues to be the right button. If, however, you are left-handed, have switched the mouse button functions, and keep the mouse on the left side of the keyboard, the left mouse button becomes the secondary mouse button. In both cases, we are talking about the outermost button furthest from the keyboard. Calling this button the secondary button (rather than the outermost button) calls attention to the fact that, in Excel, you use the primary mouse button much more often than the secondary mouse button. See also *primary mouse button* and *shortcut menus*.

selection: The chosen element, such as a cell, cell range, nonadjacent selection, file, directory, dialog box option, graphics object, or text. To select an element, highlight it by dragging the mouse or pressing keystroke shortcuts. You normally select an element before choosing the actions you want to apply to that element.

sheet tabs: The tabs that appear at the bottom of each workbook window. To select a new sheet (worksheet, chart, and so on) in your workbook, you click its tab. To display new sheet tabs, you use the tab scrolling buttons. Excel indicates which sheet is the active one by displaying the sheet name in bold on its tab. To rename sheet tabs (which are normally given names such as Sheet1, Sheet2, and so on), double-click a tab and enter the new name in the Rename Sheet dialog box; then select OK or press Enter. See also *tab*.

shortcut menus: Also known as *context menus*, these menus are attached to certain things on the screen — namely, the toolbar, worksheet cell, or parts of a chart that are open in a chart window. These menus contain quick lists of command options related to the object they're attached to. To open a shortcut menu and choose its commands, you must click the object with the secondary mouse button.

size box: The little square box in the lower-right corner of a workbook window that is neither minimized nor maximized. Use the size box to manually adjust the size of any open document window by dragging it until the window is the size and shape you want.

spreadsheet application: A type of computer program that enables you to develop and perform all sorts of calculations between the text and values stored in a document. Most spreadsheet programs like

Excel also include charting and database capabilities. *Spreadsheet* is also commonly used as an alternative term for *worksheet,* so see also ***worksheet.***

status bar: The line at the bottom of the Excel window. The status bar displays messages, such as Ready, or a short description of the menu option you have chosen, and it indicates any active modes, such as CAPS or NUM when you press the Caps Lock or Num Lock key.

style: If you've got it, flaunt it. Also known to some of us as a group of formatting instructions, all bundled together, that you can apply to the cells in a worksheet. Use styles to save time and keep things consistent. Styles can deal with the number format, font, alignment, border, patterns, and protection of the cells.

tab: You find tabs in two places in Excel: on some larger dialog boxes, such as the Format Cells or Options dialog boxes, and attached to the bottom of each worksheet in a workbook. In the case of dialog box tabs, you simply click a tab to display its set of options on the top of all the others in the dialog box. In the case of sheet tabs, you click a tab to display its sheet on top of all the others in the workbook. See also ***dialog box*** and ***sheet tabs***.

title bar: The top bar of a program window, workbook window, or dialog box that contains its title. You can move an active window or dialog box around the screen by dragging its title bar.

toolbar: A series of related tools (buttons with icons) that you simply click to perform common tasks such as opening, saving, or printing a document. Excel comes with several built-in toolbars that you can use

as-is or customize. You can create toolbars of your own design, using predefined tools or blank tools to which you assign macros. You can display them in their own little dialog boxes that float around the active document window; you can also dock them along the perimeter of the screen. See also ***docking.***

window: A framed area on-screen that contains the program (called a *program window*) or the workbook (called a *workbook window*) that you're working with. The Excel program window typically contains a title bar, Control menu, menu bar, Standard toolbar, open document windows (with the active one on top), and status bar. The program and workbook windows can be resized and moved around the screen as needed.

workbook: An Excel file containing multiple, related sheets, such as worksheets, charts, and macro sheets. When you start a new workbook, Excel automatically puts three blank worksheets in it (named Sheet1 through Sheet3) and gives the workbook a temporary name (such as Book1, Book2, and so on). You can then add or remove worksheets as needed as well as add chart and or module/macro sheets as needed. When you save the workbook, you can then give the workbook a permanent filename. See also ***chart***, ***file***, and ***worksheet***.

worksheet: Also called a *spreadsheet.* This is the primary document for recording, analyzing, and calculating data. The Excel worksheet is organized in a series of columns and rows. Each new workbook you open contains three blank worksheets. See also ***workbook.***

Index